Multilingual Europe: Facts and Policies

Multilingual Europe: Facts and Policies

edited by
Guus Extra
Durk Gorter

Mouton de Gruyter
Berlin · New York

Mouton de Gruyter (formerly Mouton, The Hague)
is a Division of Walter de Gruyter GmbH & Co. KG, Berlin.

♾ Printed on acid-free paper which falls within the guidelines
of the ANSI to ensure permanence and durability.

Library of Congress Cataloging-in-Publication Data

Multilingual Europe : facts and policies / edited by Guus Extra,
Durk Gorter.
    p. cm. − (Contributions to the sociology of language ; 96)
Includes bibliographical references and index.
ISBN 978-3-11-020512-1 (hardcover : alk. paper)
ISBN 978-3-11-020513-8 (pbk. : alk. paper)
    1. Multilingualism − Europe.   2. Linguistics minorities − Europe.
I. Extra, Guus.   II. Gorter, D. (Durk).
P115.5.E85M846 2008
306.44'6094−dc22
                                                         2008026197

ISBN 978-3-11-020513-8

Bibliographic information published by the Deutsche Nationalbibliothek

The Deutsche Nationalbibliothek lists this publication in the Deutsche
Nationalbibliografie; detailed bibliographic data are available in the Internet
at http://dnb.d-nb.de.

© Copyright 2008 by Walter de Gruyter GmbH & Co. KG, D-10785 Berlin
All rights reserved, including those of translation into foreign languages. No part of this
book may be reproduced in any form or by any means, electronic or mechanical, including
photocopy, recording or any information storage and retrieval system, without permission
in writing from the publisher.
Cover design: Martin Zech, Bremen. Photo provided by NASA.
Printed in Germany.

Acknowledgements

We would like to express our thanks to Karin Berkhout and Hans Verhulst at Tilburg University (the Netherlands) for their support in the preparation of this Volume. Karin Berkhout (at *Babylon, Centre for Studies of the Multicultural Society*) took meticulous care of the final layout and formatting of the manuscript, and Hans Verhulst (in the *Department of Language and Culture Studies*) went over the English as *lingua franca* in a number of contributions.

Guus Extra and Durk Gorter

Contents

Introduction

The constellation of languages in Europe:
an inclusive approach   3
Guus Extra and Durk Gorter

Section I. Official state languages

English as lingua franca in Europe today   63
Juliane House

French and France: language and state   87
Dennis Ager

Polish in Poland and abroad   111
Justyna Leśniewska and Zygmunt Mazur

Language constellations across the Baltic Republics:
a comparative review   135
Gabrielle Hogan-Brun

Section II. Regional minority languages

Catalan in Spain   157
F. Xavier Vila i Moreno

Frisian in the Netherlands   185
Durk Gorter, Cor van der Meer and Alex Riemersma

Hungarian as a minority language   207
Susan Gal

Sámi languages in the Nordic countries and Russia   233
Mikael Svonni

Section III. Immigrant minority languages

New minority languages in the United Kingdom 253
Viv Edwards

Immigrant minority languages in Sweden 271
Lilian Nygren-Junkin

Immigrant languages in Italy 293
Monica Barni and Carla Bagna

Immigrant minority languages in Europe:
cross-national and cross-linguistic perspectives 315
Guus Extra and Kutlay Yağmur

Contributing authors 337
Author index 339
Subject index 345

Introduction

The constellation of languages in Europe: an inclusive approach

Guus Extra and Durk Gorter

1. Introduction

Although we are fully aware of the fact that the European constellation of languages includes more than the languages of the European Union (henceforward EU), the EU is the supranational agency for which both facts and policies across Europe can be covered. At the EU level, the number of national member-states does not equal the number of national or "official state" languages. Some countries have more than one official state language and several languages are shared by two or more countries. All official state languages of the EU are also working languages for official documents and regulations, primarily to avoid a democratic deficit. According to the EU's English website, the cost of maintaining the EU policy of multilingualism (in particular the cost of translation and interpretation services) was € 1123 million in 2005, which amounts to 1% of the annual EU budget, or € 2.28 per person in 2005. In congruence with the eastward extension of the EU, English is on the rise as *lingua franca* for transnational communication, both at the institutional level and at the level of public and interpersonal communication. In addition to the national languages, there are various types of minority languages occurring across the EU member-states. We will refer to these languages as regional minority (RM) and immigrant minority (IM) languages.

Linguistic diversity is conceived as a constituent characteristic of European identity (Arzoz 2008). However, some languages play a more important role in the European public and political discourse on "celebrating linguistic diversity", the motto of the European Year of Languages (2001). The constellation of languages in Europe actually functions as a descending hierarchy (see Craith 2006 for similar considerations):

— English as *lingua franca* for transnational communication;
— national or "official state" languages of European countries;
— regional minority (RM) languages across Europe;
— immigrant minority (IM) languages across Europe.

In the official EU discourse, RM languages are referred to as *regional or minority* languages and IM languages as *migrant* languages. Both concepts are problematic for a variety of reasons (see Barni and Bagna, this Volume, on migrant *vs.* immigrant languages). Whereas the national languages of the EU with English increasingly on top are celebrated most at the EU level, RM languages are celebrated less and IM languages least. IM languages are only marginally covered by EU language promotion programmes and – so far – are mainly considered in the context of provisions for learning the national languages of the "migrants' countries of residence".

The theme of this introductory chapter will be addressed from phenomenological, demographic, sociolinguistic, and educational points of view. Both multidisciplinary and cross-national perspectives will be offered on two major domains in which language transmission occurs, i.e., the domestic domain and the public domain. The home and the school are typical of these domains. At home, language transmission occurs between (parents and) children; at school this occurs between (teachers and) pupils. Viewed from the perspectives of majority language *versus* minority language speakers, language transmission becomes a very different issue. In the case of majority language speakers, language transmission at home and at school are commonly taken for granted: at home, parents usually speak an informal variety of this language with their children, and at school, the formal variety of this language is usually the only or major subject and medium of instruction. In the case of minority language speakers, there is usually a much stronger mismatch between the language of the home and that of the school. Whether parents in such a context continue to transmit their language to their children is strongly dependent on the degree to which these parents, or the minority group to which they belong, conceive of this language as a core value of cultural identity.

Four major themes will be addressed in this introductory chapter: the discourse on national languages and minority languages (Section 2), the definition and identification of population groups in multicultural contexts (Section 3), the status of RM languages at home and at school (Section 4), the status of IM languages at home and at school (Section 5), European policies and perspectives on plurilingualism (Section 6) and the structure and contents of this book (Section 7).

2. National languages and minority languages

2.1. The linkage between languages and nation-states

Europe's identity is to a great extent determined by cultural and linguistic diversity (Haarmann 1995). Table 1 serves to illustrate this diversity in terms of EU (candidate) member-states with their estimated populations (ranked in order of decreasing numbers) and corresponding official state languages.

Table 1. Overview of 30 EU (candidate) member-states with estimated populations and official state languages (EU figures for 2007)

Nr	Member-states	Population (in millions)	Official state language(s)
1	Germany	82,5	German
2	France	60,9	French
3	United Kingdom	60,4	English
4	Italy	58,8	Italian
5	Spain	43,8	Spanish
6	Poland	38,1	Polish
7	Romania	21,6	Romanian
8	The Netherlands	16,3	Dutch (Nederlands)
9	Greece	11,1	Greek
10	Portugal	10,6	Portuguese
11	Belgium	10,5	Dutch, French, German
12	Czech Republic	10,3	Czech
13	Hungary	10,1	Hungarian
14	Sweden	9,0	Swedish
15	Austria	8,3	German
16	Bulgaria	7,7	Bulgarian
17	Denmark	5,4	Danish
18	Slovakia	5,4	Slovak
19	Finland	5,3	Finnish
20	Ireland	4,2	Irish, English
21	Lithuania	3,4	Lithuanian
22	Latvia	2,3	Latvian
23	Slovenia	2,0	Slovenian
24	Estonia	1,3	Estonian
25	Cyprus	0,8	Greek, Turkish
26	Luxembourg	0,5	Luxemb., French, German
27	Malta	0,4	Maltese, English
	Candidate member-states	Population (in millions)	Official state language
28	Turkey	72,5	Turkish
29	Croatia	4,4	Croatian
30	Macedonia	2,0	Macedonian

As Table 1 makes clear, there are large differences in population size amongst EU member-states. German, French, English, Italian, Spanish and Polish belong to the six most widely spoken official state languages in the present EU, whereas Turkish would come second to German in an enlarged EU. Table 1 also shows the close connection between nation-state references and official state language references. In 27 out of 30 cases, distinct languages are the clearest feature distinguishing one nation-state from its neighbours (Barbour 2000), the only exceptions (and for different reasons) being Belgium, Austria, and Cyprus. This match between nation-state references and official state language references obscures the existence of different types of minority languages that are actually spoken across European nation-states (Haberland 1991; Craith 2006). Many of these languages are indigenous minority languages with a regional base; many other languages stem from abroad without such a base. As mentioned before, we will refer to these languages as regional minority (RM) languages and immigrant minority (IM) languages, respectively (Extra and Gorter 2001). As all of these RM and IM languages are spoken by different language communities and not at state-wide level, it may seem logical to refer to them as community languages, thus contrasting them with the official languages of nation-states. However, the designation "community languages" would lead to confusion at the surface level because this concept is already in use to refer to the official state languages of the EU. In that sense, the designation "community languages" is occupied territory, at least in the EU jargon.

A number of things need to be kept in mind. First of all, within and across EU member-states, many RM and IM languages have larger numbers of speakers than many of the official state languages mentioned in Table 1. Moreover, RM and IM languages in one EU nation-state may be official state languages in another nation-state. Examples of the former result from language border crossing in adjacent nation-states, such as Finnish in Sweden or Swedish in Finland. Examples of the latter result from processes of migration, in particular from Southern to Northern Europe, such as Portuguese, Spanish, Italian or Greek. It should also be kept in mind that many, if not most, IM languages in particular European nation-states originate from countries outside Europe. It is the context of migration and minorisation in particular that makes our proposed distinction between RM and IM languages ambiguous. We see, however, no better alternative. In our opinion, the proposed distinction leads at least to awareness raising and may ultimately lead to an inclusive approach in the European conceptualisation of minority languages.

2.2. Language and identity

Contrary to many popular views, the concepts of "nation" and "nation-state" in the modern sense are relatively recent phenomena (Haarmann 1991; Wright 2000, 2004). Barbour (2000) discusses the distinction between these two concepts in terms of a population and a legally defined entity, respectively. Nations have frequently developed from ethnic groups, but nations and ethnic groups do not coincide. Ethnic groups are often subsets of nations or they function as collective entities across the borders of nation-states. Fishman (1989), Gudykunst (1988) and Riley (2007) go into the link between ethnic identity and (non-national) language use. The construction and/or consolidation of nation-states has ingrained the belief that a national language should correspond to each nation-state, and that this language should be regarded as a core value of national identity. Equating language with national identity, however, is based on a denial of the co-existence of majority and minority languages within the borders of any nation-state and has its roots in the German Romanticism at the end of the 18th and the beginning of the 19th century (cf. Fishman 1973: 39–85, 1989: 105–175, 270–287, Edwards 1985: 23–27, and Joseph 2004: 92–131 for historical overviews). Equating German with Germany was a reaction to the rationalism of the Enlightenment and was also based on anti-French sentiments. The concept of nationalism emerged at the end of the 18th century; the concept of nationality took hold only a century later. Romantic philosophers like Johan Gottfried Herder and Wilhelm von Humboldt laid the foundation for the emergence of a linguistic nationalism in Germany on the basis of which the German language and nation were conceived as superior to the French language and nation. The French, however, were no less reluctant to express their conviction that the reverse was true. Although every nation-state is characterised by heterogeneity, including linguistic heterogeneity, nationalistic movements have always invoked this classical European discourse in their equating languages with nations (cf. renewed references in Germany to such concepts as *Sprachnation* and *Leitkultur*). For recent studies on language, identity and nationalism in Europe we refer to Barbour and Carmichael (2000), Gubbins and Holt (2002), Schneider (2005) and Stevenson and Mar-Molinero (2006), and for a comparative study of attitudes towards language and national identity in France and Sweden to Oakes (2001).

During the 20th century, the relationship between language and national identity in Europe underwent strong changes (Oakes 2001):

- in the national arenas of the EU member-states: the traditional identity of these nation-states has been challenged by major demographic changes (in particular in urban areas) as a consequence of international migration and intergenerational minorisation;
- in the European arena: the concept of a European identity has emerged as a consequence of increasing cooperation and integration at the European level;
- in the global arena: our world has become smaller and more interactive as a consequence of the increasing availability of information and communication technology.

Major changes in each of these three arenas have led to the development of concepts such as transnational citizenship and transnational multiple identities (see, e.g., Ghuman 2003 on South Asian youngsters growing up in Western countries). Inhabitants of Europe no longer identify exclusively with singular nation-states, but give increasing evidence of multiple transnational affiliations. At the EU level, the notion of a European identity was formally expressed for the first time in the *Declaration on European Identity* of December 1973 in Copenhagen. Numerous institutions and documents have propagated and promoted this idea ever since. The most concrete and tangible expression of this idea to date has been the introduction of a European currency in 2002 and the (rejected) proposal for a European Constitution in 2004. In discussing the concept of a European identity, Oakes (2001: 127–131) emphasizes that the recognition of the concept of multiple transnational identities is a prerequisite rather than an obstacle for the acceptance of a European identity. The recognition of multiple transnational identities not only occurs among the traditional inhabitants of European nation-states, but also among newcomers and IM groups in Europe. At the same time, we see a strengthening of regional identities in many regions in Europe, in particular those where a RM language is in use.

Multiple transnational identities and affiliations will require new competences of European citizens in the 21st century. These include the ability to deal with increasing cultural diversity and heterogeneity (Van Londen and De Ruijter 1999). Plurilingualism can be considered a core competence for such an ability. In this context, processes of both convergence and divergence occur. In the European and the global arena, English has increasingly assumed the role of *lingua franca* for international communication (Oakes 2001: 131–136, 149–154; House, this Volume). The rise of English has occurred at the cost of all other official state languages of Europe, including French and German (Ammon 2007). At the same time, growing numbers of newcomers to the national arenas of EU member-states make use of the language repertoires of their countries of origin and destination.

RM and IM languages have much more in common than is usually thought. We find issues on their sociolinguistic, educational, and political agendas such as their spread, their domestic and public vitality, the determinants of language maintenance *versus* language shift towards majority languages (Fishman 2001), the relationship between language, ethnicity and identity, and the status of minority languages in schools, in particular in the compulsory stages of primary and secondary education. Many RM languages did not become designated as *minority* languages until the 18th and 19th centuries, when, during the processes of state-formation in Europe, they found themselves excluded from the state level, in particular from general education. RM languages did not become official languages of most of the states that were then established. Centralising tendencies and an ideology of *one language – one state* have threatened the continued existence of RM languages. The greatest threat to RM languages, however, is the lack of intergenerational transmission. When parents stop speaking the ancestral language with their children, it becomes almost impossible to reverse the ensuing language shift. Education can thus be a threat, but it can also be a major factor in the maintenance and promotion of a minority language. For most RM languages, some kind of educational provisions have been established in an attempt at reversing ongoing language shift. Only in the last few decades have some of these RM languages become relatively well protected in legal terms, as well as by affirmative educational programmes, both at the level of various member-states and at the level of the EU at large.

There have always been speakers of IM languages in Europe, but these languages have only recently emerged as community languages spoken on a wide scale in urban Europe, due to intensified processes of international migration and intergenerational minorisation. Turkish and Arabic are good examples of so-called "non-European" languages that are spoken and learned by millions of inhabitants of the EU. Although IM languages are often conceived of and transmitted as core values by IM language groups, they are less protected than RM languages by affirmative action and legal measures in, for example, education. In fact, the learning and certainly the teaching of IM languages are often seen by majority language speakers and by policy makers as obstacles to integration and as a threat to the national identity.

Table 2. Nomenclature of the field (source: Extra and Yağmur 2004: 19)

Reference to the people
— national/historical/regional/indigenous/old minorities *versus* non-national/non-historical/non-territorial/non-indigenous/new minorities
— non-national residents
— foreigners, étrangers, Ausländer
— (im)migrants
— newcomers, new Xmen (e.g., new Dutchmen)
— co-citizens (instead of citizens)
— ethnic/cultural/ethnocultural minorities
— linguistic minorities
— allochthones (e.g., in the Netherlands), allophones (e.g., in Canada)
— non-English-speaking (NES) residents (in particular in the USA)
— anderstaligen (Dutch: those who speak other languages)
— coloured/black people, visible minorities (the latter in particular in Canada)
Reference to their languages
— community languages (in EU jargon versus Australia)
— migrant languages (in EU jargon)
— ancestral/heritage languages (common concept in Canada)
— national/historical/regional/indigenous/old minority languages *versus* non-territorial/non-regional/non-indigenous/non-European/new minority languages
— autochthonous *versus* allochthonous minority languages
— lesser used/less widely used/less widely taught languages (in EBLUL context)
— stateless/diaspora languages (in particular used for Romani)
— languages other than English (LOTE: common concept in Australia)
Reference to the teaching of these languages
— instruction in own language (and culture)
— mother tongue teaching (MTT)
— home language instruction (HLI)
— community language teaching (CLT)
— regional minority language instruction versus immigrant minority language instruction
— enseignement des langues et cultures d'origine (ELCO: in French/Spanish primary schools)
— enseignement des langues vivantes (ELV: in French/Spanish secondary schools)
— muttersprachlicher Unterricht (MSU: in German primary schools)
— muttersprachlicher Ergänzungsunterricht (in German primary/secondary schools)
— herkunftssprachlicher Unterricht (in German primary/secondary schools)

At the European level, guidelines and directives regarding IM languages are scant and outdated. Despite the possibilities and challenges of comparing the status of RM and IM languages, amazingly few connections have been made in the sociolinguistic, educational, and political domains (Extra and Gorter 2001).

As yet, we lack a common referential framework for the languages under discussion. From an inventory of the different terms in use, we learn that there are no standardised designations for these languages across nation-states. Table 2 gives a non-exhaustive overview of the nomenclature. The concept of "lesser used languages" has been adopted at the EU level; the *European Bureau for Lesser Used Languages* (EBLUL), established in Dublin, speaks and acts on behalf of "the autochthonous regional and minority languages of the EU". Table 2 shows that the utilised terminology varies not only across different nation-states, but also across different types of education.

2.3. The spread of national languages

As mentioned before, most official state languages are spoken on the territory of one European country only. An exception is German, which is a (co-)official language in four EU member-states (Germany, Austria, Luxembourg and Belgium), in two non-EU states (Switzerland and Liechtenstein) and also a recognised RM language in five other EU-states (Czech Republic, Denmark, Hungary, Italy and Slovakia), but not in Poland and Slovenia. In Europe, several languages are at the same time the dominant official language in one state and also spoken in the neighbouring areas of adjacent states, e.g., French in the Aoste valley of Italy, Ukrainian across the border in Slovakia, or Italian in western parts of Slovenia and southern parts of Switzerland. Also Hungarian and Polish are well spread beyond their state borders (see Gal, and Leśniewska and Mazur, this Volume). Often these cross-border languages are recognised as official (minority) languages; sometimes they are not recognised at all.

In addition to the geographic dispersion of languages, which is related to state formation, administrative borders and migration, languages have also spread across the continent as "modern foreign languages", mainly through secondary education and universities (and English increasingly through primary education), but also through cultural promotion of the languages in, for example, adult courses. German, French, and English stand out in Europe because all three receive much support to encourage the learning of these languages as foreign languages abroad and to promote the culture of their respective nation-states.

First of all, German is the language that has the most speakers of the EU (Table 1): over 90 million in Germany and Austria together, plus minority populations in Denmark, Belgium, Czech Republic, Hungary, Italy, Poland, Slovakia and Slovenia. Secondly, French has a long tradition of centralised language policies (Ager, this Volume). This includes the promotion of French abroad as a model case of a strong policy to spread and support the language in political, economic, social, legal, educational and cultural ways. Thirdly, English is in a league of its own when it comes to the spread of the language. Today it is the most common *lingua franca* in Europe in a multitude of international contacts (House, this Volume). All three languages have strong institutions that promote the spread of these languages. The aims and functions of the agencies that promote German, French and English are in many ways comparable. A short characterisation is given below.

The mission of the Goethe Institute is to "promote the study of German abroad and (to) encourage international cultural exchange" (Goethe website 2008). Its headquarters are located in Berlin. In 2008, the Institute was represented in 83 countries through 147 Goethe Institutes. Its activities are funded mainly by the Foreign Office of the German government. "Language work" is one of its major tasks, framed in the context of international cultural co-operation and the image of Germany abroad. The Goethe Institute aims to make German culture more accessible to "people who speak other languages". In terms of its language policy, it also wants "to consolidate the status of the German language in the world", not only through promoting German as a foreign language for learners, but also through "upgrading German in international organisations" (Goethe website 2008). The Goethe Institute claims to contribute to world multilingualism through the promotion of German. Next to the Goethe Institute there are other agencies such as the *Institut für Deutsche Sprache* in Mannheim or the *Deutsche Akademie für Sprache und Dichtung* in Frankfurt; both of these are more research-oriented and aimed less at language promotion.

For French, several organisations exist to promote and protect the French language in France and abroad. The *Délégation Générale à la Langue Française et aux Langues de France* (DGLFLF, General Delegation for French and the Languages of France) is there to ensure the primacy of French on the territory of the French state (Ager, this Volume). The DGLFLF also recognises RM languages as part of the linguistic diversity of the country, but seems to define their role mainly in terms of local culture and literature. For the DGLFLF to include a variety as *langue de France* it has to fulfil the criteria that it is spoken by French citizens for a sufficiently long period of time, that it is part of the common wealth and that it is not an official language of another nation-state. Flemish, Basque, Corsican and Tahitian are included as "languages of France", as well as dialectal Arabic, Berber and Yiddish (DGLF website 2008; DeWitte 2004).

For the promotion of the French language around the world, the *Organisation Internationale de la Francophonie* (OIF) and the *Alliance Française* are the most important agencies. The OIF is an organisation where, in 2008, 55 member-countries and 13 observers collaborated in which French is the official language or where the French language and culture have an important (historical) presence. In most of those countries French is not the majority language. Its impact is much wider than merely the promotion of the French language, because it emphasizes political, economic, cultural and scientific collaboration. Yet many members share French as a common language and promotion of French as an international language is among its explicit priorities. The aim of the *Alliance Française* is to propagate the learning of French as a second or third language (for details see Ager, this Volume). It has a global network of centres in over 130 countries. China and Russia are both top priorities for the *Alliance Française*.

Like the Goethe Institute for German and the *Alliance Française* for French, the British Council has an explicit task to support the use and knowledge of English internationally (Graddol 2006). The British Council is the main agency for the advancement of educational and cultural relations of the United Kingdom with other countries. It was set up in 1934 and is an integral part of the UK's foreign affairs efforts. The British Council is funded by the UK government and obtains revenues from the services it provides. Its annual turnover in 2006/2007 was 551 million British pounds (approximately 825 million euros); almost half of the revenues come from teaching English and administering examinations. In this way, the "English industry" produces an important source of foreign income of Britain. In the context of EU policies on the enhancement of plurilingualism for all EU citizens (see Section 6.3), British Council language policies across Europe are moving away from English only to promoting English as a second, foreign and even first language embedded in plurilingual competencies. In 2008, the British Council had offices in 228 places in 108 countries around the world, with headquarters in London and Manchester. It also ran 185 libraries to back up its activities.

Thus, the spread of German, French and English are supported by strong institutions with a global reach. In contrast, a language such as Polish, which takes up 6th place among the most spoken languages of the EU, has no body at all to support the learning of the language abroad (Leśniewska and Mazur, this Volume). Many other languages also have organisations to promote language learning and knowledge of the culture, such as the *Dante Alighieri* for Italian, the *Cervantes* for Spanish, the *Taalunie* for Dutch and the *Language Councils* in the Nordic countries. There are also organisations more similar to *La Francophonie* such as the CLLP for Portuguese speaking countries, the *Unione Latine* for Romance language promotion, or the Turcophone TIKA. Since 2003, major language organisations in the member-states of the EU are represented in the *European Federation of National Institutes of Language* (EFNIL). The EFNIL wants to promote linguistic diversity and takes as its point of reference the official state languages. The organisation "recognises that education, the media and public discourse play central roles in the dissemination and development of national languages" (EFNIL website 2008).

3. Definition and identification of population groups

3.1. The problem of statistical criteria

Collecting reliable information about the diversity of population groups in EU countries is no easy enterprise. What is, however, more interesting than numbers or estimates of the size of particular groups, are the *criteria* for determining such numbers or estimates. Throughout the EU it is common practice to present data on RM groups on the basis of (home) language use and/or ethnicity, and to present data on IM groups on the basis of nationality and/or country of birth. However, *convergence* between these criteria for the two groups emerges over time, due to the increasing period of migration and minorisation of IM groups in EU countries. Due to their prolonged/permanent stay, there is strong erosion in the utility of nationality or birth-country statistics.

Comparative information on population figures in EU member-states can be obtained from the Statistical Office of the EU in Luxembourg (*EuroStat*). An overall decrease of the indigenous population has been observed in most EU countries over the last decade; at the same time, there has been an increase in the IM figures. For a variety of reasons, however, reliable and comparable demographic information on IM groups in EU countries is difficult to obtain. Seemingly simple questions like *How many Turkish residents live in Germany compared to France?* cannot easily be answered. For some groups or countries, no updated information is available or no such data have ever been collected. Moreover, official statistics only reflect IM groups with legal resident status. Another source of disparity is the different data collection systems being used, ranging from nationwide census data to administrative (municipal) registers or to more or less representative statistical sample surveys (Poulain 2008). Most importantly, however, the most widely used criteria for IM status – nationality and/or country of birth – have become less valid over time because of an increasing trend towards naturalisation and births within the countries of residence. In addition, most residents from former colonies already have the nationality of their country of immigration.

In the context of our reference to nation-states, we will refer to nationality rather than citizenship. Even if the two concepts are often used as synonyms nowadays, we should be aware of their historical and contextual difference in denotation (Guiguet 1998). Nationals belong to a nation-state but they may not have all rights linked with citizenship (e.g., voting rights); in this sense, citizenship is a more inclusive concept than nationality.

For a discussion of the role of censuses in identifying population groups in a variety of multicultural nation-states, we refer to Kertzer and Arel (2002). Alterman (1969) offers a fascinating account of the history of counting people from the earliest known records on Babylonian clay tables in 3800 BC to the USA census in 1970. Besides the methods of counting, Alterman discusses at length who has been counted and how, and who has not been counted and why. The issue of mapping identities through nationwide periodical censuses by state institutions is commonly coupled with a vigorous debate between proponents and opponents about the following "ethnic dilemma": how can you combat discrimination if you do not measure diversity? (Kertzer and Arel 2002: 23–25). Amongst minority groups and academic groups, both proponents and opponents of measuring diversity can be found (cf. Blum 2002 on this debate in France):

— proponents argue in terms of the social or scientific need for population data bases on diversity as prerequisites for affirmative action by the government in such domains as labour, housing, health care, education or media policies;
— opponents argue in terms of the social or scientific risks of public or political misuse of such data bases for stereotyping, stigmatisation, discrimination or even removal of the "unwanted other".

Kertzer and Arel (2002: 2) argue that the census does much more than simply reflect social reality; rather it plays a key role in the construction of that reality and in the creation of collective identities. At the same time, it should be acknowledged that the census is a crucial area for the politics of representation. Census data can make people aware of underrepresentation. Language rights are often a key demand for minority groups on the basis of (home) language databases.

Decennial censuses became a common practice in Europe and the New World colonised by Europeans in the first part of the 19th century. The USA became the first newly established nation-state with a decennial census since 1790. The first countries to include a language question in their census, however, were Belgium in 1846 and Switzerland in the 1850s, both being European countries with more than one official state language. At present, in many EU countries, only population data on nationality and/or birth country (of person and/or parents) are available. In 1982, the *Australian Institute of Multicultural Affairs* recognised the above-mentioned identification problems for inhabitants of Australia and proposed including questions in the Australian census on birth country (of person and parents), ethnic origin (based on self-categorisation in terms of which ethnic group a person considers him/herself to belong to), and home language use. For a discussion of the concepts of ethnicity and ethnic identity in a variety of multicultural contexts we refer to Guibernau and Rex (1997), Jenkins (1997) and Verkuyten (2006). Fishman (1989) and Edwards (1985) are key references on the link between ethnicity and (home) language use. In Table 3, the four criteria mentioned are discussed in terms of their major (dis)advantages.

First of all, Table 3 reveals that there is no simple road to solving the identification problem. Moreover, inspection of the criteria for multicultural population groups is as important as the actual figures themselves. Seen from a European perspective, there is a top-down development over time in the utility and utilisation of different types of criteria, inevitably going from nationality and birth-country criteria in present statistics to self-categorisation and home language in the future. The latter two criteria are generally conceived as complementary criteria. Self-categorisation and home language references need not coincide, as languages may be conceived to variable degrees as core values of ethnocultural identity in contexts of migration and minorisation.

Table 3. Criteria for the definition and identification of population groups in a multicultural society (P/F/M = person/father/mother) (source: Extra and Gorter 2001: 9)

Criterion	Advantages	Disadvantages
Nationality (NAT) (P/F/M)	— objective — relatively easy to establish	— (intergenerational) erosion through naturalisation or double NAT — NAT not always indicative of ethnicity/ identity — some (e.g., ex-colonial) groups have NAT of immigration country
Birth country (BC) (P/F/M)	— objective — relatively easy to establish	— intergenerational erosion through births in immigration country — BC not always indicative of ethnicity/identity — invariable/deterministic: does not take into account dynamics in society (in contrast to all other criteria)
Self-categorisation (SC)	— touches the heart of the matter — emancipatory: SC takes into account person's own conception of ethnicity/ identity	— subjective by definition: also determined by the language/ethnicity of interviewer and by the spirit of the times — multiple SC possible — historically charged, especially by World War II experiences
Home language (HL)	— HL is significant criterion of ethnicity in communication processes — HL data are prerequisite for government policy in areas such as public information or education	— complex criterion: who speaks what language to whom and when? — language is not always a core value of ethnicity/identity — useless in one-person households

3.2. Experiences in European Union countries

The data presented in this Section have been derived from the analysis of two comprehensive documents published by the European Commission and EuroStat (2004; 2005). In 23 out of 27 EU countries nationwide censuses with variable intervals are still in use. Scandinavian countries and the Netherlands rely on yearly updated administrative (municipal) registers in combination with periodical sample surveys. Other countries combine nationwide census data with administrative register data and/or sample survey data (Austria, Belgium, France, Latvia, Slovenia).

The following parameters are used in all or many EU countries for the definition and identification of population groups:

— *(dual) citizenship or nationality*: the category of (dual) citizenship or nationality is used in all EU countries; in North-Western European countries these two concepts are commonly used as synonyms nowadays; in Southern, Middle and Eastern European countries, however, these two categories are commonly used distinctively: in these countries citizenship refers to what is termed nationality or citizenship in North-Western Europe, whereas (ethnic) nationality refers to what is termed ethnicity in North-Western Europe; in the Czech Republic, for instance, the nationality question asks for an indication of *what nationality you consider yourself to be*, which is different from the citizenship question (see also Leśniewska and Mazur, this Volume);
— *birth country / place*: this is a common category in all EU countries; in some countries, this question refers explicitly to the country/place of (permanent) residence of *your mother when you were born*;
— *ethnicity*: ethnicity or ethnic nationality is asked for in 13 EU countries, 3 of which consider this question to be voluntary/optional;
— *language*: one or more language questions are asked in 17 EU countries, 2 of which consider this/these question(s) to be voluntary/optional;
— *religious denomination*: religious denomination questions are asked in 15 EU countries, 6 of which consider this question to be voluntary/optional.

Table 4 gives an overview of the *status quo* with respect to the latter three parameters across EU countries. It should be noted that data collection on some or all of these questions in some EU countries is considered to be in conflict with privacy legislation and/or illegal, while in other countries such questions are taken to generate crucial information.

Table 4. Identification of ethnicity, language and religious denomination in 27 EU countries

EU countries	Ethnicity/ ethnic nationality	Language	Religious denomination
Austria	–	+	+
Belgium	–	–	–
Bulgaria	*	*	*
Cyprus	+	+	+
Czech Republic	+	+	+
Denmark	–	–	–
Estonia	+	+	*
Finland	–	+	+
France	–	–	–
Germany	–	–	+
Greece	–	–	–
Hungary	*	*	*
Ireland	+	+	+
Italy	–	–	–
Latvia	+	+	–
Lithuania	+	+	+
Luxembourg	–	–	–
Malta	–	+	–
Netherlands	–	–	–
Poland	+	+	–
Portugal	–	–	*
Romania	+	+	+
Slovakia	+	+	+
Slovenia	*	+	*
Spain	–	+	–
Sweden	–	–	–
United Kingdom	+	+	*

* = voluntary/optional question

A closer inspection of the operationalisation of the three parameters referred to in Table 4 leads to the following conclusions.

Detailed ethnicity questions are asked in the United Kingdom and Ireland. In the United Kingdom, 5 categories are distinguished, i.e., *White, Mixed, Asian (British), Black (British), Chinese/Other*, in all cases with subcategories. Similar questions are asked in Ireland. Hungary lists 14 categories (plus *other*) and asks *which of these nationalities' cultural values and traditions do you feel affinity with?* Estonia lists 6 (plus *other*) *ethnic nationalities*, and Cyprus lists *Greek-Cypriot, Armenian, Maronite, Latin* and *Turkish-Cypriot*.

Questions on religious denomination are asked in terms of *belief, church, faith, religion* and/or *religious affiliation/community/confession/ denomination*, and in terms of *religion/religious denomination you were brought up in*. The latter – additional – question is only asked in Scotland.

Table 5 gives an overview of the operationalisation of the language questions asked for in 17 out of 27 EU countries. Two main conclusions emerge from Table 5. First of all, the three most commonly asked questions on language use relate to mother tongue (11 countries), (other) language(s) spoken (frequently) (6 countries) and language(s) (most frequently) spoken at home (5 countries).

Table 5. Operationalisation of language questions in 17 EU countries

EU countries	Mother tongue	(Other) language(s) spoken (frequently)	Language(s) (most frequently) spoken at home	Language(s) spoken with family members or friends	Speak well/ average/ a little	Understand/ Speak/ Read/ Write
Austria	–	–	+	–	–	–
Bulgaria	+	–	–	–	–	–
Cyprus	–	+	–	–	–	–
Czech Republic	(1)	–	–	–	–	–
Estonia	+	+	–	–	–	–
Finland	+	–	–	–	–	–
Hungary	+	+	–	+	–	–
Ireland	–	(2)	–	–	–	–
Latvia	+	+	–	–	–	–
Lithuania	+	+	–	–	–	–
Malta	–	–	+	–	+	–
Poland	–	–	+	–	–	–
Romania	+	–	–	–	–	–
Slovakia	+	–	–	–	–	–
Slovenia	+	–	+	–	–	–
Spain	(3)	–	(3)	–	–	(4)
United Kingdom	–	–	–	–	–	(5)

(1) Indicate the language spoken by your mother or guardian when you were a child
(2) Only Irish; if yes, daily within/outside the educational system/weekly/less often/never
(3) Both language questions in the Basque County, Navarre and Galicia, for Basque/ Galician
(4) In Catalonia, Valencia and the Balearic Islands for Catalan
(5) Only in Wales and Scotland, for Welsh and Gaelic respectively

Secondly, Hungary makes the most investments in finding out about language use. In addition to these findings, it should be mentioned that in some countries collecting home language data is in fact in conflict with present language legislation. This holds in particular for Belgium, where no census data on language use have been collected since 1947 and traditional language borders between Dutch, French and German have been allocated and fixed in the law.

3.3. Experiences in non-European immigration countries

Various types of criteria for identifying population groups in multicultural societies have been suggested and used outside Europe in countries with a longer immigration history, and as a result of this, with a longstanding history of collecting census data on multicultural population groups (Kertzer and Arel 2002). This holds in particular for non-European immigration countries in which English is the dominant language, like Australia, Canada, South Africa, and the USA. To identify the multicultural composition of their populations, these countries employ a variety of questions in their periodical censuses. In Table 6, an overview of (clusters of) questions is provided; for each country, the given census is taken as the norm. Both the type and number of questions are different for each of these countries. Canada takes up a prime position with the highest number of questions.

Table 6. Overview of (clusters of) census questions in four multicultural countries (source: Extra and Yağmur 2004: 67)

Questions in the census	Australia 2001	Canada 2001	SA 2001	USA 2000	Coverage
1 Nationality of respondent	+	+	+	+	4
2 Birth country of respondent	+	+	+	+	4
3 Birth country of parents	+	+	−	−	2
4 Ethnicity	−	+	−	+	2
5 Ancestry	+	+	−	+	3
6 Race	−	+	+	+	3
7 Mother tongue	−	+	−	−	1
8 Language used at home	+	+	+	+	4
9 Language used at work	−	+	−	−	1
10 Proficiency in English	+	+	−	+	3
11 Religious denomination	+	+	+	−	3
Total of dimensions	7	11	5	7	30

There are only three questions that are asked in all countries while two questions are asked in only one country. There are four different questions asked about language. The operationalisation of questions also shows interesting differences, both between and within countries over time (see Clyne 1991 for a discussion of methodological problems in comparing the answers to differently phrased questions in Australian censuses from a longitudinal perspective).

Questions about ethnicity, ancestry and/or race have proven to be problematic in all of the countries under consideration (Spencer 2006; Ansell and Solomos 2008). In some countries, ancestry and ethnicity have been conceived of as equivalent, cf. USA census question 10 in 2000: *What is this person's ancestry or ethnic origin?* Or, take Canadian census question 17 in 2001: *To which ethnic or cultural group(s) did this person's ancestors belong?* Australian census question 18 in 2001 only involved ancestry and not ethnicity, cf. *What is the person's ancestry?* with the following comments for respondents: *Consider and mark the ancestries with which you most closely identify. Count your ancestry as far as three generations, including grandparents and great-grandparents.* As far as ethnicity and ancestry have been distinguished in census questions, the former concept related most commonly to present self-categorisation of the respondent and the latter to former generations. The diverse ways in which respondents themselves may interpret both concepts, however, remains a problem that cannot be solved easily.

According to Table 6, South Africa remains as the only country where a racial question is asked instead of a question on ethnicity and/or ancestry. The paradox in South Africa is that questions on ethnicity are often considered to be racist, while the racial question (in terms of *Black/White/Coloured/Indian*) from the earlier Apartheid era has survived. Although the validity of questions about ethnicity, ancestry and/or race is problematic, at least one question from this cluster is needed to compare its outcomes with those of questions on language. Language is not always a core value of ethnicity/identity and multiculturalism may become under-estimated if it is reduced to multilingualism. For this reason, one or more questions derived from cluster 4–6 in Table 6 are necessary complements of one or more questions derived from cluster 7–10.

Whereas, according to Table 6, "ethnicity" is mentioned in recent censuses of only two countries, four language-related questions are asked in one to four countries. Only in Canada has the concept of "mother tongue" been included (census question 7). It is defined for respondents as *the language first learnt at home in childhood and still understood*, whereas questions 8 and 9 are related to the language *most often* used at home/work. Table 6 shows the added value of language-related census questions for the definition and identification of multicultural populations, in particular the added value of the question on home language use compared to questions on the more opaque concepts of mother tongue and ethnicity. Although the language-related census questions in the four countries under consideration differ in their precise formulation and commentary, the outcomes of these questions are generally conceived as cornerstones for educational policies with respect to the teaching of English as a first or second language and the teaching of languages other than English.

Table 6 also shows the importance of comparing different groups using equal criteria. Unfortunately, this is often not the case in the public or political discourse. Examples of such unequal treatment are references to *Poles vs. Jews*, *Israelis vs. Arabs*, *Serbs* and *Croatians vs. Muslims*, *Dutchmen vs. Turks* (for Dutch nationals with Turkish ethnicity), *Dutchmen vs. Muslims*, or *Islam vs. the West* (where does the West end when is the world a globe?). Equal treatment presupposes reference to equal dimensions in terms of Table 6.

3.4. Conclusions and outlook

The presented overview in Sections 3.2 and 3.3 shows that large-scale home language surveys are both feasible and meaningful, and that the interpretation of the resulting databases is made easier by transparent and multiple questions on home language use. These conclusions become even more pertinent in the context of gathering data on multicultural *school* populations. European experiences in this domain have been gathered in particular in Great Britain and Sweden. In both countries, extensive municipal home language statistics have been collected through local educational authorities by asking school children questions about their oral and written skills in languages other than the dominant language, and about their participation in and need for education in these languages.

An important similarity in the questions about home language use in these surveys is that the outcomes are based on reported rather than observed facts. Answers to questions on home language use may be coloured by the language of the questions themselves (which may or may not be the primary language of the respondent), by the ethnicity of the interviewer (which may or may not be the same as the ethnicity of the respondent), by the (perceived) goals of the sampling (which may or may not be defined by national or local authorities), and by the spirit of the times (which may or may not be in favour of multiculturalism). These problems become even more prominent in a school context in which pupils are respondents. Apart from the problems mentioned, the answers may be coloured by peer-group pressure and they may lead to interpretation problems in attempts to identify and classify languages. For a discussion of these and other possible effects, we refer to Nicholas (1988) and Alladina (1993). The problems referred to are inherent characteristics of large-scale data gathering through questionnaires about language-related behaviour and should be compensated by small-scale data gathering through observing actual language behaviour. Such small-scale ethnographic research is not an alternative to large-scale language surveys, but a necessary complement. For a discussion of (cor)relations between reported and measured bilingualism of IM children in the Netherlands, we refer to Broeder and Extra (1998).

Given the decreasing significance of nationality and birth-country criteria in the European context, the combined criteria of self-categorisation (ethnicity) and home language use are potentially promising alternatives for obtaining basic information on the increasingly multicultural composition of European nation-states. As a result, *convergence* will emerge between the utilised criteria for the definition and identification of IM and RM groups in such societies. The added value of home language statistics is that they offer valuable insights into the distribution and vitality of home languages across different population groups and thus raise the awareness of multilingualism (Nicholas 1994).

4. Regional minority languages at home and at school

4.1. Regional minority languages across Europe

The distribution of RM language groups in the EU can only be presented through an approximation because we are faced with a lot of diversity in both the availability and the quality of the data on language use. In some member-states, large-scale reported figures are available because there have been questions on language in several censuses, as a result of which data were collected over a longer period of time; in other states, only rough estimates can be obtained, either from insiders in the language group (frequently language activists who may want to overestimate the figures) or by outsiders (for example state officials who may have an interest in deliberately underestimating the number of speakers).

✱ numerically small language communities

Figure 1. Geographic spread of RM language groups across EU member-states (source: Mercator Research Centre)

Figure 1 serves as visual illustration of the geographic distribution of RM language groups and is taken from the Mercator Research Centre's website. Different typologies for RM languages exist. Thus, we could rank these languages according to geographic spread (Edwards 1991, 2007), perceived strength on some key variables (Nelde et al. 1996), language family (e.g., Celtic, Romance, Germanic or Slavic) or simply by group size. We opt for a simple typology and will distinguish five categories of RM languages within the EU (Ó Riagáin 2001; Gorter 1996; Grin and Moring 2002). For each type of language group we will give examples and the most reasonable estimates available. Figures for numbers of speakers are problematic (see Section 3.1). In some cases, such figures are based upon recent census outcomes or surveys of sufficient scale and reliability. Other figures, due to the lack of other data, are based on informed estimates by experts on a particular language group. In some cases whether or not a language should be included may even be under dispute, because languages may be considered by some as dialects of another language (e.g., Scanian in the south of Sweden, or Veneto in the north of Italy). Other language groups could be split up further, for instance the Sámi languages (Svonni, this Volume), or Frisian, which for some outsiders comprises the varieties of Frisian in the Netherlands and North Frisian and Saterfrisian in Germany. Frisian is then considered as one language, even though the speakers of these different varieties cannot understand each other and if asked about it would disagree that they speak the same language (Gorter, Van der Meer and Riemersma, this Volume). Sometimes varieties are taken together as one language group by almost general agreement, but for some politicians to distinguish between Catalan and Valencian can be an important political issue (Vila, this Volume). Similarly, Limburgian used to be perceived as a collection of several different dialects in the Netherlands, but in 1998 the Limburgian language was recognised by the government of the Netherlands as a regional language in terms of the *European Charter for Regional or Minority Languages* (see Section 4.3); in Belgium, where very similar varieties are spoken, the state government has not followed this recognition and it is not likely to do so in the future either. Several collections of statistics about RM languages in (mainly Western) Europe can be found in Breatnach (1998), Euromosaic (1996) and Tjeerdsma (1998), as well as in the Ethnologue (Gordon 2005).

In our typology, five categories of RM languages in the EU are distinguished. The first category are so-called "unique" RM languages. These are languages spoken in only one EU member-state. Examples of language groups in this category are Breton (160,000) and Corsican (166,000) in France; North Frisian (8,000), Saterfrisian (2,000) and Sorbian (20,000) in Germany; Friulan (550,000), Ladin (30,000) and Sardinian (1,000,000) in Italy; Frisian (325,000) in the Netherlands (Gorter, Van der Meer, Riemersma, this Volume); Kashubian (52,000) in Poland; Galician

(1,160,000) and Asturian (360,000) in Spain; Scottish Gaelic (59,000), Scots (1,500,000), Welsh (582,000) and Cornish (300) in the United Kingdom.

The second category concerns those RM languages that are spoken in more than one EU member-state (but are not official state languages). To this category belong languages like Basque in Spain (Basque Autonomous Community 620,000, Navarre 50,000) and in France (Iparralde 70,000); Catalan in Spain (Catalonia 4 million, Balearic Islands 428,000, Valencia 1,9 million, Aragon 48,000), in France (102,000) and in Italy (20,000) (Vila, this Volume); Occitan in Spain (4,000), in France (3,500,000) and in Italy (50,000); Sami in Sweden (18,000) and in Finland (3,000) (Svonni, this Volume); Low-Saxon in the Netherlands (1,8 million) and Low-German (8 million) in Germany.

The third category concerns RM languages which are a minority language in one state, but the official and dominant language in another, neighbouring state (the latter not necessarily being a member-state of the EU). There are a lot of such languages, and the linguistic relationship between the dominated and dominant language differs from case to case. Some of these languages might perhaps also be considered as examples of the first category. Multiple cases are, for instance, Albanian in Italy (100,000) and Greece (80,000); Croatian in Italy (2,000) and Austria (25,000); German in Belgium (100,000), Czech Republic (50,000), Denmark (20,000), France (975,000), Italy (320,000), Poland (500,000) and Denmark (20,000); Polish in Germany (200,000+), Czech Republic (50,000), Lithuania (200,000) and Latvia (57,000), now also in the UK and Ireland (Leśniewska and Mazur, this Volume). Other examples are Berber (25,000) and Portuguese (3,600) in Spain; Dutch (80,000) in France; Danish (50,000) in Germany; Greek (11,000) in Italy; Lithuanian in Poland (30,000).

The fourth category consists of three languages with a special status; they are official state languages: two are official working languages of the EU and one is not. These are Luxembourgish (359,000), which is official in Luxembourg next to German and French; Luxembourgish is also spoken in France (35,000). Irish became an official language of the EU in 2007. There are an estimated 1,6 million speakers who have some ability in Irish, and 340,000 speakers who use it on a daily basis. Irish is also spoken in the United Kingdom (in Northern Ireland by 165,000 speakers who have some knowledge, of whom perhaps 25,000 use it regularly). Maltese (400,000) is also an official language of the EU since Malta became a member-state in 2004. In Malta, both English and Maltese are official languages and Italian is widely spoken as well. The social status of Maltese is comparable to but also different from that of Luxembourgish and Irish.

The fifth category consists of non-territorial minority languages, which exist in smaller or larger numbers in almost all EU member-states; the most prominent ones are Romani and Yiddish.

This typology refers mainly to the geographic dimension related to state boundaries and partially to legal status (level of recognition). In that sense, the typology has its inherent limitations. The distinctions may be gradual and some language groups may not fit in very well (e.g., Slovenian, Croatian or Czech). Our aim is to present a typology here for the purpose of making the diversity of contexts visible across Europe (see also Gorter et al. 1990).

The sociolinguistic status of RM languages is only partially determined by demographic size. Their social status and vitality are also characterised by a combination of other factors such as use in the family, legal status, government policies, presence in traditional and new media and in cultural life, existence of a standard variety, level of literacy, economic development, language attitudes and ideology, institutional support and level of organised language activism. The demographic and sociolinguistic status are related to the status of these languages in education. The level of educational provision may in turn influence the numerical development and the social status of RM languages.

4.2. Regional minority languages at home

There are many publications on the status and use of RM languages in Europe (e.g., Gorter et al. 1990; Nelde, Strubell and Williams 1996; O'Reilly 2001a, 2001b; Hogan-Brun and Wolff 2003; Williams 2005; Ureland, Lodge and Pugh 2007). In a number of European countries, a periodical census includes one or more questions on language and ethnicity, but in other countries no such questions are asked. An additional tool for obtaining data is a sociolinguistic survey. There are some RM language communities where such surveys are carried out at regular intervals (Nelde, Strubell and Williams 1996). Here, we give some examples.

In Ireland there is a tradition of both a census that contains questions on language abilities and language use (NISRA 2004) and regular sociolinguistic surveys (Ó Riagáin and Ó Gliasáin 1994). The Irish case is thus well documented. In language policy studies, Irish "is regularly presented as the classic case of the failure of language management" (Spolsky 2004).

In Wales there is also a tradition of census data. A question on speaking Welsh has been included in the census since 1891, when 54% of the population reported to be able to speak Welsh. Since then the proportion of people speaking Welsh has declined, and in 2001 about 21% reported the ability to speak Welsh. In 2001, 39% of the children aged 10–15 reported to be able to speak Welsh compared to 25% of 16–19 year olds (Office for National Statistics 2005). Language use surveys provide deeper insight into the relation between language competence and actual use and the relevance of this relationship for language planning (Williams and Morris 2000). In the United Kingdom, the next decennial census will be held in 2011 and the Office for National Statistics carried out a household questionnaire in 2007 to test the planned procedures (*www.statistics.gov.uk/censustest*). Questions 12–15 refer to "national identity", ethnicity, religion and language skills, respectively. With respect to the latter, a distinction is made between English, Welsh, Other language (to be specified in an open box), and British/Other Sign Language; in the first three cases, a further distinction is made between *no ability/understand/speak/read/write*. The format and nature of the 2011 UK census are still under negotiation. At the time of writing, no decision had been made on the number and type of language questions, neither on English nor on languages other than English.

In Spain, the census has questions on the official languages of the Autonomous Communities in the Basque County, Catalonia and Galicia. In the Basque County, for example, the regional government has carried out large-scale surveys in 1990, 1995, 2000 and 2005, which also cover Navarre and Iparralde (the Basque parts in France). According to the most recently published survey (Euskararen Jarraipena III 2003), the percentage of Basque-Spanish or Basque-French bilinguals for the whole of the Basque County (in Spain and France) is 22%, and 14.5% report to be "passive bilingual". With a few exceptions, the rest of the population are monolingual in either Spanish or French. The number of bilinguals in the Basque Autonomous Community is increasing and it is now 29.4% of the population. The Basque Government actively encourages the use of Basque as language of instruction. At present, 89% of primary school children and 78% of secondary school children have Basque as language of instruction (Cenoz, forthcoming). Apart from promoting the use of Basque in education, the Basque Government has created specific institutions to teach and promote the use of Basque in other sectors such as government services, the media or private companies. This policy has had some effect in restoring the status of Basque and reversing language shift. In spite of the support given by the Basque Government, Basque is still a language at risk and according to the 2001 survey, only 11.9% of the population use Basque more than Spanish and 6.8% of the population report that they use Basque as much as Spanish (Euskararen Jarraipena III 2003).

The Netherlands has not had a census since 1971 and never had a question on language use. In the province of Friesland large-scale surveys were carried out at regular intervals in 1967, 1980 and 1994 (Gorter 1994). A "quick scan" in 2007 showed that the figures have not changed much over the last few years. Approximately 94% of the population can understand Frisian, 74% can speak Frisian, 75% can read it and 28% can write it at least "reasonably" (Province of Fryslân 2007; Gorter, Van der Meer and Riemersma, this Volume). Over a time span of almost 40 years, a slow decline has been observed in speaking proficiency and some increase in writing abilities. There is, however, an increased language shift among younger generations towards Dutch as their first language. The use of Frisian shows an uneven pattern over differing social domains. In the domains of the family, the work place and the village community, Frisian demonstrates a relatively strong position, with a small majority of the population still using Frisian. In the more formal domains of education, the media, public administration and law, Dutch clearly dominates (Gorter 2001; Gorter, Van der Meer and Riemersma, this Volume).

The Euromosaic (1996) project has provided a general overview of 48 RM language communities in the EU. In about half of these cases, data were also collected through small-scale sociolinguistic surveys. In 1999, after Austria, Finland and Sweden had joined the EU, the Euromosaic study was extended and again in 2004, resulting in about 90 RM language groups in ten new member-states. The *European Language Survey Network* has developed a core module of 28 questions that can be used as a standard for questionnaires in any RM language community in Europe in order to obtain a basic overview of the language situation (ELSN 1996; Gorter 2008).

4.3. Regional minority languages at school

In the *European Framework Convention on National Minorities* and in the *European Charter for Regional or Minority Languages* we find a kind of European standard. The groups covered by these two treaties are RM languages. The Framework Convention which has been operative since 1998 outlines its aims in a general way and provides a standard for the member-states that become signatories. As far as education is concerned, there is first of all the encouragement "to foster knowledge of the culture, language and history of the national minorities, also among the majority" (Article 12) as well as "the recognition of the right to learn the minority language" (Article 14). This means that all citizens have to be informed, through the school curriculum, about minorities, and also that members of an RM group have a right to receive at least some minimal RM language teaching provision.

In March 1998, the Council of Europe's *European Charter for Regional or Minority Languages* came into operation. The Charter functions as an international instrument for the comparison of legal measures and facilities of member-states in this policy domain (Craith 2003), and is aimed at the protection and the promotion of "the historical regional or minority languages of Europe." The concepts of "regional" and "minority" languages are not specified in the Charter and IM languages are explicitly excluded from the Charter. States are free in their choice of which RM languages to include. Also, the degree of protection is not prescribed; thus, a state can choose loose or tight policies. The result is a wide variety of provisions across EU member-states (Grin 2003).

The European Charter is much more elaborate on the use of language in education than the European Framework Convention. The Charter offers the adhering states the opportunity of choice between different alternatives (Woehrling 2006). Even if a state has chosen one of the presented goals for education, the languages that are actually used in the curriculum can vary. The complexity can be summarised as a typology with four categories: 1) no RM language teaching at all; 2) the RM language as subject and the dominant language as medium of instruction; 3) both the RM language and the dominant language as medium of instruction; and 4) the RM language as the medium of instruction and the dominant language as subject. The fifth logical possibility, no teaching of the dominant language, does not occur.

The number of RM languages in Europe for which there is no educational provision at all has decreased over the last few decades. In many cases, teaching takes place only on a very limited scale, sometimes restricted to pre-primary education (e.g., Saterfrisian in Germany). The most frequent pattern is category 2, where the RM language is (only) a subject. Categories 3 and 4 contain fewer language groups, and especially in category 4, whenever it occurs (e.g., the Basque County, Catalonia and Wales), the pattern may be limited to particular levels of the educational system or to specific types of schools.

What is most important is the result of RM language schooling. Does schooling indeed lead to increased RM language use and language transmission, or has it rather promoted the shift to the dominant language? Few studies have been carried out throughout Europe on this topic. In the case of transitional education, where only little attention is given to the RM language (e.g., one lesson per week at primary level), this approach may actually work as an encouragement to use the dominant language. In such cases, speaking the RM language may be conceived of as a "learning deficit" which has to be remedied through education. In the case of stronger provisions for RM language teaching, the RM language is commonly conceived of as an enrichment and as worthy of revitalisation and promotion. The outcome of such education contributes to cultural pluralism, and in principle, pupils do become bilingual and biliteral. Examples of such well-established RM languages are Catalan, Basque, Welsh, and Swedish (in Finland).

5. Immigrant minority languages at home and at school

5.1. Immigrant minority groups across Europe

As a consequence of socio-economically or politically determined processes of migration, the traditional patterns of language variation across Western Europe have changed considerably over the past few decades. A new pattern of migration started in the 1960s and the early 1970s, and it was mainly economically motivated. In the case of Mediterranean groups, migration initially involved contract workers who expected – and were expected – to stay for a limited period of time. As the period of their stay gradually became longer, this pattern of economic migration was followed by a second pattern of social migration as their families joined them. Subsequently, a second generation was born in the immigrant countries, while their parents often remained uncertain or ambivalent about whether to stay or to return to their country of origin. These demographic shifts over time have also been accompanied by shifts of designation for the groups under consideration – "migrant workers", "immigrant families", and "immigrant minorities", respectively (see also Table 2).

As a result, many industrialised Western European countries have a growing number of IM populations which differ widely, both from a cultural and from a linguistic point of view, from the indigenous population. In spite of more stringent immigration policies in most EU countries, the prognosis is that IM populations will continue to grow as a consequence of the increasing number of political refugees, the opening of the internal European borders, and political and economic developments in Central and Eastern Europe and in other regions of the world. In the year 2000, about one third of the population under the age of 35 in urbanised Western Europe had an immigration background.

Within the various EU countries, four major IM groups can be distinguished: people from Mediterranean EU countries and Mediterranean non-EU countries, people from former colonial countries, and political refugees. An overall decrease of the indigenous population has been observed in all EU countries over the last decade; at the same time, there has been an increase in the immigration figures. Although free movement of migrants between EU member-states is legally permitted and promoted, most immigrants in EU countries originate from non-EU countries.

At the EU level, comparable cross-national data are available only on non-national population groups in EU member-states (Poulain 2008; EuroStat 2006). In 2004, their number was around 25 million, just under 5.5% of the total EU population. The largest numbers of foreign citizens reside in Germany, France, Spain, the United Kingdom and Italy. The citizenship structures of foreign populations in the EU member-states vary greatly. As well as geographical proximity, the composition of the non-national population in each country, examined against the proportion of the five largest groups of non-nationals, strongly reflects their history, in particular labour migration, recent political developments and historical links. For example, the largest non-national groups include Turkish citizens in Germany, Denmark and the Netherlands; citizens of former colonies in Portugal (citizens of Cape Verde, Brazil and Angola) and in Spain (Ecuadorians and Moroccans); migrants from Albania in Greece; citizens from other parts of the former Yugoslavia in Slovenia; Czech citizens in Slovakia; and citizens from former Soviet Union countries in Estonia, Latvia and Lithuania.

5.2. Immigrant minority languages across Europe

Given the overwhelming focus on second-language acquisition by IM groups, there is much less evidence on the status and use of IM languages across Europe as a result of processes of international migration and intergenerational minorisation. In contrast to RM languages, IM languages have no established status in terms of period and area of residence, nor do they have influential pressure groups at the EU level. Also in contrast to RM languages, hardly any systematically collected data are available on IM languages across European nation-states. Typological differences between IM languages across EU nation-states do exist, e.g., in terms of the status of IM languages as EU or non-EU languages, or as languages of former colonies. Taken from the latter perspective, e.g., Indian languages are prominent in the United Kingdom, Maghreb languages in France, Congolese languages in Belgium, and Surinamese languages in the Netherlands.

Tosi (1984) has carried out an early case study on Italian as an IM language in England. Churchill (1986) has offered an early cross-national perspective on the education of IM children in the OECD countries, while Reid and Reich (1992) have carried out a cross-national evaluative study of 15 pilot projects on the education of IM children supported by the European Commission. Most studies in Europe have focused on a spectrum of IM languages at the level of one particular multilingual city (Kroon 1990; Baker and Eversley 2000), one particular nation-state (LMP 1985; Alladina and Edwards 1991; Extra and Verhoeven 1993a; Extra and De Ruiter 2001; Caubet, Chaker and Sibille 2002; Extra et al. 2002; Dewitte 2004), or one particular IM language at the state or European level (Tilmatine 1997 and Obdeijn and De Ruiter 1998 on Arabic in Europe, or Jørgensen 2003 on Turkish in Europe). A number of studies have taken both a cross-national and a cross-linguistic perspective on the status and use of IM languages in Europe (e.g., Husén and Opper 1983; Jaspaert and Kroon 1991; Extra and Verhoeven 1993b, 1998; Gogolin and Kroon 2000; Extra and Gorter 2001; Luchtenberg 2004; Extra and Yağmur 2004).

There have also been comparative studies on dealing with linguistic diversity in Europe and abroad. Examples of such studies are Pauwels, Winter and Lo Bianco (2007) and Barni and Extra (2008): the focus of the former study is on maintaining minority languages in cross-continental contexts, the focus of the latter on mapping linguistic diversity in such contexts. A fascinating study on the vitality of IM languages in New York City was published by García and Fishman (2002).

5.3. Immigrant minority languages at school

Being aware of cross-national differences in denotation (see Table 2, Section 2.2), we use the notion of *community language teaching* (henceforward CLT) when referring to IM languages at school. Our rationale for using the concept of CLT rather than the concepts of *mother tongue teaching* or *home language instruction* is the inclusion of a broad spectrum of potential target groups. First of all, the status of an IM language as a "native" or "home" language can change through intergenerational processes of language shift. Moreover, in secondary education, both minority and majority pupils are often *de iure* (although seldom *de facto*) admitted to CLT (in the Netherlands, for instance, Turkish is a secondary school subject referred to as "Turkish" rather than "home language instruction"; compare also the concepts of *Enseignement des Langues et Cultures d'Origine* and *Enseignement des Langues Vivantes* in French primary and secondary schools, respectively, in Table 2).

Across many EU countries, there has been an increase in the number of IM pupils who speak a language at home other than or in addition to the dominant school language in primary and secondary education. Schools have responded to this home-school language mismatch by paying more attention to the learning and teaching of the dominant language as a second language. A great deal of energy and money is being spent on developing curricula, teaching materials, and teacher training for second-language education. CLT stands in strong contrast to this, as it is much more susceptible to an ideological debate about its legitimacy. While there is consensus on the necessity of investing in second-language education for IM pupils, there is a lack of support for CLT. IM languages are commonly considered sources of problems and deficiencies, and they are rarely seen as sources of knowledge and enrichment. Policy makers, local educational authorities, headmasters, and teachers of "regular" subjects often have reservations about or negative attitudes towards CLT. On the other hand, parents of IM pupils, CLT teachers, and IM organisations often make a case for including IM languages in the school curriculum. These differences in top-down and bottom-up attitudes emerge in many EU nation-states.

Across Europe, vast contrasts occur in the status of IM languages at school, depending on particular nation-states, or even particular federal states within nation-states (as in Germany), and depending on particular IM languages, being official state languages in other European (Union) countries or not. Most commonly, IM languages are not part of mainstream education. In Great Britain, for example, IM languages are not part of the "national" curriculum, and they are dealt with in various types of "supplementary" or "complementary" education at out-of-school hours (e.g., Martin et al. 2004; Edwards, this Volume).

From a historical point of view, many EU countries show a similar chronological development in their argumentation in favour of CLT. CLT was generally introduced into primary education with a view to family remigration. This objective was also clearly expressed in *Directive 77/486* of the European Community, on 25 July 1977. The Directive focused on the education of the children of "migrant workers" with the aim "principally to facilitate their possible reintegration into the Member-State of origin". The Directive excluded all IM children originating from non-EU countries, although these children formed and form the majority in many European primary schools. At that time, Sweden was not an EU member-state, and CLT policies for IM children in Sweden were not directed towards remigration but modelled according to bilingual education policies for the large minority of Finnish-speaking children in Sweden.

During the 1970s, the above argumentation for CLT was increasingly abandoned. Demographic developments showed no substantial signs of families remigrating to their source countries; instead, processes of family reunion and family formation took place in the target countries. This development resulted in a conceptual shift, and CLT became primarily aimed at combating disadvantages. CLT had to bridge the gap between the home and the school environment, and to encourage school achievement in "regular" subjects. Because such an approach tended to underestimate the importance of other dimensions, some countries began to emphasize the intrinsic importance of CLT from cultural, legal, or economic perspectives:

— from a cultural perspective, CLT contributes to maintaining and advancing a pluriform society, in line with the fact that many IM groups consider their own language as a core value of their cultural identity;
— from a legal perspective, CLT meets the internationally recognised right to language transmission and language maintenance;
— from an economic perspective, CLT leads to an important pool of profitable knowledge in societies with an increasingly international orientation.

Comparative cross-national references to experiences with CLT in the various EU member-states are rare (Reich 1991, 1994; Reid and Reich 1992; Fase 1994; Tilmatine 1997; Broeder and Extra 1998; Schneider 2005), or they focus on particular groups (Tilmatine 1997; Obdeijn and De Ruiter 1998). With a view to the demographic development of European nation-states into multicultural societies and the similarities in CLT issues, more cross-national comparative research would be desirable, in the domain of both primary and secondary education. Extra and Yağmur (2004: 129) suggested a range of CLT status parameters for such research, outlined in Table 7.

Table 7. Status parameters for community language teaching (CLT) in primary and secondary schools (source: Extra and Yağmur 2004: 129)

CLT parameters	Research questions for primary and secondary schools
1 Target groups	Are target groups specified in terms of (which) countries of origin and/or (which) home languages/mother tongues? Is CLT also accessible (*de iure*) for and utilised (*de facto*) by indigenous pupils?
2 Arguments	Are arguments given in terms of a struggle against (which) deficits and/or in terms of (which) multicultural policy?
3 Objectives	Are objectives specified in terms of (which) language skills and/or metalinguistic skills?
4 Evaluation	Does evaluation of the pupils' achieved skills take place, and if so, how and when? Do pupils get grades/report figures for achieved skills in their regular school reports?
5 Enrolment	Is there a minimal enrolment requirement for CLT? If so, is this figure determined per class, per school, or per municipality? How high is this minimal enrolment figure?
6 Curricular status	Is CLT perceived as "regular" education? Is CLT offered instead of other subjects and/or at extra curricular hours?
7 Funding	For which target groups and/or languages is CLT funded by national, regional or local educational authorities? For which target groups and/or languages is CLT funded by consulates/embassies of countries of origin?
8 Teaching materials	Do such materials origin from the country of residence and/or from countries of origin?
9 Teacher qualifications	Are such qualifications dependent on regulations in the country of residence and/or in countries of origin?

In Chapters 11 and 13 of this Volume, the outcomes of national and cross-national research on each of these parameters in various EU countries will be presented by Nygren-Junkin, and Extra and Yağmur, respectively.

6. European policies and perspectives on plurilingualism

6.1. European Union institutions as agents of plurilingualism

Language diversity is considered to be a key property of Europe's identity and promoting language learning and pluralism belongs to the main activities of European institutions in the domain of language policies. The two major European agencies on promoting plurilingualism are the European Union and the Council of Europe (henceforward EU and CE), with seats in Brussels/Belgium and Strasbourg/France, respectively. The major language policy agencies within these two institutions are the *Unit for Multilingualism Policy* of the Directorate of Culture, Multilingualism and Communication in Brussels and the *Language Policy Division* in Strasbourg, complemented by the programmes of the *European Centre for Modern Languages* in Graz/Austria. Baetens-Beardsmore (2008) gives an overview of both EU and CE language promotion initiatives.

In the EU, language policy is the responsibility of individual member-states and the EU does not have even the beginnings of a common language policy. EU institutions play a supporting role in this field, based on the "principle of subsidiarity". Their role is to promote cooperation between the member-states and to promote the European dimension in national language policies. The EU encourages all its citizens to be plurilingual; specifically, it encourages them to be able to speak two languages in addition to their "mother tongue". Although the EU has limited influence in this area as the content of educational systems is the responsibility of individual member-states, a number of EU funding programmes actively promote language learning and linguistic diversity. The major domains where the EU has dealt with language issues are the following ones: the status of EU languages as official and working languages, the use of EU languages by and within EU institutions, translation services and terminology harmonisation, language learning and teaching, and the protection of linguistic diversity. In each of these domains, EU institutions have shown a strong commitment to plurilingualism (see Coulmas 1991: 1–39 for a historical overview, and Hogan-Brun, this Volume, for the Baltic States).

The same holds for many CE initiatives and recommendations, in particular in the domain of language learning and teaching. Major examples are the development of a *Common European Framework of Reference for Languages* and the *European Language Portfolio*. The former sets European standards for different modes and levels of language proficiency, the latter describes individual language repertoires and aims at raising the awareness of plurilingualism in educational contexts. For a discussion of properties of linguistic diversity and the cultural and economic importance of maintaining multilingualism in Europe and other parts of the world, we refer to Skutnabb-Kangas (1995; 2002) and Nelde (2007). A recent study on the economic effects of a lack of foreign language skills in European enterprises was carried out by CILT (2007).

In September 2006, the European Commission decided to set up a *High Level Group on Multilingualism* in order to develop a new EU framework strategy for this domain. Their final 2007 report is available at the EU website. A second *Group of Intellectuals for Intercultural Dialogue* reflected on multilingualism and advocated the idea of a personal adoptive language for all EU citizens. Their 2008 report is also available at the EU website. From January 2007, the European Commission has a special Commissioner for Multilingualism. In 2008, this post was held by the Romanian Leonard Orban. The main priorities in the Commissioner's portfolio are to encourage language learning and to promote linguistic diversity. EU initiatives in this domain have been the *Socrates* and *Leonardo da Vinci* programmes. Until 2006, the EU also provided most of the financial support to the *European Bureau for Lesser Used Languages*, and for the *Mercator* networks of universities active in research on such languages in Europe. In 2004, the Commission launched a feasibility study on the creation of a *European Agency for Language Learning and Linguistic Diversity*. The study proposed two options: creating an agency or setting up a European network of *Languages Diversity Centres*. The Commission decided in favour of the second option and is examining the possibility of financing such a network on a multi-annual basis. Finally, although this is not an EU treaty, some EU member-states have ratified the *European Charter for Regional or Minority Languages* (see Section 4.3).

6.2. European citizens on language proficiency and language learning

Since 1973, the European Commission has been monitoring the evolution of public opinion in the member-states, thus helping the preparation of texts, decision-making and the evaluation of its work. For this purpose, both standard and special *Eurobarometers* are implemented across all EU member-states. In the language domain, two special Eurobarometers are particularly relevant. One was carried out in 15, the other in 29 countries, and they were both published by the European Commission (2001; 2006). Our focus will be on the latter. The 2006 Eurobarometer 243 is based on late 2005 findings, collected in 27 EU countries plus 2 candidate EU countries (Croatia and Turkey) in face-to-face interviews in people's homes. For each country, a stratified sample was defined derived from European and/or national population statistics offices, taking into account such variables as gender, age (15 plus), region and size of locality. The total sample consisted of 28,694 respondents, based on approximately 500 (Cyprus, Luxembourg, Malta) to 1000 interviews per country.

Two critical issues in data gathering are, as usual, the selection of informants and the type of data collected. First, residents were selected with a sufficient command of the national languages, leading to an under-representation of RM and/or IM groups. Secondly, what informants report that they are able to do does not necessarily correspond to what they actually do; this obviously also obtains in the present domain of investigation. Here, we present the major outcomes of the 2006 Eurobarometer 243. Languages other than the "mother tongue" (a widely used but problematic concept in itself, see Section 3.3), will be referred to as AL, i.e., additional languages:

— 56% of Europeans can hold a conversation in at least one AL, 28% in at least two, 11% in at least three, and 4% in none; for at least one AL, Luxembourg, Slovakia and Latvia have the highest rankings (>95%), the UK and Ireland the lowest (<40%);
— in 9 out of 29 countries, over half of Europeans can hold a conversation in at least two AL, which corresponds to the long-term objectives of the European Commission;
— a plurilingual European has the following characteristics: young, well-educated, motivated to learn, and born in another EU country or having parents from other EU countries than the country of residence;
— English (38%) is the most widely-spoken AL throughout Europe, in particular in Sweden, Malta and the Netherlands (>87%); 14% indicate that they know either French or German as AL;
— over half of Europeans evaluate their AL skills as (very) good, in particular their skills in English; 59% indicate that they have learned at least one AL at secondary school, 24% at primary school; a significant share of Europeans learn these languages only at school; this highlights the role of the educational system, and language teaching in particular, in promoting plurilingualism;
— 83% believe that AL skills are or could be useful for them personally; 53% perceive such skills as being very useful; 68% rate English to be

the most useful AL, leaving French (25%), German (22%) and Spanish (16%) far behind;
- 77% consider English also to be the most useful AL that children should learn; 33% mention French, 28% German and 19% Spanish; support for children to acquire AL skills appears to be strong; however, the range of languages perceived as useful for children appears to be narrow;
- most Europeans believe that the best age to start AL learning is from the age of 6 onwards, i.e., at primary school; the age group of 6–12 receives the widest support both when the first (55%) and the second (64%) AL are considered;
- the effect of a plurilingual background is again visible; those who are born in another EU country than the country of residence or outside Europe are more likely to opt for an early start in AL learning; this trend is also apparent with respondents whose parent or parents are born in another country than the respondents' country of residence.

The last part of the study offers a cross-section of public opinion on issues related to plurilingualism already introduced before. Support for some of the principles underpinning the Commission's plurilingualism policy is analysed, along with respondents' perceptions of the situation in their respective countries and their support for plurilingual policies at the country level. The respondents were presented with five statements that illustrate some of the key principles behind the policies targeted at promoting plurilingualism in Europe. All statements receive the support of the majority of Europeans but to a varying extent, as Table 8 makes clear.

Table 8. Attitudes towards plurilingualism in Europe (source: Special Eurobarometer 243: 53, European Commission 2006)

Statements	Tend to agree	Tend to disagree	Don't know
Everyone in the EU should be able to speak one AL	84%	12%	4%
All languages spoken within the EU should be treated equally	72%	21%	7%
Everyone in the EU should be able to speak a common language	70%	25%	5%
The European institutions should adopt one single language to communicate with European citizens	55%	40%	5%
Everyone in the EU should be able to speak two AL	50%	44%	6%

The wide support for the third statement can be partly understood in the light of the opinion of the majority of Europeans that English is the most useful language to know and, also a language that children should learn. The (lesser) support for the last statement is in line with the European Commission's ideas on trilingualism for all European citizens.

6.3. The enhancement of trilingualism for all EU citizens: an inclusive approach

As mentioned in Section 6.1, language policy within the EU, has largely been considered a domain that should be developed within the boundaries of each EU member-state, derived from the "principle of subsidiarity". Proposals for an overarching EU language policy were laboriously achieved and are non-committal in character (Coulmas 1991). The most important declarations, recommendations or directives on language policy, each carrying a different charge in the EU jargon, used to show a clear hierarchy in the recognition of the status of official EU languages, "indigenous" or RM languages and "non-territorial" or IM languages (in the decreasing order mentioned). In the most recent EU documents since 2007, this is less obvious.

For various reasons, the development of an educational policy regarding RM and IM languages was, and continues to be, a complex and challenging task. In view of the multicultural composition of many schools, this task involves the organisation of multilingual rather than bilingual education (Coelho 1998; García, Skutnabb-Kangas and Torres-Guzmán 2006). Experiences with, and the results of research into, an exclusively bilingual context are therefore only transferable to a limited degree. Bilingual education in majority languages and RM languages has been an area of interest and research for a long time (Baetens-Beardsmore 1993; Baker 2006). More recently, local and global perspectives are taken into consideration that go beyond bilingualism for RM groups and focus on plurilingualism and plurilingual education. Apart from majority and RM languages, the focus is commonly on the learning and teaching of English as a third language from a perspective of *glocalisation*, and in this way on promoting trilingualism from an early age on (Cenoz and Genesee 1998; Cenoz and Jessner 2000; Beetsma 2002; Ytsma and Hoffmann 2003).

It is remarkable that the teaching of RM languages is generally advocated as a matter of course for reasons of fairness, social cohesion, group identity or economic benefit, while such reasoning rarely is an argument in favour of teaching IM languages. The 1977 guideline of the Council of European Communities on education for "migrant" children (*Directive 77/486*, dated 25 July 1977) is now completely outdated. It needs to be put in a new and increasingly multicultural context and it needs to be extended to pupils originating from non-EU countries who form the large part of IM children at European primary schools. Besides, most of the so-called "migrants" in EU countries have taken up citizenship of the countries in which they live, and in many cases they belong to second or third generation groups. Against this background, there is a growing need for overarching human rights for every individual, irrespective of their ethnic, cultural, religious or language background. For similar inclusive approaches to IM and RM language rights we refer to Grin (1995) and Craith (2006).

There is a great need for educational policies in Europe that take new realities of multilingualism into account. Processes of internationalisation and globalisation have brought European nation-states to the world, but they have also brought the world to European nation-states. This bipolar pattern of change has led to both convergence and divergence of multilingualism across Europe. On the one hand, English is on the rise as the *lingua franca* for international communication across the borders of European nation-states at the cost of all other official state languages of Europe, including French. In spite of many objections against the hegemony of English (Phillipson 2003), this process of convergence will be enhanced by the extension of the EU to Eastern Europe. Within the borders of European nation-states, however, there is an increasing divergence of home languages due to large-scale processes of global migration and intergenerational minorisation. Although these two processes of convergence and divergence seem to be contradictory trends, they can actually be counterbalanced (Fishman 1989: 220).

The call for differentiation of the monolingual *habitus* (Gogolin 1994) of primary schools across Europe originates not only *bottom-up* from IM parents or organisations, but also *top-down* from supra-national institutions which emphasize the increasing need for European citizens with a transnational and multicultural affinity and identity. Plurilingual competencies are considered prerequisites for such an affinity and identity. Both the European Commission and the Council of Europe have published many policy documents in which language diversity is cherished as a key element of the multicultural identity of Europe – now and in the future. This language diversity is considered to be a prerequisite rather than an obstacle for a united European space in which all citizens are equal (but not the same) and enjoy equal rights (Council of Europe 2000). The maintenance of language diversity and the promotion of language learning and plurilingualism are seen as essential elements for the improvement of communication and for the reduction of intercultural misunderstanding.

The European Commission (1995) in a so-called *Whitebook* opted for trilingualism as a policy goal for all European citizens. Apart from the "mother tongue", each citizen should learn at least two "community languages". In fact, the concept of "mother tongue" referred to the official languages of particular member-states and ignored the fact that for many inhabitants of Europe mother tongue and official state language do not coincide (Tulasiewicz and Adams 2005). At the same time, the concept of "community languages" referred to the official languages of two other EU member-states. In later European Commission documents, reference was made to one foreign language with high international prestige (English was deliberately not referred to) and one so-called "neighbouring language". The latter concept always related to neighbouring countries, never to next-door neighbours. UNESCO adopted the term "multilingual education" in 1999 (*General Conference Resolution* 12) for reference to the use of at least three languages, i.e., the mother tongue, a regional or national language, and an international language in education.

In a follow-up to the European Year of Languages in 2001, the heads of state and government of all EU member-states gathered in March 2002 in Barcelona and called upon the European Commission to take further action to promote plurilingualism across Europe, in particular by promoting the learning and teaching of at least two additional languages from a very early age (Nikolov and Curtain 2000). The resulting *Action Plan 2004–2006*, published by the European Commission (2003), may ultimately lead to an inclusive approach in which IM languages are no longer denied access to Europe's celebration of language diversity. A recent initiative, supported by the Council of Europe and coordinated by the European Centre for Modern Languages in Graz (Austria), has been the *Valeur* project 2004–2007. Its ambitions were to bring together information on educational provisions for non-national languages in more than 20 European countries, to focus on the outcomes of these provisions for students by the time they have left school, to identify good practices and draw conclusions about how provision can be developed, to promote a greater awareness of the issues involved, and to create a network for developing new initiatives (McPake et al. 2007).

In particular the plea for the learning of three languages by all EU citizens, the plea for an early start to such learning experiences, and the plea for offering a wide range of languages to choose from, open the door to the above-mentioned inclusive approach. Although this may sound paradoxical (Phillipson 2003), such an approach can also be advanced by accepting the role of English as *lingua franca* for transnational communication across Europe. Against this background, the following principles are suggested for the enhancement of plurilingualism at the primary school level (see also Extra and Yağmur 2004: 406).

1 In the primary school curriculum, three languages are introduced for all children:
   - the official standard language of the particular nation-state (or in some cases a region) as a major school subject and the major language of communication for the teaching of other school subjects;
   - English as *lingua franca* for international communication;
   - an additional third language selected from a variable and varied set of priority languages at the national, regional and/or local level of the multicultural society.
2 The teaching of all these languages is part of the regular school curriculum and subject to educational inspection.
3 Regular primary school reports contain information on the children's proficiency in each of these languages.
4 National working programmes are established for the priority languages referred to under (1) in order to develop curricula, teaching methods and teacher training programmes.
5 Some of these priority languages may be taught at specialised language schools.

This set of principles is aimed at reconciling *bottom-up* and *top-down* pleas in Europe for plurilingualism, and is inspired by large-scale and enduring experiences with the learning and teaching of English (as L1 or L2) and one *Language Other Than English* (LOTE) for all children in the State of Victoria, Australia (Extra and Yağmur 2004: 99–105). The *Victorian School of Languages* in Melbourne has led to an internationally recognised break-through in the conceptualisation of plurilingualism in terms of making provisions feasible and mandatory for all children (including L1 English-speaking children), in terms of offering a broad spectrum of LOTE provision (in 2005, more than 40 languages were taught), and in terms of government support for this provision derived from multicultural policy perspectives.

When in the European context each of the above-mentioned languages should be introduced in the curriculum and whether or when they should be subject or medium of instruction, has to be spelled out according to particular national, regional or local demands. Derived from an overarching conceptual framework, priority languages could be specified in terms of both RM and IM languages for the development of curricula, teaching methods and teacher training programmes. Moreover, the increasing internationalisation of pupil populations in European schools requires that a language policy be introduced for *all* school children in which the traditional dichotomy between foreign language instruction for indigenous majority pupils and home language instruction for IM pupils is put aside. Given the experiences abroad (e.g., the *Victorian School of Languages* in Australia), language schools can become centres of expertise where a variety of languages are taught, if the students' demand is low and/or spread over many schools. In line with the proposed principles for primary schooling, similar ideas could be worked out for secondary schools where learning more than one language across European nation-states is already an established curricular practice. The above-mentioned principles would recognise plurilingualism in an increasingly multicultural environment as an asset for all youngsters and for society at large. The EU, the Council of Europe, and UNESCO could function as leading transnational agencies in promoting such concepts. The UNESCO *Universal Declaration of Cultural Diversity* (updated in 2002) is very much in line with the views expressed here, in particular in its plea to encourage linguistic diversity, to respect the mother tongue at all levels of education, and to foster the learning of more than one language from a very early age.

7. Structure and contents of this book

Multilingualism in Europe is a theme that has attracted increasing attention from both researchers and policy makers in recent years. The present chapter serves as an introduction to major themes that are addressed in the following chapters. It is impossible to deal with all aspects of multilingualism in Europe, but a number of relevant case studies will be presented. The selection of case studies is based on geographical spread of countries and languages on the one hand and on the availability of expert knowledge on the other. Twelve case studies have been grouped in three parts. The first part deals with four cases of official state languages: English, French, Polish and the languages of the three Baltic States. The discussion is not limited to the status of these languages as the official language of one country. On the contrary, the discussions cover a much wider area and also look into the position of these languages abroad, where they may be a *lingua franca*, as in the case of English, or a minority language as in the case of Polish. The second part concerns RM languages. The cases of Catalan, Frisian and Sámi are examples of unique minority languages that are not official state languages elsewhere, but, as the case of Catalan shows, they may be similar. The case of Hungarian makes clear that an official state language can also function as indigenous minority language in other geographical spaces. The third part of the book deals with IM languages. The cases of the United Kingdom, Sweden and Italy present contrasting perspectives. The concluding chapter presents an overview of IM languages across Europe. In some more detail the chapters put forward the points below.

Although English is the official state language of the United Kingdom and a marker of identity for many British residents, the focus of the initial chapter in the first part of this book is different. Juliane House develops a framework for English as a *lingua franca* and its properties, in which English is not primarily a language of identification, but a language for "transactional communication". The debate about English as a threat to multilingualism is discussed from socio-political, linguistic, psycholinguistic and pedagogic perspectives. House concludes that the use of English as a *lingua franca* in Europe is not necessarily a threat to multilingualism. European language policy should take a "third way" where English functions as a "co-language" and other languages continue to flourish alongside.

In terms of its role in Europe, the ambitions of the French language may be called similar to those of English. In his chapter, Dennis Ager provides detailed information on French in France and abroad. He discusses the changes French has undergone along the dimensions of ageing, urbanisation, the labour market and immigration, as well as the beliefs and attitudes towards languages in terms of insecurity and image. He also discusses the language policies of the government towards French and towards minority languages. Ager concludes that French has a secure future, despite all the changes it is still undergoing.

A case that is much less well known is the status of the Polish language, discussed by Justyna Leśniewska and Zygmunt Mazur. Polish is the national state language of Poland, but abroad it is also an indigenous RM language as well as a recent IM language. Even if Poland is linguistically very homogenous, there are about ten small indigenous minority languages. The Polish language is seen as the core element of national identity and is strongly protected by law. Polish communities exist in some 80 countries. Since Poland joined the EU in 2004, a large number of Poles have migrated and still migrate to other EU countries. The Poles have the belief that they should learn foreign languages rather than expect others to learn Polish.

In her chapter, Gabrielle Hogan-Brun gives an outline of the changing language dynamics of Estonian, Latvian and Lithuanian in official and private domains. The common fate of these languages has led to strikingly similar outcomes in the three Baltic Republics in terms of language development and use, and in terms of language policy. In each Republic, this has resulted in a substantial increase in the visibility and the use of these languages since independence. In each Republic, attitudes to language have changed. The post-Soviet period has allowed for some language revival for minority groups. However, while Lithuania has undergone some positive developments of social integration, the consequences of language policy in Estonia and Latvia continue to pose problems.

In the second part of the book, the focus is on RM languages. Two types of studies are presented: case studies on RM languages *within* the borders of nation-states (Catalan and Frisian) and on RM languages *across* the borders of nation-states (Hungarian and Sámi). Xavier Vila introduces the case of the Catalan language in Spain. After a short historical overview and an outline of the legal framework, he presents the differences in policies between the autonomous communities of Catalonia, Valencia, the Balearic Island and Aragon as well as the position of the central state. Vila illustrates the main dilemmas of language policy with the example of language in education. Recent patterns of immigration pose new challenges to language policies. Overall, Catalan has gained ground and is in many respects no longer a minority language. The Catalan experience is according to Vila "well within reach for many middle-sized European linguistic communities".

An example of such a middle-sized language is Frisian in the Netherlands. Durk Gorter, Cor van der Meer and Alex Riemersma give an outline of the sociolinguistic status of Frisian. Data from a recent survey show that Frisian is undergoing a gradual decline. At the same time, the province is becoming more multilingual through the greater presence of IM languages and English. The developments of status and corpus planning are sketched in detail. Notwithstanding its small presence, the field of education is important for the promotion of Frisian. It is concluded that the strength of Frisian and thus its chances for survival rank at an intermediate position among RM languages in Europe.

Susan Gal makes clear in her chapter that the speakers of Hungarian abroad belong to both IM and RM groups. As IM groups, small numbers of Hungarian speakers are present in Western Europe, North and South America as well as in Israel and Australia. Hungarian speakers also constitute one of Europe's largest RM groups living in seven different nation-states: Slovakia, Ukraine, Romania, Serbia, Croatia, Slovenia and Austria. The chapter provides a brief overview of their complex demographic, sociopolitical and sociolinguistic circumstances. Gal includes an orientation to four research perspectives in terms of demographic and educational perspectives, political processes, and sociolinguistic practices and problems. She also deals with differences in language ideologies and valuations and language use patterns.

Whereas Hungarian has a status as a minority language in many nation-states outside Hungary, the Sámi people and their languages are spread as a much smaller community over extensive areas of northern Norway, Sweden, Finland and Russia. In his chapter, Mikael Svonni deals with the history and demography of Sámi speakers, the Sámi languages and dialects, and their present legal status. He describes language use in general, in education, in the mass media, in literature and in administration. Finally, he deals with the process of language shift and with prerequisites for the Sámi to maintain their language. According to Svonni, circumstances for the North Sámi for developing their language are favourable, while the speakers of the other Sámi languages and dialects have a much weaker position. The speakers of the smaller Sámi languages are well aware of their language being endangered. Svonni concludes that in order to prevent extinction "considerably more support and greater resources are required from the majority society but also from the Sámi communities themselves".

In the third part of the book, the focus shifts from RM to IM languages. In her chapter on the United Kingdom, Viv Edwards examines the impact of two large waves of migration in the 1960s and around the new millennium. She prefers the term "new minority languages" over "immigrant", "community" or "additional" languages. Also in this case, precise numbers of speakers are difficult to establish but at least 300 languages other than English are spoken in England among over 700,000 school children. Edwards discusses a number of indicators of the ethnolinguistic vitality of these languages, including religion, the economy, the media and the arts. She pays particular attention to education. Religious institutions fulfil an important cultural and welfare role. Ethnic economies are an important feature of life in the UK and knowledge of languages other than English is also recognised as offering businesses a competitive edge. Minority radio and TV, like the minority press, satellite TV and the Internet play a key role in language transmission. In cultural life in the UK, new minorities have had an enormous impact. In education, the responsibility for the organisation of classes has fallen on minority communities themselves and they have been relatively successful there. New minority languages are increasingly seen as important elements in cultural cohesion. Edwards concludes that there is a new discourse of inclusion and a significant softening of attitudes.

The chapter by Lilian Nygren-Junkin deals with IM languages in Sweden. Present-day Sweden has one of the highest proportions of IM groups in Europe, although reliable data are hard to obtain. Data on home language use are indispensable tools for educational policies. After a brief overview of patterns of immigration, the focus is on nine parameters for the teaching of IM languages, i.e., in terms of target groups, arguments, objectives, evaluation, enrolment, curricular status, funding, teaching materials, and teacher qualifications. The child may be a first, second or third generation immigrant, but is entitled to home language instruction as long as he/she has developed some proficiency. The acquisition of bilingual skills is supplemented with the aim of developing a bicultural identity. Nygren-Junkin points to better integration as being essential to the maintenance of the linguistic capital Sweden has in its IM population.

In their chapter, Monica Barni and Carla Bagna discuss the case of IM languages in Italy. Their objective is to describe the trends over the last 30 years. They point out that IM languages are helping to strengthen linguistic pluralism, but that this is not recognised. The cases of Chinese and Romanian in Rome and Florence are treated in detail. In contrast to what Viv Edwards says in her chapter about the United Kingdom, Barni and Bagna report that in Italy it is still difficult to perceive IM languages as "new" minority languages.

In the final chapter, Extra and Yağmur present a summary of the outcomes of the *Multilingual Cities Project*, a cross-national and cross-linguistic survey study in six multicultural European cities. The aims of the MCP were to compare multiple data on the status of IM languages at home and at school. Home language surveys were carried out among primary school children. The findings have yielded a wealth of hidden evidence on the distribution and vitality of IM languages at home and at school. The findings also show that making use of more than one language is a way of life for an increasing number of children across Europe. The outcomes of the project make clear that the traditional concept of language diversity in Europe should be reconsidered and extended, and that comparative cross-national research in this domain would be highly desirable.

References

Alladina, Safder
   1993   South Asian languages in Britain. In *Immigrant Languages in Europe*, Guus Extra and Ludo Verhoeven (eds.), 55–65. Clevedon: Multilingual Matters.

Alladina, Safder and Viv Edwards (eds.)
   1991   *Multilingualism in the British Isles* (Volume 1: The older mother tongues and Europe; Volume 2: Africa, the Middle East and Asia). London/New York: Longman.

Alterman, Hyman
   1969   *Counting People. The Census in History*. New York: Harcourt.

Ammon, Ulrich
   2007   Do you speak European? In *Culture Report: Progress Europe*, Sebastian Körber, Jenni Roth and Detlef Thelen (eds.), 178–184. Stuttgart: Institut für Auslandsbeziehungen.

Ansell, Amy and John Solomos
   2008   *Race and Ethnicity: The Key Concepts*. London/New York: Routledge.

Arzoz, Xabier (ed.)
   2008   *Respecting Linguistic Diversity in the European Union*. Amsterdam: John Benjamins.

Baetens Beardsmore, Hugo.
   1993   *European Models of Bilingual Education*. Clevedon: Multilingual Matters.
   2008   Language promotion by European supra-national institutions. In *Bilingual Education: Multilingual and Multicultural Children and Youths in 21st Century Schools*, Ofelia García (ed.). New York: Blackwell.

Baker, Colin
   2006   *Foundations of Bilingual Education and Bilingualism (4th ed.)*. Clevedon: Multilingual Matters.

Baker, Philip and John Eversley (eds.)
   2000   *Multilingual Capital. The Languages of London's Schoolchildren and their Relevance to Economic, Social and Educational Policies*. London: Battlebridge Publications.

Barbour, Stephen
   2000   Nationalism, language, Europe. In *Language and Nationalism in Europe*, Stephen Barbour and Cathie Carmichael (eds.), 1–17. Oxford: Oxford University Press.

Barbour, Stephen and Cathie Carmichael
   2000   *Language and Nationalism in Europe*. Oxford: Oxford University Press.

Barni, Monica and Guus Extra (eds.)
2008   *Mapping Linguistic Diversity in Multicultural Contexts.* Berlin/New York: Mouton de Gruyter.

Beetsma, Danny (ed.)
2002   *Trilingual Primary Education in Europe.* Ljouwert: Fryske Akademy.

Blum, Alain
2002   Resistance to identity categorization in France. In *Census and Identity. The Politics of Race, Ethnicity, and Language in National Censuses*, David Kertzer and Dominique Arel (eds.), 121–147. Cambridge: Cambridge University Press.

Breatnach, Diarmaid (ed.)
1998   *Mini Guide to Lesser Used Languages of the European Union.* Dublin: EBLUL.

Broeder, Peter and Guus Extra
1998   *Language, Ethnicity and Education. Case Studies on Immigrant Minority Groups and Immigrant Minority Languages.* Clevedon: Multilingual Matters.

Caubet, Dominique, Salem Chaker and Jean Sibille (eds.)
2002   *Codification des Langues de France.* Paris: l'Harmattan.

Cenoz, Jasone
forthc. *Towards Multilingual Education: Basque Educational Research in International Perspective.* Clevedon: Multilingual Matters.

Cenoz, Jasone and Fred Genesee (eds.)
1998   *Beyond Bilingualism. Multilingualism and Multilingual Education.* Clevedon: Multilingual Matters.

Cenoz, Jasone and Ulrike Jessner (eds.)
2000   *English in Europe. The Acquisition of a Third Language.* Clevedon: Multilingual Matters.

Centraal Bureau voor de Statistiek (CBS)
2000   *Allochtonen in Nederland 1999.* Voorburg: CBS.

Clyne, Michael
1991   *Community Languages: The Australian Experience.* Cambridge: Cambridge University Press.

Churchill, Stacy
1986   *The Education of Linguistic and Cultural Minorities in the OECD Countries.* Clevedon: Multilingual Matters.

CILT, the National Centre for Languages
2007   *ELAN: Effects on the European Economy of Shortages of Foreign Language Skills in Enterprise.* London: CILT.

Coelho, Elizabeth (ed.)
1998   *Teaching and Learning in Multicultural Schools: An Integrated Approach.* Clevedon: Multilingual Matters.

Coulmas, Florian (ed.)
   1991   *A Language Policy for the European Community. Prospects and Quandaries*. Berlin/New York: Mouton de Gruyter.

Council of Europe
   2000   *Linguistic Diversity for Democratic Citizenship in Europe. Towards a Framework for Language Education Policies. Proceedings Innsbruck (Austria) May 1999*. Strasbourg: Council of Europe.

Craith, Máiréad Nic
   2003   Facilitating or generating linguistic diversity. The European charter for regional or minority languages. In *Minority Languages in Europe. Frameworks, Status, Prospects*, Gabrielle Hogan-Brun and Stefan Wolff (eds.), 56–72. Hampshire: Palgrave Macmillan.
   2006   *Europe and the Politics of Language. Citizens, Migrants and Outsiders*. Hampshire: Palgrave Macmillan.

Dewitte, Philippe (ed.)
   2004   Langues de France. *Hommes & Migrations* 1252.

DGLF
   2008   *http://www.culture.gouv.fr/culture/dglf/* [accessed March 5, 2008].

Directive 77/486
   1977   *Directive 77/486 of the Council of the European Communities on the Schooling of Children of Migrant Workers*. Brussels: CEC.

Edwards, John
   1985   *Language, Society and Identity*. Oxford: Basil Blackwell.
   1991   Socio-educational issues concerning indigenous minority languages: terminology, geography and status. In *European Lesser Used Languages in Primary Education*, Jantsje Sikma and Durk Gorter (eds.), 207–226. Leeuwarden: Mercator Education/Fryske Akademy.
   2007   Societal multilingualism: reality, recognition and response. In *Handbook of Multilingualism and Multilingual Communication*, Peter Auer and Li Wei (eds.), 447–467. Berlin/New York: Mouton de Gruyter.

EFNIL
   2008   *http://www.eurfedling.org* [accessed March 7, 2008].

ELSN
   1996   *European Language Survey Network. A Comparative Analysis of Four Language Surveys (Ireland, Friesland, Wales & the Basque Country)*. Dublin: ITE.

Euromosaic
   1996   *The Production and Reproduction of the Minority Language Groups of the EU*. Luxembourg: Office for Official Publications of the European Communities [*http://www.uoc.edu/euromosaic*]

European Commission
1995   *Whitebook. Teaching and Learning: Towards a Cognitive Society.* Brussels: COM.
2001   *Europeans and Languages. Special Eurobarometer Report 54.* European Commission: Brussels.
2003   *Promoting Language Learning and Linguistic Diversity. An Action Plan 2004–2006.* Brussels: COM.
2006   *Europeans and Their Languages. Special Eurobarometer Report 243.* European Commission: Brussels.
European Commission and EuroStat
2004   *Documentation of the 2000 Round of Population and Housing Censuses in the EU, EFTA and Candidate Countries, Parts I-III and Annexes.* Luxembourg: Office for Official Publications of the European Communities.
2005   *Population and Housing Censuses 2001. Results at National and Regional Level with Documentation and Detailed Tables.* Luxembourg: Office for Official Publications of the European Communities (CD-ROM).
EuroStat
2006   Non-national populations in the EU Member States. *Statistics in Focus* 8: 1–3.
Eusko Jaurlaritza III
2003   *Euskararen Jarraipena. La Continuidad del Euskera. La Continuité de la Langue Basque* (Volume III). Vitoria-Gasteiz: Gobierno Vasco.
Extra, Guus and Durk Gorter (eds.)
2001   *The Other Languages of Europe. Demographic, Sociolinguistic and Educational Perspectives.* Clevedon: Multilingual Matters.
Extra, Guus and Jan Jaap de Ruiter (eds.)
2001   *Babylon aan de Noordzee. Nieuwe Talen in Nederland.* Amsterdam: Bulaaq.
Extra, Guus and Ludo Verhoeven (eds.)
1993a   *Community Languages in the Netherlands.* Amsterdam: Swets and Zeitlinger.
1993b   *Immigrant Languages in Europe.* Clevedon: Multilingual Matters.
1998   *Bilingualism and Migration.* Berlin/New York: Mouton De Gruyter.
Extra, Guus and Kutlay Yağmur (eds.)
2004   *Urban Multilingualism in Europe: Immigrant Minority Languages at Home and School.* Clevedon: Multilingual Matters.
Extra, Guus, Rian Aarts, Tim van der Avoird, Peter Broeder and Kutlay Yağmur
2002   *De Andere Talen van Nederland.* Muiderberg: Coutinho.
Fase, Willem
1994   *Ethnic Divisions in Western European Education.* Münster/New York: Waxmann.

Fishman, Joshua
 1973 *Language and Nationalism. Two Integrative Essays.* Rowly, Mass.: Newbury House.
 1989 *Language and Ethnicity in Minority Sociolinguistic Perspective.* Clevedon: Multilingual Matters.
 2001 *Can Threatened Languages be Saved? Reversing Language Shift, Revisited: a 21st Century Perspective.* Clevedon: Multilingual Matters.
García, Ofelia and Joshua Fishman (eds.)
 2002 *The Multilingual Apple: Languages in New York City (2nd ed.).* Berlin/New York: Mouton de Gruyter.
García, Ofelia, Tove Skutnabb-Kangas and Maria Torres-Guzmán (eds.)
 2006 *Imagining Multilingual Schools. Language in Education and Glocalization.* Clevedon: Multilingual Matters.
Ghuman, Paul
 2003 *Double Loyalties. South Asian Adolescents in the West.* Cardiff: University of Wales Press.
Goethe Institute
 2008 *http://www.goethe.de/enindex.htm* [accessed April, 10, 2008]
Gogolin, Ingrid
 1994 *Der Monolinguale Habitus der Multilingualen Schule.* Münster/New York: Waxmann.
Gogolin, Ingrid and Sjaak Kroon (eds.)
 2000 *"Mann schreibt wie man spricht". Ergebnisse einer International Vergleichende Fallstudie über Unterricht in Vielsprachigen Klassen.* Münster/New York: Waxmann.
Gordon, Raymond (ed.)
 2005 *Ethnologue: Languages of the World*, Fifteenth edition. Dallas, Tex.: SIL International. Online version: *http://www.ethnologue.com/.*
Gorter, Durk
 1994 A new sociolinguistic survey of the Frisian language situation. *Dutch Crossing. A Journal of Low Countries Studies* 18 (2): 18–31.
 1996 Information, documentation and research on bilingual education for regional or minority languages in the European Union. In *Language Regulations in Multi-Ethnic Societies*, 21–33. International Conference Proceedings, Chisinua (Helsinki Citizens' Assembly of Moldova).
 2001 Policy and teaching of Frisian as a minority language. In *Actas da VIII Conferencia Internacional de Linguas Minoritarias*, Xesús Lopez et al. (eds.), 295–301, Santiago de Compostela.
 2008 Frisian in the Netherlands. In *Mapping Linguistic Diversity in Multicultural Contexts*, Monica Barni and Guus Extra (eds.), Berlin/New York: Mouton de Gruyter.

Gorter, Durk, Jarich Hoekstra, Lammert Jansma and Jehannes Ytsma (eds.)
   1990   *Fourth International Conference on Minority Languages* (Vol. 1: General papers; Vol. 2: Western and Eastern European papers). Clevedon: Multilingual Matters.
Graddol, David
   2006   *English Next*. London: British Council.
Grin, François
   1995   Combining immigrant and autochthonous language rights: a territorial approach to multilingualism. In *Linguistic Human Rights. Overcoming Linguistic Discrimination*, Tove Skutnabb-Kangas and Robert Phillipson (eds.), 31–48. Berlin/New York: Mouton de Gruyter.
   2003   *Language Policy Evaluation and the European Charter for Regional or Minority Languages*. Hampshire: Palgrave Macmillan.
Grin, François and Tom Moring
   2002   *Final Report: Support for Minority Languages in Europe*. Brussels: European Bureau for Lesser Used Languages.
Gubbins, Paul and Mike Holt
   2002   *Beyond Boundaries. Language and Identity in Contemporary Europe*. Clevedon: Multilingual Matters.
Gudykunst, William (ed.)
   1988   *Language and Ethnic Identity*. Clevedon: Multilingual Matters.
Guibernau, Montserrat and John Rex (eds.)
   1997   *The Ethnicity Reader: Nationalism, Multiculturalism and Migration*. Cambridge/Oxford: Polity Press.
Guiguet, Benoît
   1998   Citizenship and nationality: Tracing the French roots of the distinction. In *European Citizenship, An Institutional Challenge*, Massimo la Torre (ed.), 95–111. The Hague: Kluwer Law International.
Haarmann, Harald
   1991   Language politics and the new European identity. In *A Language Policy for the European Community. Prospects and Quandaries*, Florian Coulmas (ed.), 103–119. Berlin/New York: Mouton de Gruyter.
   1995   *Europäische Identität und Sprachenvielfalt*. Tübingen: Max Niemeyer.
Haberland, Hartmut
   1991   Reflections about minority languages in the European Community. In *A Language Policy for the European Community. Prospects and Quandaries*, Florian Coulmas (ed.), 179–213. Berlin/New York: Mouton de Gruyter.

Hogan-Brun, Gabrielle and Stefan Wolff (eds.)
    2003   *Minority Languages in Europe. Frameworks, Status, Prospects.* Hampshire: Palgrave Macmillan
Husén, Torsten and Sylvia Opper (eds.)
    1983   *Multicultural and Multilingual Education in Immigrant Countries.* Oxford: Pergamon Press.
Jaspaert, Koen and Sjaak Kroon (eds.)
    1991   *Ethnic Minority Languages and Education.* Amsterdam/Lisse: Swets and Zeitlinger.
Jenkins, Richard
    1997   *Rethinking Ethnicity. Arguments and Explorations.* London: Sage.
Jørgensen, J. Normann (ed.)
    2003   *Turkish Speakers in North Western Europe.* Clevedon: Multilingual Matters.
Joseph, John
    2004   *Language and Identity: National, Ethnic, Religious.* Hampshire: Palgrave Macmillan.
Kertzer, David and Dominique Arel
    2002   *Census and Identity. The Politics of Race, Ethnicity, and Language in National Censuses.* Cambridge: Cambridge University Press.
Kroon, Sjaak
    1990   *Opportunities and Constraints of Community Language Teaching.* Münster/New York: Waxmann.
Linguistic Minorities Project (LMP)
    1985   *The Other Languages of England.* London: Routledge and Kegan.
Luchtenberg, Sigrid (ed.)
    2004   *Migration, Education and Change.* London/New York: Routledge.
Martin, Peter, Angela Creese, Arvind Bhatt and Nirmala Bhojani
    2004   *Complementary Schools and their Communities in Leicester. Final Report.* School of Education, University of Leicester.
McPake, Joanna, Teresa Tinsley, Peter Broeder, Laura Mijares, Sirkku Latomaa and Waldemar Martyniuk
    2007   *Valuing All Languages in Europe.* Graz: European Centre for Modern Languages.
Nelde, Peter
    2007   Maintaining multilingualism in Europe: Propositions for a European language policy. In *Maintaining Minority Languages in Transnational Contexts*, Anne Pauwels, Joanne Winter and Joseph Lo Bianco (eds.), 59–77. London: Palgrave Macmillan.
Nelde, Peter, Miquel Strubell and Glyn Williams
    1996   *Euromosaic. The Production and Reproduction of the Minority Language Groups in the European Union.* Luxembourg: Office for Official Publications of the European Communities.

Nicholas, Joe
  1988   British language diversity surveys (1977–1987). A critical examination. *Language and Education* 2: 15–33.
  1994   *Language Diversity Surveys as Agents of Change*. Clevedon: Multilingual Matters.
Nikolov, Marianne and Helena Curtain (eds.)
  2000   *An Early Start. Young Learners and Modern Languages in Europe and Beyond*. Strasbourg: Council of Europe.
NISRA
  2004   Household Projections for Northern Ireland: 2002–2025. Belfast: Northern Ireland Statistics Research Agency. URL: *http://www.nisra.gov.uk/statistics/financeandpersonnel/DMB/ publications/householdexec.pdf*.
Oakes, Leigh
  2001   *Language and National Identity. Comparing France and Sweden*. Amsterdam/Philadelphia: John Benjamins.
O'Reilly, Camille (ed.)
  2001a   *Language, Ethnicity and the State. Volume 1: Minority Languages in the European Union*. Hampshire: Palgrave.
  2001b   *Language, Ethnicity and the State. Vol. 2, Minority Languages in Eastern Europe post-1989*. Hampshire: Palgrave.
Ó Riagáin, Pádraig
  2001   Irish language production and reproduction 1981–1996. In *Can Threatened Languages be Saved?*, Joshua Fishman (ed.), 195–214. Clevedon: Multilingual Matters.
Ó Riagáin, Pádraig and Micheál Ó Gliasáin
  1994   *National Survey on Languages 1993: Preliminary Report*. Dublin: Institiúid Teangeolaíochta Éireann.
Obdeijn, Herman and Jan Jaap de Ruiter (eds.)
  1998   *Le Maroc au Coeur de l'Europe. L'Enseignement de la Langue et Culture d'Origine (ELCO) aux Éleves marocains dans cinq Pays Europeens*. Tilburg: Tilburg University Press, Syntax Datura.
Office for National Statistics
  2005   *The Official Yearbook of the United Kingdom of Great Britain and Northern Ireland*. London: Office for National Statistics. Available at *http://www.statistics.gov.uk/StatBase/Product.asp?vlnk=5703* [accessed April 10, 2008].
Pauwels, Anne, Joanne Winter and Joseph Lo Bianco (eds.)
  2007   *Maintaining Minority Languages in Transnational Contexts*. London: Palgrave Macmillan.
Phillipson, Robert
  2003   *English-only Europe? Challenging Language Policy*. London/New York: Routledge.

Poulain, Michel
- 2008 European migration statistics: definitions, data and challenges. In *Mapping Linguistic Diversity in Multicultural Contexts*. Monica Barni and Guus Extra (eds.). Berlin/New York: Mouton de Gruyter.

Province of Fryslân
- 2007 *De Fryske Taalatlas 2007. Friese Taal in Beeld*. Ljouwert: Provinsje Fryslân.

Reich, Hans
- 1991 Developments in ethnic minority language teaching within the European Community. In *Ethnic Minority Languages and Education*, Koen Jaspaert and Sjaak Kroon (eds.), 161–174. Amsterdam/Lisse: Swets and Zeitlinger.
- 1994 Unterricht der Herkunftssprachen von Migranten in anderen europäischen Einwanderungsländern. In A. Dick (Hrsg.), *Muttersprachlicher Unterricht. Ein Baustein für die Erziehung zur Mehrsprachigkeit*, 31–46. Wiesbaden: Hessisches Kultusministerium.

Reid, Euan and Hans Reich
- 1992 *Breaking the Boundaries. Migrant Workers' Children in the EC*. Clevedon: Multilingual Matters.

Riley, Philip
- 2007 *Language, Culture and Identity. An Ethnolinguistic Perspective*. London: Continuum.

Schneider, Britta
- 2005 *Linguistic Human Rights and Migrant Languages*. Angewandte Sprachwissenschaft, Band 17. Frankfurt am Main: Peter Lang.

Skutnabb-Kangas, Tove
- 1995 Introduction. In *Multilingualism for All*, Tove Skutnabb-Kangas (ed.), 7–20 (European Studies on Multilingualism, Vol. 4). Lisse: Swets and Zeitlinger.
- 2002 *Why Should Linguistic Diversity be Maintained and Supported in Europe? Some Arguments*. Strasbourg: Council of Europe.

Spencer, Stephen
- 2006 *Race and Ethnicity. Culture, Identity and Representation*. London: Routledge.

Spolsky, Bernard
- 2004 *Language Policy*. Cambridge: Cambridge University Press.

Stevenson, Patrick and Clare Mar-Molinero (eds.)
- 2006 *Language Ideologies, Policies and Practices: Language and the Future of Europe*. Hampshire: Palgrave Macmillan.

Tilmatine, Mohand (ed.)
- 1997 *Enseignement des Langues d'Origine et Immigration Nord-Africaine en Europe: Langue Maternelle ou Langue d'Etat?* Paris: Inalco/Cedrea-Crb.

Tjeerdsma, Rommert
    1998   *Mercator Guide to Organizations*. Leeuwarden: Mercator Education/Fryske Akademy.
Tosi, Arturo
    1984   *Immigration and Bilingual Education. A Case Study of Movement of Population, Language Change and Education within the EEC*. Oxford: Pergamon Press.
Tulasiewicz, Witold and Anthony Adams (eds.)
    2005   *Teaching the Mother Tongue in a Multilingual Europe*. London: Continuum.
UNESCO
    1999   *http://www.unesco.org/education/imld_2002/resolution_en.shtml*
    2002   *Universal Declaration of Cultural Diversity*. Paris: UNESCO.
Ureland, Sture, Anthony Lodge and Stefan Pugh (eds).
    2007   Language Contact and Minority Languages in Europe. *Studies in Eurolinguistics,* Vol. 5. Berlin: Logos Verlag.
Van Londen, Selma and Arie de Ruijter
    1999   Ethnicity and identity. In *Culture, Ethnicity and Migration*, Marie-Claire Foblets and Ching Lin Pang (eds.), 69–79. Leuven/Leusden: Acco.
Verkuyten, Michael
    2006   *The Social Psychology of Ethnic Identity*. Hove/New York: Psychology Press.
Williams, Glyn
    2005   *Sustaining Language Diversity in Europe*. Hampshire: Palgrave Macmillan.
Williams, Glyn and Delyth Morris
    2000   *Language Planning and Language Use (Welsh in a Global Age)*. Cardiff: University of Wales Press.
Woehrling, Jean-Marie
    2006   *The European Charter for Regional or Minority Languages. A Critical Commentary*. Strasbourg: Council of Europe.
Wright, Sue
    2000   *Community and Communication. The Role of Language in Nation State Building and European Integration*. Clevedon: Multilingual Matters.
    2004   *Language Policy and Language Planning. From Nationalism to Globalisation*. Hampshire: Palgrave Macmillan.
Ytsma, Jehannes and Charlotte Hoffmann (eds.)
    2003   *Sociolinguistic Perspectives on Third Language Acquisition*. Clevedon: Multilingual Matters.

Section I
Official state languages

English as lingua franca in Europe today

Juliane House

In this chapter, I will first briefly describe the language policy of the European Union (EU) as a framework for considerations of the role of English as a *lingua franca* in Europe today. Secondly, I will clarify the term *English as a lingua franca* (ELF). Thirdly, I will discuss the claim that ELF is a serious threat to multilingual communication and multilingualism in the world and in Europe from four perspectives, i.e., the socio-political, the linguistic, the psycholinguistic and the pedagogic perspective. Finally, I will draw some conclusions from this discussion.

1. Language policy in the European Union

In the Charter of Fundamental Rights the EU declares that it respects linguistic diversity, and that linguistic diversity is a fundamental value of the EU. Despite this commitment, there is no common European language policy because language policy is understood to be the responsibility of the European member-states. The member-states are however supported in their decisions on language policy by many EU institutions which explicitly encourage all their citizens to become multilingual and follow the so-called "M+2" principle (Europeans should master two other languages over and above their mother tongue). In support of this ideal, the EU has instituted a number of programs (Lingua, Erasmus, Socrates, etc.) to promote diversity, mobility, multilingualism and multiculturalism – all of them mainstays of the (unofficial) European language policy.

There are at present 23 official languages in the European Union (with immigrant languages being ignored) and all languages in the EU can also function as working or procedural languages, i.e., as languages that have legal status in the EU as a supra-national organisation and thus function as a legitimate means of communication. However, in different EU organs the actual number of working language varies: the EU Commission has three working languages: English, French and German, but operates entirely multilingually for public information purposes. The Official Journal of the EU however is published in all 23 official languages, and in the European Parliament all documents must be fully multilingual – a huge translation and interpreting machinery is required to keep up this commitment to diversity. In view of the cumbersome (and costly) translation and interpreting processes in many organs of the European Union, I have suggested elsewhere (House 2003, 2006c) that it would be more efficient to operate in EU institutions with but one language, the only realistic candidate being English. In a similar but more moderate stance, Van Els (2005) has recently proposed to reduce the EU working languages for oral and in particular informal consultations to English, and he claimed that such a measure would not only increase efficiency of operations, be politically desirable but also be in the interests of the EU and its individual citizens. This viewpoint has earlier been put forward famously by Jürgen Habermas (1998), who alongside his propagation of a de-nationalisation of Europe has suggested to use English as a de-nationalised, unifying language for Europe.

However, Ammon (2006) in his replique to Van Els (2005) – speaking for many others – has pointed out that the opposition to English as the only working language in the European Union is too strong and widespread in Europe for any simple one-language solution. These objections lie probably less in a deep emotional commitment to a multilingual Europe but rather in the economic and political advantage which the continued use and spread of one's own national language in Europe would bring, i.e., in the type of traditional linguistic nationalism Habermas and other postnationalists argue against. Another reason for the unabated antagonism in Europe against the official recognition that English is the default option in many multilingual encounters is the continuous refuelling of the argument that using English inhibits the maintenance and equality of other European languages (Phillipson 2006: 82). As we will see in the following sections, this must not necessarily be the case.

Despite the deeply entrenched concern in the EU with upholding and increasing diversity and multilingualism in Europe, it is common knowledge that some languages in the European context are more equal than others. While French occupied a prestigious position in the past, it is now without doubt the English language which holds a special position in the European linguistic landscape. According to the Eurobarometer of the European Community (February 2006), only 13% of the European population speaks English as a mother tongue, but nearly 40% speak English as a second or foreign language, and over 50% claim they are able to speak and understand English. Further, in 19 out of 29 countries included in the poll it is English which is the most widely known language after the respective mother tongues. The penetration of English is most noticeable in Scandinavia and in the Netherlands, where just below 90% of the population say they know English. European citizens also think that they speak English better than any other second or foreign language, and 77% of European citizens believe that their children should learn English, and that English is the uncontested number one language in Europe, although there are regional differences in the level of English knowledge: in the Northern and Western member states of the EU English is more widely known than in Eastern and Southern Europe.

Comparing these figures with other major European languages, we can see that there is a wide gap indeed: although for instance German is the language most widely spoken in Europe as a native tongue (18% of Europeans in various European countries), only 14% of Europeans master it as a second or foreign language. And French is the mother tongue of only 12% of the European population, with 14% speaking French as a second or foreign language. To summarise, there is no doubt that for communication purposes it is English which is most widely used in Europe. It is used by many European citizens as a means of trans-local, trans-regional and trans-national communication – just as it is used in this way worldwide. Given the spread of English across Europe, it is more than strange – but of course also telling – that in many official policy recommendations emerging from the organs of the European Union, English is often deliberately not mentioned, e.g., in the so-called *Whitebook* that emerged from the European Commission (1995) pushing the M+2 objective for all citizens of Europe. One plausible interpretation of this surprising blindness to reality is the deliberate attempt to defend the linguistic interests of powerful European nation-states, most obviously France.

Multilingualism is not evenly distributed across the member-states of the EU. Nor is it evenly spread across social strata. High levels of competence in more than one language tend to occur primarily with persons who live in smaller member-states with more than one official language and whose mother tongue belongs to the lesser-used languages. As to the citizens who best fit the proclaimed ideal of the "multilingual European", they are young, well-educated, born in a country which is not the country they currently reside in, who have a strong motivation to learn languages and use languages on the job. All others master their mother tongue and – at best – some English.

Although immigrant languages do not have a recognised status in the EU, their speakers are commonly bilingual: They speak their mother tongue and the majority language of their country of residence. And very often they also acquire a third language, most frequently English (Simsek 2008), which they recognise as a useful *lingua franca* in Europe. In an insightful state-of-the art review of immigrant languages in Europe in which he urges the inclusion of these languages in the "celebration of language diversity", Guus Extra (2006: 37) also makes the point that the use of ELF in Europe need not clash with the European tenet of multilingualism and multiculturalism. In line with the Action Plan suggested by the European Commission (2003) as a means of promoting multilingualism across Europe, Extra lists three necessary steps: learning three languages, an early start to language learning activities and offering a wide range of languages to choose from. Following these actions would open the door to an approach in which immigrant languages in Europe would be included. And he continues "Although this may sound paradoxical, such an approach can also be advanced by accepting the role of English as *lingua franca* for intercultural communication across Europe" (2006: 37).

2. English as a lingua franca in the world and in Europe today

The concept of a *lingua franca* in its original sense is very different from the role which the English language is currently playing on the world stage. In its original meaning, a *lingua franca* – the term comes from Arabic *lisan al farang* – was simply an intermediary or contact language used, for instance, by speakers of Arabic with travellers from Western Europe. Its meaning was later extended to describe a language of commerce, a rather stable variety with little room for individual variation. This meaning is clearly not applicable to today's global English, whose major feature is its enormous functional flexibility and spread across many different linguistic, geographic and cultural areas, as well as its openness for foreign forms (Firth 1996). ELF in both international and intranational cases of communication can be regarded as a special type of intercultural communication where there is no consistency of form that goes beyond the participant level, i.e., each combination of interactants seems to negotiate and govern their own variety of *lingua franca* use in terms of proficiency level, degree of code-mixing, degree of pidginisation, etc. One might even go as far as saying that with every Korean, Italian and German, Dutch and French individual who uses English as a mediating language, there arises a unique and genuine speech community where the roles and rules of mutual understanding have to first be established.

Such formal (and functional) flexibility coupled with a truly global spread has led to another new, and indeed remarkable, feature: That the number of non-native speakers of English is now substantially larger than its native speakers (the ratio is about 4 to 1, tendency rising). The fact that English is increasingly NOT owned by its native speakers makes for a parallel increase in the diversification of the English language through a series of acculturation and nativisation processes. The linguistic consequences of such large-scale processes of convergence are numerous non-native varieties. And this means that there is no monolithic "hegemonic" English voice – but rather a diversity of different voices which reflect differences in the social, economic and political backgrounds of its speakers. The so-called "inner circle" in Braj Kachru's famous three-circles-model (Kachru 1992) consisting of the previously most influential group, i.e., native speakers of English and the dominant, hegemonic variety they speak is steadily losing influence in the world today.

ELF can further not be described as a language for specific purposes, a sort of pidgin or a creole language, and it certainly is not some kind of "foreigner talk", nor is it a type of learner language. The interlanguage paradigm introduced in the late 1960s in applied linguistics with its focus on the deficits of learners of a foreign language *vis à vis* the native norm is not valid in the context of ELF.

Instead of the learner it is rather the multilingual individual and his or her "multicompetence" (Cook 1992), who is to be taken as a norm or yardstick for describing and explaining ELF communication. Here we can look for support from the rich literature on bilingualism, where the notion of a "simultaneous activation" of speakers' native tongue and ELF in the cognitive structures of bilingual and multilingual subjects is widely accepted today (Grosjean 2001).

Another interesting suggestion with regard to capturing the notion "ELF" comes from Widdowson (2003), who has suggested that ELF is a type of "register", a term well known from Hallidayan systemic functional linguistics, and from stylistics, the idea being that when the English language as a "virtual language" is employed in different contexts of use, for different purposes, by different people, it fulfils different functions and is changed accordingly.

In sum, we can say that the main characteristic of ELF is its multiplicity of voices. ELF is a language for communication, i.e., a medium that can be given substance with different national, regional, local, and individual cultural identities. English as such does not carry these identities; it does not function as a language of identification. When English is used as a language for communication, it is in principle neutral with regard to the different socio-cultural backgrounds of its users, and has thus undoubtedly great potential for international understanding – precisely because in ELF communication there is no fixed norm, and because *lingua franca* speakers must always work out anew – in different communities of practice (Wenger 1998; House 2003a) – a joint linguistic, intercultural and behavioural basis for their communication.

3. The debate about the use and misuse of English as a lingua franca in Europe viewed from four perspectives

3.1. The socio-political perspective

It is useful to ask why it should be English and not any other language which is currently the world's most frequently employed *lingua franca*. David Crystal (1997) has pointed out that the British empire, present day US global power, and an ever increasing technology-driven need for easy international border-crossing communication as well as a preference for a type of "neutral ground" (Svartvik and Leech 2006) have paved the way for the English language. This holds particularly true in countries with very many different languages and dialects (such as, e.g., India). Another reason often given is that English is preferred by many people because it is supposedly "a simple code" – a rather dubious reason (cf. the recent discussion in Spielmann 2007).

But what are we to make of the claim made by proponents of "ecolinguistics" or "liberation linguistics" that ELF poses a threat to other languages, that it is in effect a "killer language", a perfidious agent of linguistic dominance and imperialism? Here one needs to point out that since ELF is a language with the currently widest communicative range, many people – if not most – choose to use it out of their own free will, and they more often than not make an intuitive distinction between ELF as a language for communication and their native language(s) as their language(s) for cultural and linguistic identification. These indigenous languages and ELF are then NOT in competition, rather they supplement each other, there is never a stark either-or situation. (cf. Kramsch 2002 who gives some interesting examples of this perceived difference between the native language and ELF).

But what about the linguistic and the human right to use one's mother tongue in Europe whenever one so wishes? This is of course always possible; there are no restrictions and sanctions on the use of any language. However, the decision to use or avoid using any given language depends on many situational, cognitive and affective factors. In contemporary Europe, individuals are in principle free to choose. As concerns ELF, speakers know what they are doing when they use ELF – and they do it in the majority of cases to their own advantage. De Swaan (2001) characterises the linguistic-human rights stance versus the utilitarian stampede for ELF poignantly and insightfully when he writes:

> Recently, a movement to right the wrongs of language hegemony has spread across the Western world, advocating the right of all people to speak the language of their choice, to fight 'language imperialism' abroad and 'linguicism' at home, to strengthen 'language rights' in international law. Alas, what decides is not the right of human beings to speak whatever language they wish, but the freedom of everyone else to ignore what they say in the language of their choice (2001: 52).

Giving ELF users a bad conscience because they make profitable use of ELF as a language of wider communication frequently puts them – unnecessarily – into a sort of double-bind situation, as the present author has often experienced herself at conferences and as colleagues from many countries have testified. Here is an example taken from an e-mail message I have recently received from a colleague in Hong Kong:

> I always feel that non-native speakers of English caught in a kind of double bind. I got criticised at school and at university if I didn't speak English, but I also got criticised (mostly by those who pretended to be politically correct) if I spoke English. I was only in the last few years that I stopped wishing I had two mouths. English, I believe, can never replace our mother tongue, certainly not where the emotional intensity of feelings is concerned.

The omnipresence of ELF in Europe and elsewhere also gives rise to the following paradoxical situation: Using ELF as a language for communication often strengthens the use of indigenous languages for identification purposes and as a vehicle of protest against ELF dominance. We therefore witness today strong counter-currents, even in the modern pop music scene, saturated with English language products and the Internet, once thought to be classic ELF dominated killer media. Instead of large-scale language loss, we are thus confronted with a merging of ELF and native varieties (e.g., Bloch 2004; Lam 2004).

3.2. The linguistic perspective

One of the main arguments against the use of ELF in Europe and elsewhere is that ELF speakers are at a severe disadvantage *vis à vis* native speakers of English. They will never be able to express themselves with the finesse and subtlety they have at their disposal in their native tongue, and often suffer from the "reduced personality" syndrome. However, we may ask, is this necessarily so? Here it is advisable to abandon rumours, ideologised expectations and projections and rather look at some results of empirical studies that have examined how ELF speakers actually perform in interactions (cf. Baumgarten and House 2007; Firth 1996; House 1999, 2002b, 2003a, 2007a; Lesznyák 2004 to name but a few).

Summarising results of the seminal study by Firth (1996), we can say that there are surprisingly few instances of miscommunication, misunderstandings and repairs in ELF interactions – which is in stark contrast to the findings of most native-non-native interactions, including my own (cf., e.g., House 1996b, 2003b). Further, ELF speakers exhibit a markedly tolerant "Let-it-Pass" behaviour (Firth's 1996 term), which makes ELF interaction "robust" and "normal" – and this despite the "seemingly linguistically lawless nature" of their talk (Firth and Wagner 2007).

Let me illustrate some recent empirical investigations of ELF interactions with a description of the Hamburg ELF project, which I have carried out for the past seven years. Here we have collected different types of data from international students of various disciplines at the University of Hamburg (age 20–34):

1. L1 English interactions
2. Interactions between L1 English speakers and ELF speakers
3. ELF interactions between speakers of many different L1s
4. Retrospective interviews for collaborative interpretation of data 1–3.

The results of data set 3 (the ELF data), which interests me in the context of this chapter, largely confirm previous findings. However, a number of further interesting characteristics of the use of ELF were added to previous findings.

(1) Transfer of L1 discourse conventions

For example: East Asian speakers' specific topic management, which results in a number of non-sequitur turns-at-talk – a phenomenon consistently ignored by the other participants, such that it never leads to a breakdown of the conversation (cf. data excerpt 1). In this excerpt, as in the following ones, length of pauses and other non-verbal phenomena will be described in brackets, laughter via the symbol @, and the points focussed on in the analysis given will be highlighted in bold print.

Data excerpt 1

Joy: *Does maybe the nationalism erm in Quebec*

Wei: ***For us we*** *don't have problem I mean* ***Asian people Chinese for example***

Brit: *I've seen several movies in Japanese recently like Manga Comics are very popular*

Wei: *Since perhaps twenty years (2 sec) a lot of* ***Chinese people*** *began to learn a second foreign language it's..*

Joy: *When you speak English so you can @ translate in English or you can use the one language and not three languages*

Wei: *You know the problem is* ***Taiwan Hongkong and Mainland China*** *and the different and the difference (2 sec) how to say and the very different history this is the problem*

Brit: *But people have an interest in keeping their languages (1 sec) like Wales or erm in Ireland they try to revive the Gaelic Irish (2sec) I think it's got something to do with identity*

Wei: *I think in* ***South-East Asia*** *perhaps the first foreign language be English and a second foreign language perhaps* ***Japanese*** *or German (5sec)*

(2) Frequency of occurrence of multi-functional gambit "Represent" (Edmondson 1981)

In the Hamburg ELF data, (parts of) previous speakers' moves are very often "represented". This can be interpreted as a) a strategy with which speakers' working memory in comprehension and production is supported, b) a coherence-creating strategy with which lexical-paradigmatic clusters are systematically built up, c) a signal of receipt and a confirmation of comprehension, d) a meta-communicative procedure that strengthens interactants' awareness of their own and others' talk (cf. data excerpt 2). Represents (in the literature also known as "echo"-, "mirror"- or "shadow"- elements) typically occur in genres such as psycho-therapeutic interviews, instructional discourse and aircraft control discourse, where information is deliberately and routinely restated to create coherence and ensure understanding. The fact that ELF speakers use this convention shows that their strategic communicative competence is very well developed, indeed.

Data excerpt 2

Joy: *And you mean that English (2sec) is really getting important or taken for the education because the grammar is syntactic erm the grammar **is very easy***

Wei: ***is easy is very easy***

(3) Solidarity and consensus via co-construction of utterances

The Hamburg ELF data reveal a strong and consistent demonstration of consensus in the face of marked cultural differences. This consensual tendency leads to a feeling of community and group identity. ELF seems to be used as an egalitarian tool ("We're all in the same boat"). Speakers routinely support each other, they even pay each other compliments ("My English is I think very bad" – "No no no it's much better than mine!", [Firth and Wagner 2007]) (cf. data excerpts 3 and 4).

Data excerpt 3

Joy: *I recently read an article in a Korean erm (2 sec) Moment (4 sec).*

Brit: *Newspaper, Internet?*

Joy: *Yes thank you @ erm the article is about new foreign language education in Japan*

Data excerpt 4

Mau: *I think it begins erm of course with the colonialism I think too because the history of this development how the language in the very early period erm (3 sec)*

Joy: *Build up this basis*

Mau: *Yes*

Joy: *To be a world language*

Mau: *Yes*

(5) Strategically modified use of discourse marker "you know" (cf. House 2007)

The marker *you know* is used in ELF talk as a routinised self-serving strategy a) to make salient various coherence relations and b) to "fumble" for words. It is thus NOT used – as we know from the rich literature on discourse markers (cf., e.g., Edmondson 1981) – as a polite hedge or a sociocentric expression with which speakers appeal to knowledge shared with their addressees.

The data reveal an amazing rate of co-occurrence of *you know* tokens with the conjunctions *but*, *because* and *and*. Here is an example of a typical use of *you know* in this corpus.

Data excerpt 5

H: *No matter how many people speak in the university they some of them speak really well English **but you know** the real life it's different and you have to learn English*

S: *yes ehm (1s)*

A: *This institute where you're working at is this the only possibility to erm learn English...*

The second function of *you know* in the Hamburg ELF data is its use as a "fumble" in the sense of Edmondson (1981) and as a fumble also simultaneously indicating a coherence relation. This is illustrated in data excerpt 6 below.

Data excerpt 6

> B: *I mean if I'm the only male here but (laughs) I know models actually they **you know** they look maybe good but they're not interesting as a body it's just **you know** like having a nice lamp in the corner it's **you know** its it's a visual effect but it's it's it's very surfacey it **you know** it's not a woman it's more an object it's **you know** it's more an object=*
>
> G: *=Not like a person with mind something like this*

As opposed to the use of *you know* as a gambit or discourse marker in non-ELF English discourse, *you know* in ELF talk is thus primarily used both as a routinised fumble and a relational phrase to help speakers structure their own output, and to monitor their own progression in discourse – a clear sign of ELF speakers' making the most of their often less than optimal competence in English.

In conclusion, I propose on account of the evidence in the Hamburg ELF data that ELF users' strategic competence is admirably intact. ELF users are able to carry out meaningful, normal discourse and they do not appear to suffer from a "reduced personality" syndrome. ELF is for them simply a useful tool whenever no other common language is available.

Another argument against ELF use is that ELF "contaminates" other languages. This argument can be relativised on the basis of the results of another empirical research project currently conducted at the University of Hamburg: The project "Covert Translation" supported by the German Science Foundation's (*Deutsche Forschungsgemeinschaft*) Research Center on Multilingualism (*Sonderforschungsbereich Mehrsprachigkeit* SFB 538) since 1999 (cf. Baumgarten, House and Probst 2004; Bührig and House 2004, 2007; Küppers 2007; Böttger 2008). The initial hypothesis of this project is as follows: Due to ELF's global dominant status and the massive uni-directional translation movement from English into other languages, ELF influences – over and above the well-known lexical invasions – communicative norms and preferences in other languages via translations. For example, German communicative styles (House 1996a, 2006a, 2006b) will be adjusted to Anglophone ones (see Table 1).

Table 1. Communicative Styles English – German

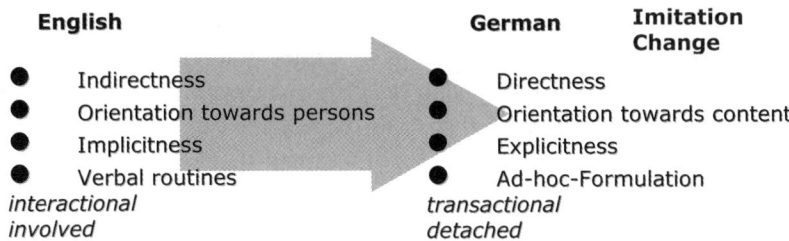

English	German	Imitation Change
• Indirectness	• Directness	
• Orientation towards persons	• Orientation towards content	
• Implicitness	• Explicitness	
• Verbal routines	• Ad-hoc-Formulation	
interactional	*transactional*	
involved	*detached*	

In the project "Covert Translation" we have constructed a tripartite diachronic (1978–2006) corpus of original English and original German texts as well as German translations of English texts (to a lesser degree also French and Spanish original and translated texts) in the (potentially vulnerable) genres popular science and business communication of about 1 million words. The analysis of this data consists of a combination of qualitative and quantitative methods, with the qualitative method relying on the present author's model of translation analysis (House 1977, 1997), the quantitative method comprising frequency counts and the renewed qualitative method using detailed re-contextualised analyses of the translation relation in individual texts.

While the first phase of this project with its analyses of some 80 texts showed initially no influence of English communicative norms on German ones, analyses of texts dated from the beginning of the new millennium did indeed reveal an impact of Anglophone norms on German texts (but not on French and Spanish ones) in the areas of subjectivity and addressee orientation. These areas were subsequently operationalised for quantitative analyses and statistical operations to comprise such phenomena as personal deixis, coordination, modality, mental processes, pronominal adverbials and other coherence markers.

In the second phase of the project we concentrated on quantitative analyses. They revealed interesting changes, e.g., in the use of the coordinate conjunction *And* and *Und* in sentence-initial position over the past 25 years (Baumgarten 2007), but also in the use of other functional categories such as personal pronouns, expressions of modality and conjunctions.

An example of Phase 3, the re-contextualised qualitative analysis of the translation relation, is our analysis of the occurrence of personal pronouns, which showed an interesting increase in the economic texts (cf. Baumgarten and Özçetin, in press). We found that while in the majority of cases the

English personal pronoun *we* was translated as the formal and functional equivalent *wir* in German, there were also interesting variations, where, e.g., *we* is expressed in a non-equivalent structure. This is for instance the case when congruent realisations of states of affairs in English are rendered by grammatical metaphors in German, or when inanimate noun phrases in subject position (common in English) are dispreferred in German. These variations show that stylistic preferences of German speakers and language specific aspects of the German language are retained. The most surprising finding is however that there is a higher frequency of *wir* in the German economic texts, which thus exhibit a stronger orientation towards persons and a presence of writer-reader interaction.

The overall results of the Hamburg covert translation project work to date suggest that there is an increased frequency of certain linguistic means (speaker-hearer deixis, modality, connectivity) of realising subjectivity and addressee orientation in German translations and comparable, original German texts over the past 25 years in the genres popular science and business communication, and that this increase might eventually change the nature of communicative styles in German texts, and may in the future also spread to texts and communicative norms in other European languages.

How are we to interpret these results? Can we conclude that there is a change in communicative norms because of a direct contact with the English language in translation? However, no mono-causal interpretation of the results is possible, particularly as in some cases original texts have changed more than translations. Instead, at least three explanatory hypotheses offer themselves:

— *The Booh-Factor*: Translation as the Mediator of the English Take-over.
  ▶Translation EFFECTS change.

— *The X-Factor*: Universal Impact of Globalisation: Translation as a mere reflector of adaptation to Anglophone norms, not an instigator thereof.
  ▶Translation REFLECTS change.

— *The Green-Factor*: Translation as cultural conservation amidst the threat of Anglicisation of other European languages.
  ▶Translation RESISTS change.

At the present time, we cannot reasonably favour any one of these hypotheses. What needs to be done is to compare the results described above to reference corpora in the languages involved for benchmarking purposes. This is what we will pursue in our work in this project in the future.

3.3. The psycholinguistic perspective

Recently, claims have been made that the massive influx of English lexis into other European languages influences processes of thinking and concept formation in these languages, and that in certain fields of knowledge it might well become difficult if not impossible in the future to express scientific and everyday concepts in languages other than English (e.g., Ehlich 2006), which means that speakers' L1-mediated knowledge is being exposed to "acts of organised violence" through the omnipresence of English in everyday life. This claim is, it seems to me, compatible with the strong Humboldt-Sapir-Whorf hypothesis (the so-called "linguistic relativity hypothesis") which, put in a simplified way, ascribes one's native language a strong and unavoidable influence on thinking and behaviour. This strong linguistic relativity hypothesis has been and can be refuted for at least the following three reasons:

— The universal possibility of translation (Jakobson 1966);
— The fact that languages in performative use are "anachronisms", i.e., their forms do not normally rise to our consciousness (Ortega y Gasset 1960);
— Converging evidence suggests that multilinguals possess a "deep" common conceptual store to which "lower level" language-specific systems are attached (Grosjean 2001; Myers-Scotton 2006).

In other words, there is always a way out of the conditioning influence of one's native and indeed any other language, through language itself, its creativity and flexibility and through the amazing richness of the human brain.

This optimistic stance is supported by, among others, neurolinguistic studies of translation (Altarriba 1992; Price, Green and von Studnitz 1999) showing that multilinguals move regularly and flexibly from L1 to L2, and vice versa: The two systems are distinct but essentially permeable. And with expert users, processing is often "quite shallow", i.e., semantic-conceptual processing does not occur at all (Sanford and Graesser 2006). Further, there is no proof at present of the assumption that there is a link between only one particular language – the native tongue – and thinking and conceptualising. An increased use of ELF at all educational levels and especially at the tertiary level of education must therefore not necessarily inhibit knowledge in students' indigenous languages. However, any excessive and unnecessary use of English, for instance at scientific get-togethers in non-English speaking European countries, might well be avoided, and alongside internationally recognised publications in the English language, it might be sensible and advisable to also publish articles and give lectures in the respective native languages, whenever this possibility offers itself. Arguments often heard by scholars that they can no longer express their thoughts in their native language because they only write in English, can be rejected more often than not as stemming from a simple lack of motivation, laziness, vanity or all of these combined.

3.4. Pedagogic perspectives

Is the use of English as a medium of instruction in non-Anglophone universities in Europe dangerous for the respective native languages? While there certainly is a tendency in many European countries to increasingly offer courses (particularly at graduate level) partially or entirely taught in English, there is now also a movement away from "English only" towards at least some type of instruction in a country's national language(s) prior to, alongside or following instruction in English (Motz 2005a, 2005b; Priegnitz 2007; Soltau 2007). This is a model that needs to be encouraged – again it is a compromise approach, not a dogmatic either-or stance. Demonising instruction in English is counter-productive, economically inadvisable and hopelessly isolationist.

Mention must be made of an alternative idea to using ELF, which is gaining ground in Europe: the EUROCOM or "Semi-communication" model, i.e., making use of speakers' receptive competence in their interlocutors' language. This model implies that speakers of different native languages each speak their own language, and rely on their interlocutors' receptive competence for successful communication to take place (Ten Thije and Zeevaert 2007). How successful this model is, depends to a large degree on the typological closeness of the languages involved (it is said to work well in Scandinavia for instance) and, of course, on the degree of knowledge in the respective second or foreign languages. There is no real competition between the EUROCOM model and the use of ELF in Europe, as their employment depends on different conditions and contexts.

As concerns the promotion of language learning in Europe, the suggestions made by Extra and Gorter in the final part of their Introduction to this Volume, with respect to enhancing multingualism at primary level are worth quoting here again, because they give ELF the place it deserves in Europe's linguistic landscape:

1. In the primary school curriculum, three languages are introduced for all children:
   - the official standard language of the particular nation-state (or in some cases a region) as a major school subject and the major language of communication for the teaching of other school subjects;
   - English as *lingua franca* for international communication;
   - an additional third language selected from a variable and varied set of priority languages at the national, regional and/or local level of the multicultural society.
2. The teaching of all these languages is part of the regular school curriculum and subject to educational inspection.
3. Regular primary school reports contain information on the children's proficiency in each of these languages.
4. National working programmes are established for the priority languages referred to under (1) in order to develop curricula, teaching methods and teacher training programmes.
5. Some of these priority languages may be taught at specialised language schools.

4. Conclusions

The use of ELF in Europe is not necessarily a threat to multilingualism in the world. ELF is no more and no less than a useful tool for interlingual and intercultural communication – it is an additional language, never a substitute for European citizens' mother tongues.

Neurolinguistic studies of translation and code-switching do not support the assumption that ELF inhibits or damages conceptualisation in native languages. It is the responsibility of the intellectual elite of non-Anglophone countries to make sure that publications in English will be accompanied and supplemented by publications in their respective native languages.

ELF is both a pheno- and a genotypically hybrid language: Transfer from L1 is widespread such that ELF users' native languages can be said to be well and alive "underneath the English surface" in any ELF talk.

Because of ELF speakers' inner dialogicity, evaluation norms should not be any longer inner circle English speakers' competence, but rather multilingual experts' use of ELF. Acceptance policies of publication organs as well as institutions employing teachers of English should therefore no longer follow rigid native English speaker norms or consider exclusively native English speakers for teaching posts.

Studies of the influence of ELF on other languages show that for instance German norms – but interestingly not French or Spanish ones – are open to English influence to a certain degree and in certain domains. However, no claims for their origin can be made at the present time.

There is an understandable association of ELF with global US economic power. However, it should not be forgotten that the English language is but an instrument, i.e., it should not be identified with that power. What we need is neutral descriptions based on research (as, e.g., illustrated above) rather than value judgements. Power transported via language can of course lead to a deplorable linguistic sameness, as can be witnessed today for instance in the service encounters in global (US American owned) chains, where people in many countries are increasingly confronted with exaggerated consumer-oriented "friendliness" (Cameron 2000). But we also see today mounting resistance to such communicative nivellation foisted upon traditional communicative norms in other linguacultural communities.

Language policies in Europe should opt for a sensible and realistic "third way" steering clear of the extremes of fighting ELF for its dangerous "linguistic imperialism" and accepting ELF uncritically and wholesale for its benefits. In present day Europe, ELF is not used instead of other European languages; it does not "kill" other European languages. Rather it functions as a kind of "co-language" (cf. Fishman's 1977 early characterisation), an additional tool employed in conjunction with, but not necessarily in opposition to, a multitude of native languages. European citizens' native languages will continue to be used and flourish alongside ELF. On this view, then, the use of ELF in Europe is but a special (often default) form of transactional communication.

References

Altarriba, Jeanette
- 1992 The representation of translation equivalents in bilingual memory. In *Cognitive Processing in Bilinguals*, Richard Jackson Harris (ed.), 157–174. Amsterdam: North-Holland.

Ammon, Ulrich
- 2006 Language conflicts in the European Union. On finding a politically acceptable and practicable solution for EU institutions that satisfies diverging interests. *International Journal of Applied Linguistics* 16 (3): 319–338.

Baumgarten, Nicole
- 2007 Converging conventions? Macrosyntactic conjunction with English *and* and German *und*. *Text & Talk* 27 (2): 139–170.

Baumgarten, Nicole and Demet Özçetin
- in press Linguistic variation through language contact in translation. In *Language Contact and Contact Languages*, Peter Siemund and Noemi Kintana (eds.). Amsterdam: Benjamins.

Baumgarten, Nicole and Juliane House
- 2007 Speaker stances in native and non-native English conversation. In *Receptive Multilingualism*, Jan ten Thije and Ludger Zeevaert (eds.), 195–216. Amsterdam: Benjamins.

Baumgarten, Nicole, Juliane House and Julia Probst
- 2004 English as lingua franca in covert translation processes. *The Translator* 10 (1): 83–108.

Bloch, Joel
- 2004 Second language cyber rhetoric: A study of Chinese L2 writers in an online usenet group. *Language Learning & Technology* 8 (3): 66–82.

Böttger, Claudia
- 2008 *Lost in Translation? An Analysis of the Influence of English as the Lingua Franca of Multilingual Business Communication*. Hamburg: Kovac.

Bührig, Kristin and Juliane House
- 2004 Connectivity in translation: Transitions from orality to literacy. In *Multilingual Communication*, Juliane House and Jochen Rehbein (eds.), 87–114. Amsterdam: Benjamins.
- 2007 Linking constructions in discourse across languages. In *Connectivity in Grammar and Discourse*, Jochen Rehbein, Christiane Hohenstein and Lukas Pietsch (eds.), 345–366. Amsterdam: Benjamins.

Cameron, Deborah
- 2000 *Good to Talk? Living and Working in a Communication Culture.* London: Sage.

Cook, Vivian
    1992   *Linguistics and Second Language Acquisition.* New York: St. Martin's Press.

Crystal, David
    1997   *English as a Global Language.* Cambridge: Cambridge University Press.

Edmondson, Willis James
    1981   *Spoken Discourse. A Model for Analysis.* London: Longman.

Ehlich, Konrad
    2006   *Kultur-Globalisierung und die Zukunft der Sprache(n).* Plenary lecture given at the 37th Annual Congress of the Gesellschaft für Angewandte Linguistik (GAL), Münster, September 2006.

European Commission
    1995   *Whitebook. Teaching and Learning: Towards a Cognitive Society.* Brüssel: COM.
    2003   *Promoting Language Learning and Linguistic Diversity: An Action Plan 2004–2006.* Brüssel: COM.

Extra, Guus
    2006   Dealing with multilingualism in multicultural Europe: immigrant minority languages at home and school. In *Reconfiguring Europe. The Contribution of Applied Linguistics*, Constant Leung and Jennifer Jenkins (eds.), 21–40. London: Equinox.

Firth, Alan
    1996   The discursive accomplishment of normality on 'lingua franca' English and conversation analysis. *Journal of Pragmatics* 26: 237–260.

Firth, Alan and Johannes Wagner
    2007   Second/foreign language learning as a social accomplishment. Elaborations on a reconceptualized SLA. *Modern Language Journal* 91 (s1): 800–819.

Fishman, Joshua
    1977   English in the context of international societal bilingualism. In *The Spread of English*, Joshua A. Fishman, Robert Cooper and Andrew Conrad (eds.), 329–336. Rowley, Mass: Newbury House.

Grosjean, Francois
    2001   The bilingual's language modes. In *One Mind, Two Languges: Bilingual Language Processing*, Janet Nicol (ed.), 1–22. Oxford: Blackwell.

Habermas, Jürgen
    1998   *Die Postnationale Konstellation. Politische Essays.* Frankfurt/Main: Suhrkamp.

House, Juliane
    1977 (1981 2d. ed.) *Translation Quality Assessment. A Model for Analysis.* Tübingen:Narr.

1996a	Contrastive discourse analysis and misunderstanding. In *Contrastive Sociolinguistics*, Marlis Hellinger and Ulrich Ammon (eds.), 345–362. Berlin: Mouton de Gruyter.
1996b	Developing pragmatic fluency in English as a foreign language. Routines and metapragmatic awareness. *Studies in Second Language Acquisition* 18: 225–252.
1997	*Translation Quality Assessment: A Model Revisited.* Tübingen: Narr.
1999	Misunderstanding in intercultural communication: Interactions in English as a lingua franca and the myth of mutual intelligibility. In *Teaching and Learning English as a Global Language*, Claus Gnutzmann (ed.), 73–93. Tübingen: Stauffenburg.
2002a	Maintenance and convergence in covert translation English-German. In *Information Structure in a Cross-Linguistic Perspective*, Bergljot Behrens et al (eds.), 199–213. Amsterdam: Rodopi.
2002b	Communicating in English as a lingua franca. In *EUROSLA Yearbook 2,* Susan Foster-Cohen (ed.), 243–261. Amsterdam: Benjamins.
2003a	English as a lingua franca: A threat to multilingualism? *Journal of Sociolinguistics* 7 (4): 556–578.
2003b	Misunderstanding in intercultural university encounters. In *Misunderstanding in Social Life. Discourse Approaches to Problematic Talk*, Juliane House, Gabriele Kasper and Steven Ross (eds.), 22–56. London: Longman.
2006a	Communicative styles in English and German. *European Journal of English Studies* 10: 249–267.
2006b	Text and Context in Translation. *Journal of Pragmatics* 38: 338–358.
2006c	Unity in Diversity: English as a lingua franca for Europe. In *Reconfiguring Europe. The Contribution of Applied Linguistics*, Constant Leung and Jennifer Jenkins (eds.), 87–104. London: Equinox
2007	(Inter)subjectivity in English lingua franca discourse: The case of *you know*. Paper given at the 10th International Pragmatics Congress, Göteborg, July 2007. To appear in *Journal of Intercultural Pragmatics* 2008.

Jakobson, Roman
    1966   On linguistic aspects of translation. In *On Translation*, R. Brower (ed.), 232–239. New York: Oxford University Press.

Kachru, Braj (ed.)
    1992   *The Other Tongue. English across Cultures* (2nded.). Chicago: Chicago University Press.

Kramsch, Claire
    2002   Language Thieves. In *In Sachen Deutsch als Fremdsprache*, Hans Barkowski and Renate Faistauer (eds.), 91–103. Hohengehren: Schneider.

Küppers, Anne
    2007   *Zur Verwendung der Personaldeixis in deutschen und französischen Aktionärsbriefen. Eine kontrastiv-quantitative Korpusanalyse.* Magisterarbeit, Universität Hamburg.

Lam, Wan Shun Eva
    2004   Second language socialization in a bilingual chatroom: Global and local considerations. *Language Learning & Technology* 8 (3): 44–65.

Lesznyák, Ágnes
    2004   *Communication in English as an International Lingua Franca.* Norderstedt: Books on Demand.

Motz, Markus
    2005a   *Ausländische Studierende in Internationalen Studiengängen: Motivation, Sprachverwendung und sprachliche Bedürfnisse.* Bochum: AKS Verlag.
    2005b   *Englisch oder Deutsch in internationalen Studiengängen?* Frankfurt/Main: Lang.

Myers-Scotton, Carol
    2006   *Multiple Voices.* Oxford: Blackwell.

Ortega y Gasset, José
    1960   *Miseria y Esplendor de la Traducción. Glanz und Elend der Übersetzung.* München: Langewiesche-Brandt.

Phillipson, Robert
    2006   Figuring out the Englishization of Europe. In *Reconfiguring Europe. The Contribution of Applied Linguistics*, Constant Leung and Jennifer Jenkins (eds.), 65–86. London: Equinox.

Price, Cathy, David Green and Roswitha von Studnitz
    1999   A functional imaging study of translation and language switching. *Brain* 122: 2221–2235.

Priegnitz, Frauke
    2007   *Die Motivation ausländischer Studierender für den Hochschulstandort Deutschland.* Magisterarbeit, Universität Hamburg.

Sanford, Anthony and Arthur Graesser
    2006   Shallow processing and underspecification. *Discourse Processes* 42 (2): 99–108.

Simsek, S. Cigdem Sagin
    2008   *Turkish-German Bilingual Students' Acquisition of English.* Muenster: Waxmann.

Soltau, Anja
    2007   *Englisch als lingua franca in der wissenschaftlichen Lehre: Charakteristika und Herausforderungen englischsprachiger Masterstudiengänge in Deutschland.* Unveröffentlichte Dissertation, Universität Hamburg.

Spielmann, Daniel
    2007   *English as Lingua Franca: A Simplified Code?* Magisterarbeit, Universität Hamburg.

Svartvik, Jan and Geoffrey Leech
    2006   *English. One Tongue, Many Voices.* London: Palgrave Macmillan.

De Swaan, Abram
    2001   *Words of the World.* Cambridge: Polity Press.

Ten Thije, Jan and Ludger Zeevaert (eds.)
    2007   *Receptive Multilingualism.* Amsterdam: Benjamins.

Van Els, Theo
    2005   Multilingualism in the European Union. *International Journal of Applied Linguistics* 15 (3): 263–281.

Wenger, Etienne
    1998   *Communities of Practice.* Cambridge: Cambridge University Press.

Widdowson, Henry
    2003   *Defining Issues in English Language Teaching.* Oxford: Oxford University Press.

French and France: language and state

Dennis Ager

1. Introduction

The French state has long considered the French language, and hence language policy, as of fundamental importance. That this should be so derives from three historical "myths" which found the role of the State. First, France is a nation-state, combining ethnicity and powerful centralised government, with the French language as one of its most important unifying symbols. Second, this same Republic and its language may one day disintegrate. Third, it is the destiny of France to be a great country, able and willing to give leadership to the world. French state attitudes to language and hence language policy are still based on all three underlying beliefs, which we have elsewhere called "Identity, Insecurity and Image" (Ager 1999).

How far are these beliefs still relevant? Have the known changes in the French population and social structure, in the relative standing of countries internationally in both politics and economics affected the vitality of language or its nature? Are they changing the state's traditional policies?

We examine first the French language community and the changes it has undergone. Second, the community's values, beliefs, and attitudes towards languages. Third, the changes affecting the official standard language and its place within the language ecology. Finally, the policies governments adopt towards language. Our concern is with "metropolitan" France, the mainland including Corsica, except where dependent territories or other Francophone states are specifically mentioned.

88 Dennis Ager

2. The French language community is changing

2.1. The population of France

2.1.1. Organisation

Traditionally one of the most centralised countries in Europe, under its President and Parliament France now has 22 Regions, 96 Departments and 36,571 Communes, each governed by an elected Council with executive Presidents for Regions and Departments and an executive Mayor for Communes. Education and policing, and much government, is still mainly centralised on Paris although regional centres such as Lyon, Lille and Bordeaux are growing in importance. Overseas, French dependent territories, the remains of the Empire, are now organised in four Departments (DOM), "integral" parts of France which are also Regions (ROM): Guadeloupe, Guyane, and Martinique in the Caribbean, and Réunion off the coast of Africa. The former TOM or overseas territories have now become *Pays d'Outre-Mer* (POM) (overseas countries) or Territories (TOM), with varying status and organisation: French Polynesia and New Caledonia in the Pacific, Mayotte in the Indian Ocean, St. Pierre et Miquelon off the coast of Canada and Terres Australes in Antarctica. New Caledonia will vote on its possible independence in 2014, while French Polynesia has very nearly achieved internal autonomy. The 22 metropolitan administrative Regions nearly, but not quite, correspond to historical counties, dukedoms or "countries" in which languages different from French may have been used. In both DOM and POM, where French is the only official language, indigenous languages were and are many and varied while French-based Créoles are widely used. Table 1 and 2 give some basic statistics.

Table 1. Population of France as at 01.01.2007 (INSEE)

Areas	Population
Metropolitan France	61,538,000
DOM-ROM	1,854,000
ex-TOM	710,000
Total	64,100,000

Table 2. Population, recognised regional languages and growth since 1999 (calculated from INSEE, DGLF)

Region	Population	Population growth
Alsace (Alsace regional languages)	1,734,000	+4.3%
Mayenne, Sarthe (approximately the Gallo region)	850,000	+4.3%
Bretagne (Breton)	2,906,000	+5.6%
Corsica (Corsican)	260,000	+6.6%
Department of Moselle (Moselle regional languages)	1,023,000	+1.2%
Southern and Central regions (approximately Occitan) i.e., Languedoc-Roussillon, Limousin, Midi-Pyrénées, Provence-Alpes-Côtes d'Azur, Rhône-Alpes minus the Departments noted below as Basque)	14,701,000	+2.2%
Pyrénées Orientales, Hautes-Pyrénées, Landes (Basque)	1,009,000	+7.1%
For the overseas areas noted below, the figures refer to the population in 2004		
DOM-ROM (Créole)	1,790,000	
POM (Pays d'Outre-Mer)	484,000	
of which French Polynesia (Tahitian)	249,000	

Although no monolingual speakers of regional languages remain, and there are no accurate figures for bilingual speakers, the figures of Table 2 show that the traditional regions still retain large enough populations to provide an adequate base for language maintenance or revival.

2.1.2. Changes in the structure of the population

Static at 40 million between 1890 and 1946, the population added 13 million between 1946 and 1976, but only a further 6 million over the next thirty years. Within this growth the population has aged; immigration has increased, then decreased; social structure has changed through occupational change; and urbanisation has greatly increased. We shall deal with these four factors in turn, taking and calculating all figures from the INSEE website except where separately shown.

Ageing

Life expectancy, at 75 in 2000, is projected to rise to 84.1 by 2050. Fecundity remains static, at 1.8 children per woman, slightly below the replacement rate. The growth in overall population means therefore that the ageing of the population is due to a lower death rate: whereas in 1950 the proportion of those aged over 60 was 16.2%, in 2007 it was 21.3%. Conversely, the proportion of those under 20 was at its highest for post-war years in 1970 (33.2%) and has dropped to 24.7% in 2007.

Urbanisation

In the centre of Paris, the population density in 2005 was 20,436 people per square kilometre, with an increase of 1.4% since 1999. In the Paris suburbs though the increase was between four and six percent; around Lyon the increase was 4.7%; for Marseilles it was 3.9%. By contrast, the lowest population densities are in essentially rural regions like Corsica (32 people per square kilometre) or near Limoges (43). The urban-rural difference is noticeable in the Auvergne, a region of four departments where the Puy-de-Dôme containing Clermont-Ferrand has a density of 78, while the other three (Allier (47), Cantal (26) and Haute-Loire (44)) are much lower. Urbanisation in France has been based since 1958 on ZUP (Priority urbanisation zones), building concentrated, uniformly designed and often poorly serviced blocks around towns, particularly Paris, many of which are now classed as "sensitive areas". During the 1960s and 1970s these attracted a high proportion of immigrants, and the predominant age group is now of young second generation immigrants, often with half the employment ratio of other areas. Group loyalty is to the *quartier* (neighbourhood), a street culture is the norm, and education standards often lower with a consequential feeling of entrapment since schools recruit from the neighbourhood. Such concentration of the population creates sociolinguistic networks using specific non-standard social varieties. Conversely, since services and amusements are in the town centres, contacts take place between the social groups, ensuring awareness of each other's linguistic practices (Armstrong and Jamin 2002: 123).

Social and occupational change

The decrease in the proportion of the population involved in agriculture has been striking over the last fifty years. In the French socio-professional classification system, those counted in agriculture dropped from over 3,000,000 in the 1950s to 1,470,904 in 1982 and to 642,167 in 1999. The economic results of agriculture have not declined, and success has been achieved by more intensive methods and more machinery; agriculture remains one of France's main sources of income.

A second change involves an increase in management and intellectual professions, and a concomitant decrease in worker proportions. Even between 1990 and 1999, the former increased by 17.5% while the latter decreased by 7.4%. The nature of the traditional French elite has been well studied (e.g., Birnbaum 1994). Three characteristics make it special to France: the centralisation of power in Paris; the nature of the higher educational system; and the important role of the state in the industrial and commercial field. Centralising power in Paris means that it is easy for social or political networking to create a tightly knit group of managerial cadres in the civil service, business and the cultural industries, sharing similar social and educational backgrounds and views (Bourdieu 1982). Higher education in France consists of two "streams": the universities, and the *grandes écoles* ('great schools'), originally established before the Revolution and developed under Napoleon to train senior civil servants to serve the state (PPS 2007: 936). The double system is "designed to serve existing French elites and their offspring, while masquerading as a meritocracy" (Maclean, Harvey and Press 2006: 103), and the most successful path for entry to the *grandes écoles* is via the top ten secondary schools (*lycées*), all based in Paris. Both such *lycées* and such higher education reinforce the networking of the elite. This is again reinforced by the *grands corps*, major branches of the civil service, which recruit from the *grandes écoles* and particularly the *École Nationale d'Administration* (ENA) while it is easy, and encouraged, to move between the civil service, state enterprises, private business and politics. ENA graduates include top professional diplomats and administrators, senior political figures (Chirac, François Hollande, Ségolène Royale) and chief executives (AXA, Barclays France, Renault, Air France). The close integration of the French elite has been blamed, along with other factors, for the "immobility" of French policy in many fields as the elite tries to prevent changes which do not benefit them.

On the other hand, a major feature of the second half of the 20th century has been increased social mobility and social mixing. Not merely has this meant breaking the boundaries between traditional social classes; it has also meant greater contacts between rich and poor, elite and the middle man.

Immigration

Theoretically, immigration was suspended in 1974, since when family reunification has been the main source. The annual rate of immigration has fluctuated, although in recent years INSEE claims it is constant at about 50,000. In 2003, the majority (26,768) gave family reunion as their reason for immigrating, with only 6,500 entering for permanent employment. Illegal immigration, by definition, is impossible to calculate with any accuracy: estimations vary from a few thousands to millions.

The source of immigration is of course a matter of prime political interest, with a concentration of discussion on "visible" rather than "invisible" immigrants. Until 1968 the majority of the foreign population of France came from neighbouring countries. By 1990 Europeans counted for 41%, Maghrebins for 39%, other Africans for 12% and Asians for 7% (Hargreaves 1995: 11). Overall, Hargreaves estimated that about ten million people in a population of 57 million were immigrants, their children or grandchildren in 1990: most were of course now French citizens. Modern immigration, in France as elsewhere, is no longer a permanent change of country: often immigrants retain contact with their "home" country, return "home" and spend long periods "there" as well as "here".

Table 3. Immigration by nationality and relevant language(s), as at 2006 (INSEE)

Source	Population	Relevant language(s)
Africa, of which	2,108,000	Arabic, various African languages
Morocco	625,000	
Tunisia	222,000	
Congo	93,000	
Ivory Coast	52,000	
Cameroon	50,000	
European Union (27), of which	1,786,000	
Portugal	567,000	Portuguese
Spain	276,000	Spanish
Germany	128,000	German
UK	125,000	English
Asia, of which	690,000	
Turkey	222,000	Turkish
Vietnam, Laos, Cambodia	162,000	Vietnamese, Laotian, Cambodian
Sri Lanka, India	58,900	Various Indian, Tamil
USA	33,000	English
Haiti	30,000	Creole
Total immigrants	4,959,000	
As percentage of the total population	8.1%	

2.2. Outside France

Various attempts have been made to estimate the numbers of French speakers in the world. The *Organisation Internationale de la Francophonie* (OIF) claims 200 millions (L1, L2 and L3), including speakers in France; the French Foreign Ministry declares that French is the only language apart from English spoken on the five continents, by 175 million people including 115 million L1 users, and claims that a quarter of the world's countries use it as a language of reference (55 members of the OIF plus 13 observers) (MAE). The majority of L1 speakers of French live in metropolitan France, so French is unlike English, Spanish or Portuguese, where the bulk of speakers live outside the country of the language's origin.

Main concentrations of the French language in Europe, where social changes in recent years have been similar to those in France, are in parts of Belgium, Switzerland, Italy and Andorra. In Belgium, the French-speaking and the Flemish-speaking communities find it difficult to work together. Outside Europe the main concentration is in Quebec, where for 40 years independence from the Federal state has been discussed and where Quebeckers have for long felt dominated by Anglophone interests. The significant social change here is in urbanisation, but also in constant increases in the proportion of the population speaking French inside, and a decrease outside, Quebec. While there is a declining memory of French in the Far East as well as for instance in Louisiana, it is in North, West and Central Africa that many countries use French as the official language, and indeed as a popular language in some. The decolonisation process of the 1960s inevitably led to a decrease in the use of official French. France has retained commercial, diplomatic and indeed military contact with much of Africa. Changes in the population and in the social structure and employment patterns of African Francophone countries have meant greater impoverishment, the closing of much education and increasing reliance on Western aid.

Everywhere outside France the growing influence of English as an international language is evident, as are economic and social attitudes based on American procedures and thinking. The international use of French does have consequences for the standard language, in France as well as elsewhere, in that for example some dictionaries of the standard language now include terms from African, Quebec or Belgian varieties.

Since French is an official language in many international institutions (United Nations and its agencies, European Union, Olympic Games), its official form is a widely used diplomatic language. In these institutions many delegates and representatives however have a choice of languages, and French must compete with other official languages. When delegations have a choice, more now opt for a language other than French: in 2001, for example, 36 countries wished to receive correspondence in French, 19 in Spanish, and 130 in English of the 185 UN members expressing a preference.

3. The bases for French language policy: beliefs and attitudes

3.1. Nationalism and identity

The French concept of identity is based on the geographical construct of a Hexagon with "natural" frontiers, and a social construct involving a unified population voluntarily empowering its representatives to form a cohesive society. This "Frenchness" has been defined as successfully combining two diverse political strands: that established during the Revolution, seeing the nation as the result of personal choice, a social pact between reasoning individuals who accept the Revolution's Declaration of Human Rights as the summit of human achievement; and a more recent, more right-wing view of the nation as an ethnic entity with a long history and shared myths, memories and taboos (Fysh 1997: 85). In the Revolutionary, "left-wing" view, the French language is seen as representing reason and democracy, a human right for all humanity and not just France. Following the political Right, the language is just as important, a creation of intellectual and cultural perfection, but also both a fundamental part of the French personality and representing the best of what is specifically French. In the discourse of identity, recurrent terms include: France itself; the symbols of the state (tricolour flag, national anthem, the French language); greatness (*grandeur*) and glory (*gloire*); the Republican values (Liberty, Equality and Fraternity); and the right of the individual to give or refuse his or her consent (*c'est mon droit*). As a concept of national identity, it is hard-headed, pragmatic and homogeneous; one of its consequences is that those who work for the state consider themselves to be the state (*L'Etat, c'est moi*).

In these respects French nationalism and the resulting identity politics are quite different from the German and Romantic tradition, and even more so from "mosaic" societies such as the UK or the USA. A negative view of the French nation and society stresses its inbuilt immobilism: since citizens voluntarily and individually "establish" the state, it must be perfect, and change to cope with developments is impossible without major chaos, even violence as in recurring street "battles". Subgroups of any nature are anathema, and foreigners must assimilate. On the positive side, every citizen is individually responsible for his social contract; sovereignty lies with the people; and all citizens are equal. Similarly, each citizen is free, has the same rights as others and society is inclusive.

3.2. Insecurity

Insecurity about language has a long history in France: complaints that French is not used, is not properly used, is declining in quality date at least from the 16th century, when the term "Defence of French" was first used. Since then books complaining about the imminent demise of French have appeared with regularity, and are the inspiration of language defence organisations such as the modern *Défense de la Langue Française*, run by the French Academy. We identified four types of insecurity, each with a long history but each still valid today (Ager 1999: 15–115):

— Fear of the regional languages: during the French Revolution it seemed obvious to those in Paris that the language of freedom and democracy was French, while Breton, Basque and other regional languages were symbols for attacks on the state. They should be destroyed.
— Fear that social outsiders such as women, the poor, the young, or immigrants would wish to create their own communities with their own rules. They should be ignored.
— Fear that these same social outsiders would not accept the specifically French definition of inclusiveness and would destroy social stability. They should be assimilated.
— Fear of English: in the twentieth and twenty first centuries the English-speaking countries, at first Britain and now the United States, have been demonised as "barbarians at the gate" for their "single mode of thought" (*pensée unique*) beliefs in economic free-trade and cultural openness. They should be opposed, and hopefully crushed.

In language terms, the fear is that the standard language might be replaced or degraded. Insecurity also means that users are so unsure of their own language use that they have recourse to language "authorities", and fear to innovate. For Gadet (2003: 20–23) "French is obviously a language like others, but the sociolinguistic particularity which makes it somewhat special is strong support for the ideology of the standard". Defence of the standard requires that other language varieties, or even other languages, are condemned as threatening "proper" French, with metaphors of rape, contamination, war, and chaos. It is such condemnation that terrifies learners and makes French seem a "difficult" language to learn, and may militate against its spread overseas. The overall reaction to insecurity has been one of aggressive protectionism and purism within the citadel, allied to a warlike opposition to all threats, real or imagined.

3.3. Image

An image is the reflection, in observers' minds, of an identity, for example of a country or of a language. The image can be manipulated, as in advertising, and most people, organisations and countries try to thus portray themselves in the most favourable light possible. The image of the language traditionally projected internally is of a binding force at the basis of the French nation-state, a liberating, democratic tool available to all to enable them to achieve their full potential. For those abroad, the more recent, post-colonial image is of a means of access for all to an alternative vision of the world free from cultural, economic or military domination. However paradoxical, the state thus projects both a conception of intrinsic worth and an "international", "democratic" and "modern" flavour. The discourse of image-building is centered on the idea of *rayonnement*, the radiation outwards of France's glory and greatness, aiming always at ensuring the presence, prestige, and influence of France.

4. The official language

4.1. The linguistic ecology of France

The linguistic ecology of metropolitan France involves an official standard language, regional languages spoken only within, or in some cases also spoken outside, France, and immigrant languages. Users deploy verbal repertoires, making use of linguistic variables which have become marked as correlating with external variables such as time, space, class, style, channel and situation (Gadet 2003). The standard language is often defined as the public use of educated Parisians. It was standardised through selection (the Francien dialect of the *Ile de France*), codification (by the Court and the French Academy in the 17th century), elaboration (but very sparingly, by Diderot and the *Encyclopédie* in the 18th century and subsequently), and acceptance (through intensive education in the 19th century) (Lodge 1993). As Gadet notes (2003: 18), "The ideology of the standard prizes uniformity as the ideal state for a language, and the perfect form of this is the written".

The three main dialectal divisions of French are *Langue d'oïl* (North); *Franco-Provençal* (Centre East) and *Langue d'Oc* (South). Within these, there are numerous dialects, which have been practically extinct since the 1920s, but have left considerable and marked differences in pronunciation particularly between the North and the South.

Ten regional languages or language groups are recognised by DGLF as in Table 2. The DGLF decisions are sometimes contested as attempts by the state to oversimplify or to make choices for political reasons. There are continuing disagreements between specialists and among language activists over terminology, particularly in the case of *Occitan/Provençal*, and over language boundaries, for example in the Alsace and Moselle regions. There is little information on how far immigrant languages are used.

4.2. Changes in the language

Two main questions arise at this point: how far the French language is changing in response to the drivers of change we identified above – ageing, urbanisation, occupational change, and immigration; and whether these changes are so great, and so negative, that standard French is in danger.

4.2.1. Ageing

Logically, ageing should produce a slowing down of drastic change, the use of more rather than less formal language and retention of the forms of the past. Attitudinally, the simple dichotomy is strengthened, opposing the "pure" form (*causer à*) and the "debased" one (*causer avec*), and discovering a language crisis as the young refuse to accept a uniform, homogenised, and unchanging norm. The ageing of society reaffirms the generation gap as the language use of the young rejects what they see as a restrictive norm.

Official French is by definition for use in public, formal situations such as the law, education and government, in both speech and writing. In some of these domains it is "frozen" or unchanging, with a prescribed vocabulary, grammar and discourse structure, and even repeated attempts to modernise administrative language are unlikely to affect it. In addition, the strong formality of French educational practices, and the stress on language correctness where the written form is taken as the correct one, mean that there is widespread awareness of the norm, to the extent of maintaining a common norm of pronunciation as well as characteristics of spoken French such as clear diction. To this extent French is indeed fairly static.

On the other hand, the spoken/written differences are quite large in French, and the spoken forms are undoubtedly becoming more recognised as writing becomes no longer the normal form of widespread social interaction. The written language makes use of conjunctions, the spoken of intonation. Left dislocation (*Marie, sa femme, tu connais?* 'Do you know Mary, his wife?'), and the replacement of interrogative inversion by simple intonation are both more frequent than before 1950. Many grammatical forms of the written language are simply no longer used in the spoken: the imperfect of the subjunctive has disappeared, the past definite is replaced by the perfect; *ne* has disappeared from negation.

Usage typical of younger members of society has become more common in a number of ways, particularly in the appearance of a final mute *e* (*bonjour e*), a rising intonation at the end of statements, slang formations such as *verlan* (syllable inversion); use of relative *que*; and less awareness of social interaction, sometimes producing unintended impressions of aggressiveness, rapidity, or "sloppiness". On the other hand, "prestigious" liaison has become more frequent in cases where it is unexpected (*il faut t comprendre*).

4.2.2. Urbanisation

Urbanisation has produced two opposing developments: the creation of close-knit neighbourhood networks with jargons of their own, and the opposite, the easier mixing of social classes and groups. Networks often use or even create their own forms as a way of isolating themselves from others: *verlan* is much used in Paris, very little in Marseilles or Grenoble.

The disappearance of final *l* and *r*, of the negative particle *ne*, or of the unstressed *schwa*, all socially marked characteristics of informal or of lower social class usage, while still anathematised, are all increasing in frequency in the standard language, perhaps associated with greater urbanisation and a more youthful population. Elision and reduction are both more common, perhaps in relation to the speed of modern urban life, as is abbreviation, which is normally right-hand syllable deletion (*impec* for *impeccable*). Non-etymological *-o* often appears (*prolo* for *prolétaire*). The language is changing also in grammar and lexis: *tarif étudiant* for *tarif pour l'étudiant* ('student rate'); acronyms (ZUP); new vocabulary, from *télé* ('tele, television set') to *mèl* ('e-mail') and *internet*. English has affected spoken French to the extent of creating a new phoneme (*-ng* as in *le living*), as well as in widespread borrowing. Contacts between users, whether through media or directly, aid the spread of such features (Armstrong and Jamin 2002: 123).

4.2.3. Occupational change

The disappearance of agricultural and unskilled professions should produce a move towards the standard and a disappearance of rurally marked forms, while a higher proportion of better educated and more elitist people could produce greater awareness of international events and other countries, as well as attitudinal change, possibly towards acceptance of modern media and its linguistic forms.

The standard word-group pattern of stressing the word- or group-final syllable is changing, perhaps under the influence of pronunciation in the audio-visual media, towards stressing the most emotionally loaded or significant syllable or word, while adjectives are moving from post- to prenominal order. Modern technology has influenced writing, from the use of reduced forms as in e-mail or texting, to the adoption of journalistic forms and vocabulary (*sécuriser* 'to reassure'; use of acronyms; order of words). The language of advertising is widespread, with its occasional linguistic creativity (*roule cool*). Modern technology, too, has sometimes aided in the creation of symbolic languages, such as sign language (not exclusively used for or by the deaf) or the use of symbols and icons, for example on computer screens or consumer goods.

4.2.4. Immigration

The presence of first generation immigrants is likely to affect language use in the street culture, where new arrivals congregate, borrowing terms from immigrant languages and adapting French to the norms of the foreign language, sometimes creating an interethnic *lingua franca* (Gadet 2003: 91–94). Thus variable affrication (*dzh* for *d* in *dire*), and glottalisation of *r*, to an extent traceable to Arabic, seem to be characteristic of inner city and youthful populations (Armstrong and Jamin 2002). Similarly words appear from African languages (*go* 'girl') or Arabic (*kif* 'cannabis, pot'). Code-switching and mixing are frequent: *obligé tu viens* for 'you should come';

je veux pas choufer using an Arabic verb; the use of ritual insults, characteristic of Arabic and other languages. One feature of these linguistic developments is that they no longer represent an intermediate and short-lived stage but seem durable changes in the language.

4.2.5. Is the official language disappearing or declining in quality?

Yes

Maurice Druon, then Secretary of the French Academy, was capable of declaring even in 2004 that French had been raised to a level of "clarity, precision, subtlety, elegance, charm, politeness ... which has made it the universal language, that which every cultured person owed it to themselves to know and was delighted to use, often preferring it to their native language". There are frequent press articles and books repeating such beliefs and condemning "degradation".

Threats against the standard language can be classified as lexical, grammatical or stylistic, whether in spoken or written French, although much of the protestation is directed at radio and television and hence at the spoken. In grammar, "degradation" is exemplified in word order, in the loss of interrogative inversion, in unfinished phrases, in the loss of forms like the imperfect subjunctive, in inaccuracies of noun-adjective agreement. In style, complaints recur about carelessness, vulgarity if not obscenity, slang, unfinished phrases, inappropriate liaisons in the spoken form, stumbling and garbled expression. But it is in lexis that the majority of complaints occur, and in particular against an invasion of Anglo-American. Druon indeed regards the problem as being that the French no longer feel pride in their language, in themselves or in their international power. But another source of danger is mass education, which no longer provides a guarantee of economic success. The media, as well as modernism generally, are the other main sources of the crisis. The threats are supposedly to the genius of the language; to its purity; to its logic, and to its aesthetic value. There is little doubt that general public opinion supports the view that language use is becoming worse.

No

Those who consider there is no crisis of quality either consider that purism has nothing to do with linguistics and everything to do with social or political ideology, or feel that those who despair of present-day French are simply unaware of real usage and particularly of the need for language variety to match communicative situation and purpose. They note that of the five types of purism commonly recognised France is prone to use three: archaic, elitist and xenophobic, but not ethnographic nor reformist purism. Critics of such purism point to ignorance of linguistic as well as sociolinguistic facts. Thus many of the condemned forms, like *verlan*, in fact have a long and respectable history within French; many "English" forms have their origins in French (budget); every user of any language deploys his or her verbal repertoire in many different domains and with many different communicative purposes. Critics also have a stronger point to make: that it is precisely the commentators who have driven the French to the level of insecurity they now demonstrate: "some people expect *résout* or *résolu* when they hear *solutionne* or *solutionné*, too "popular" for them because it is used by people who can't manage morphology and therefore don't know how to, and don't dare to, use *résoudre*" (Houdebine-Gravaud 1995: 103).

In a conference dedicated to the "quality" of French, linguists condemned the purists. For Culioli (1995: 53), "what is striking is the absence of respect (for varietal forms)"; "whatever equates quality to a unique, historical model, is destined to be ignored". His conclusion was that "we have the language we deserve, in the sense that it corresponds to the social practices we have". For Boutet, similarly (1995: 86), the reality is of a heterogeneous language with several norms, and a definition of quality requiring a language form to fulfil its linguistic, rather than social, function.

Overall, about 10% of the population are illiterate in the UNESCO definition, in difficulty with reading; about 5% overall in serious difficulty with 19% among those aged 55–65, and 4.5% of those aged 17–19 (INSEE 2002, MINED, *Note d'Evaluation* 06.03 and *L'Etat de l'Ecole*, 2007: 17). On an international comparison made in 2000 these figures are better than the average, but place France in the middle of the range of scores in written comprehension (MINED: Dossier 123). These figures have not changed much since the Espérandieu report of 1984, when the French government accepted that the priorities placed on education since 1789, and particularly on education in French, had still not produced a completely literate nation (Ager 1996: 78–80).

5. Language policies

Following Spolsky (2004: 63–74) we deal here with six aspects of language policy in France: constituent or administrative policy (the organisations); the status of French; language management; policy towards the regional languages; language acquisition management; diffusion policy; and the effectiveness of policy.

5.1. The main organisations

The French Academy, taken over by Cardinal Richelieu in 1635, is one of the oldest European language policy instruments established by any state. Forty "immortals", illustrious representatives of culture but also from other fields, were brought together to write a dictionary, a grammar, a rhetoric and a poetics, and told to give explicit rules and ensure the language could deal with arts and sciences. Marginalised for years, the Academy returned to centre stage in the 1990s and now, theoretically at least, heads the state language policy organisations. Its aim is to defend French.

Under de Gaulle and later Mitterrand language policy began to concentrate on the issue of ensuring French could resist domination by international English. The first institution was the "High Committee for the Defence and Expansion of French", and was set up following reports on the three topics which have remained of major interest: Anglicisms in French, the role of French in international organisations, and the future of France's colonial empire. After changing name and status several times, the *Délégation Générale à la Langue Française et aux Langues de France* (DGLF: General Delegation for French and the Languages of France) now has two main roles: to implement the 1994 Toubon Law and to organise the Terminology Commissions.

5.2. The status of French

Currently, the status of French is ensured by the 1992 addition to the Constitution, which states that "The language of the Republic is French". This clause has prevented the ratification of the European Charter for Regional or Minority Languages (Extra and Gorter, this Volume), and is cited in attempts to prevent implementation of free trade, cultural imports, protocols on patents and even some international contacts. In 1994 the main instrument of legislation on the status of French, the "Toubon Law", was passed and now forms the basis of status policy for French in France. "French is an essential element of France, the language of teaching, work, commerce and the public service, and is the special link for the Francophone community" states the first of its 24 clauses, which require French to be used in commerce, publicity, public notices, contracts including employment contracts and in the workplace, in science and in education except for the teaching of regional or foreign languages. "French" is not defined in official legislation, although parliamentary debates noted that terms derived from the regional languages (*kouign aman* – a Breton sweet cake) and established borrowings (whisky) counted as French.

A significant aspect of the Toubon Law was its insistence that French should be official in order to protect the rights of the consumer and the worker as well as the citizen. This particular slant enabled the government of the time to include measures which in other countries and at other times have been regarded as proto-fascist, protectionist, dictatorial or offensive to the rights of minorities. The existing Consumer Protection and Repression of Fraud mechanisms ensure implementation, thus avoiding setting up any special system to ensure compliance but nonetheless ensuring the Act has teeth.

5.3. Language management

Corpus policy for French was and remains part of the remit of the French Academy: it was supposed to make French fit for use in arts and sciences. This implied ensuring that vocabulary was adequate to name and discuss new developments as they arose, although the main result of the standardisation process which took place in the 17th and 18th centuries was to restrict vocabulary, producing the classical restraint and dislike of neologism that typifies French today. The Academy soon became too inefficient, since fifty years passed between new editions of its dictionary. It no longer tries to produce a grammar, although it does make language advice available on its website.

It became clear in the 1970s that new technology, as well as new social developments, needed new terminology to describe objects and processes. Every Ministry now has its own Terminology Commission, agreeing the appropriate terms, which often involve approving translations from English. The DGLF has a general commission for other aspects of corpus work, and after a decision by the Constitutional Council, approved new terms must be used by the government, including diplomats, but private citizens may not be obliged to use them. Other corpus work is undertaken by private dictionaries – Robert and Larousse are the best known – and now include Francophone terms from other countries. There is also a *Conseil Supérieur de l'Audiovisuel*, charged with ensuring "the defence and illustration of French, the use of French and respect for French and the spread of Francophony" in state radio and television.

5.4. The regional languages

At the time of the Revolution, and possibly until 1951, the state's policy towards the regional languages was to encourage language shift towards French by a mixture of overt and covert coercion and bribery. In 1951 some regional languages were allowed into schools. Although France has not ratified the *European Charter for Regional or Minority Languages*, in practice it provides support for them in education, usually in co-operation with the relevant Region. Bilingual teaching is provided in some schools in association with parents' groups, affecting 8,206 children in 6 languages in 2005/2006; regional languages are accepted as Baccalaureate examination subjects; and are available in higher education. Total staff involved was 287, giving 11,965 hours of teaching.

The DGLF notes that its location in the Ministry of Culture "invites one to consider languages in their capacity to produce works of art: more as tools of artistic creation than as means of communication". It declares that "the policy of valuing the languages of France proves our country's commitment in favour of European plurilingualism", and notes that a law to give legal recognition to regional languages is a necessary prerequisite for new action in this field.

5.5. Language acquisition

The teaching of French is a priority of the educational system, the first pillar of seven competencies required since 2006 by the end of compulsory schooling (MINED: Socle Commun). Mastery of French, "the basis of all education", is based on "mastery of vocabulary, grammar and syntax, involving exercises in conjugation, dictations, public speaking as part of learning the rules of language", leading to "mastery of the language involving clear and precise expression in speaking and writing, including awareness of literature in French". The outline of the syllabus lists the knowledge to be acquired, the competencies to establish, and the attitudes to encourage. For perhaps the first time this brief explanatory document makes clear in everyday language the aims of education in French and the method by which these are to be acquired. As an example, the skills for spoken language are given as

— speaking in public;
— participating in a dialogue, a debate, taking into account the views of others and making one's own views known;
— presenting individual or collective work (exposition, experience, demonstrations);
— reformulating a text, spoken or written;
— adapting speech, in attitude and level of language, to the communication situation (place, intended listener, effect sought);
— reciting heritage texts from memory (literary texts, quotations).

In terms of international comparisons, one might suggest that the French document stresses traditional skills and methods. Indeed, critics of the French educational system have long pointed to its conservatism.

Policy for foreign languages stresses the European dimension and the necessity for two languages in most streams of the Baccalaureate. A wide selection of languages is theoretically available, and parents may request teaching in certain circumstances, although the latest statistics available (for 2004) show that 97% studied English, mostly as first foreign language, 40% Spanish, 16% German. Nearly all pupils in secondary schools studied a foreign language, 96% a second language, and 6% a third (MINED).

5.6. Diffusion

Policy for the French language abroad is conducted by France, often working with the OIF. Both represent "the best examples of an active diffusion policy" (Spolsky 1994: 71). Traditionally, the policy stressed education in French, for elites, and regarded other languages as either inferior or irrelevant to the task of civilisation. These policy lines continue, through educational organisations like the *Alliance Française* or the government network of cultural institutes, through OIF activities or through TV5 and aid arrangements.

France "conducts an active policy aiming to promote linguistic diversity in the European Union and preserving the place of French" (Report 2006: 89). As elsewhere, "linguistic diversity" and "the promotion of French" go closely together, since French diplomacy sees the main advantage of diversity as being the reduction of the hegemonic influence of international English. Policy for French outside France has a number of strands, including work in diplomacy, in international institutions and organisations, and in education.

France maintains the largest cultural network in the world, with 436 establishments including 283 *Alliances Françaises* and 745,000 learners. France spends 50 million Euros on five ambitious initiatives, training 10,000 teachers in Asia and Africa, helping to train European civil servants, creating educational centres in the Maghreb, developing information and communication technologies.

Apart from education, in EU institutions, "the policy of recruiting French candidates" and "the daily action" (of French staff in negotiations) "can delay the tendency towards monolingualism" (Report 2006: 89). Pressure to make French the reference language for European law heightened in 2004, while under the cover of supporting "multilingualism" a number of pro-French actions, particularly in education, are supported financially and politically.

In the United Nations and its agencies, similar action promotes the use of French and guards the rights of Francophone staff. A particular effort has been directed towards the use of French in the Olympic Games.

The OIF now claims 68 members, representing states and "governments" such as Quebec, and including observers. Although it is now mainly a political organisation, it retains language-related activities, such as the 2006 Code of Conduct for OIF members involving the use of French by delegations, demands for French versions of documents, the recruitment of French-speaking staff, training for international civil servants, and systematic noting of breaches in multilingual usage. Among other actions, the OIF tries to persuade its European members to use and promote French in the institutions. OIF educational funding aimed at helping the teaching and learning of French at an early stage is considered by Chaudenson (2007: 138) to be too low. He notes it as 1.7 million Euros, or 1.7 centimes per child to educate, or 50,000 Euros per state for the 35 states most in need. Chaudenson deplores what has practically become the end of OIF educational efforts, to find the organisation becoming simply another arena for international political disputes.

5.7. The effectiveness of policy

The 2007 Report on the Toubon Law notes that in 2006 the DGLF examined 10,923 breaches of the law in commercial cases, leading to 804 formal reminders of the law, 131 court cases and 59 guilty verdicts. The highest number of guilty verdicts was in 1997, with 127; the lowest 42 in 2001. In the workplace, firms were ordered to provide translations into French of manuals and trade unions were active in identifying cases. In advertising, of 1,892 cases requiring modification in 2006/2007, 372 contravened the language policy. In science, 9.6% of references in the citation database organised by France were in French, 76% in English. A large number of convictions might mean that the policy is effective; on the other hand it might mean that the general public is ignoring the provisions of the law.

In certain areas, particularly in scientific research, transport and aircraft manufacture, the relevant groups mainly ignore it, while the state turns a blind eye. Indeed, if the law were fully applied, French scientific research would make no impression internationally. In aircraft manufacture Airbus, Dassault and other French manufacturers would be out of work if the law were applied, and in air transport at least one serious incident in 2003 was caused by non-use of English in Roissy-Charles-de-Gaulle airport. In some cases European or international agreements prevail over French legislation; in others, commercial or diplomatic advantage seems preferable to a strict observance. The European Commission has several times objected to the law on the grounds of European fair competition law, and similar laws in other countries have been declared un-European.

6. Conclusion

In France, French has for centuries been *une affaire d'Etat*, whatever the government and its political colour. Its future is assured, despite the changes it is undergoing. In Francophone countries outside France, mostly multilingual, with French in a situation of competition or conflict with other languages, its future is very dependent on local circumstances. In some countries there are language defence organisations for French, although in general they are less extreme than those based in France and users generally see little problem in accepting neologisms and borrowings.

In Europe the prestige of the Parisian norm is so well established that users in other countries tend to have some insecurity about their own version, although not to the extent of rejecting it altogether. Speakers of

French seem unlikely to shift to other languages, and the language generally retains its full vitality.

In Quebec, French is in good shape, despite the popular form's differences in pronunciation and in lexis with the French of Paris. The language is actively used in official circumstances: in Parliament, in the law, in education. Indeed, Quebec French is used and is important in all domains and is "managed" by specific language planning organisations under the protection of the political world. The danger seen, and actively opposed, is the influence of American English which might overpower French in Quebec, as it has done in New England.

In North Africa French is widely used and is in little danger of disappearance, despite its associations with the colonial era and its accompaniment, and in some cases replacement, by Arabic as the state's official language. In most African countries French is in more danger, partly through the power of the English-speaking states such as Nigeria and South Africa, partly through the growth of English as an international language, and partly because of the collapse of African educational systems. In both North Africa and in many other African countries French is the language of the elite and has become a marker of social advancement, which also protects it from disappearance. In some areas varieties other than the official exist and are used, such as a well-developed popular French in Senegal.

The use of French in international institutions is tracked in the annual DGLF Report. At least theoretically, 21 languages are equally official in the European Commission and its agencies, where, for the DGLF, "the preponderance of English is becoming absolute" (Report 2006: 87). In the United Nations and its agencies six languages are theoretically equally official. In practice most documents are produced in English and translated. Nonetheless, it is French that is most used after English: in UNESCO's Executive Council plenary sessions in 2006 delegates used languages as follows: English 46, French 34, Spanish 11, Arabic 5, Chinese 3, Russian 2.

In the remainder of the world the nine UNESCO measures of vitality nearly all indicate a drop for French: in the absolute number of speakers, in proportions of speakers in the total population, in the availability of materials, in response to new domains and media, in type and quality of documentation, in governmental and institutional attitudes, in domain shift, in attitudes and in intergenerational language transmission. But none of these indicators could remotely indicate that French is in any danger of disappearance. Still, there are over a hundred million L1 speakers, with a world usage rank of about twentieth overall in a list of several thousand languages. Material, written and in modern media formats, on French and in French is plentiful. French has responded to new domains and media with a flood of French-language material; documentation on and in French is extensive; governmental attitudes could not be more supportive, while the policies of the major institutions all support French. French is used in all domains; intergenerational transmission, and community attitudes, are perhaps less supportive than they used to be but by no means negative. By comparison with the languages that really are in danger of disappearance, or even with a major language like Hindi, the indicators for the future of French outside France and its main communities give no cause for concern whatsoever. The only danger facing French is that overzealous protectionism may damage the language and its prospects.

Note

French official social statistics are maintained in a number of databases, accessible by Internet. Where these are referenced in the text without further information, references are as shown below, derived from consultation in October/December 2007.

- DGLF: Délégation Générale à la Langue française et aux Langues de France: *www.culture.gouv.fr/culture/dglf/*
- DLF: Défense de la Langue Française: *www.langue-francaise.org*
- INSEE: Institut National des Statistiques et des Etudes Economiques: *www.insee.fr*
- MAE: Ministère des Affaires Etrangères: *www.diplomatie.gouv.fr*
- MINED: Ministère de l'Education Nationale: *www.education.gouv.fr*
- OIF: Organisation Internationale de la Francophonie: *www.francophonie.org*

References

Ager, Dennis E.
    1996   *Language Policy in Britain and France*. London: Cassell.
    1999   *Identity, Insecurity and Image. France and Language*. Clevedon: Multilingual Matters.
Armstrong, Nigel and Mikaël Jamin
    2002   Le français des banlieues. In *French In and Out of France*, Kamal Salhi (ed.), 107–136. Oxford: Peter Lang.
Birnbaum, Pierre
    1994   *Les Sommets de l'Etat; Essai sur l'Élite du Pouvoir en France*. Paris: Seuil.

Bourdieu, Pierre
  1982   *Ce que Parler Veut Dire*. Paris: Fayard.
Boutet, Josiane
  1995   Qualité de la langue et variation. In *La Qualité de la Langue? Le Cas du Français*, Jean-Michel Eloy (ed.), 73–86. Paris: Champion.
Chaudenson, Robert
  2007   La place de la langue française dans la francophonie. *Hérodote* 3 (126): 129–141.
Culioli, Antoine
  1995   Peut-on théoriser la notion de "Qualité de la Langue"? In *La Qualité de la Langue? Le Cas du Français*, Jean-Michel Eloy (ed.), 51–64. Paris: Champion.
Fysh, Peter
  1997   Gaullism and Liberalism. In *Political Ideologies in Contemporary France*, Christopher Flood and Laurence Bell (eds.), 73–102. London: Cassell.
Gadet, Françoise
  2003   *La Variation Sociale en Français*. Paris: Ophrys.
Hargreaves, Alec
  1995   *Immigration, 'Race' and Ethnicity in Contemporary France*. London: Routledge.
Houdebine-Gravaud, Anne-Marie
  1995   L'unes langue. In *La Qualité de la Langue? Le Cas du Français*, Jean-Michel Eloy (ed.), 96–120. Paris: Champion.
Lodge, Anthony
  1993   *French: from dialect to standard*. London: Routledge.
Maclean, Mairi, Charles Harvey and Jon Press
  2006   *Business Elites and Corporate Governance in France and the UK*. Hampshire: Palgrave Macmillan.
PPS (Problèmes Politiques et Sociaux)
  2007   Universités et Grandes Écoles. *Problèmes Politiques et Sociaux,* n° 936.
Report
  Annual *Rapport au Parlement sur l'Emploi de la Langue Française*. Paris: Délégation Générale à la Langue Française et aux Langues de France.
Spolsky, Bernard
  2004   *Language Policy*. Cambridge: Cambridge University Press.

Polish in Poland and abroad

Justyna Leśniewska and Zygmunt Mazur

1. The Polish language

Polish, the official language of Poland, where it is spoken by about 38 million people, belongs to the six most widely spoken official state languages in the present EU (Extra and Gorter, this Volume). Polish is a member of the West Slavic group of the Slavic branch of the Indo-European family of languages. It is written in the Roman alphabet and modified by means of diacritical marks to obtain additional graphemes; the spelling was standardised by two reforms, in 1918 and 1936 (Bajerowa 2001: 38). Polish is a highly inflected language, which goes together with a very flexible word order. The Slavic base of Polish vocabulary has been enriched by many borrowings over the centuries, from Latin, German, Italian, French, Russian, Ukrainian, and, most recently, from English. The earliest extant texts written in Polish date back to 1136 (proper and place names in a papal document), the oldest known sermons and translations of psalms date back to the 14th century, and the earliest Polish dictionary dates back to 1526. Polish developed rapidly in the 16th century, when the masterpieces of Polish Renaissance literature were composed, despite the fact that the official language of Poland at that time was still Latin.

2. Polish in Poland

2.1. Demographic and demolinguistic perspectives

Poland's population (the total size of which was 38,230,000 in 2002, the year of the last census) is ethnically homogeneous to an exceptional degree and predominantly Roman Catholic (89% of the population [Mały rocznik 2007: 132]). According to the 2002 census (Raport 2003: 40), an overwhelming 96.7% of the population declared they were of Polish nationality, around 1.23% declared they were of other nationality and 2.03% did not specify any nationality. Among the 1.23% who declared to be of a nationality other than Polish, the most frequent answers were: Silesian

(173,153), German (152,897), Belarusian (48,700), Ukrainian (31,000), Roma (12,900), Russian (6,103), Lemko (5,863), Lithuanian (5,846), Kashubian (5,062), and Slovak (2,000). As can be seen, three minorities (Silesian, Lemko, Kashubian) are ethnic groups not related to another country in Europe, while the remaining minorities declare their nationalities to be of other European nation-states.[1]

The 2002 census also investigated the language spoken at home and revealed that Poland is a linguistically homogeneous country. An overwhelming majority of the population of Poland use Polish at home (37,405,300 people or 97.8% of the country's population, a number which exceeds the number of people who declared to be of Polish nationality, which means that at least some of the people who declared to be of a different nationality use Polish at home). Only 52,500 people (0.14%) declared that they only use a language/languages other than Polish at home (the remaining 2.02% are subjects for whom no data concerning languages spoken at home could be obtained). Moreover, the Polish language is used as *the only language at home* in most cases (36,894,400 people or 96.5%). The languages other than Polish that were named most often (whether in combination with Polish, with another foreign language, or as the only language used at home) were German (204,600 respondents) and English (89,900 respondents) (Raport 2003: 41), outnumbering by far any other foreign languages.

Similar data was obtained in the Eurobarometer study conducted towards the end of 2006, in which 98% of the Polish population named Polish as their mother tongue, 1% named another official EU language, and 1% named a language other than any official EU language (Special Eurobarometer 2006). Poland thus emerges as a classic example of a country in which the mother tongue of the overwhelming majority of the people is the state language.

2.2. Recent changes in Polish and the language norm

The last 20 years have been a period of rapid change for the Polish language, which reflects the major change of the political system from a totalitarian regime to a democracy, and the accompanying changes in society. The transition to a free market economy has brought countless new vocabulary items into the language, connected with trade, technology, or lifestyle, as well as new modes of discourse characteristic of, for example, advertising or marketing. Globalisation and integration with other EU countries have increased language contact and cross-linguistic influence. If this were not enough, communication has been greatly affected by the arrival of the Internet. At the same time, the model of language communication and the language awareness of the Polish nation have been changing. Bartmiński (2001: 13) observes that post-1989 changes in the Polish language include the rejection of the totalitarian model of communication, characterised by the dominance of the censored monologue in the mass media and of irony and parody in private conversations. The language of administration and politics, the so-called *nowomowa* 'new speech' was widely perceived as a language of lies, presenting a false picture of reality, which had the effect of undermining the trust in language as a medium of communication in general. The regaining of independence, Bartmiński notes, has lowered the need for the national-religious-patriotic discourse used previously to keep up the spirit of opposition and the struggle for independence, and democracy has encouraged the mode of dialogue in language.

While some language changes are seen as welcome, others are perceived by many linguists as detrimental to the Polish language, in particular the excessive borrowing from English and the vulgarisation of the language (see, e.g., Bajerowa 2001 for a discussion of the "poverty" of contemporary Polish). The general approach is normative and prescriptive (for a discussion see, e.g., Markowski and Puzynina 2001); in lexicography, this emphasis on language correctness has resulted in the divergence of language description from actual language use. Only recently did a new dictionary (Markowski 1999) introduce the distinction between two kinds of language norm, which enabled the inclusion of many language forms characteristic of the informal register.

Dubisz (2002: 93) notes that at the beginning of the 20th century standard Polish was used by about 20–25% of the Polish community, with another 50–60% aspiring to use it. A century later, standard Polish is used by about 80% of the community, but two variants of it have evolved: the official one, precise and exact, and the unofficial (colloquial) one. Dubisz predicts a further increase in the number of users of standard Polish, with the expansion of the unofficial variety, and reduction of the role of the official variety.

2.3. Regional varieties of Polish

Generally speaking, Polish as a language is to a great extent unified and standardised (Bajerowa 2001: 47). The Communist regime contributed to the unification of Polish by undermining the class system and strongly promoting the *one language – one state* ideology. Regional monority (henceforward RM) languages unique to Poland (e.g., Kashubian) were treated as dialects of Polish. The dispute over the status of Kashubian continues to the present day (Majewicz and Wicherkiewicz 1999), but most Polish sources (e.g., Handke 2001) list it as one of the five main dialects of Polish, alongside the *mazowiecki* 'Mazovian', *wielkopolski* 'Great Polish', *małopolski* 'Little Polish', and *śląski* 'Silesian' dialects – the former two spoken in the North, and the latter two in the south of Poland. The distribution of the five dialects has been relatively stable throughout centuries, and still mirrors the original geography of the Slavic tribes who used them (Handke 2001: 203). Kashubian is most markedly different from contemporary standard Polish, while Silesian is most varied internally, consisting as it does of a large number of local variants. Whatever their linguistic make-up, however, the status of Kashubian and Silesian is obviously different from that of the other three dialects since they are used by speakers with a sense of regional identity (as shown by the census data mentioned above), which makes them RM languages.

The current situation, therefore, is the result of two different trends: on the one hand, we are witnessing a certain strengthening of the position of RM languages such as Kashubian; on the other hand, other regional and dialectal differences in Polish are generally disappearing. At present, dialects of Polish are intelligible throughout Poland, the differences between them are mostly limited to pronunciation, and their distribution is very strongly determined by social status (Pisarek 2001). Commonly perceived as indicating low social status and lack of education, they are spoken mostly by those inhabitants of a given region who choose to remain in their hometown; those who leave tend not to make an effort to retain the ability to speak the dialect they grew up with. The status of Polish dialects remains low despite the fact that some of the Polish literature was written in dialect. In this sense, the situation of Polish dialects is strikingly different from, for example, that of Bavarian in Germany.

Polish in Poland is geographically diversified also in another way (Handke 2001: 216); apart from the existence of dialects, there is some regional variation in standard Polish, which is different from dialectal differences, as it occurs in all registers and social strata in connection with a particular geographical location. Regional variation is mostly limited to slight differences in accent (not perceptible to all speakers of Polish), and some much quoted lexical differences, mostly in the semantic fields of fruit, vegetables, food and cooking (e.g., *ostrężyny* [Kraków] *vs. jeżyny* [Warsaw and Poznań] for "blackberries"). However, while before the Second World War regional variation in Polish lexis was very strong, at present it has become very rare (Bajerowa 2001: 45), and the regional division does not hold for all speakers. Dubisz (2002: 93–94) predicts that regional variation, already slight, will continue to fade, and that the current tripartite division (standard language: mixed codes: folk dialect) will be substituted by the bipartite division of standard language *vs.* mixed codes.

2.4. Polish in national education

Practically all of Polish education is conducted in Polish. In 2006, RM languages were taught at 1,068 primary and secondary schools, and were learnt by 49,036 pupils (Mały rocznik 2007: 238). This is not much, considering the fact that the numbers include inter-school groups which organise additional classes of RM languages, and that Poland has over 30,300 primary and secondary schools altogether. At tertiary level, classes are conducted in foreign languages only in some subjects, most notably in the foreign languages departments of universities and teacher training colleges. The school-leaving examinations (*matura*), which need to be taken at the end of secondary school by those who wish to pursue their education at the college or university level, include Polish as an obligatory subject (which includes the knowledge of Polish language and literature, and tests the ability to write in Polish).

3. The language policy of Poland

3.1. The language ethos

In a survey conducted in 2005, Poles were asked the question *why should we care about the language we use?* By far the most frequent answer, given by 35.4% of the respondents, was "because the language holds the nation together" (*Co Polacy sądzą...*), which shows that the Polish language is still seen as the core element of national identity. The specificity of Polish history, with the long struggle for independence, and the experience of having to maintain nationality without statehood when Poland was partitioned, contributed to the particularly strong connection between language and the concepts of nationality and the motherland. Bartmiński (2001: 15) gives a large number of quotations from writers, philosophers and others who reveal the central place ascribed to language in the models of Polish national identity and notes that the perception of Polish among Poles is essentially Romantic (see Extra and Gorter, this Volume, who observe that the equalisation of language and national identity has its roots in German Romanticism from around 1900).

3.2. The Polish Language Act

The language ethos mentioned above is reflected in Polish legislation. The justification given for the introduction of the Polish Language Act (passed by Parliament on October 7, 1999) is that the Polish language is the basic component of national identity and national culture. The Act also makes a reference to history, evoking the fact that both during the partitions and during WWII the partitioning and occupying powers made systematic efforts to weaken the Polish language as a means of destroying the Polish nation.

The Act declares Polish to be the official language of Poland, which must be used by all authorities, public administration, and public institutions (Article 4).[2] All public activity in Poland must be carried out in Polish, unless specific regulations permit otherwise. Polish should be used in relations with public administration and other entities performing public functions. All authorities, institutions and organisations operating in Poland and taking part in public life are obliged to protect the Polish language. As specified in Article 3 of the Act, the protection of Polish primarily involves the following:

1) encouraging proper use of the language and the development of language skills among the users of the language, and ensuring that there are conditions conducive to the proper growth of the language as a tool of communication;
2) counteracting the vulgarisation of the language;
3) promoting respect for regional varieties and local dialects, and preventing the attrition of these dialects;
4) the promotion of Polish abroad;
5) supporting the teaching of Polish in Poland and abroad.

The Act also states that Polish is the language of education and dissertations in all types of public and private schools, colleges and universities, and other educational institutions, unless specific regulations state otherwise (Article 9) and that all signs and information materials in public institutions and administrative offices, as well as in means of public transport, must be in Polish (though there may be translations into other languages accompanying these signs, as specified by appropriate regulations) (Article 10). The Act also introduces a state examination for foreigners wishing to obtain a certificate of their proficiency in Polish (further specified in the 2003 Amendment to the Act).

While the above statements were fairly uncontroversial, some of the new legislation provoked some criticism. Article 8 of the Act required all agreements to be concluded in Polish if one of the parties was a Polish entity and the agreement was to be executed in Poland. It was possible for foreign language versions of the agreement to exist, but the Polish version would be binding, unless provisions of the agreement provided otherwise. Likewise, the Act required the Polish language to be used in legal transactions when at least one party was a Polish entity[3] (Article 7). As a result, the Act "created many difficulties in business relations, and from the very beginning many opinions were expressed in favour of changing it", while the need to draw up a Polish version of every agreement "caused particularly severe problems in transactions on the international professional market: negotiations were delayed due to the need to translate entire swathes of documentation into Polish and then to agree on the Polish language version. This inevitably increased transaction costs" (Mężykowski 2004). The regulation also violated EU law, being a restriction on the freedom of transfer of goods and services, and had to be changed before Poland entered the EU in May 2004.

The 2004 Amendment to the Polish Language Act abolished the problematic requirement to use Polish in all legal transactions and agreements in Poland if at least one of the parties is Polish, but retained the obligation to use Polish in transactions with consumers and in exercising provisions of the labour law, if the consumer or the person providing work is domiciled in Poland at the time when the agreement is concluded, and if the agreement is to be executed in Poland. In transactions other than consumer and labour relations, Polish should be used only if governmental or other public authorities or institutions are involved. The change has made legal transactions easier, but the legislation still raises some doubts; for example, it does not define what is meant by the term "consumer" or by the phrase "executed in Poland". It has been pointed out that the definitions of the term "consumer" available elsewhere differ from one another (Mężykowski 2004).

The Act makes it necessary for all foreign descriptions of goods and services introduced to the market to have a simultaneous Polish language version. This applies specifically to the names of goods and services, offers, advertisements, instruction manuals, information about the characteristics of goods and services, guarantees, invoices, bills and receipts. There are some exceptions, however, namely trade names and trade marks, commercial names, proper names, indications of the country of origin of the goods and services, as well as foreign-language daily papers, magazines, books, and computer software (except their descriptions and accompanying instructions), artistic and academic activity, and customary scientific and technical vocabulary. Also, teaching at schools and universities may be carried out in a foreign language if this is allowed by specific regulations (Article 11).

The implementation of the Act is ensured by trade inspectors and by the Office for the Protection of Competition and Consumers. Non-compliance with the Act, especially the exclusive use of a foreign language in legal transactions, may subject the party to a fine of up to 100,000 PLN (ca. 28,000 Euros) (Article 15).

3.3. The Polish Language Council

The Polish Language Act of 1999 (Articles 12–14) also named the consultative and advisory body responsible for protecting the Polish language, shaping the language policy of the country and dealing with all matters connected with the use and development of the Polish language: the Polish Language Council (*Rada Języka Polskiego*). The Council had been established in September 1996 as a committee of the Polish Academy of Sciences (PAN). At that time, it consisted of 30 members, mostly scholars (predominantly linguists, but also representatives of other subjects in the humanities and the sciences) as well as journalists, writers, and actors. The Council was established as an advisory body, which was to give opinions on Polish names for new products and services, solve problems connected with the use of Polish in new areas of science and technology (for example in computer sciences), and give opinions on the form of texts in public communication, especially in the media and in administration. It was decided that the Council would cooperate with the government, especially with the ministries responsible for education and culture, and that it was going to produce, at least every two years, a report for the Parliament and the Senate about the current state of the Polish language. Some other aims of the Council were also specified at the time, among them the promotion of Polish and the teaching of Polish, popularising the knowledge about the Polish language and its varieties, raising awareness of language norms and of the criteria for assessing language correctness, suggesting language forms suitable in particular contexts, and deciding on doubtful cases in lexis, grammar, pronunciation, spelling and punctuation, as well as stylistics.

The Council, which at present numbers 38 members, has so far given over 1,000 opinions, introduced some minor reforms of Polish spelling, and clarified a number of issues concerning the correct use of Polish[4]. It publishes conference proceedings and specially commissioned reports about the state of the Polish language in various fields, such as the media, the Church, the administration, advertising, the sciences, etc. (Pisarek 1999). The Council also plays a part in forming the school curriculum with respect to Polish language teaching (Mikołajczuk and Puzynina 2004). The Council answers questions by governmental bodies, institutions and organisations; it advises individuals and registry offices about what names can be given to newborn children. The Council also cooperates with other governmental institutions, for example the Polish Committee for Standardisation and the Office for the Protection of Competition and Consumers. About 300 institutions subscribe to the newsletter published by the Council (not counting registry offices). The Council cooperates with the translators working for EU institutions in solving problems of terminology and organises training courses for EU translators working with Polish. Also, it takes part in the work of the European Federation of National Institutions for Language (EFNIL).

One of the aims of the Council is to prevent the "deterioration of Polish", both as a public language (here the introduction of large numbers of English words is seen as the greatest danger) and as a private language (where the greatest damage is done by the spread of vulgar language and slang). The policy is executed by means of various programs for the general public, such as competitions for short written texts, or electing the "Master of Polish Speech" from among actors, journalists and politicians.

4. Language of the Polish diaspora

4.1. Overview

As far as the use of Polish outside Poland is concerned, two separate fields of enquiry emerge: firstly, Polish as used in the Polish diaspora (whose members acquire Polish at least to some extent at home) and, secondly, Polish as a foreign language studied by speakers of other languages, unrelated to the Polish community (who make a conscious decision to study Polish, and learn it mostly in an instructional setting). This section will be devoted to the former of these areas of interest, while the latter will be discussed further on in a separate section.

Polish communities outside Poland differ greatly from one another, as a result of their different origins, as well as different political, social and demographic situations. According to Dubisz (1997: 19), there are Polish communities in 80 countries in the world, the bigger ones of which are listed below and divided, as in most publications on the topic (e.g., Dubisz 1997a, 2001; Walczak 2001), into two groups of very different character:

— Indigenous Polish ethnic communities, or communities resulting from repatriation: in Latvia, Lithuania, Belarus, Ukraine, Russia, Kazakhstan, Czech Republic, Slovakia, Hungary, and Romania;
— Polish people in the diaspora, resulting from waves of emigration from Poland, both in Europe and overseas. In Polish, these people are often called *Polonia* (though sometimes, if very rarely, the term *Polonia* is used to mean all Polish communities abroad).

The number of speakers of Polish in the world is notoriously difficult to estimate even roughly, as is the number of people of Polish origin, and the available statistics vary widely. The most often quoted numbers of speakers of Polish outside Poland center around 2 million in Europe and around 8 million in the rest of the world. Of course, different criteria of what it means to speak Polish result in very different estimates.

Data about emigration from Poland (Walczak 2001: 564) tell us that about 5 million Poles emigrated from the partitioned Poland in the late 19th and early 20th centuries, before the outbreak of the First World War. Another 5 million left during WW I, and 2 million left between the wars, while 1 million returned. About 5 million Poles found themselves outside the country's borders as the result of WW II. There was relatively little emigration after the war, when Poland was behind the Iron Curtain, altogether about 600,000 until 1980. Between 1980 and the end of the century another million people left. This gives us, very roughly, over 17.5 million speakers of Polish leaving for other countries since the late 19th century. Most typically, children of the early emigrants would speak some Polish, and the grandchildren very little; exactly how many of these 17 million people or their descendants still speak Polish is not known. Apart from these speakers, we have the indigenous communities mentioned as group 1 above. On top of this, in most recent years – since Poland joined the EU in 2004 – a very large number of Poles have left Poland to work in other EU countries. The most recent poll of the Public Opinion Research Centre, from March 2007, revealed that about 2 million Poles currently residing in Poland have worked abroad since Poland's accession to the EU in 2004 (Praca Polaków za Granicą 2007: 2), and that about 1,200,000 Poles were working abroad at the moment the survey was conducted, mostly in the UK (26%), Germany (16%) and Ireland (10%). These 1.2 million workers are native speakers of Polish who have left Poland very recently, so in terms of language use they are likely to be very similar to Poles in Poland.

Table 1. Different estimates of the size of Polish communities abroad

		1	2	3		4
1	USA	10,600,000	9,385,233	8.200,000	(2,500,000)	6,542,844
2	Germany	2,000,000	290,000	600,000	(600,000)	241,300
3	Brazil	1,800,000	1,500,000	450,000		650,000
4	France	1,050,000		900,000	(300,000)	650,000
5	Belarus	900,000	400,000			418,000
6	Canada	900,000	820,000	400,000	(130,000)	404,000
7	Ukraine	900,000	144,130			219,000
8	UK	500,000	750,000	170,000	(170,000)	155,000
9	Argentina	450,000	500,000			120,000
10	Lithuania	300,000	250,000			257,994
11	Russia	300,000	73,000			94,600
12	Australia	200,000	150,900	140,000	(70,000)	122,000
13	Czech Rep.	100,000	52,000			69,000
14	Kazakhstan	100,000	47,293			80,000–100,000
15	Sweden	100,000				40,000
16	Italy	100,000	50,790			80,000
17	Ireland	80,000	63,276			
18	Latvia	75,000	57,000			63,000
19	Belgium	70,000				47,500
20	Netherlands	60,000	39,500			3,184

Table 1 is provided as an illustration of the wide divergences which obtain in the estimates of the size of Polish communities abroad. Column 1 presents numbers given by the *Wspólnota Polska* organisation, based on "updated estimates made by Polonia organisations, Polish embassies, publications about emigration from Poland and national censuses" (*Polacy za granicą*). Column 2 presents numbers quoted by Wikipedia – based mostly on data from national censuses, but also other sources. Column 3 presents data from Walczak (2001: 568): estimates of the size of the communities and, in parentheses, the number of people who use Polish as their mother tongue. Column 4 presents data from Dubisz (1997: 32–36).

4.2. Language of indigenous Polish communities abroad

The origin of the indigenous Polish communities abroad goes back to the process of settlement of the Polish people in territories which were then on the peripheries of the Polish language area, that is, either belonged to Poland or were close to Poland's borders. In most cases, these communities were cut off from Poland by the post-WW II borders and now form national minority groups in the Czech Republic, Slovakia, and in the former USSR republics: the Ukraine, Belarus, Lithuania and Latvia. Another group of communities which belong to this group came into being as the result of forced deportation of Poles by the Soviet authorities far into the USSR: to Siberia and Kazakhstan.

The scope of this chapter does not permit a detailed analysis of the language of each of the ethnic Polish communities outside Poland; however, all communities have certain characteristics in common. In general, they are shrinking and Polish is disappearing, even if this is a slow process. Dzięgiel (2003: 35–36) gives the following numbers of those who declared to be of Polish nationality in the Ukraine (based on census data): in 1959 363,300 Poles, in 1970 295,100, in 1989 219,200 and in 2001 144,100. Dzięgiel (2003: 75) found that Polish in the Ukraine is diminishing, with very minor exceptions; for most people who can speak Polish the dominant language is Ukrainian; in many villages the inhabitants display a residual knowledge of Polish, for example, they use Polish greetings and attend mass in Polish, but use Ukrainian in everyday life. Karaś (2001) found that in Lithuania the older generation is usually bilingual, the middle one is familiar with Polish, while members of the youngest generation often do not speak Polish at all or learn Polish (at Sunday schools for example) only because of the wishes of their parents or grandparents.

Efforts have been made to describe the Polish of indigenous Polish communities and to record the speech of their members. Karaś (2001), for example, contains transcribed texts recorded in 28 towns in the Kaunas region in Lithuania. Dzięgiel (2003: 169) notes that the Polish language in the Ukraine was not examined until the 1990s, when it was already too late to register many of the local varieties of Polish, as they had disappeared together with those who had used them. On the other hand, some kind of revival of interest in Polish has been taking place since 1989 (Rieger 2001: 576), as is illustrated by the appearance of new Polish schools, newspapers and associations.

Most importantly, the Polish spoken by indigenous communities is often derived from dialects of Polish, brought from Poland by emigrant farmers. Another important characteristic of these communities is that they are strongly internally differentiated according to social status, education, etc., and linguistically still reflect the social division between the peasants and the gentry that was crucial at the time when these communities thrived. In the region north of Kaunas in Lithuania the dialects of Polish spoken by people aged 45–90 were found to differ according to the social background of the subjects, and broadly fell into three categories: the peasants, the lesser gentry and the landowners/intelligentsia (Karaś 2001). Dzięgiel (2003) notes that the Polish spoken in the Ukraine falls into two distinct categories: the Polish of the gentry (*polszczyzna szlachecka*) and that of the peasants (*polszczyzna chłopska*).

In general, studies of the Polish spoken by indigenous communities in Europe shows how often linguistic reality is determined by historical, social and political factors. For example, in Belarus, after the Second World War, the Polish minority was repatriated to Poland. Practically all the intelligentsia and the landowning gentry left, as did most of the inhabitants of cities and wealthier farmers. Only the least educated and poorest people stayed behind, mostly peasants (Eberhardt 2007). This influenced the kind of Polish that was spoken in Belarus after the repatriation – it was the language of one particular social group. The way this language developed further was affected by the fact that the institutions which could help with the preservation and the teaching of Polish – Polish schools, cultural or educational institutions and organisations, the Roman Catholic church – were closed and outlawed.

Another very interesting feature of indigenous communities is that the sense of being of Polish nationality/origin is much more common than the ability to speak Polish, which may be surprising in view of the fact, described above, that Polish nationality is very often defined in reference to the Polish language. According to the 1999 census conducted in Belarus, of the 294,090 people who declared to be of Polish nationality in the Grodno district, only over 55,129 (18.7%) consider Polish their mother tongue an only 16,406 use Polish at home (5.6%) rather than Belarusian or Russia (Eberhardt 2007). Dzięgiel (2003: 35–36) quotes census data about ho many of those who declared to be of Polish nationality in the last Ukrainian census considered Polish their main language: "in 1959: 68,200 (19%), in 1970: 44,000 (15%), in 1989: 27,500 (12.5%) and in 2001: 18,000 (12.9%)."

This does not seem like much (by comparison, in 1926, about half of the Polish population declared Polish as their main language), but of course the census does not provide information on those who speak Polish, but not as their main language. It is worth noting that Polish national identity in the Ukraine is most strongly determined by Roman Catholicism, as contrasted with the Orthodox or Greek Catholic faith of the Ukrainians, to such an extent that the terms "Polish" and "Roman Catholic" are sometimes used as synonyms (Dzięgiel 2003). This is noteworthy, given the fact that the practice of religion was strictly forbidden and the churches could not be used until the restitution of the churches in the 1990s (Dzięgiel 2003: 50).

In some countries, Polish communities are more linguistically uniform than in others. For example, the Polish community in the Ukraine is strikingly heterogeneous (as compared, for example, to the relatively homogeneous variety of Polish in Lithuania), due to the fact that the Polish population of every village had come to the Ukraine at a different time, from a different part of Poland, and also because of the influence of the many different dialects of Ukrainian.

The status of Polish in the indigenous communities is a complicated issue. In the region north of Kaunas, for example, Polish originally appeared as the language of the landowners and gentry, and gradually spread among the peasants, which led to the appearance on the linguistic map of Lithuania of a Polish-speaking "island". As a result, the older generation still has a strong perception of the prestige of Polish as the language of the gentry, a perception completely absent among the younger generation (Karaś 2001: 22).

4.3. Polish of emigrant communities

The first important difference between the Polish of the indigenous communities described above and the *Polonia* communities in other parts of the world is that while the Polish of the former is derived from regional and dialectal varieties of Polish, the Polish spoken by the latter group is to a greater extent based on standard Polish, modified by the influence of the language of the particular target country. The *Polonia* communities are most numerous in English-speaking countries, followed by French-speaking and then German-speaking countries.

Another important difference is that the *Polonia* communities in Western Europe and the rest of the world have a stronger wish to become integrated into the culture of the host country, while most members of the indigenous communities may be reluctant to do so. It seems that in countries like Ukraine and Belarus, where the Polish minority experienced Stalinist repression, deportation, famine, and even genocide, the sense of national identity was sharpened to such an extent that individuals may be unwilling to fully identify with the culture of their country of residence, even if they are no longer able to communicate in Polish. According to Dubisz (1997b: 369), this attitude is strongest in the East-Slavic language sphere (in Belarus, Ukraine, Latvia, Lithuania, Russia, Kazakhstan), while in the countries south of Poland (Czech Republic, Slovakia, Romania, Hungary) the attitude is mixed: there is some resistance towards integration, but also present is the willingness to become integrated into the culture of the target country, typical of the *Polonia* communities in Western Europe and overseas.

Another feature common to many *Polonia* communities is that they are strongly internally differentiated according to many features, such as social position, the sense of belonging to a particular "wave" of emigration (i.e., "old" emigration *vs.* "new" emigration), and – most importantly – according to generation. The emigration generation originally is monolingual, then learns the language of the new country to some extent. The *Polonia* generation, as it is called in many research studies, is usually bilingual, exposed to Polish mostly as spoken by the local group. This leads to the occurrence of two primary varieties of Polish abroad: the emigration variety and the *Polonia* variety (Dubisz 1997a: 21).

The rate at which emigrants lose their first language differs depending on a large number of different individual and social factors. An important role is played by the size and density of the particular community. As Walczak (2001: 566) notes, the Polish immigrants in Chicago, for example, were able to function in Polish in all spheres of life until at least the 1930s. Most usually, however, the language of the new country gradually replaces the mother tongue, first as the language of work and then also in other functions. For the second generation of emigrants, even if Polish is the first language in chronological terms, it quickly loses the status of the main language.

From the point of view of language norm (Dubisz 1997a: 22), the Polish of the *Polonia* has a complicated character; its speakers display a very uneven level of language awareness, and a varied level of competence. Most of the time they treat the local variety as the language norm, and do not relate to the norms of standard Polish, although upon reflection they express one of two contradictory views: either that the Polish spoken abroad should be identical to the language spoken in Poland (the purist standpoint), or that it should develop in a natural way, reflecting the contact with the language of the target country (the naturalistic standpoint).

The language situation of the Polish diaspora has changed recently as a result of the large number of Poles who have left Poland in order to work in other EU countries. This wave of emigration significantly enlarged the Polish communities in Britain and Germany, and resulted in the appearance of a new country on the map of the Polish communities in the world: Ireland. According to the 2006 Irish census, there were 63,276 Poles living in Ireland, which made them the dominant group among migrants from the new EU states. However, the number is very likely to be much higher: some 120,000 according to the Polish survey mentioned above, perhaps even close to 200,000 (Singleton et al. 2007).

While the emergence of Polish as a minority language in Ireland is a very recent development, some research has already been carried out with respect to the attitudes of the Polish community towards second language acquisition and native language maintenance. Singleton et al. (2007) report that while migrant workers in Ireland (as elsewhere) tend to get low-wage jobs that are below their educational qualifications, they are generally content with their life in Ireland, and see coming to Ireland as a positive experience. The subjects in the study were willing to become part of Irish society on a long-term or even permanent basis, despite the relatively short duration of their stay and the fact that they rated their English language proficiency as low to medium. As Extra and Gorter note (this Volume), the transmission of an IM language depends on whether the parents in immigrant families conceive of this language as a core value of cultural identity. This bodes well for the maintenance of Polish in Ireland, since the subjects in the Singleton et al. study said that it was very important for their children to speak Polish (89.8%), more often than they expressed the view that speaking English was very important for their children (72.9%).

4.4. The teaching of Polish as a foreign language

It must be emphasised here that while the Polish diaspora involves a great number of people and is present almost everywhere in the world, and the use of Polish there has been studied by a number of linguists[5], the study of Polish as a foreign language, by learners unrelated to Polish communities, is carried out on a rather modest scale, and has been investigated to a very limited extent. Walczak (2001: 564) notes that it is difficult to make any meaningful generalisations about such learners, since they are not numerous and include very different individual cases. According to the State Committee for the Certification of the Knowledge of Polish as a Foreign Language, the number of people learning Polish as a foreign language is growing, and it can be estimated at around 10,000 in the whole world, about one third of whom is studying Polish at universities and language schools in Poland (*O języku polskim*). On the other hand, we may assume that at least some Polish is acquired by those who come to Poland to study, even if learning Polish is not the primary aim of their visit. Statistics on the number of foreign students in Poland are available (Mały rocznik 2007: 247) and they show that the number of such students has grown from 6,563 in 2000 to 11,752 in 2007. Interestingly, the number of foreign students who declare Polish ancestry remains more or less the same every year (around 3,5 thousand), which suggests that Poland is becoming a more attractive place to study also among those who have no family ties with Poland, which may indirectly contribute to an increase in the interest in the Polish language. It seems that women constitute the majority of Polish as a foreign language learners in Poland (70% according to Miodunka 2005: 51).

An important development in the teaching of Polish as a foreign language was the introduction in 2004 of examinations which enable speakers of other languages to obtain certificates of proficiency in Polish that are consistent with the Common European Framework of Reference for Languages (CEFR) and the European Language Portfolio program (ELP) (Martyniuk 2005). The work on certification standards has had yet another benefit: it inspired the revision of current Polish language teaching programs and materials and the preparation of new ones (Lipińska and Seretny 2005). The examinations turned out to be most popular among German and Ukrainian learners of Polish (Miodunka 2005: 52). By the end of 2006, the exam had been taken by 651 learners from 40 countries. Surprisingly, learners of Polish origin constitute only about 20% of all candidates. Miodunka (2005: 52) comments that, sadly, people of Polish origin "seem to continue to doubt the usefulness of the language of their ethnic and national origin in the international educational and labour market."

As far as university studies in Polish outside Poland are concerned, the situation has been described as "highly unsatisfactory" (Mazur 2000: 19). Only a few universities (with the largest Polish departments and the longest traditions of Polish studies, in Paris, Moscow, Lvov and Vilnius) – were found to carry out a full programme of Polish studies (Polish language, linguistics and literature – what is referred to as "Polish philology" in Poland) and the level of proficiency in Polish in some smaller departments was very disappointing. According to Mazur, this is due to many factors, such as lack of staff, low initial level of Polish among the students, very traditional programmes and courses, and – sadly – a lack of support from Poland.

5. Perspectives for the future

Pawłowski (2005: 14–15) mentions several perspectives from which the position of Polish and the prospects for its growth can be evaluated. In terms of demographic considerations, Polish has a strong position as the sixth biggest mother tongue in the EU, and the largest Slavic language. With respect to geographic factors, Poland has a favourable location in the middle of Europe. From a linguistic point of view, Polish has the advantage of using the Roman alphabet, as opposed to Russian for example; more generally speaking, it shares the common Indo-European roots and a large proportion of "international" lexis with other EU languages (see also Satkiewicz 1998). When it comes to cultural factors, however, things begin to look bleak: Polish has a very low position in terms of the cultural associations other EU citizens have with the language. Like all Slavic languages, it is associated with backward and poor countries; moreover, Polish culture and any Polish achievements (whether in the arts or in the sciences) are little known outside Poland. When one considers economic factors, Poland's low GNP and high unemployment rate (relative to other EU countries) do not make Poland an attractive job market; nor does the knowledge of Polish improve one's professional prospects. Lastly, the position of Polish must be seen in the light of the current position of Russian. Pawłowski quotes western European sources which still consider Russian the primary foreign language of Central and Eastern Europe. The widespread Western stereotype of Russian as the *lingua franca* of the region dies hard, despite the reality in countries like Poland where Russian is likely to be known only by some of those who completed their education by the end of the 1980s, and is no longer taught on a large scale.

As was mentioned above, the overall number of speakers of Polish (both as L1 and L2) is usually estimated at around 48–50 million people. Dubisz (2002: 92), on the basis of the growth index so far and the forecasts of demographic growth[6], predicts that the Polish community may reach 70–80 milllion by the end of the 21st century.

It has been suggested that the language policy of Poland should be aimed at making it the *lingua franca* of the Central-Eastern region of Europe (Dubisz 2002; Pawłowski 2005). Whether or not this is a realistic idea, it would require a change in Poland's language policy, which currently seems to be primarily defensive, geared towards protecting Polish from the "corruption" of foreign language influence. The promotion of Polish, though included in the Polish Language Act, is insufficient. For example, although it has been postulated by many (e.g., Pawłowski 2005: 22), Poland does not have an institution that would promote the Polish language in the world (such as the Goethe Institut or the British Council). The problem may partly result from the fact that, despite the very strong ethos of Polish as a national language, the language does not enjoy a high prestige in contemporary Polish society, as evidenced by the omnipresence of foreign or pseudo-foreign words (mostly English, less commonly French or Italian), in the names of new apartment buildings, shopping malls, shops, restaurants, labels of clothes or shoes produced in Poland. It must also be stressed that, as a rule, Poles do not expect foreigners to speak Polish, and are very willing to learn foreign languages: in the Eurobarometer (2006: 7) study, Poles were the nation which was the most supportive (75%) of the idea that everyone in the EU should speak two foreign languages apart from their mother tongue (as compared to, for example, 31% in France or 27% in Sweden). It seems that the Poles' attitude towards their mother tongue is characterised by, on the one hand, a strong association between language and nationality, and on the other, by the belief that they should learn foreign languages rather than expect others to learn Polish.

Notes

1. The definition of nationality given for the purpose of the census was as follows: "Nationality is a declarative (based on subjective feeling), individual characteristic of every person, expressing this person's emotional, cultural or genealogical (related to parentage) relationship with a particular nation." (Raport 2003: 39)
2. The Polish Language Act of 1999 replaced the decree of November 30, 1945, about Polish as the national language.
3. Where a Polish entity is a natural person domiciled in Poland, or a legal person or entity without legal personality conducting business in Poland.
4. Information about the Polish Language Council is taken from the Council's website, *http://www.rjp.pan.pl*.
5. At least since the early 1990s. One of the first important studies of Polish abroad was Miodunka (1990).
6. It should be noted that as far as vital statistics are concerned, Poland has a very low total fertility rate (1.267) (p 124) and the rate of only 1.012 live births per death) (123).

References

Bajerowa, Irena
    2001   Język ogólnopolski XX wieku [Standard 20th-century Polish]. In *Współczesny język polski* [Contemporary Polish], Jerzy Bartmiński (ed.), 23–48. Lublin: Wydawnictwo Uniwersytetu Marii Curie-Skłodowskiej.

Bartmiński, Jerzy (ed.)
    2001   *Współczesny język polski* [Contemporary Polish]. Lublin: Wydawnictwo Uniwersytetu Marii Curie-Skłodowskiej.

Bartmiński, Jerzy
    2001   Język w kontekście kultury [Language in the context of culture]. In *Współczesny język polski* [Contemporary Polish], Jerzy Bartmiński (ed.), 13–22. Lublin: Wydawnictwo Uniwersytetu Marii Curie-Skłodowskiej.

Dubisz, Stanisław (ed.)
    1997   *Język polski poza granicami kraju* [Polish Abroad]. Opole: Uniwersytet Opolski.

Dubisz, Stanisław
    1997a   Język polski poza granicami kraju – wstępne informacje i definicje [Polish abroad: Basic information and definitions]. In *Język polski*

1997b   *poza granicami kraju* [Polish Abroad], Stanislaw Dubisz (ed.), 13–46. Opole: Uniwersytet Opolski.

1997b   Język polski poza granicami kraju – próba charakterystyki kontrastowej [Polish abroad: An attempt at contrastive analysis]. In *Język polski poza granicami kraju* [Polish Abroad], Stanislaw Dubisz (ed.) 324–376. Opole: Uniwersytet Opolski.

2001   Język polski poza granicami kraju [Polish abroad]. In *Polszczyzna XX wieku. Ewolucja i perspektywy rozwoju* [20th-century Polish: Evolution and the Perspectives of Development], Stanisław Dubisz and Stanisław Gajda (eds.), 199–210. Warszawa: Elipsa.

2002   Development of the Polish Language and the European Integration. *The Polish Foreign Affairs Digest* 2 (4/5): 87–96.

Dzięgiel, Ewa

2003   *Polszczyzna na Ukrainie* [Polish in the Ukraine]. Warszawa: Semper.

Eberhard, Piotr

2007   *Polacy na Białorusi: Liczebność i rozmieszczenie ludności polskiej według ostatnich spisów powszechnych* [Poles in Belarus: The number and distribution of the Polish population according to latest census data]. Retrieved on December 20, 2007, from *Świat Polonii* (website of the "Wspólnota Polska" Association) *http://www.wspolnota-polska.org.pl/index.php?id=pwko01.*

Handke, Kwiryna

2001   Terytorialne odmiany polszczyzny [Regional varieties of Polish]. In *Współczesny język polski* [Contemporary Polish], Jerzy Bartmiński (ed.), 201–221. Lublin: Wydawnictwo Uniwersytetu Marii Curie-Skłodowskiej.

2001   *Język polski na Kowieńszczyźnie. Historia, sytuacja socjolingwistyczna, cechy językowe, teksty* [Polish in the Kaunas Region: History, Sociolinguistic Situation, Linguistic Characteristics, Texts]. Warsaw/Vilnius: Elipsa.

Lipińska, Ewa and Anna Seretny

2005   Od "z" do "a" – czyli od certyfikacji do programów nauczania [From z to a – or from certification to the curriculum]. In *Nauczanie języka polskiego jako obcego i polskiej kultury w nowej rzeczywistości europejskiej* [The Teaching of Polish as a Foreign Language and the Teaching of Polish Culture in the New European Reality], Piotr Garncarek (ed.), 31–41. Warsaw: Uniwersytet Warszawski.

Majewicz, Alfred F. and Tomasz Wicherkiewicz

1999   *Polityka językowa na Kaszubach na tle prawodawstwa wobec mniejszości w jednoczącej się Europie (diagnoza i postulaty)* [Language Policy in Kaszuby in View of Minority Legislation in the United Europe]. Stęszew: II.EOS.

Mały rocznik statystyczny Polski [Concise Statistical Yearbook of Poland]
2007   Warsaw: Główny Urząd Statystyczny [Central Statistical Office].

Markowski, Andrzej (ed.)
1999   *Nowy słownik poprawnej polszczyzny PWN* [New PWN Dictionary of Correct Polish]. Warszawa: Państwowe Wydawnictwa Naukowe.

Markowski, Andrzej and Jadwiga Puzynina
2001   Kultura języka [Language culture]. In *Współczesny język polski* [Contemporary Polish], Jerzy Bartmiński (ed.), 49–72. Lublin: Wydawnictwo Uniwersytetu Marii Curie-Skłodowskiej.

Martyniuk, Waldemar
2005   Certyfikacja znajomości języka polskiego jako obcego w kontekście europejskiej polityki językowej [The certification of Polish as a foreign language knowledge in the context of the European language policy]. In *Nauczanie języka polskiego jako obcego i polskiej kultury w nowej rzeczywistości europejskiej* [The Teaching of Polish as a Foreign Language and the Teaching of Polish Culture in the New European Reality], Piotr Garncarek (ed.), 42–49. Warsaw: Uniwersytet Warszawski.

Mazur, Jan
2000   Stan i perspektywy polonistyki w świecie [The Current State and Future Perspectives of Polish Studies in the World]. In *Polonistyka w świecie: Nauczanie języka i kultury polskiej studentów zaawansowanych* [Polish Studies in the World: The Teaching of the Polish Language and Culture to Advanced Students], Jan Mazur (ed.), 15–26. Lublin: Wydawnictwo Uniwersytetu Marii Curie-Skłodowskiej.

Mężykowski, Michał
2004   *Polish Language. The Warsaw Voice* (online edition). Published 26 May 2004. Retrieved December 20, 2007, from http://www.warsawvoice.pl/view/5723/.

Mikołajczuk, Agnieszka and Jadwiga Puzynina (eds.)
2004   *Wiedza o języku polskim w zreformowanej szkole* [The Knowledge About the Polish Language in Reformed Schools]. Warsaw: Nowa Era.

Miodunka, Władysław (ed.)
1990   *Język polski w świecie. Zbiór studiów* [Polish Abroad: Collected Studies]. Warszawa / Kraków: Państwowe Wydawnictwo Naukowe.

Miodunka, Władysław
2005   Wartość języka polskiego na międzynarodowym rynku edukacyjnym i rynku pracy. Uwagi na marginesie certyfikacji jezyka polskiego jako obcego [The value of Polish in the international and labour market: Comments on the certification of Polish as a foreign language]. In *Nauczanie języka polskiego jako obcego i polskiej kultury w nowej rzeczywistości europejskiej* [The Teaching of Polish as a

Foreign Language and the Teaching of Polish Culture in the New European Reality], Piotr Garncarek (ed.), 50–57. Warsaw: Uniwersytet Warszawski.

O języku polskim [About the Polish language]
- 2007 Retrieved on December 20, 2007, from the website of *Pańtwowa Komisja Poświadczania Znajomości Języka Polskiego jako Obcego* [State Committee for the Certification of the Knowledge of Polish as a Foreign Language], http://www.buwiwm.edu.pl/certyfikacja/index.html

Pawłowski, Adam
- 2005 Język polski w Unii Europejskiej: szanse i zagrożenia [Polish language in the European Union: chances and threats]. *Poradnik Językowy* 10: 3–27.

Pisarek, Walery
- 1999 *Polszczyzna 2000: Orędzie o stanie języka polskiego na przełomie tysiącleci* [Polish 2000: A Report of the State of the Polish Language at the Turn of the New Millenium]. Kraków: Ośrodek Badań Prasoznawczych, Uniwersytet Jagielloński.
- 2001 *Następstwa członkostwa UE dla małego języka* [The Consequences of EU Membership for a Small Language]. A summary. Retrieved on December 20, 2007, from the Polish Language Council website, http://www.rjp.pl/?mod=dokumenty&id=4

Polacy za granicą [Poles abroad]
- 2007 Retrieved on December 20, 2007, from *Świat Polonii* (website of the "Wspólnota Polska" Association), http://www.wspolnota-polska.org.pl/index.php?id=pwko

Praca Polaków za Granicą [Poles working abroad]
- 2007 Warsaw: Centrum Badania Opinii Społecznej [Public Opinion Research Center].

Rada Języka Polskiego (The Polish Language Council)
- 2007 *Co Polacy sądzą o języku polskim – wyniki badania CBOS* [What do Poles think about the Polish language? – Results of a survey by the Public Opinion Research Center] retrieved on December 20, 2007, from: http://rjp.pan.pl/index.php?option=com_content&task=view&id=48&Itemid=60

Raport z wyników Narodowego Spisu Powszechnego Ludności i Mieszkań 2002 [A report on the results of the 2002 census]
- 2003 Warsaw: Główny Urząd Statystyczny [Central Statistical Office].

Rieger, Janusz
- 2001 Język polski na Wschodzie [Polish in the East]. In *Współczesny język polski* [Contemporary Polish], Jerzy Bartmiński (ed.), 575–590. Lublin: Wydawnictwo Uniwersytetu Marii Curie-Skłodowskiej.

Satkiewicz, Halina
1998 Zapożyczenia leksykalno-semantyczne – przeszkoda czy zaleta w promocji języka polskiego [Lexical-semantic borrowings: an aid or an obstacle in the promotion of Polish]. In *Promocja języka i kultury polskiej w świecie* [Promotion of Polish Language and Culture in the World], Jan Mazur (ed.), 43–55. Lublin: Wydawnictwo Uniwersytetu Marii Curie-Skłodowskiej.

Singleton, David, Agnieszka Skrzypek, Romana Kopeckova and Barbara Bidzinska
2007 *Attitudes towards and perceptions of English L2 acquisition among Polish migrants in Ireland*. Paper given at the Royal Irish Academy symposium ("In/difference") at the University of Limerick in November 2007.

Special Eurobarometer: Europeans and their Languages
2006 Published February 2006 by the European Commission. Retrieved December 20, 2007, from *http://ec.europa.eu/public_opinion/ar chives/ebs/ebs_243_sum_en.pdf*.

Walczak, Bogdan
2001 Język polski na Zachodzie [Polish in the West]. In *Współczesny język polski* [Contemporary Polish], Jerzy Bartmiński (ed.), 563–574. Lublin: Wydawnictwo Uniwersytetu Marii Curie-Skłodowskiej.

Language constellations across the Baltic Republics: a comparative review[1]

Gabrielle Hogan-Brun

This chapter reviews the changing dynamics of Estonian, Latvian and Lithuanian in their national contexts. They represent two distinct language families and have at times been subject to different influences and threats in their development (for further, detailed information see Hogan-Brun 2005d). Estonian belongs to the Finno-Ugric languages while Latvian and Lithuanian are Baltic languages; the latter are closely related but not mutually intelligible. The common fate of these three languages has produced remarkably similar outcomes in terms of language development and language use, and ultimately of (constitutionally anchored) language policy. Local language management activities aim to preserve and strengthen the state language and culture, reduce the effects of former enforced Russification and meet the present day challenges of globalisation while also supporting minority rights. As a result of these efforts the overall visibility and use of these languages have increased considerably in each republic since their restitution of independence. Titular language competence among resident speakers of other languages has also grown, either for integrative or intrumental purposes. On the whole, Lithuania's state language policy lends more support to its relatively small minorities than Latvia's or Estonia's that were focused on during European Union (EU) accession negotiations. Tensions that have arisen between language policy and practice are similar in kind, but different in intensity in the three republics.

---

1. This chapter was compiled while on a Visiting Fellowship offered by the National Europe Centre at ANU Canberra.

1. Introduction

Language and culture have played a central role in the re-construction and consolidation of national identity in the Baltic Republics prior to and after the restoration of sovereignty. Hence long-term language and integration policies were set in motion across the Baltic following independence in 1990/1991 to deal with the complex ethno-demographic legacy of the Soviet past. Proficiency in "national" languages is considered to be a key element or even pre-requisite for social cohesion and integration and to reverse the state of asymmetric bilingualism. The increasing use of the national languages in the public sphere of the Baltic Republics was propelled by legal requirements that demand their deployment in this domain, and also because of their growing prestige. All public (and some private) sector employees must be proficient in their state language according to specific language knowledge categories. To this end state agencies were created to ensure that the population be provided with adequate language learning facilities. Titular language competence (at the lower intermediate level) is also asked of applicants for citizenship. As a consequence Baltic national language policies have produced marked changes in language use since the restitution of independence two decades ago. Steadily increasing levels of bilingualism with the titular language have been observed among speakers of minority languages, particularly the younger generation who has acquired appropriate linguistic knowledge at school.

In each republic, over time the central criteria evolved into the creation of social conditions that would ultimately ease accession to the EU. However, expectations during EU accession negotiations that acceeding members conform with Western approaches to multiculturalism presented a new challenge, together with the impact of globalisation. Baltic national language legislations were scrutinised by Western organisations and at times sharply criticised, both from within and beyond the Baltic Republics. The protection of minority and citizenship rights became a particular issue as they are considered key elements of democratic politics. Recommendations were produced by the *Organisation for Security and Cooperation in Europe* (OSCE) to address Estonia's and Latvia's citizenship requirements which were, and remain, more restrictive than Lithuania's to deal with their greater share of Russian-speaking people. Prompted by EU accession conditionalities, some of these regulations were subsequently liberalised to some extent. Metuzāle-Kangere and Ozolins (2005) offer more details on this and give a critical evaluation of the repercussions of EU pressures on local language regime politics. For a discussion of the transferability of

Western models of minority rights and multicultural citizenship see also Hogan-Brun (2005c).

In what follows we sketch the current language dynamics in the Baltic Republics, both in the official and private domains. Against the background of recently changing language settings and language legislation generally we introduce state language assessment procedures that were introduced as part of naturalisation requirements, for language proficiency in the professional and occupational fields, and through education. These formal requirements are then complemented with an overview of actual language practices in this changing environment. In our analysis of the current language constellations in the Baltic countries we are mainly adopting an interpretive and analytical perspective. Demographic and sociolinguistic data are briefly touched upon to provide the necessary context but these sets of data were more extensively reviewed in Hogan-Brun (2005d). An authoritative volume on comparative aspects of the languages in the Baltic is presented in Dini (2000). Furthermore, there is a range of literature available that can be consulted for a fuller understanding of historic conditions, which have over the centuries affected and reshaped the demographic composition and fabric of the three Baltic countries. Sociohistorical and socio-political developments in the Baltic generally are documented in Hiden and Salmon (1991), Dini (1991), Lieven (1993), Gerner and Hedlund (1993), and Norgaard (1996). Plasseraud (2003) gives a wide-ranging account on the evolving situation of minorities in the Baltic. Language and social processes in the Baltic countries surrounding their EU accession are discussed in Hogan-Brun (2005a), and a critical analysis of Baltic-wide language politics and practices is presented in Hogan-Brun et al. (2007).

2. Changing language settings

Changing socio-political configurations in the Baltic have resulted in multiple layers of language contact throughout the centuries. Poles, Russians, Germans and Swedes were among the actors who sought to extend their control along the Eastern shore of the Baltic Sea, which led at times to the relegation of Estonian, Latvian and Lithuanian to semi-public and private settings. While the intensity and dynamics of such contacts varied over time, these republics have evolved as multinational polities with challenging multilingual problems.

In 1918, the Balts seized simultaneously the opportunity of the collapse of both Russia and Germany to forge their statehoods. Estonian, Latvian and Lithuanian were legislated as the sole national (or official titular) language in their own territory. However, the three fledgling republics lost their inter-war independence in 1940, when they were incorporated into the Soviet Union for half a century. The language ecologies evolved differently in the three countries under Communist immigration and population transfer policies when a marked increase in speakers of Russian paralleled a decrease of the native people. Due to the larger influx of Soviet immigrants in Latvia and Estonia, the resulting demographic changes experienced there were more dramatic than in Lithuania. By 1989, the indigenous population had sunk to 61.5% from 92.4% in Estonia, to 52% from 73.4% in Latvia and to 83.45% from 84.2% in Lithuania (Hogan-Brun et al. 2007: 504). A large Russophone group (mainly Belarusians, Ukrainians, Jews and Poles) had also emerged, who used Russian as a *lingua franca* in both public and private life. Russian functioned as the main language and had to be used in all official and public contexts. At the time of the restoration of independence in 1990/1, 34.8% of the total population in Estonia, 42.5% in Latvia and 11.66% in Lithuania claimed Russian as their first language (Hogan-Brun and Ramonienė 2003: 31). Of those who did not consider the national language of their country of residence to be their first language, some (most Russians) were monolingual; others were bilingual (mother tongue/Russian) or trilingual (mother tongue/national language of country of residence/Russian). While the Baltic countries were afforded some (limited) flexibility in adopting unique education policies reflecting language and culture during the fifty years of Communist rule, a process of language substitution nevertheless evolved that favoured the language of the ruling power. This led to the prevalence of asymmetrical bilingualism (on the part of the titular nationals in the Baltic States), a limitation of the function of the local languages, and their ideological stigmatisation (Ozolins 2002: 1).

As the Soviets began to lose their control over the Communist Bloc, and spurned by Gorbachev's *glasnost* ideology, cultural and linguistic independence started to be re-asserted in the Baltic Republics, together with political sovereignty. In 1989, national language directives were adopted to end the hegemony of Russian. These were subsequently revised and strengthened to secure the status and expand the sociolinguistic function of the titular languages, while at the same time providing protection for the languages and cultures of the national minorities. Once Estonian, Latvian and Lithuanian had regained official status, all work in state entities, organisations and enterprises was to be conducted in the respective titular languages. Speakers of other languages were particularly affected by the sudden change, as language proficiency became a key for employment, chiefly in the public sector. Hence many members from these communities needed to move from monolingualism or bilingualism with Russian to bilingualism or trilingualism with the titular language of their host country. To certify professional linguistic competence and as part of naturalisation requirements, state language exams were introduced. The implementation of the emerging language laws started to be monitored nationally by language inspectors.

Today, some 35% of Latvia's population consist of Russophones. Estonia's Russophone communities amount to 28% and Lithuania mainly hosts Russophones (6.3%) and slightly more Poles (6.7%) (Hogan-Brun et al. 2007: 505). These groups, whose languages and cultures are protected by law, are at various stages of integration in each country. In general, attitudes amongst community representatives towards the titular language of their host country have become more positive, and an increasing number of people have acquired some mastery of it during the last two decades. Several factors account for this overall increase in bilingualism with the state language among the minority populations: the steady demand for the naturalisation of non-nationals (such procedures involve a language test), nationwide work-related language competency certification requirements, a natural decrease in older (monolingual) immigrant settlers and the simultaneous succession of a younger generation with acquired linguistic knowledge at school.

To sum up, the prestige of Estonian, Latvian and Lithuanian has increased considerably during the last two decades, and minority representatives tend to be eager to acquire some mastery of their host country's titular language. While cultural openness and integrative orientations certainly play a role for many, learners are chiefly instrumentally motivated because they tend to perceive the mainstream language as a means to power and social mobility. In the next section we shall focus on the role of the larger legislative context in the promotion of such rational choice perspectives.

3. Language legislation in the Baltic Republics

The means to re-establish after the restitution of independence the constitutionally anchored official status and sociolinguistic functionality of the titular languages are strikingly similar across the Baltic and have emerged out of a centralist approach. The main objective of national language policy is to guarantee the status of Estonian, Latvian and Lithuanian as the only official language in each republic, respectively, as enunciated in each Constitution and detailed in the several language laws. This has been a complex process, involving an inversion of the Soviet period language hierarchy.

Current language policies are implemented through national State Language Laws: Estonia's was passed in 1995, Latvia's in 1999 (both with subsequent amendments) and Lithuania's in 1995. The texts of these State Language Laws are available online and can be accessed via the websites listed in the reference section to this chapter. These laws regulate the use of the titular language in the main spheres of public life and stipulate its status as well as stating the legal implications for violations of the law. As earlier versions of these laws were gradually refined, other language regulations specifying the required levels of language proficiency were also instituted for acquisition of citizenship, in education and in the professional and occupational fields. We now present a brief overview of these state language assessment procedures (for more details see Hogan-Brun et al. 2007).

3.1. Language and citizenship

Estonia's citizenship law was first passed in 1993 (revised into the current version in 1995), Latvia's in 1994 (revised in 1998 after much debate and pressure from Russia and the European Union), and Lithuania's in 1991. The website addresses for each of these laws are provided in the reference section. Naturalisation Boards with nationwide administrative branches were also established. Lithuania's citizenship legislation diverges from that in its sister republics. Though theoretically Lithuanian legislation could have emulated that of the other Baltic Republics, the country has been in a position to opt for inclusive citizenship policies since it hosts a relatively small percentage of immigrant communities who already tend to have an adequate command of the state language. The majority of Lithuania's non-native population was, therefore, able to acquire citizenship through a naturalisation process offering the so-called "zero option" which permitted all individuals normally resident in the republic at the time of the restitution of independence in 1990 to become Lithuanian citizens. In contrast, the more heterogeneous neighbouring Baltic Republics introduced stricter citizenship criteria pertaining to the immigrant population that had settled there during the Soviet occupation. By law, those who were Latvian/Estonian citizens in 1940, and their descendants, can automatically claim Latvian/Estonian citizenship. The legal status of those immigrants who were permanent residents in Estonia and Latvia but who had not been naturalised is termed "non-citizens" (Estonian: *mittekodanikud*; Latvian: *nepilsoņi*). In Lithuania, the adoption of the "zero option" has meant that very few persons there belong to this category.

Naturalisation requirements in all three republics differ slightly and involve the successful completion of a State Language competence examination. In Lithuania, this examination is pitched at the lower intermediate level (which corresponds to Level A2 of the Common European Framework of Reference for Languages (CEFRL)), in Latvia at the intermediate level (CEFRL level A), and in Estonia at the elementary (oral and written) proficiency level. Since the inception of naturalisation in 1993 more than 11,000 persons who successfully have passed the examinations have been granted citizenship in Lithuania (*Valstybinės kalbos mokėjimo kategorijos* 2003). In comparison, 114,000 non-citizens have naturalised in Latvia since 1995 (Social integration in Latvia 2006) and 145,470 non-citizens in Estonia (Citizenship in Estonia, *http://www.vm.ee/estonia/pea_172/kat_399/4518.html*). Free language tuition is offered to those applying for citizenship in Latvia and Estonia. In Lithuania, on the other hand, tuition is free only for Lithuanians and their families returning from exile. The examination involves a fee, with reductions for such categories of candidates as the unemployed, the disabled, and students.

3.2. Occupational language use

In addition to the above described language laws, other language regulations specifying the required levels of language proficiency were also instituted in the professional and occupational fields. These requirements (ranging from basic listening comprehension to full proficiency in the titular language) for various professional categories were introduced for individuals who held relevant positions but who had not attended titular language education institutions, i.e., who had been schooled through the Russian education stream during the Soviet period. Since these requirements were applied without reference to the individuals' ethnicity, Estonians, Latvians and Lithuanians who had attended Russian-stream education also needed to sit these language attestation tests. The original ambit thereof in Estonia and Latvia pertained to all those who were in positions of contact with the public, whether in private or in public institutions; in Lithuania this requirement only concerned officials in public institutions. Ensuing from international pressure deriving from the OSCE and the EU, these laws in Estonia and Latvia were amended by introducing the principles of public interest and proportionality, so that language restrictions would be proportionate to the communicative needs involved (Adrey 2005: 460).

The levels, profile and pace of language attestation are almost exactly identical in each Republic. The only material difference is that in Lithuania such language attestation was only for personnel in the public sector, while in Estonia and Latvia it initially covered all persons having public contact in both the public and private sectors. The following parallel characteristics can be observed across the board in occupational language competence (for more information see Hogan-Brun et al. 2007: 566):

— The identification of personnel needing to pass such occupational language tests was based not on ethnicity or citizenship criteria but on whether or not personnel had attended the titular language education system; those who had gone through the Russian school system had to provide proof of their competence in the national languages, even if they were members of the titular group.
— In all three Baltic States, the period of most extensive testing occurred from the early to the mid 1990s when over 200,000 tests were taken and passed in Estonia, more than twice as many in Latvia and about 25,000 in Lithuania. More recently, the numbers have decreased significantly.
— Initially the three Baltic States did have slightly different formulations of the levels of language proficiency required for various grades of personnel (Estonia tested at six levels, Latvia and Lithuania at three levels); however, the occupations identified for testing at the various levels were similar across the three countries. More recently, all three states have adopted the Common European Framework proficiency levels.
— There have also been moves in each country to strengthen titular language learning in Russian stream (and other minority-medium) schools, including success in the final secondary school examinations; those passing this final examination in the titular language subject are seen as having the equivalent of the occupational language attestation.

As we shall see below, one factor that will increase access to citizenship and the professions in the Baltic countries, will be the various coordinating measures that are being taken to align citizenship and occupational language tests with school-based language teaching and testing. Students will be exempt from occupational language tests and the language component of the citizenship test if they successfully pass the titular language examination in their final year of secondary education.

4. Language and education

Due to the differing national demographic composition in the Baltic Republics, education policies vary considerably, and decisions are made with respect to the existence of a hybrid school population. New school curricula were drawn up over the years in order to find adequate and useful solutions for these societies in transition. Across the Baltic, students from the main minority and immigrant communities are offered schooling in the medium of their first language, where the titular language is a compulsory subject. While supporting first language instruction for children from those communities, all education models derive from a progressive change to the national language as the predominant one at university level. In each republic, pupils of non-mainstream schools are also required to take an exam in the titular language when graduating. These tests have been integrated with general language proficiency certifications that are a requirement for job seekers and for those wishing to pursue further education. A comparative study of various models of minority and immigrant language-medium education and the challenges and implications of bilingual schooling in the three Baltic Republics is provided in Hogan-Brun (2007).

Attitudes of parents from the minority and immigrant communities towards the choice of schools for their offspring have changed gradually over the years. Seeing their children's future directly linked to success in the overall society, these parents have increasingly started to send them to mainstream schools. Such a move is stronger in Lithuania, but it is also found in Estonia. This trend has brought about a number of unexpected challenges, necessitating the formulation of appropriate educational policies to address particularly the need of teaching the national languages as second languages, or in mixed first language settings. Hence new models of bilingual – and in Estonia, immersion – schooling at the primary and secondary levels were introduced as additional educational options. Teachers were offered training, curricula were formulated and textbooks were written to provide the necessary infrastructure. Minority schools, where instruction is chiefly held in the community languages, are being retained alongside this new scheme.

4.1. The titular language as a subject

In each republic the titular language is now a compulsory subject throughout all levels of schooling to the end of the final secondary education or the vocational qualification examinations. Proficiency assessment systems for state language competence have been developed and introduced in all three Baltic States. In addition, all public tertiary education is only in the titular language, with a small number of international higher education institutions (e.g., some business schools) offering courses mainly in English. The introduction of the titular languages into the Russian stream and other minority-medium schooling system has been a particular challenge in terms of conceptualisation of second language methodology (an entirely new experience in this region), materials preparation, teacher education and curriculum organisation.

At the same time, the necessity to learn other languages has been widely recognised and encouraged, echoing the situation before World War II when more than one foreign language was the usual fare in education. Across the Baltic, students are now offered a greater range of languages at schools such as English, French and German as a first choice (and English, French, German, Russian, Italian or, in some establishments, some other languages as a second choice). In the mid-nineties, a policy decision was taken not to offer Russian as a first foreign language any longer. It now lags in popularity behind English, which enjoys high prestige amongst students. But there has lately been a renewed demand for Russian, which will no doubt continue to be a *lingua franca* in the Baltic and among people from the former Soviet republics. The future range of schooled bilingualism among the population is therefore sure to expand – albeit mostly on a diglossic level – and involve a promotion of western-oriented language and cultural sensitivity (Kaplan and Baldauf 1997: 219).

4.1.1. Estonia

Estonian as a second language aims to promote competence in Estonian on the Common European Framework level B2 by the end of primary education and level C1 at the outset of secondary schooling. As in both sister republics, a national compulsory Estonian language examination has been introduced for completion of secondary education. Here too, this objective has necessitated the development of curricula for Estonian as a second language and relevant teaching methods and materials. With the support of the Ministry of Education and that of several municipalities teachers at

Russian schools were offered opportunities (mainly in the shape of in-service provision) to upgrade their training and retraining in bilingual teaching methods.

At the present time, Estonian is the main medium of instruction across all levels in over 500 schools in the country. During the last two decades, however, the overall amount of the teaching of Estonian as a native language has gradually decreased. This drop has produced a concern among teachers of Estonian with respect to quality loss in relation to the literary standard of Estonian as well as to functional and critical literacy. Hence, a new curriculum that offers a greater focus on orthography, text comprehension and literature was introduced from the academic year 2002/2003. The number of lessons per week has been set at 19 for primary education in grades 1–3, with a decrease to 15 in grades 4–6 and to 12 in grades 7–9. At the secondary school level (grades 10–12), six courses, each consisting of 35 lessons respectively, are offered both on the subject of the Estonian language and also on literature in Estonian (Hogan-Brun et al. 2007: 562).

As paralleled in Lithuania and Latvia, Estonian is also the main medium of instruction in higher education. Some educational programs are taught in English, and several private higher education institutions use Russian. In order to improve the quality of language used in management and business, a course on practical Estonian (involving tasks linked to text creation and processing) will shortly be made mandatory for all students. For those coming from secondary schools with a language of instruction other than Estonian, an introductory course on academic Estonian language is provided.

4.1.2. Latvia

With Latvian now taught as a core subject in all mainstream school systems, a pass in the final Latvian language examination is required in Russian-medium schools to complete secondary education. Latvian is also the exclusive language of public higher education, though a limited number of non-government or foreign higher education institutions use other languages, mostly English (as in the Stockholm School of Economics in Riga). Foreign languages are taught from the first year of Latvia's 9-year primary school curriculum, with a second foreign language introduced in mid-primary school. These two languages are then continued throughout general secondary education (years 10 to 12). Russian has not disappeared, but now is arrayed alongside other choices.

In Grade 3, approximately 12.5% of the time in the curriculum is spent on a foreign language, compared to the EU average of 15.7%. By Grade 6 this figure rises to 20% on a foreign language (as opposed to 12.3% in the EU) and, in Grade 9, 14.7% of time is devoted to a foreign language, compared to the EU average of 13.2%. This strong language learning pattern is continued to the end of secondary education (Hogan-Brun et al. 2007: 561).

A crucial practice in Latvia, as in all three Baltic States, has been the development of a titular second-language methodology, of materials and support. In 1996, the *National Program for Latvian Language Teaching* (NPLLT) was introduced to develop professional training activities for teachers to produce Latvian as a second language methodologies and materials for schools, to teach Latvian as a second language (LAT2) and to individuals in various occupational groups who have not attended Latvian medium education but who are none the less required to meet standards of language competence as part of language attestation procedures and to stimulate public debate and contact with community groups on language issues. The National Agency of Latvian Language Training (NALLT; *http://www.lvava.lv*) is now continuing this work.

4.1.3. Lithuania

Lithuania's students who pass the state language examination receive certificates equivalent to those of state language competence for adults. The examination, which has been administered centrally since 2001, assesses the communicative competence of the learners in four areas of language activity: listening, speaking, reading and writing. It grants access to Lithuanian-medium tuition in all disciplines at national higher educational establishments and universities. According to the Law on Higher Education, the only language of instruction in public higher education institutions is Lithuanian, with some exceptions for special study programmes (e.g., English or other foreign languages) and courses for foreign/exchange students.

Mirroring the above situation, Lithuanian is taught as a compulsory subject in all schools throughout the country. In primary education, 34% of the time in the curriculum is spent on Lithuanian; in basic schools 18%, and at the secondary level 11–16% (depending on student choice). The curriculum for minority-medium schools sets the percentage of time to be spent on

Lithuanian as a second language at a lower level, respectively 11%, 10% and 10–12% (Kalbų mokymo politikos aprašas 2006: 84).

The Ministry of Education and Science has proposed to introduce a single examination of Lithuanian as a mother tongue for mainstream schools, and of Lithuanian as a state language for minority schools, but this is still under discussion. Guidelines for this reform are currently being prepared for a planned implementation. However, there are a number of complex problems relating to differences in the curricula for teaching Lithuanian as a mother tongue and as a second language that still need to be addressed. A comparative analysis was carried out by a working group formed by the Ministry of Education and Science in 2005–2006, on the secondary school curricula, education standards and the examination content used for mainstream and minority schools. Then, in April 2006 a single pilot examination was organised for 2,000 students from 80 schools (52 with Lithuanian as a medium, 14 with Polish and 14 with Russian). Results have revealed that students from minority schools are not yet prepared for a common examination. The decision was therefore taken to further unify curricula, syllabi and examination requirements in mainstream and minority schools and to stage an additional pilot examination (*bandomasis egzaminas*) in 2008 (Bulajeva and Hogan-Brun, forthcoming 2008).

5. Language practice

As illustrated above, the increasing use of the national languages in the Baltic Republics was largely propelled by legal requirements that demanded the deployment of the respective languages in the public sphere – an idea strongly supported by the growing prestige of the languages. State programs exist to provide the population with adequate language learning opportunities. Many minority representatives are instrumentally motivated to learn their state language in order to gain status and economic success, others display integrative orientations, seeking to identify with their overall society (see Hogan-Brun and Ramonienė 2005a). As a result, steadily increasing levels of bilingualism with the titular language amongst speakers of minority languages have been observed in all three republics. This is particularly evident amongst the members of the younger generation who have acquired appropriate linguistic knowledge at school. However, as a result of the removal of compulsory Russian from the school curricula a situation has arisen where the succeeding generation is growing up with less competence in Russian.

On the other hand observations point to the fact that language habits in localities with greater, largely self-sufficient ethnic densities are changing at a somewhat slower rate (Hogan-Brun and Ramonienė 2005b; Metuzāle-Kangere and Ozolins 2005; Verschik 2005). Sizeable (mainly Russophone – consisting chiefly of Belarusians and Ukrainians – and also Russian) language groups remain, particularly in Latvia and Estonia, and to a lesser extent also in Lithuania. These communities exist mostly in the larger towns, and in some country locations (northeastern Estonia; eastern Latvia; and southeastern and eastern Lithuania which also hosts a large Polish community). In these environments, Russian is still widely shared as a means of communication. The language dynamics in these language communities still require thorough investigation. While recent census returns contain language-related information, few data have so far become available on actual (as opposed to reported) levels of state language competence and practice. Research therefore needs to focus more on this aspect in order to provide baseline information for the formulation and implementation of appropriate policies.

5.1. Estonia

As the census data (Estonian Census 2000) show Estonians and Russians are both characterised by high language loyalty (97.9% and 98.2% respectively), while knowledge of the national languages (both as a first and as a second language) of other minority language groups (except Finns) is steadily decreasing. Of these, fewer than 40% have sustained the language of their own national affiliation, with most others shifting to Russian and, during recent years, to Estonian. Thus the number of Russian first language speakers is almost 400,000, which is considerably higher than the number of Russian nationals (330,000), at the cost of the languages of third (i.e., non-Estonian and non-Russian) nationalities. Knowledge of the Estonian language too has increased modestly. According to the results of the census, the share of non-Estonians who are able to speak Estonian has risen steadily over recent years, from 14% in 1989 to 37% in 2000. Among Russians some 44% claimed competence in Estonian in the 2000 census, as against 15% in the 1989 census (Verschik 2005). Though these figures point to a significant shift towards bilingualism they need to be treated with some caution since they are based on self-reports and also because the census questionnaire excluded the possibility of declaring multiple identity/several mother tongues. But as findings by Verschik (2005) show, language habits are changing in more subtle ways too. In place of the characteristic Soviet period encounter in which an Estonian would always address a Russian speaker in Russian, highly diverse encounter strategies are emerging, including reverse politeness (using each other's major language), or greater common initiation in Estonian. However, Vihalemm (2002) argues that the instrumental value of Estonian still remains ambivalent, and that Estonian and Russian communities are still highly segregated, with most Estonian-Russian interaction still taking place in Russian.

5.2. Latvia

The census (Latvian Census 2000) demonstrated that 79% of the population now assessed themselves as having competence in Latvian, a significant increase of 17% over the 1989 Census figure. Yet the peculiarity of the Latvian situation is that the national language is not necessarily the most widely spoken language. According to the 2005 report on the state language policy guidelines for 2005–2014, many residents of Latvia (some 81%) report to have a command of the Russian language, which often prompts the choice of the language for communication. English on the other hand is mastered by some 14%, German by just 8% of residents, with other languages (French, Swedish, Norwegian, Polish) lagging behind (Latvia State Language Agency 2005: 24, in Hogan-Brun et al. 2007: 574). The political nature of language policy in Latvia has ensured that studies of attitudes about bilingualism remain at the forefront of public attention as well as of scholarly investigation. Studies undertaken by the Baltic Social Research Institute (BSZI) provide the most comprehensive overall tracking of reported monolingual and bilingual use in large representative samples (*http://www.bszi.lv/downloads/resources/ language/Language_2003.pdf*).

The surveys show both steady increases in knowledge of Latvian among minorities, supporting the census findings, and in the far more complicated dynamics of the situational uses of Latvian or Russian in various domains. When correlated to age, the tendencies demonstrate an increasing bifurcation between youth and the older group. The younger cohorts show continual improvement in their knowledge of Latvian, with successive increases each year among those claiming fluency in Latvian at the higher levels. The data also point to steady but smaller increases among those between 35–49 years of age but to largely unaltered language conpetencies for those over 50 in this constituency.

5.3. Lithuania

The census data (Lithuanian Census 2000) show that the majority of Lithuanians and Russians declare the language of their own nationality as their native language. Numerous Poles on the other hand, who in Soviet times had switched to Russian as the language of power now declare Russian as their first language. Among non-native speakers of Lithuanian over half of them (50–66%) now declare it to be their second language. Two thirds of Lithuanians and three quarters of Poles use Russian as their second language. Polish is less popular as a second language. Research findings (Kasatkina and Leončikas 2003: 271) point to the fact that many (mainly Russian) members of the minority communities consider a good command of Lithuanian to be a necessary precondition to pursue a career in Lithuania. Clearly the use of Lithuanian predominates in the country as a whole. In the densely multilingual and multi-ethnic region of eastern and southeastern Lithuania there is evidence that a growing number of residents are also adopting the state language, both in the public and in the semi-public spheres. Findings from a recent major survey on language attitudes and use in this region including the capital Vilnius show that attitudes towards Lithuanian are overall positive. Here, Russian (still) figures as the most widely shared language but increasingly *in tandem* with Lithuanian. In this plurilingual environment, many individuals, particularly Poles, possess several (bilingual/trilingual) language competencies to varying degrees, with a fairly fluid boundary between languages, where one language (formerly Russian, now increasingly Lithuanian) in the various settings is widely shared (for more information see Hogan-Brun and Ramonienė 2005a).

As this overview shows the nature of language loyalties is complex locally in the wake of repeated phases of assimilation in the past. Overall, there is no direct connection between language preferences and national affiliation amongst the so-called third ethnicities in the Baltic. Many non-Russians are competent in Russian and even have Russian as their first language. The vast majority of both titular nationals and Russians have their respective language as a first language, but a majority of titular nationals have competence in Russian and a majority of Russians in Latvia and Lithuania report competence in the titular language, with Russians in Estonia appearing to be somewhat behind in this respect.

6. Summary

This review on the language constellations in the current settings of the Baltic has sought to foreground the inter-connectedness of changes in language use, language ideology and language legislation in this region. From studies we can infer that some people seem to have accepted the legitimacy of recently introduced language laws (Rose 2000: 48f; Hogan-Brun et al. 2007: 596). Observations from findings cited in the previous section also show that attitudes to language use have changed to varying extents in each republic over the years, and that a degree of (linguistic) accommodation among speakers of minority languages appears to have evolved variously. In part it could be argued that this is the result of competitive assimilation, spurned by supporters of extrinsic motivation as a means to obtain material benefits and better jobs through the mainstream society. No doubt such pragmatic attitudes to language and integration are likely to continue.

Overall, data consistently attest to the degree of Russification the local populations have undergone and suggest that these individuals' first language does not often coincide with their nationality. However, the post-Soviet period has allowed for some language revival for the resident minorities, with schools now providing instruction in a wide range of minority languages. Many of these minorities are found to be in support of various aspects of recently emerged language policy and often desire to reverse the processes of Russification they have had to undergo previously. However, while overall positive signs of the consolidation of society have been observed in Lithuania, the implications for language policy and practice of the more complex language constellations in the demographically more heterogeneous settings of Estonia and Latvia continue to present a challenge.

References

Adrey, Jean-Bernard
    2005   Minority language rights before and after the 2004 EU enlargement: The Copenhagen Criteria in the Baltic States. *Journal of Multilingual and Multicultural Development* 26 (5): 453–468.

Baltic Institute of Social Research
    2003   *Language 2003*. Available at *http://www.bszi.lv/downloads/resources/language/Language_2003.pdf*

Bulajeva, Tatjana and Gabrielle Hogan-Brun
    2008   Language and Education Orientations in Lithuania post-EU Accession. *International Journal of Bilingual Education and Bilingualism*.

Citizenship in Estonia. Estonian Ministry of Foreign Affairs
    2007   Retrieved 10 August 2007 from *http://www.vm.ee/estonia/pea_172/kat_399/4518.html*.

Common European Framework of Reference for Languages (CEFRL).
    2008   Retrieved 15 January 2008 from *http://www.coe.int/t/dg4/linguistic/CADRE_EN.asp*.

Dini, Pietro
    2000   *Baltų kalbos. Lyginamoji istorija* [The Baltic Languages. Comparative History]. Vilnius: Mokslo ir enciklopedijų leidybos institutas.
    1991   *L'anello Baltico. Profilo delle nazioni Baltiche Lituania, Lettonia, Estonia* [The Baltic Ring: Profile of the Lithuanian, Latvian and Estonian Nations]. Genova: Marietti.

Estonia. Citizenship Law
                  Available at *http://www.vm.ee/estonia/pea_172/kat_399/4518.html*

Estonian Census 2000
    2000   Available at *http://pub.stat.ee/px-web.2001/I_Databas/Population_Census/Population_Census.asp*

Gerner, Kristian and Stefan Hedlund
    1993   *The Baltic States at the End of the Soviet Empire*. London: Routledge.

Hiden, John and Philip Salmon
    1991   *The Baltic Nations and Europe. Estonia, Latvia and Lithuania in the 21st Century*. London/New York: Longman.

Hogan-Brun, Gabrielle
    2005a   Language and social processes in the Baltic Republics surrounding EU accession (Special Issue guest-edited by G. Hogan-Brun). *Journal of Multilingual and Multicultural Development* 25 (6).
    2005b   The language situation in Lithuania. Baltic Sociolinguistic Review. Special Issue, *Journal of Baltic Studies* 36 (3).
    2005c   The Baltic Republics and language ideological debates surrounding their EU accession. In *Language and Social Processes in the Baltic Republics Surrounding EU Accession* (Special Issue guest-editor G. Hogan-Brun), *Journal of Multilingual and Multicultural Development* 26 (5): 367–377.
    2005d   Baltic Sociolinguistic Review, *Journal of Baltic Studies* XXXVI/3 (G. Hogan-Brun: guest editor).
    2007   Education in the Baltic States: Contexts, practices and challenges. *Comparative Education* 43 (4): 553–570.

Hogan-Brun, Gabrielle and Meilutė Ramonienė
2003   Emerging language and education policies in Lithuania. *Language Policy* 2: 27–45.
2005a   Perspectives on language attitudes and use in Lithuania's multilingual setting. In *Language and Social Processes in the Baltic Republics Surrounding EU Accession* (Special Issue guest-edited by Gabrielle Hogan-Brun), *Journal of Multilingual and Multicultural Development* 26 (5): 425–441.
2005b   The language situation in Lithuania. In *Baltic Sociolinguistic Review* (Special Issue guest-edited by G. Hogan-Brun), *Journal of Baltic Studies* XXXVI/3: 345–370.
Hogan-Brun, Gabrielle, Uldis Ozolins, Meilutė Ramonienė and Mart Rannut
2007   *Language Policies and Practices in the Baltic States*. Polity series of Current Issues in Language Planning 8: 4. Clevedon: Multilingual Matters.
Kalbų mokymo politikos aprašas [Language education policy profile]
2006   Retrieved 1 December 2006 from *http://www.smm.lt*
Kaplan, Robert and Richard Baldauf
1997   *Language Planning from Practice to Theory*. Clevedon: Multilingual Matters.
Latvia. Citizenship Law
        Available at *http://www.np.gov.lv/en/faili_en/Pils_likums.rtf*
Latvia. State Language Agency
2005   *Guidelines of the State Language Policy for 2005-2014* Riga: State Language Agency. Available at *http://vva.valoda.lv/*
Latvian Census 2000
2000   *http://data.csb.lv/EN/Database/popcensus/popcensus.asp*
Law on the Estonian State Language
        Available at *http://seadus.ibs.ee/aktid/rk.s.19950221.512.19990701.html*
Law on the Latvian State Language
        Available at *http://www.ttc.lv/New/lv/tulkojumi/E0120.doc*
Law on the Lithuanian State Language
        Available at *http://www3.lrs.lt/cgi-bin/preps2?Condition1=21941&Condition2=*
Lithuania. Citizenship Law
        Available at *http://www.legislationline.org/legislation.php?tid=11&lid=1050&less=false*
Lithuanian Census
2000   *http://www.std.lt/Surasymas/Rezultatai/index_pirm_e.htm*
Lieven, Anatol
1993   *The Baltic Revolution. Estonia, Latvia, Lithuania and the path to independence*. New Haven: Yale University Press.

Metuzāle-Kangere, Baiba and Uldis Ozolins
  2005   The language situation in Latvia from 1850–2004. In *The Baltic Sociolinguistic Review*, Special Issue guest-edited by Gabrielle Hogan-Brun, *Journal of Baltic Studies* 36 (3): 317–344.
National Agency of Latvian Language Training (NALLT)
  2006   Retrieved 14 January 2006 from *http://www.lvava.lv*
National Program for Latvian Language Teaching (NPLLT).
  2006   Retrieved 14 January 2006 from *http://www.lvavp.lv*
Norgaard, Ole
  1996   *The Baltic States After Independence.* Cheltenham: Edward Elgar.
Ozolins, Uldis
  2002   Post Imperialist Language Situations: The Baltic Republics". *World Congress on Language Policies,* Barcelona. 24 June. Retrieved 2 March 2004 from *http://www.linguapax.org/congres/taller/taller1/Ozolins.html*
Plasseraud, Yves
  2003   *Les Etats Baltiques. Les Sociétés Gigognes. La dialectique minorités-majorités.* Crozon: Editions Arméline.
Rose, Richard
  2000   *New Baltic Barometer IV: A Survey Study.* Studies in Public Policy. Glasgow: University of Strathclyde.
Social integration in Latvia: Towards mutual understanding and cooperation
  2006   Retrieved August 10, 2007. *http://www.mfa.gov.lv/en/news/Newsletters/Integration/2006/59*
Valstybinės kalbos mokėjimo kategorijos [The categories of state language knowledge]
  2003   Retrieved 2 December 2006 from. *http://www.pprc.lt/vkm/kategor.htm*
Verschik, Anna
  2005   The language situation in Estonia. In *Baltic Sociolinguistic Review,* (Special Issue edited by G. Hogan-Brun), *Journal of Baltic Studies* 36 (3): 283–316.
Vihalemm, Triin
  2002   Usage of language as a source of societal trust. In *The Challenge of the Russian Minority: Emerging Multicultural Democracy in Estonia*, Marju Lauristin and Mati Heidmets (eds.), 199–217. Tartu: Tartu University Press.

Section II
Regional minority languages

Catalan in Spain[1]

F. Xavier Vila i Moreno

1. Introduction

The traditional Catalan-speaking area includes the eastern part of the Iberian Peninsula, the Balearic Islands, a small part of southern France (the Department of Eastern Pyrenees, *Catalunya Nord* in Catalan) and the city of Alghero (*l'Alguer*) in Sardinia, Italy (Figure 1). The area is spread over four countries: Spain, France, Italy and Andorra. In Spain, the focus of this Chapter, the Catalan language area covers Catalonia (with the exception of the Valley of Aran in the Pyrenees, where *Aranese* Occitan is spoken), most of Valencia (also called the Valencian Country or Valencian Community), the Balearic Islands, a stretch of land in Aragon on the border with Catalonia, known as La Franja, and a handful of hamlets in Murcia known as *Carxe/Carche*.

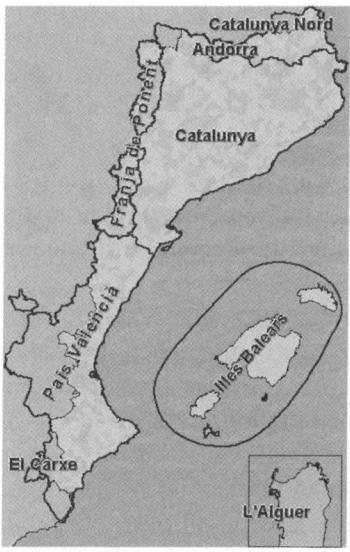

Figure 1. The Catalan-speaking territories
   (Source: *http://www.demolinguistica.cat/demoling/index.php*)

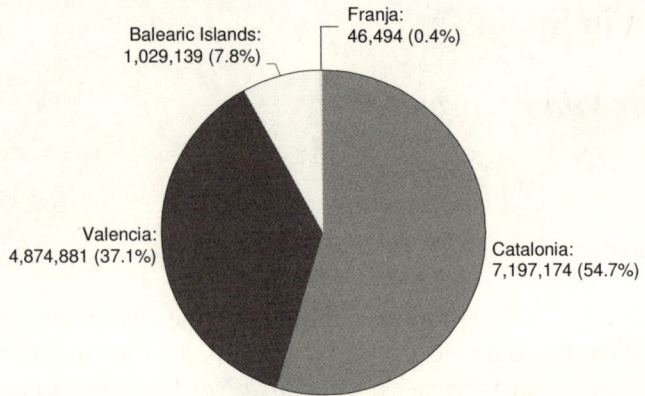

Figure 2. Population in Spain's Catalan-speaking territories, 2007 (Source: The population census (*Estimación del padrón*) of 1 January 2007, National Statistics Institute. Provisional data)

In 2007, the population living in areas of Spain in which Catalan is spoken amounted to around 13 million people. Catalan is the language that evolved from the Latin spoken by Roman settlers and the indigenous people two thousand years ago in the eastern part of the Tarraconense province. The language spread to the Balearic Islands and to Valencia in the thirteenth century when the Arabic-speaking kingdoms there were annexed to the dual Crown formed by Catalonia and Aragon.[2] Between that time and the mid-twentieth century, Catalan was the area's predominant language, in demolinguistic terms at least. In purely quantitative terms, the only significant minority during this period were the Arabic-speaking peasants who remained in Valencia after the *Reconquista* and were eventually expelled in 1659.

Castilian, a Romance language like Catalan, was born and developed in the kingdom of Castile. Castilian reached the Catalan court in 1412 when Ferdinand of Trastámara, a Castilian landowner, was crowned king of the Catalan-Aragonese confederation. This event had little immediate impact in a monarchy where the royal power was severely curtailed by the Catalan Parliament. In fact, Catalan reached its greatest splendour in the fourteenth century; the language was used in all areas of life and Castilian was practically non-existent in the Catalan states of the time.

The position of Castilian changed significantly during the sixteenth and seventeenth centuries. First, the dynastic union between Ferdinand of

Aragon and Isabel of Castile, who married in 1476, took the court to Castile. Second, cultural activities in Valencia, the capital of Catalan culture at the time, came under severe pressure from the Inquisition and were harshly repressed after the revolt of the *Germanias*. Third, the economic centre of the Habsburg Empire moved westwards to the Atlantic Ocean, and the Catalan states faced stagnation and recession. Within a few decades, the Catalan culture that had produced the philosopher Raymundus Lullius and inaugurated the modern novel with *Tirant lo Blanc* – to quote Cervantes, "the greatest book in the world" – lost its vibrancy and was superseded by imported Castilian culture, in a period known as the *Decadència*. However, this decline only affected higher culture: Catalan continued to be the language used in institutional life and everyday affairs by the overwhelming majority of the population.

The institutional position of Castilian was greatly reinforced after the Spanish War of Succession (1700–1714). After the war, Philip V issued the *Nueva Planta* decrees, which put an end to the autonomy of the kingdoms of the Crown of Aragon. Over the next two hundred years, there were innumerable official attempts on the part of the Spanish authorities to spread the use of Castilian and to displace Catalan (Ferrer 1985). These efforts combined explicit language policies, such as the obligatory use of Castilian in government or the courts, with many seemingly non-linguistic measures; for example, since 1875, all males were expected to "serve" in the Spanish army, often in mixed units in which, far away from their home, Catalan recruits had to learn Castilian.

By the end of the nineteenth century, the use of Castilian in the Catalan language territories remained fragile, crucially dependent on the State's activities. Castilian was the language of government, the educational system, and the Catholic Church in Valencia and La Franja – but not in the other areas, where Catalan remained firmly established. Castilian was also the language of most of the press and scholarly culture. But, for the overwhelming majority of the population, Castilian remained a second language, a foreign language even. The majority of the population had little contact with State agencies. The educational system, in theory made compulsory and universal in 1857, had still reached less than half of the population by 1900, and could not guarantee the learning of Castilian. The refined, cultured environments where intellectuals conversed in Castilian were far removed from most of the population. Even more importantly, in demographical terms, *Castilians*[3] were few and far between in the Catalan-speaking territories; most of them were government employees, whose presence was only noted in the great cities or in military garrisons. There are no demolinguistic data available, but it seems likely that, at the beginning of the twentieth century, native speakers of Castilian numbered less than 5% of the population (Vila 2006: 141).

2. The period of maximum subordination

The transformations that began during the nineteenth century gathered momentum in the twentieth century. In the first place, the presence of the centralist State became more and more keenly felt in everyday life. Between 1900 and 1975 (in fact, between 1714 and 1975) the Catalan-speaking territories only enjoyed six and a half years of self-government, all limited to Catalonia. Spain's two twentieth-century dictatorships were strongly anti-Catalan. The school system played a significant role in imposing State language policies (Monés 1995).

Secondly, the Catalan-speaking territories became a modern, industrial, urban society. New spheres of activity and business appeared and increasingly made their mark on the linguistic landscape: publicity, labeling, industrial bureaucracy, legal matters, and mass media. In 1924, the first radio station appeared (Radio Barcelona); in 1932–1933 the first spoken films were produced; in 1959, television came to Barcelona. Catalan was only intermittently allowed in all these new spheres of life during the short periods of freedom.

Thirdly, during the twentieth century, the Catalan language area became a focus of immigration from the rest of Spain, and the number of Castilian speakers rose sharply in all territories (Figure 3).

By 1975, Catalan was in a very delicate position. Official activities were carried out in the State language. For the first time in history, Castilian had been actively learnt by all Catalan speakers, and literacy in that language approached 100%. Immigration had brought in millions of Castilian speakers and, although an appreciable minority of them had learnt Catalan, most of them remained monolingual and were raising a second generation of Castilian-speaking locals. Contact with Castilian was rapidly eroding language loyalty and even language quality among Catalan speakers, especially among the new generations. However, in spite of official prohibition, Catalan speakers clung to their language for in-group purposes, including formal events such as bank transactions (Figure 4).

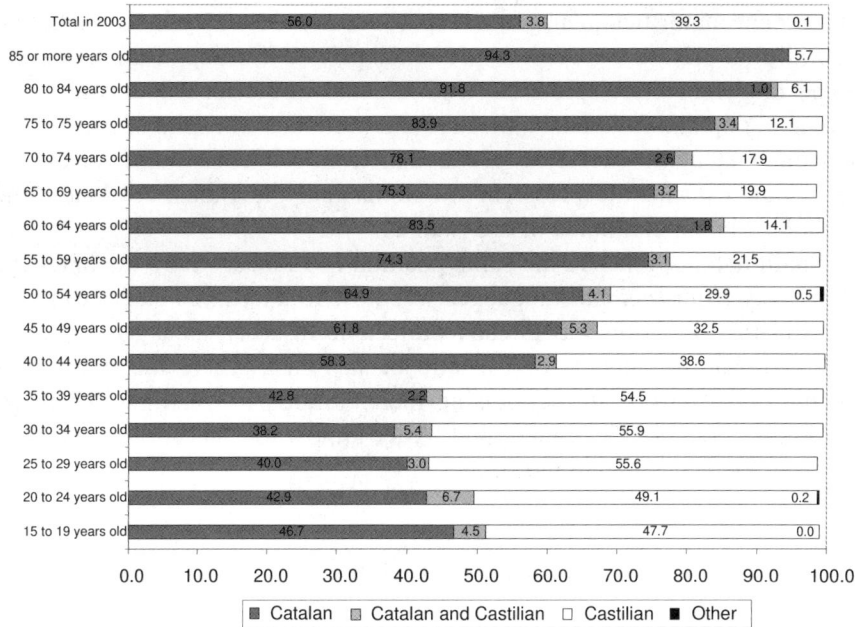

Figure 3. First language of people born in Catalonia during the twentieth century, in groups of 5 years, in % (Source: *Estadística sobre els Usos Lingüístics a Catalunya 2003*)

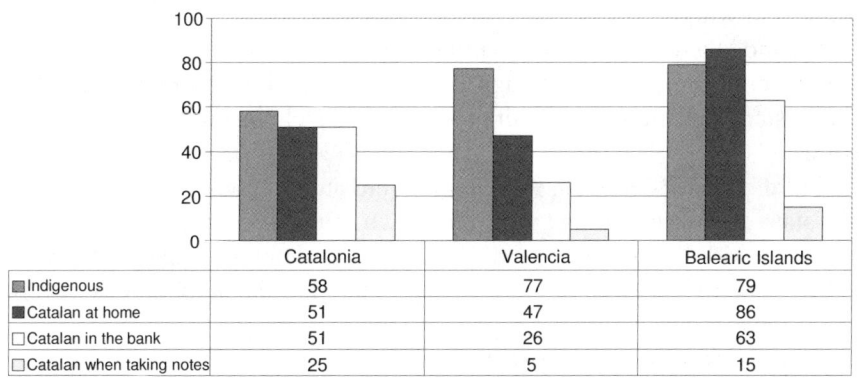

Figure 4. Percentage of indigenous population and use of Catalan in Catalonia, Valencia and Balearic Islands in 1978 (Source: Census 1970 en CIS 1978, in Rodríguez 1979)

Significant minorities managed to reproduce some literacy in Catalan, and a handful of private associations promoted private learning of the language. Some modern cultural products were created in the local language – for example, pop and folk music, theatre, and literature – in spite of censorship and the systematic exclusion of Catalan from modern cultural media, in particular TV and the press. In Catalonia and the Balearic Islands, the Catholic Church continued to use Catalan.

Spain had not reached the same position as France, where the language shift away from *regional* languages was now in a terminal stage. But progress in this direction was already noticeable in urban areas such as Alacant (Alicante), Valencia or Castelló de la Plana, where the indigenous middle classes were already raising their children in Castilian. Then, on November 20th, 1975, Franco died. After almost four decades of dictatorship, democracy began to return.

3. The 1978 Constitutional framework for language policies

On December 6th 1978[4], the draft Constitution proposed by the first democratic parliament, elected the previous year, was approved by referendum, ushering in a new political system. Some elements of the new regime are of crucial importance to understand the dynamics of language policies that have emerged in the Catalan language area of Spain since 1978.

First of all, democracy and freedom of speech turned language policy into a prominent political and electoral issue. Policies would no longer be explicable without politics.

Second, there was the separation of powers. Since 1978, language issues entered the courts, although the proverbial slowness of Spain's judicial system constituted a hindrance to the development of any language policy.

Third, since 1978 Spain was divided into autonomous communities, i.e., sub-state territorial entities with their own legislative and executive powers, each with its own Statute of Autonomy indicating its areas of competence.[5] One of the areas of competence granted to the autonomous governments was language policy.

Fourth, the new political scenario redistributed power among social actors; the armed forces and the Catholic Church lost part of their social control, and many other agents appeared or gained autonomy: political parties, free trade unions, free mass media, consumers' associations, and so on.

What were the explicitly linguistic provisions of the 1978 Constitution? In fact, language issues appear very early in the Constitution – indeed, they appear in the preliminaries, section 3:

> 1. Castilian is the official Spanish language of the State. All Spaniards have the duty to know it and the right to use it.
>
> 2. The other Spanish languages shall also be official in the respective Self-governing Communities in accordance with their Statutes.
>
> 3. The richness of the different linguistic modalities of Spain is a cultural heritage which shall be specially respected and protected.

The Constitution recognises the existence of languages other than Castilian, allows for them to be official in their territories, and engages the State in affirmative action to protect linguistic diversity. Protection of diversity is further enshrined in Chapter 2 *Rights and freedoms*, section 20:

> 3. The law shall regulate the organisation and parliamentary control of the mass communication means under the control of the State or any public agency and shall guarantee access to such means by the significant social and political groups, respecting the pluralism of society and of the various languages of Spain.

But the 1978 Constitution is not egalitarian: Castilian is recognised as *the* (only) language of the State, and its speakers are granted the right to use it throughout the country. The *other* languages, not even explicitly named, *may* become official, but only in (part of) their original territories. The model sketched here adopts the principle of monolingual territoriality for Castilian in its homeland, and applies the principle of personality to the other territories. Non-Castilian speakers are also obliged to learn Castilian, while nothing is explicitly said about the linguistic duties of Castilian speakers.

Arriving after three hundred years of centralist policies, the Constitution represented an opportunity for democracy and self-government, but its provisions were liable to multiple interpretations; indeed, its approval in 1978 signalled the starting point of a process of constant (re)interpretation in many areas, including language policy.

4. Language policies in each autonomous community

The current political model grants the autonomous governments the opportunity to develop their own language policies within the framework established by the 1978 Constitution. Some of these policies have worked to maintain Catalan as a minority language within its territory. Others have tried to redress the years of persecution and the imbalance which may derive from a restrictive interpretation of the Constitution.

4.1. Catalonia: ridding Catalan of its minority status

Language policies in Catalonia have aimed to enable Catalan to shake off the minority status granted by State policies. The 1979 Statute of Autonomy of Catalonia was a giant step towards normalizing the language situation (Milian 2007). This Statute[6] devotes a whole article to language issues (article 3). This article states that Catalan and Castilian are official in their own right; this makes systematic duplication of messages in each language unnecessary.[7] The official status of each language derives from different sources: Catalan is official because it is *the* language of Catalonia,[8] while Castilian is official as a consequence of its being the official language of the Spanish State. The government commits itself to affirmative action to achieve the "normal and official" use of both languages. Finally, the language of the Aran Valley – Occitan– is recognised and protected, but not yet official.

The Statute of Autonomy paved the way for the first language policy law,[9] the Linguistic Normalisation Act, passed in 1983.[10] This law made Catalan the only official language for toponyms; introduced the principle that Catalan was the language of education; required all students to know Catalan and Castilian by the end of their compulsory education; allowed the Catalan government to promote the position of Catalan in the mass media; and made Aranese Occitan the language (*llengua pròpia*) of the Valley of Aran.

In 1982, the Catalan Government created the *Corporació Catalana de Ràdio i Televisió*, which promoted the birth of *Catalunya Ràdio* and TV3 in 1983. The latter was the first TV channel to broadcast entirely in Catalan. Up to that moment, there had been only two public channels in Spain, both of them broadcasting in Castilian. Since 1985, TV3 could be seen in the rest of the linguistic area thanks to private associations.

During the 1980s and 1990s, Catalan progressively displaced Castilian as the main language of education, especially in primary schools and at universities, and knowledge of Catalan increased steadily among the new generations, while knowledge of Castilian remained stable (see section 4.6 and Vila, in press). But the fact that the language was now systematically used in education did not guarantee the transformation of ingrained sociolinguistic customs which were the result of the language's minority status during the dictatorship, and according to which Catalan speakers felt compelled to switch to Castilian when addressing Castilian speakers. Thus, awareness grew during the 1990s that the "social use" of Catalan – i.e., basically oral, formal and informal use of the language – had to be promoted. In 1998, a new Language Policy Act[11] replaced the 1983 Act. Among other changes, this new law made Catalan the working language of Catalonia's public institutions, the normal language of primary and secondary education, Catalonia's public mass media. The Act also offered ways to promote Catalan in the private sector, especially in mass media.

In 2006, a reform of the Statute of Autonomy was approved.[12] The new Statute raises some of the principles developed during the previous years to the highest legal position below the Constitution, and introduces a number of innovations. One of the most relevant ones is the inclusion of the *duty* to know Catalan for all Catalan citizens; in this, Catalan is finally placed on an equal footing with Castilian in terms of rights and duties, in Catalonia at least. A second important provision combines what is known as the principle of *disponibilitat* (i.e., that firms should be both able and willing to serve their customers in either language) and the *right of choice* of official language (i.e., individuals can choose the language in which they wish to be served). According to the Statute, the (Spanish) State authorities are partially co-responsible for promoting Catalan in certain cases. Finally, Aranese Occitan was declared official not only in the Valley of Aran, but throughout Catalonia.

The 2006 Statute is currently being studied by Spain's Constitutional Court. Whatever the Court's final decision may be, the fact is that Catalonia has sought to implement a language policy model that interprets the 1978 constitutional framework in a way that ensures that Catalan is treated not as a minority language in Catalonia, but as a majority language.

4.2. Valencia: keeping Catalan down

Language policy in Valencia has followed quite a different path. In fact, to a large extent, local language policies have worked *against* removing Catalan's minority status.

As the 1982 Valencian Statute only included the notion of *llengua pròpia* in passing, it severely limited the possibility of constructing an autonomous language policy. Neither was the language law of 1983[13] conceived to repair the effects of linguistic subordination: it made Catalan a compulsory subject for all school children in the Catalan-speaking areas, but did not go much beyond this in promoting the language. Few initiatives were taken during the following years to promote the official use of Catalan. Indeed, today most official business is conducted in Castilian. When the new autonomous channel Canal 9 was created in 1989, it broadcast in both Catalan and Castilian. In the private sector, promotion of Catalan was almost non-existent.

Linguistic secessionism has been a key factor in blocking the promotion of Catalan in Valencia (Pradilla 2004; Climent-Ferrando 2005). Valencians have traditionally called their language "Valencian". Unlike their counterparts in Catalonia, Valencia's urban middle classes shifted from Valencian/Catalan to Castilian during the 1960s and 1970s. Thus, in the late 1970s and early 1980s, it was mostly leftist parties, trade unions and intellectuals that defended Valencian/Catalan, while sectors to the right were shifting to Castilian. At this point, to counteract the pro-Catalan/Valencian discourse of the left, certain right-wing sectors started to appeal to the regional identity. These *secessionist* sectors accused the left-wing "Catalans" of trying to annex Valencia, and claimed that Valencian was an independent language descending directly from a pre-Arabic Romance language or even from an unknown language predating Latin[14]. Several new spellings were designed to reinforce the alleged independence of Valencian. In fact, most secessionist political and cultural works were written in Castilian, but their "norms" were extremely successful in blocking the use of Catalan/Valencian, for every single text could be contested on the basis of minute, but emblematic, linguistic differences – e.g., "Should we write *València, Valéncia* or *Valencia?*"; "Should we spell *sencer* or *sancer?*" The obvious solution to this recurrent conflict was to drop the Valencian/Catalan text and to use only Castilian.

At the beginning, the ruling Socialist Party regarded secessionism as a tool with which to divide the right-wing parties. In the 1980s, though, secessionist positions were progressively embraced by parties on the right. In the end, the secessionist debate eroded the pro-Catalan/Valencian positions that had been widely supported within the Socialist Party. With time, the strongest defenders of the language were the parties to the left of the Socialists and a wide movement which included universities as well as civic and cultural organisations such as *Acció Cultural del País Valencià* and *Escola Valenciana*. These civic movements recorded a number of successes in their defence of Catalan, such as establishing Catalan TV broadcasts throughout the Valencian country, setting up publishing houses, publishing journals and magazines, organising language courses, and so on. In fact, during the 1980s, the 1990s and the first decade of the 21st century Valencian/Catalan culture flourished throughout the Valencian Country in a way unparalleled since the Golden Age of the fifteenth century. Most of these activities received little support from the autonomous authorities.

In 1995, the Socialists were replaced by the Popular Party in the Valencian government. Apparently encouraged by their comrades in Madrid – now in government, but lacking a majority and in need of the support of the Catalan parties in Parliament – the Valencian government created the *Acadèmia Valenciana de la Llengua* (Valencian Academy of the Language, not the Academy of the Valencian Language) in 1998.[15] This institution was granted maximum powers as far as "Valencian" was concerned,[16] and was allegedly given the task of ending the linguistic debates about the nature of the language. In 2003, the Academy solemnly declared that "Valencian" was the appropriate name to refer to the language Valencians shared with Catalans and Balearics; thus, in a convoluted, euphemistic fashion, the AVL ruled that Catalan/Valencian was a single language.[17] But the Valencian government rejected this verdict, insisted that Valencian was an independent language, and introduced more and more restrictions on cultural and literary exchanges.

In 2006, the Popular and Socialist Parties agreed on a reform of the Statute. This Statute introduced the term *idioma valencià* (the Valencian language) and declared it to be Valencia's own language (*llengua pròpia*).[18] At the same time, the Valencian government started an offensive to close down the aerials that transmitted Catalan TV in Valencia. Finally, on December 9th 2007, the Valencian government interrupted the broadcasts of Catalan TV channels in the area near Alacant (Alicante), replacing it with a Castilian language station. Another step had been taken to make Catalan/Valencian a minority language in Valencia.

4.3. The Balearic Islands

The Balearic Islands were slow to assert their new status as a self-governing community, and only passed their Statute of Autonomy in 1983.[19] As far as linguistic issues were concerned, this text followed the model of Catalonia and included the mention of the *llengua pròpia*. The Linguistic Normalisation Act, passed in 1986, was less ambitious than its equivalent in Catalonia.

The development of an autonomous language policy gathered speed in the mid 1990s, when the Islands were granted authority over education, and took off in 1999, when a left-wing coalition won the elections and launched a concerted programme to increase both the knowledge and the use of Catalan. But the elections in 2003 brought the Popular Party back in power. This time language policy remained active, but in a different direction, as the new government sought to gain the support of recent Castilian-speaking immigrants attracted by the real estate and tourism boom, and Catalan was relegated once again. In 2007, a new Statute of Autonomy was passed which included some minor improvements for the language.[20] In 2007, left-wing parties got back into power, and language policy seemed to change direction once more, in favour of Catalan.

4.4. La Franja (Aragon)

Language policies in La Franja, which is part of Aragon, have remained almost unchanged for the last three decades. Taking advantage of the fact that the Catalan-speakers living in the rural Franja have neither the political and cultural means nor the numbers to achieve recognition of their language, Catalan has not been declared (co-)official and hardly any linguistic rights have been granted to Catalan-speakers. At school, the language is taught as an optional subject for 1, 2 or 3 hours per week, but only at the request of parents and teachers. This has been the situation since 1985. In the 2004–2005 school year, 81% of primary and secondary school pupils in La Franja took these optional classes in Catalan.

In 2007 a new Statute of Autonomy was approved which did not include any significant improvements for Catalan. The language remains non-official in its own territory.[21] However, the government announced that in 2008, the long-promised Language Act would finally be produced and Catalan would gain official recognition in La Franja.

4.5. Catalan and the central institutions

The analysis of language policies in connection with Catalan would be incomplete without a consideration of the positions adopted by the central institutions in Spain. While there are numerous differences between the various bodies, three features can be said to have remained unchanged with regard to language issues: an exclusive interest in Castilian; preference for apparently non-language-centred measures that affect language policies; the *externalisation* of language policies.

1. Only Castilian is relevant: The language policies designed and implemented by the successive central authorities have hardly ever actively supported Catalan, Basque or Galician, at least with *de motu proprio* measures. To give only a handful of significant examples: Catalan cannot be used in the institutions of the State, such as the Spanish Parliament[22] or the Supreme and Constitutional Courts. Catalan is not used in the Armed Forces, the *Guardia Civil*, or the National Police Force, all of which are dependent on the State government. The highest authorities in the country, including the members of the Royal Family, make little use of Catalan, and only when travelling to a Catalan-speaking area. No programme in Catalan has ever been broadcast all over Spain by public radio or television. Stamps and other materials produced by *Correos de España* use only Castilian. Nor has the Spanish currency (either pesetas or euros) ever included Catalan. Iberia, Spain's public airline, hardly ever uses the language. In general terms, knowledge of Catalan is not a requirement for working for the State offices in Catalonia, Valencia or the Balearic Islands, even in the case of members of staff dealing with the public. Judges have been especially vociferous in this area, arguing that knowledge of Catalan is not necessary in order to serve as a judge in the Catalan language area.

To be sure, Castilian is the only Spanish language that seems to attract the interest of the State authorities. The last three Ministers of Education have expressed their concern about the low level of competence in Castilian in Spain, and have tried to pass legislation to increase the number of hours of Spanish classes in compulsory education. But no Minister has ever been worried by the fact that thousands of children in Valencia and La Franja finish their compulsory education almost illiterate in Catalan.

The lack of concern for the *other* languages of Spain has been made evident in the long controversies about Spain's language policies in Europe. Catalan was not included as an official language when Spain became a member of the EEC in 1986. Since then, Catalan organisations have sought official status, but with little success, not only due to difficulties in the European framework, but also due to the lack of interest shown by successive Spanish governments. It was only in 2004 when, due to pressure from their indispensable Catalan parliamentary allies, the Socialist government obtained some sort of official recognition for Catalan by the EU – though in practical terms this recognition is far weaker than that obtained by the many other languages with fewer speakers but with a State to support them. This lack of concern for languages other than Castilian was explicitly stated by the Spanish authorities in their first report submitted to the Council of Europe regarding the degree of accomplishment of the European Charter for Regional or Minority Languages[23], in which all responsibility for languages other than Castilian was systematically transferred to the autonomous communities.

2. *Language policy via non-linguistic measures*: central governments have so far avoided specific legislation on language issues. In fact, a large percentage of their language policies have been applied by means of measures which are apparently non-linguistic. The labelling of commercial products in Catalonia provides a good example. In broad terms, product labels and instructions may be written in either official language. But Spanish legislation rejects all obstacles to free domestic trade, and the requirement to use Catalan in Catalonia would be considered such an *illiberal* obstacle for firms producing goods outside the Catalan-language territories.[24] As a consequence, most products sold in the Catalan language area are labelled only in Castilian,[25] and only Catalan firms producing mostly for the Catalan market dare include Catalan in their labels. This case underlines the fact that the application of the liberal principle of State non-intervention, often used as an argument not to "interfere" with official bilingualism is currently used against Catalan.

3. *Externalisation:* most language policy lines designed by the central authorities involve third agents, such as the school system, many large companies, and civic associations. In fact, it seems fair to speak of a practice of externalising the implementation of language policies.

The reactions to TV3 may exemplify this point. The success of this channel was regarded with much suspicion by Castilian Spain. In 1988 the Spanish Parliament passed a law for private television[26] allowing three private channels that would be introduced in accordance with a technical plan to be approved at a later date. Some months later, a Royal Decree[27] stated that private TV channels should start broadcasting in the main Spanish cities, including Barcelona, Valencia and Palma, before spreading to other areas; thus, the "free market" made private Catalan TV stations and/or the use of Catalan in private TV stations "technically" unviable. The law and the decree were apparently non-linguistic, but proved devastating for Catalan.

First, television in Spanish gained an appearance of increased pluralism, with which a single, public channel could not compete. There are many kinds of programmes that private channels can produce that cannot be produced by public channels. In the long run, this made Spanish language television appear more innovative than Catalan.

Second, TV stations were eager to consume soapoperas, films, music, and cartoons. Thus, the "free market" sucked the cultural industries in Spain towards Madrid and/or towards Castilian, including TV producers and actors, and the film and music industries.

Third, private TV stations have, since their inception, followed a strictly monolingual language policy: all films are dubbed in Castilian, foreign interviewees are dubbed, all production is done only in Castilian. The only examples of bilingualism on Spanish TV channels are provided by music sung in English. Spanish language TV reproduces a monolingual ethos that makes linguistic diversity a rare abnormality. By contrast, Castilian is widely present on the Catalan-speaking TV chains, in the form of Castilian-speaking interviewees – never dubbed or subtitled – music, commercials, and so on; indeed, most soapoperas set in Catalonia tend to include some characters who speak Castilian "for the sake of realism".

Finally, the abundance of Castilian language mass media reduces the need to learn and use Catalan in Catalonia, Valencia or the Balearic Islands. In fact, throughout the Catalan language area, the consumption of Catalan TV tends to be reduced to native Catalan speakers; to most Castilian speakers, the products and characters on the Catalan stations are almost foreign.[28]

4.6. On dilemmas, conflicts and discourses

The development of the different language policies has prompted numerous dilemmas. The different language-in-education policies provide a good example.[29] The 1978 Constitution requires that children all over Spain must finish compulsory education knowing Castilian. However, autonomous communities with a language of their own are responsible for answering the following questions:

1. Should all children learn the language of the autonomous community?
2. Should school models prevent the construction of (potentially) antagonistic linguistic communities?
3. Should parents enjoy the right to select the language of education?

In Catalonia and, partially, in the Balearic Islands, the choice has been to guarantee points 1 and 2, at the expense of point 3: Catalan is the predominant language in teaching, and children are not separated according to their first language. In this way, all children become bilingual and biliterate,[30] but parents cannot choose the language of education. In Valencia, on the other hand, three different school programmes have been set up: one in Castilian, a second one in Catalan/Valencian, for native speakers, and a Catalan/Valencian immersion programme. In theory, parents can choose the language of education. But this freedom comes at a price: children attending programmes in Castilian never learn Catalan (see Section 5). Finally, in Aragon, education in Catalan is simply not available and even learning Catalan as a subject is complicated; parents must apply for it, and language courses are sometimes cancelled for arcane administrative reasons.

In short, Catalonian and Balearic language-in-education policies make school counterbalance the societal weight of Castilian in an attempt to ensure that Catalan is not in a minority position *vis-à-vis* the State language. In the Valencian and Aragonese systems, the school reaffirms the minority status imposed on Catalan.

It comes as no surprise that language issues have repeatedly entered parliaments, courts, and public debates over the last three decades. In this respect, September 12th 1993 was a turning point. On that day, the conservative newspaper *ABC* published a report entitled *Like Franco, but the other way round: persecution of Castilian in Catalonia*. Although the ultimate goal of the article was to force the Catalan government to stop supporting the minority Socialist government in Madrid, its consequences were to last, for ABC had triggered a debate that would become a persistent point of friction in contemporary Spanish political life.

It is impossible to review all the discussions about language policies in recent decades here, but at least two points should be kept in mind. First, not all actors have equal access to published opinion. In our case, pro-Castilian activists have free access to most Spanish media and enjoy considerable support in the State institutions, while pro-Catalan activists have far fewer opportunities to express their views publicly. On the other hand, the vocabulary used should be considered with caution. For instance, it is customary to represent the language policy conflicts as opposing (Catalan) *nationalists* to (Spanish) *non-nationalists, constitutionalists* or *liberals*. This opposition should be taken with a pinch of salt. It is understandable that, for strategic reasons, those seeking to promote Castilian depict themselves as *non-nationalist*; nevertheless, their rationales tend to be based on traditional imperialism and State nationalism.[31] The statements of Mr. Mariano Rajoy, leader of the Popular Party, when opposing the article of the 2006 Statute of Catalonia, which introduced the duty of knowing Catalan alongside Castilian for the citizens of Catalonia, are a case in point:

> [es] *lógico, si hay un principio inspirador que es la soberanía, y si afirmamos la nación [española], que haya el deber de conocer el idioma [castellano]*. [it is] logical, if there exists an inspiring principle which is sovereignty, and if we affirm the [existence of the Spanish] nation, that there exists the duty to know Castilian (Spanish Parliament's *Diario de Sesiones* n°. 499, session n°. 16, March 10th 2006, in Pons and Pla 2007: 200)

The rationale is crystal clear: there exists one nation, which is Spain; this nation must have one (single) language, which is Castilian; every Spaniard must know Castilian. This is what linguistic "liberalism" actually stands for in Spain: deregulation for Catalan plus maximum protection for Castilian. Indeed, it should be kept in mind that the 1978 Constitution, passed only three years after Franco's death, is built on an explicitly essentialist, nationalist assumption:

> Preliminary Title, Section 2
> The Constitution is based on the indissoluble unity of the Spanish Nation, the common and indivisible homeland of all Spaniards; it recognises and guarantees the right to self-government of the nationalities and regions of which it is composed and the solidarity among them all. [capital letters in the original; underlined here]

4.7. New immigrants, new responses?

Since the late 1990s, the Catalan language territories have attracted thousands of "new immigrants" from all over the world. At the same time, thousands of foreign residents – mostly well-off central and western Europeans – have moved to the Catalan language area in search of a better climate, and universities in the area have started to attract thousands of foreign students for short study periods (Table 1).

Language policies for the newcomers differ from area to area. In Valencia and, especially in La Franja, the authorities made little if any effort to encourage newcomers to learn Catalan. Initiatives were more vigorous in the academic world – see the *Unitat per a l'Educació Multilingüe at Alacant University*[32] – as well as among cultural and civic organisations, which designed projects for facilitating language learning, such as the *Voluntaris pel Valencià*[33] (Volunteers for Valencian).

Table 1. Evolution of foreign residents in Catalonia, Valencia and Balearic Islands 1994–2007. (Sources: Padrones 1994, 2003 and estimation for 1 January 2007. Website Instituto Nacional de Estadística: *http://www.ine.es/*. Our elaboration)

Area	1994		2003		2007	
	Number of foreigners	% of total population	Number of foreigners	% of total population	Number of foreigners	% of total population
Catalonia	83,296	1.3	623,947	9.3	966,004	13.4
Valencia	56,163	1.4	488,080	10.9	727,080	14.9
Balearic Isl.	25,895	3.3	146,046	15.4	189,437	18.4

In Catalonia and, to a certain extent, in the Balearic Islands, the arrival of the newcomers has meant a significant transformation in language policies in at least two ways. On the one hand, they injected new life into the activities of language teaching and promotion: new adult language courses were designed,[34] and campaigns were launched to encourage the use of Catalan by new immigrants – "*Tu ets mestre*", (lit. 'You are a teacher'), or *Voluntaris per la llengua*. The educational system was transformed, with a whole array of measures, such as new *aules d'acollida* (welcoming classes), and *plans d'entorn* (environmental plans) to integrate immigrant children in their local environment and to raise awareness in the community of the need to help newcomers to learn the local language.

The joint effects of globalisation and immigration required the creation of new discourses better able to explore forms of societal multilingualism and intercultural harmony (Marí 2002; Pueyo 2007). Today, new forms of civic nationalism are being developed in which the language is the vector of solidarity that goes beyond cultural diversity, rather than an old national heritage to be preserved.

5. Catalan at the beginning of the millennium

It is impossible to summarise here the progress made by Catalan in the areas of culture, officialdom, and formal uses (Pons and Vila 2005). Today Catalan is known by a majority of the population in Catalonia, Valencia, Balearic Islands and La Franja (see Figure 5). In many respects, Catalan is no longer a *minority* language in Catalonia and the Balearic Islands: it has become the predominant language of education from kindergarten to university and the local and autonomous governments.

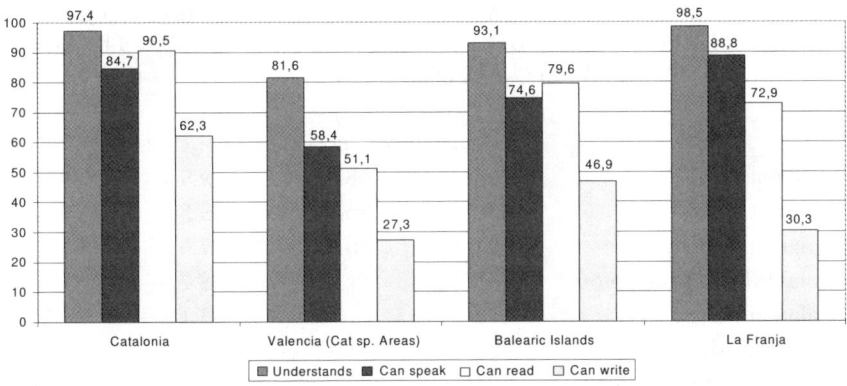

Figure 5. Knowledge of Catalan in Catalonia, Valencia, Balearic Islands and La Franja, in %, 2003–2004

It is widely used in all kinds of public and private mass media, and is well represented in the socio-economic sector. More than 8,000 books are published in Catalan each year, and Catalan is regularly found among the 10 most translated languages in the world and the 20 most used languages on the Internet. As a result of this vitality, Catalan culture was the guest of honour at the Frankfurt Book Fair in October 2007.

But three decades after the end of Franco's dictatorship, the situation of the Catalan language is still delicate. In general terms, the demolinguistic basis of Catalan was weaker in 2003–2004 than in the late 1970s, as shown by the data on "language at home" in Table 2 and Figure 4. There are three reasons for this: first, the older generations which included fewer Castilian speakers, were passing away; second, the majority of Castilian speakers did not learn and/or adopt Catalan as their everyday language of communication; and third, non-Catalan speakers continued to arrive, especially in the Balearic Islands. Indeed, Catalan may have gained ground in formal contexts – e.g. "in the bank" – especially in Catalonia,[35] but progress in status cannot counterbalance demographic movements in a context where Castilian remains compulsory and Catalan optional. In Catalonia, Catalan records gain in long-life and in intergenerational terms: compare, in Table 2, Catalan as an initial language, as the language used at home, as the language of identification (i.e., "which language do you consider as *yours*?"), and as the language used with (one's own) children. However, in the other territories, Catalan has not made progress in any of these dimensions.

Table 2. Percentages of indigenous population, language practices and identity in Catalonia, Valencia, Balearic Islands and Franja in 2003–2004 (Source: EUL 2003–2004, in Querol et al. 2007)

	Catalonia	Valencia*	Balearic Isl.	La Franja
Indigenous	71.9	68.9	59.9	89.0
Catalan at home	45.3	36.5	43.5	70.2
Catalan in the bank	59.0	30.0	47.0	31.0
Catalan when taking notes	35.7	–	18.2	9.6
Catalan initial	40.6	–	43.1	71.1
Catalan identification	48.8	–	45.6	66.6
Catalan with own children	50.9	39.3	48.3	72.2

* Catalan-speaking area

In other words: in Catalonia, where a vigorous language policy has been established, Catalan is managing to a certain extent to integrate newcomers; in the rest of the areas, processes of immigration (both from the rest of Spain and from abroad) are putting Catalan speakers in a minority position in demographic terms.

The evolution of language competence confirms the above diagnosis (see Figure 6). Knowledge of Catalan in Catalonia is gaining ground in spite of immigration, and this is especially due to the impact of schooling on the new generations.

By contrast, language-in-education policies in Valencia have not managed to promote linguistic competence – see particularly the (in)ability to write Valencian/Catalan. The situation in the Balearics stands half way between Catalonia and Valencia. Finally, knowledge of spoken Catalan in La Franja remains high due to the lack of immigration, but the ability to write Catalan remains low.

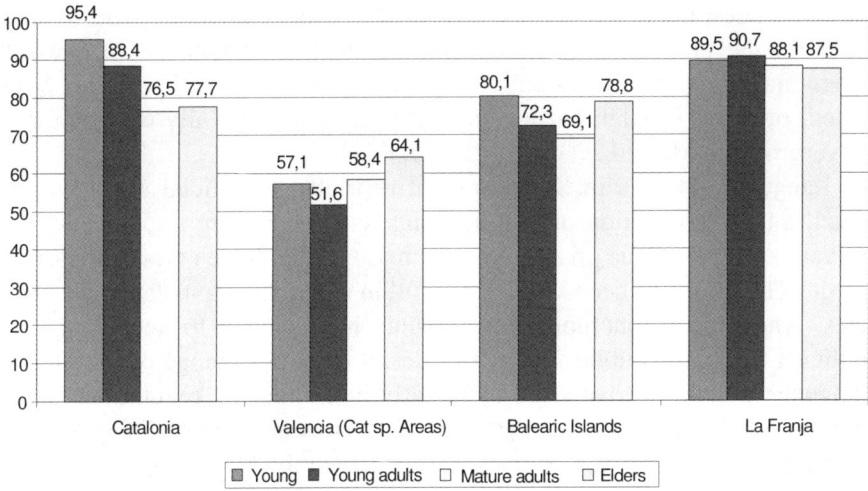

Figure 6. Ability to speak Catalan according to age in Catalonia, Valencia, Balearic Islands and Franja, 2003–2004, in %

6. Conclusion

Especially since the eighteenth century, the Spanish State has sought to impose the supremacy of Castilian throughout Spain. The fate earmarked for Catalan was that it should become a minority language and eventually disappear. Franco's dictatorship (1936/1939–1975) came close to that goal, but did not fully achieve it.

The post-Franco democratic system represented a change in course. The State embraced the defence of linguistic pluralism, although the 1978 Constitution was far from egalitarian, but it could be interpreted in a number of different ways. By themselves, the provisions of the 1978 Constitution are clearly not enough to guarantee the minimal protection of Catalan in its own territory, as proved by the case of La Franja, where Catalan is still not official. In the rest of the Catalan language area, it is only by political mobilisation that the language has achieved official status. Inevitably, then, the definition of public language policies has become heavily politicised. Not all autonomous governments have been in favour of Catalan. Some governments – especially in Catalonia – have sought to improve the status of the language, but others – for instance, Aragon and Valencia – have done little, if anything at all, to defend it. On the other hand, during the last three decades, the Spanish State has shown virtually no *motu proprio* concern for the promotion and recovery of Catalan. Catalan has progressed when and only when local and autonomous authorities and societies have acted, or when Catalan parties have been an important ally of a minority government in Madrid.

Language policies in Spain are not restricted to official agencies; indeed, a large proportion of (public) language policies are implemented by private agents, such as private schools, mass media, large corporations, and so on. The State has been very successful in externalising its language policies, while the autonomous governments have tended to keep language policies inside the public sector. Besides, a large percentage of the State's language policies derive from apparently non-linguistic regulations. Both approaches – relying on non-linguistic measures and externalising the implementation of language policies – have served the State well by reducing the visibility of its language policies.

The position of Catalan in Spain is complex and delicate: continuous immigration and the lack of State support places the language under considerable stress. Catalan is faring much better than other non-state languages in Europe, but its position is still precarious. This is especially so in Valencia, the Balearic Islands, and La Franja.

Can the Catalan experience be of use beyond its borders? Possibly. It may for instance help others to reconsider certain *idées reçues* in the social sciences. It is standard practice nowadays to blame so-called *romantic* nationalism for linguicidal policies, under the slogan "one nation, one language". In Spain, linguicidal policies have been historically implemented not in the name of any *Volksgeist* but rather in the name of "progress", "unity", "equality", and "efficiency". At least in this case, ethnolinguistic activism has for the most part resisted the (nation) State's efforts to wipe out subordinate languages: the so-called *romantic* nationalist demand "one language → one nation → one state" stands in opposition to the allegedly *non-nationalist* "one state → one nation → one language".

The Catalan experience is also a case in point for language planners who aim to make their societies thoroughly bilingual, a prospect that is well within reach for many middle-sized European linguistic communities. The Catalan case suggests that only by retaining – or regaining – a substantial number of societal functions will societal bilingualism be sustainable in the long run. Otherwise, the local language will be restricted to the local population, and increased geographic mobility will place its capacity of reproduction in grave danger. It goes without saying that State support remains crucial if languages such as Catalan are to shed their status as minority languages. To be sure, it was precisely the State that made Catalan a minority language; it remains to be seen whether Spain is able, or even willing, to put an end to this situation.

Notes

1. My thanks to professor Eva Pons for her comments on a previous version of this text.
2. Arabic had arrived in those areas with the Muslim invasion in the seventh century. The Romance dialects spoken in Valencia and the Balearic Islands seem to have disappeared at least one hundred years before these areas came back under Christian control.
3. At least up to the end of the twentieth century, the major ethnic division in the Catalan-speaking areas has been that distinguishing the locals – i.e., *Catalans, Valencians, Majorcans*, etc. – from *Castilians*, i.e., people from the former kingdom of Castile with Castilian as their first language (Woolard 1989).
4. English version in: *http://www.constitucion.es/constitucion/lenguas/ingles.html#p2*. All excerpts from the Constitution in this text come from this source.
5. Neither the judiciary nor the military powers went through a comparable process; today, both remain highly centralised and thoroughly *Castilianised*.
6. English version available in: *http://www.gencat.cat/generalitat/eng/estatut1979/index.htm*. All quotations come from this source.
7. In Catalan, this opposition is referred to as *doble oficialitat* rather than *cooficialitat*.
8. The text in Catalan says: "1. La <u>llengua pròpia</u> de Catalunya és el català." [our emphasis]. The notion *llengua pròpia* – akin to the idea of "property" – allowed Catalan legislators to introduce a nuance between Catalan and Castilian whereby the former was declared more closely connected to Catalan without declaring the other *alien*.
9. Available at: *http://bibiloni.net/legislacio/LNLC.htm*
10. The term *linguistic normalisation*, created in 1966 by the Valencian sociolinguist Lluís Vicent Aracil, had become popular during the previous decade as a label to denote the activities to promote Catalan.
11. Available at: *http://www6.gencat.net/llengcat/legis/lleipl.htm*
12. Available at: *http://www.gencat.net/generalitat/cat/estatut/*. See Argelaguet (2007) and Pons and Pla (2007).
13. Available at: *http://www.gva.es/cidaj/val/v-normas/4-1983.htm*
14. The possibility of a connection of this kind is totally rejected by both historians and linguists. See Guinot (1999).
15. *http://www.avl.gva.es/*

16. It should be remembered that the highest authority for Catalan in the whole of Spain is the Institut d'Estudis Catalans http://www.iec.cat/gc/ViewPage.action?siteNodeId=148&languageId=1&contentId=-1
17. Based on recent official surveys, Ros (2007: 111) estimates that around 38–42% of Valencian citizens consider "Valencian" to be an independent language, while 56% regard it as shared with Catalonia and the Balearic Islands. "Secessionists" are mostly found among the older generations and/or poorly educated sectors, while "unitarists" form the vast majority among the young – more than 60% between 16 and 34 years old – and those able to read and write the language.
18. In Castilian: http://www.boe.es/g/es/iberlex/normativa/estatutos_autonomia.php
19. Available at: http://www.caib.es/govern/informacio/index.do?path=/webcaib/governilles/estatut_autonomia/estatut&lang=ca
20. Available at: http://www.caib.es/govern/informacio/index.do?path=/webcaib/governilles/estatut_autonomia/estatut&lang=ca
21. Available at: http://www.cortesaragon.es/Reforma_del_Estatuto.786.0.html
22. With only a few exceptions: since the 2005 Reform of the Senate regulations, citizens and institutions may address the Senate in any official language (additional provision 4), and these languages can be used in some circumstances by Senate members (art. 59 bis 9; art. 191.2).
http://www.senado.es/reglamen/indices/reglamen_insis.html
23. Available at: http://www.coe.int/T/E/Legal_affairs/local_and_regional democracy/regional_or_minority_languages/2_Monitoring/Monitoring_table.asp#TopOfPage
24. Not to mention European regulations requiring labelling to be written in an official European language.
25. Often next to Portuguese, French, Italian, Greek, even Russian, Latvian, Kazakh, not to mention bidialectal labels in Spanish and Argentinian Castilian.
26. Available at: http://noticias.juridicas.com/base_datos/Admin/l10-1988.html
27. Available at: http://www.mityc.es/NR/rdonlyres/2D7B7F31-F996-4A82-9468-0D69D7445E4B/0/1Rd136288.pdf
28. See cultural language practices at http://www.escacc.org/escacc/ca/barometre.html
29. See a thorough discussion of language-in-education policies in the Catalan territories in Vila (in press).
30. In the Catalan context, where Castilian is dominant in mass media and the professional sphere and where Castilian speakers have traditionally been monolingual, experience and research show that Castilian children only learn Catalan in models where this language is clearly predominant. See Arnau (2004) for language competences at school levels in Catalonia.

31. Billig's (1995) notion of *banal nationalism* is clearly relevant here.
32. See *http://www.ua.es/uem/index.html*
33. See *http://www.escolavalenciana.org/voluntariat/2005/*
34. See *http://www.cpnl.cat/*
35. In Valencia, the comparison would be incorrect, because it includes the whole territory in 1978 and Valencian speaking areas only in 2004.

References

Argelaguet i Argemí, Jordi
    2007   La qüestió lingüística en els primers passos del procés de reforma de l'Estatut d'autonomia de Catalunya (1999–2003). *Revista de Llengua i Dret* 47: 145–182.

Arnau, Joaquim
    2004   Sobre les competències en català i castellà dels escolars de Catalunya: una resposta a la polèmica sobre el decret d'hores de castellà. *LSC - Llengua Societat i Comunicació*, 1: 1–7.
            http://www.ub.edu/ cusc/LSC_set.htm

Billig, Michael
    1995   *Banal Nationalism*. London: Thousand Oaks. New Delhi: Sage.

Climent-Ferrando, Vicent
    2005   *The Origins and Evolution of Language Secessionism in Valencia. An Analysis from the Transition Period until Today*. Barcelona: CIEMEN – Mercator.
            http://www.ciemen.org/mercator/pdf/wp18-def-ang.pdf

Ferrer i Gironès, Francesc
    1985   *La Persecució Política de la Llengua Catalana. Història de les mesures preses contra el seu ús des de la Nova Planta fins avui*. Barcelona: Edicions 62.

Guinot, Enric
    1999   *Els Fundadors del Regne de València*, vol. 2: Tres i Quatre.

Marí, Isidor
    2002   *Una Política Intercultural per a les Balears? Informe per al Debat*. Palma: Direcció General de Cultura, Conselleria d'Educació i Cultura (Govern de les Illes Balears); "SA NOSTRA" Caixa de Balears, Fundació "SA NOSTRA".

Milian i Massana, Antoni
    2007   El règim jurídic de la llengua catalana amb l'Estatut d'autonomia del 1979: balanç i perspectives. *Revista de Llengua i Dret*, 47: 307–351.

Monés i Pujol-Busquets, Jordi
   1995   Les colònies escolars. In *Història, Política, Societat i Cultura dels Països Catalans. Volume 8. L'època dels grans moviments socials. 1900–1930*, B. de Riquer i Permanyer (ed.), 312–315 Barcelona: Enciclopèdia Catalana.
Pons Parera, Eva and Anna M. Pla Boix
   2007   La llengua en el procés de reforma de l'Estatut d'autonomia de Catalunya (2004-2006). *Revista de Llengua i Dret*, 47: 183–226.
Pons, Eva and F. Xavier Vila i Moreno
   2005   *Informe Sobre la Situació de la Llengua Catalana (2003–2004)*. Barcelona: Observatori de la Llengua.
            http://www.observatoridelallengua.org/arxius_documents/informe6_ok.pdf
Pradilla Cardona, Miquel Àngel
   2004   *El Laberint Valencià. Apunts per a una Sociolingüística del Conflicte*. Benicarló: Onada.
Pueyo i París, Miquel
   2007   *La Política Lingüística com a Política Social*. Barcelona: Generalitat de Catalunya, Departament de la Vicepresidència, Secretaria de Política Lingüística.
Querol Puig, Ernest (coord.), Enrico Chessa, Natxo Sorolla, Joaquim Torres i Pla, with collaboration of Xavier Sanjuán, and Marina Solís
   2007   *Llengua i Societat als Territoris de Parla Catalana a l'Inici del Segle XXI. L'Alguer, Andorra, Catalunya, Catalunya Nord; la Franja, Illes Balears i Comunitat Valenciana*. Barcelona: Generalitat de Catalunya, Departament de Vicepresidència, Secretaria de Política Lingüística.
Rodríguez Osuna, Jacinto
   1979   Estudios del CIS: desarrollo regional, democracias. *Revista Española de Investigaciones Sociológicas* 6: 183–233.
Ros, Honorat
   2007   El valencià a les comarques castellanoparlants. In *A Alacant, en Valencià. Observatori de la Llengua (2003/2005)*, J.V. Forcadell Saport and F. Isabel i Vilar (eds.), 119–124. Alacant: Universitat d'Alacant.
Vila i Moreno, F. Xavier
   2006   Una, dues... moltes? Llengües inicials i transmissió lingüística a Catalunya. In *Seminari: La Multiculturalitat i les Llengües, Centre Ernest Lluch-CUIMP, 10 d'octubre 2006*, 137–155. Barcelona: Centre Ernest Lluch – Universitat Internacional Menéndez y Pelayo.
   in press Language-in-education policies. In *Language Policies in the Catalan Language Area*, E. Boix-Fuster and M. Strubell i Trueta (eds.). Berlin: Springer.

Woolard, Kathryn A.
   1989   *Double Talk. Bilingualism and the Policy of Ethnicity in Catalonia.*
              Stanford: Stanford University Press.

Frisian in the Netherlands

Durk Gorter, Cor van der Meer and Alex Riemersma

1. Introduction

Today Frisian is spoken in the province of Friesland (*Fryslân*) in the north-western part of the Netherlands. In the early Middle Ages, Frisian was spoken over a much larger area. The language area covered a narrow strip along the North Sea coast in what are now the Dutch provinces of *Zuid-Holland, Noord-Holland, Friesland* and *Groningen* and also in the adjoining area of East Friesland (*Ostfriesland*) in the north-west of Germany up to the *Weser* river. Over the ages, Frisian gradually disappeared from these areas (Niebaum 2001). The administrative borders of the province of Friesland today coincide well with the geographic area in which Frisian is spoken.

Contrary to popular belief throughout history, the area has never been a homogeneous monolingual area. Frisian evolved into a separate language somewhere between 500 and 700 AD when variants of North Sea Germanic (also called *Ingweonic*) grew wider apart (Bremmer 1997: 69–70). Historically, (West-) Frisian is closely related to English. Both languages are part of the larger West Germanic language group, which also includes Afrikaans, Yiddish, German and Dutch. (West-) Frisian does have strong linguistic relationships to Sater Frisian and North Frisian, both located in Germany. Over one thousand years, their historical development was separated. Today the three languages differ rather strongly from one another and cannot be treated as one minority language with three variants. In the rest of this chapter, we will only refer to Frisian in the Netherlands.

In the late Middle Ages, a change from Latin to the vernacular took place in many places in Europe. As a result of this transition, Frisian was widely used in writing during the 14th and 15th centuries, but there was never a monolingual literacy tradition. Most of the scribes got their training outside Friesland and many of them were multilingual in at least Frisian, Dutch and Latin (Vries 1997). When in 1498 Friesland acquired new rulers, outside influences became increasingly important. During the 16th and 17th centuries the province of Friesland became politically, economically, socially, culturally and religiously incorporated into the newly established

Republic of the Low Countries. During the 16th century, Frisian texts became scarce and a complete transition to written Dutch took place in about 80 years (Vries 1997). During the same period, many civil servants and traders settled in the province, bringing new languages with them, particularly forms of early Dutch. Due to this intensive language contact a mixed language arose in the seven major towns of Friesland. Although designated as *town-Frisian*, it is a dialect of Dutch (Jonkman 1993; Van Bree 1994). This town-Frisian is still spoken today, but it is declining rapidly and is being replaced by standard Dutch. The Frisian language itself kept a stronghold as a spoken variety in the countryside. As a result of language contact over several centuries, the development of Frisian was influenced most by Dutch. During the 17th and 18th centuries Frisian hardly functioned as a written language at all. A movement to revive Frisian began in the early 19th century (Zondag 1993). Only in the 20th century does the Frisian language regain a modest position in government, education and the media (Gorter 2001a and below).

2. Current sociolinguistic situation

For almost any minority language it is difficult to know exactly how many speakers there are. In many cases there are no statistics at all, only rough estimates which can often widely diverge between government officials, language activists and linguistic experts. In other cases, the census of a country may be just about the only source of information. In the case of the Frisian language there are no census figures because the Netherlands never included a question on language in its censuses (the last census was held in 1970). Yet in Friesland several studies were carried out that yielded fairly reliable estimates of numbers of speakers. The most recent study was carried out at the request of the provincial government in 2007 (Provinsje Fryslân 2007).

The number of speakers of a minority language can be estimated according to different criteria (Extra and Gorter, this Volume). It is common in a census to look at the number of first language (or "mother tongue") speakers. Another criterion is the number of people that are able to speak the language. A third criterion is related to language use, for instance the most commonly used language or the language currently spoken at home. In the case of the Frisian language there are recent figures relating to mother tongue and to language proficiency; for data on language use in different domains, we have to rely on figures from earlier surveys in the 1990s.

The most recent study shows that 54.3% of the adult population of Friesland has Frisian as its mother tongue, as "the language used by the parents of the interviewee while growing up" (Provinsje Fryslân 2007: 14–16). It means that just over half of the population of the province have Frisian as the language of their youth. If we extrapolate this percentage to the total population, the number of mother tongue speakers of Frisian can be calculated to be 349,000 (out of a total population of 643,000, January 2008). However, this figure needs to be adjusted. First of all, the four Wadden islands with a total of 10,000 inhabitants, few of whom speak Frisian, were not included in the survey. Secondly, it should also be taken into account that younger people less often have Frisian as their mother tongue (see below). Therefore the number of mother tongue speakers has to be adjusted downward to around 325,000. One could add a number of Frisian speakers in the adjacent area of the province of Groningen and thousands of Frisian speakers that have emigrated to the rest of the Netherlands or abroad over the past few decades. However, there are no studies that can give any reliable estimates of the number of Frisian speakers outside the province of Friesland.

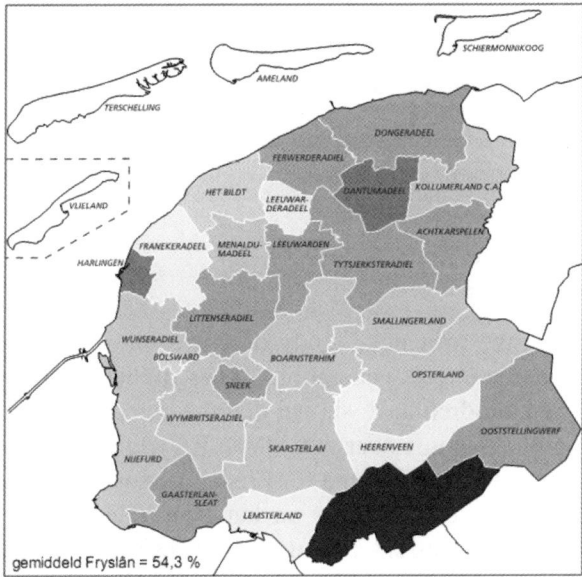

Figure 1. Geographic distribution of Frisian as a mother tongue

In Section 1, town-Frisian and some other regional variants were mentioned and it will thus not come as a surprise that Frisian as a mother tongue is not equally spread over the geographic area of the province. The ancient concentrations of Frisian and the different variants in specific municipalities or towns can still be observed in the distribution of mother tongue speakers over the 31 municipalities of Friesland. The contrast between Frisian-speaking areas and traditional dialect areas may have become less sharp but still exists. The map shows that Frisian traditionally has more speakers in the countryside and less in some of the larger towns, on the islands, in the area of It Bilt and in the two south-eastern municipalities of the Stellingwerven (in which a Low-Saxon variant is more prominent).

As we pointed out, the first estimation of the total number of speakers did not take into account the unequal distribution over the age groups. The older generation more often have Frisian as their mother tongue than the younger generation. As the survey figures show, there is a gradual decline. The percentage has gone down from almost 60% in the age bracket of 65 and orlder, to almost 50% among the age group between 18 and 29 years old. Figure 2 shows this gradual decline (Province 2007: 14).

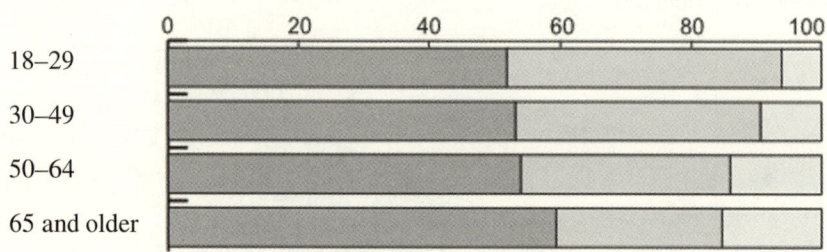

Figure 2. Mother tongue according to age group

The figures from the provincial study only include adults and do not inform us about the youngest generation. Other studies among primary and secondary school children have shown that the percentage among children around the age of 12 is just over 40% (Van Ruijven 2000; Van der Bij en Valk 2005). Thus, the overall trend for Frisian is most certainly downward. This trend is confirmed by figures on language transmission to the next generation. Of *all* the current parents, about 48% speak Frisian to their children (and about 47% speak Dutch) (Provinsje Fryslân 2007: 17). Still another study (Foekema 2004) pointed out that this situation is less black-

and-white. The study only interviewed young parents (with children under the age of 13) and prospective parents. The results showed that some parents commonly speak both Frisian and Dutch to their children; some speak more Frisian than Dutch and others the other way around. The downward trend was confirmed and estimated at a decline of 11–12% less Frisian used by current parents of young children than one generation earlier. When both parents are Frisian-speaking, in almost all cases the language of the family will be also Frisian, but when one partner is Dutch-speaking, the whole family almost exclusively speak Dutch. The study also pointed out that raising a child in Frisian is usually not a conscious choice (Foekema 2004: 8).

Proficiency in Frisian is another way to estimate the strength and the potential use of the language. In the study of 2007, this was measured by a scale that runs from "very good", via "good", "reasonable" and "with effort" to "not at all". The same scale was used in earlier surveys. Because the linguistic distance between Frisian and Dutch is relatively small, over 90% of the population, i.e., almost all inhabitants of the province, indicate that they have the ability to understand Frisian. All mother tongue speakers of Frisian are also able to speak the language (language attrition inside the province thus far is a rare phenomenon). Also, a substantial part of the population has learned to speak Frisian as a second language; 74% indicate that they are able to speak Frisian at least reasonably well. This percentage implies that about 20% have learned to speak Frisian. This learning of Frisian in many cases cannot be the result of the teaching of Frisian at school. As we will see later, the amount of Frisian at schools is just too small. The main sources are early childhood experiences with playmates or the peer group, mainly again in the countryside, or learning Frisian later in life in the work situation.

Frisian is predominantly an oral language. This circumstance is confirmed by the percentages for proficiency in reading and writing, literacy skills that are typically learned at school. Again the language distance makes learning to read Frisian relatively easy once you know how to read Dutch; so quite a few people will have taught themselves how to read Frisian. Between 75 and 46% of the adult population can read Frisian, depending on whether you accept the answer *I can read Frisian reasonably well* as a "yes" or a "no". Writing is a more technical skill that only a minority of the population have mastered. Only 10% indicated that they were able to write "very well" or "well" and another 16% dicate that they have a "reasonable" command of writing in Frisian (Provinsje Fryslân 2007: 6–7).

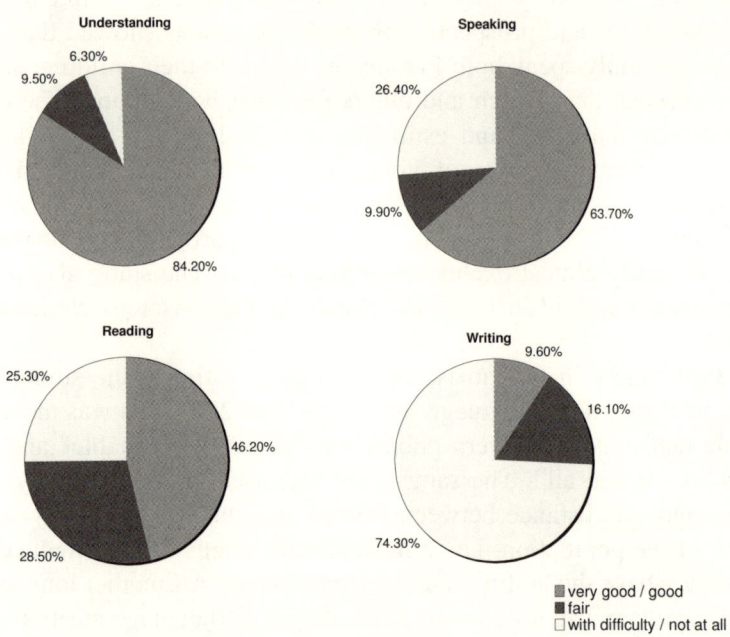

Figure 3. Level of Frisian language command

These figures for proficiency can be compared to three earlier population surveys that were carried out in 1967 (Pietersen 1969), 1980 (Gorter et al. 1984) and 1994 (Gorter and Jonkman 1995). The results of these surveys show a remarkable stability over a period of 40 years. There is a slight decrease in understanding Frisian, some decrease in speaking ability, a minor increase in being able to read and a substantial increase in the ability to write the language. There is also some shift away from the answering category "very good" towards "good" or "reasonable", which might indicate people being less certain about their oral skills.

The former sociolinguistic surveys contain many questions on language use in different situations. The patterns of language use that surface from the surveys are similar to what is found for many other minority languages in Europe. The more formal a situation is, the less likely a person who is able to speak Frisian will indeed also use the language. Moreover, language choice seems in many cases to be 'person bound'; if the interlocutor is known to be a Frisian speaker, people will accommodate.

For language use it is very important whether Frisian was learned as a first or as a second language. For instance, of the first-language speakers, 22% answered they would speak Frisian to a medical specialist in a hospital, whereas only 5% of second-language learners would use Frisian. It seems clear that such a situation is defined by most people as a "Dutch-language situation". In contrast, 85% of those who had Frisian as L1 responded they would use Frisian with the assistant in the shop where they do their daily shopping. But only 42% of L2-speakers would do the same (Gorter and Jonkman 1995). Another question in the same survey illustrates that language choice depends almost completely on the interlocutor. All respondents were asked to situate themselves in a shop in a larger town and answer the question of the language they would choose for the interaction with a shop-assistant. They were first asked *What language do you speak when you are spoken to in Frisian by the salesperson?*, and secondly, its complement: *When the salesperson speaks Dutch to you?* The results were very clear. When a salesperson addresses the respondent in Frisian, almost all Frisian speakers (with Frisian as their first language) will also use Frisian in return (98%). However, when the salesperson addresses them in Dutch, over three quarters of the Frisian speakers accommodates to the shop-assistant and answers in Dutch. Only 22% continue to speak Frisian in the case of a Dutch speaking shop-assistant. For second language learners the outcomes are totally different. Here only one-third converge to a Frisian speaking salesperson by answering in Frisian. In the case of a Dutch speaking salesperson, hardly any L2-speaker will answer in Frisian. As a rule, Dutch is the "unmarked", safe choice between strangers. It will not come as a surprise that many non-Frisians notice that they hear only little Frisian spoken in the streets of the capital of Leeuwarden.

Besides the degree of formality and the interlocutor, language attitudes also are of some importance. Attitudes towards the Frisian language vary widely among the population. Frisian speakers seem to be basically positively inclined to their language. They express a certain emotional attachment and there is widespread agreement on the "beauty" and "value" of Frisian. At the same time, speakers can wholeheartedly oppose certain specific measures to promote the use of Frisian, e.g., for education or public administration (Gorter and Jonkman 1995). Frisian is taken to be important; for instance of all of the (prospective) young parents in the study mentioned earlier, almost 60% on average agreed that Frisian was "very important" or "important" to them. Half of them would regret it a great deal if Frisian were to disappear in the future and one third would regret it to some degree (Foekema 2004: 16–17). Similar positive opinions were found in the earlier surveys (Gorter and Jonkman 1995; Gorter et al. 1984).

The number of immigrants from other countries has increased and so has the number of mother tongue speakers of foreign languages. It has been estimated that approximately 25,000 foreign-born migrants settled in Friesland in ten years time (Van der Vaart 2001: 15); they constitute 3% of the total population, a number that is much lower than in the central urbanised regions of the Netherlands. Most immigrants live in the larger towns of Friesland, not in the small villages. In the capital of Leeuwarden/Ljouwert (population 90,000), there are some 50 different languages spoken by primary school children at home (Van der Avoird et al. 2000). The five most common mother tongues among immigrants are English, Arabic, Kurdish, Hindi and Berber. Together these five languages cover 50% of all speakers of immigrant languages.

Over the last few decades, English has become increasingly important. English today is a second (or third) language rather than a foreign language. A European Union survey informs us that 87% of the Dutch population are able to carry on a conversation in English (Eurobarometer 2005: 5); this will not be much different in Friesland.

Due to trends in globalisation, almost all persons living in Friesland are confronted with English on a daily basis. Television is "English-speaking" a great deal of the time, because TV programmes are subtitled rather than dubbed. English is seen in public spaces on advertisements, in brand-names, in shops, bars, restaurants, etc. The whole linguistic landscape is permeated by English, either on its own or in combination with Dutch or other languages (Cenoz and Gorter 2006).

This combination of more immigrant languages spoken at home, and thus also in the public sphere, and English in the linguistic landscape and in the domain of popular culture and higher education by and large has led to an increase or multilingualism in the province of Friesland over the past few decades (Gorter 2001).

3. Language policy

In this section, an overview will be given of efforts to carry out corpus and status planning for Frisian, as well as of the position Frisian holds in the media, in the cultural domain and in economic and social affairs. Subsequently, Section 4 will deal with education more in detail.

3.1. Corpus planning

As with other European regional minority languages, a lot of work has been done since the 19th century to standardise Frisian. This was done among other things by means of dictionaries, grammars, text-books and by settling principles of spelling. The first dictionary of Frisian was compiled by the philologist Joast Halbertsma, (1789–1869) who unfortunately was not able to complete his dictionary. The dictionary materials were bequeathed to the provincial authorities. The Province took the responsibility of completing and publishing this work as *Friesch Woordenboek* (1900–1911). This Frisian-Dutch dictionary has served the learners and users of Frisian for many years. The dictionary also was the source for all later Frisian-Dutch and Dutch-Frisian dictionaries of the 20th century (1952–1956, 1971, 1984).

The first and most important task of the *Fryske Akademy* (founded in 1938, funded by both the provincial and the national governments) was to produce a scientific *Woordenboek der Friese taal/Wurdboek fan de Fryske taal* ('Dictionary of the Frisian language'). This dictionary has been described as "a scholarly, alphabetically arranged, historic dictionary, with Dutch as its metalanguage and covering the Frisian language from 1800–1975" (Dijkstra 2001: 151). As with similar efforts for other minority languages, this dictionary is not only a form of corpus planning, but because of its monumental character and prestige it is also part of status planning. The first volume was published in 1984; since then almost every year one volume of about 400 pages has been published. The 25th and final volume will be completed by the year 2010.

All dictionaries of Frisian in the 20th century use Dutch as the metalanguage for the description of meaning, etc. The reason given for this is that it makes the dictionary more accessible for non-Frisian readers. The use of Dutch does put Frisian in the position of a secondary, dependent language that cannot be used on its own. The first Frisian-Frisian dictionary will break through this pattern and is planned for publication in 2008.

Already in the 19th century a number of partial grammars of Frisian were published. These grammar books were mainly used for teaching Frisian as a mother tongue to adults, prescribing the orthography, phonology and morphological rules of Frisian. A number of descriptive Frisian grammars according to international linguistic standards were published by Sipma (1913), Fokkema (1948) and Cohen et al. (1959), Tiersma (1985) and Popkema (2006). A common feature of all Frisian grammars is that they are contrastive Frisian-Dutch grammars using Dutch or English as the metalanguage of description. The first textbook that contained a complete grammar was aimed at learners of Frisian as a second language (Van der Woude 1960). The *Afûk*, the institute for adult courses, has published a variety of text books and materials for first and second language learners of Frisian as well as for school children.

The first attempt to standardise the orthography of Frisian dates back to 1879. This spelling system can be characterised as phonological-etymological. After the Second World War, the *Fryske Akademy* developed a revised spelling system that was easier to learn and to apply. However, since 1969 the provincial government has taken responsibility for the orthographic system of Frisian, parallel to the Netherlands' Minister of Education, who is responsible for the spelling of Dutch.

In 1980, with the introduction of Frisian as a compulsory subject in primary education, the spelling of Frisian was simplified further. It was harmonised as much as possible with the spelling of Dutch. Today the Frisian language can be read with relative ease by those who already know Dutch. The introduction of the spell checker for Word 97 in 1998 (upgraded with a full language help function in 2004) seems to have stimulated the use of Frisian in writing. The Frisian language today has been fully codified and corpus planning is no longer a priority in language policy, except for the development of tools to increase the use of Frisian.

3.2. Status planning

During the 20th century a slow process of legal codification took place. Step by step certain provisions for the use of Frisian in the domains of education, the judiciary, public authorities and cultural affairs have been created. The Frisian language has been officially recognised as the second language of the Netherlands. Later, in 1996, that formal recognition resulted in the ratification by the Dutch state of the *European Charter for Regional or Minority Languages* as well as the *Framework Convention on the Protection of National Minorities* in 2005. However, there is no clause in the Constitution of The Netherlands about the Frisian language (nor about the Dutch language), nor is there a general Frisian language law.

According to the *Covenant on Frisian Language and Culture* (2001), the responsibility for the protection and promotion of Frisian language and culture is the common responsibility of national, provincial and local authorities. In practice, however, the province is the first actor who takes initiatives towards both the municipalities and the central government. The trend in national government policy is to decentralise the responsibility to the regions; however, without providing the regions with enough financial resources. This tendency not only creates tensions between the central and regional levels, but is also criticised by the Council of Europe in its evaluation reports on the implementation of the *European Charter for Regional or Minority Languages* (Council of Europe 2004).

Already in 1907 Frisian in education started without a legal base when a subvention for teaching some lessons outside the regular school hours was given by the provincial authorities. The Dutch state government saw no need to make arrangements for Frisian. Only some 30 years later, in 1937, Frisian obtained a modest place in the state law on the curriculum where it was mentioned as a "living dialect". This law permitted the use of Frisian in the highest grades of primary school and only for reading skills. In 1995, a new state law on education allowedFrisian as the medium of instruction for reading, writing and mathematics in grades 1 to 3. This provided a legal basis for bilingual schools that worked with a transitional model. During the 1950s–1970s about 20% of all primary schools worked with this model. In 1980, the law specified that Frisian was an obligatory part of the curriculum in all primary schools in Friesland (with exceptions for some dialect-speaking areas). Frisian has also been granted a legal place in secondary education, as a compulsory subject in the lower grades and as an optional subject for the final exams.

The first legal steps for the use of Frisian in the judiciary domain came about as the result of a street riot in the Frisian capital of Leeuwarden, when protesters were harassed by the police. That day in November 1951 is known as *Kneppelfreed* (Cudgels Friday). The immediate cause was a dispute over the use of Frisian in the courts. The final outcome was a law in 1956 that afforded a limited place to Frisian by permitting its oral use in the courts as well as in contacts with public authorities. It took another 40 years before t the written usage of Frisian was formally permitted. In 1995, a new Act on Administrative Law was passed that deals with the organisation of public administration in the Netherlands. In this act, the use of Dutch was, for the first time, established as the common rule. An exception was made for the province of Friesland, where the use of Frisian both spoken and in writing was in principle allowed in all kinds of legal documents. The Act finally created a legal base for the tradition of written Frisian in the minutes of official meetings of the provincial assembly and of many municipality councils.

Similarly, in 1997, the written use of Frisian in the courts was permitted by law. Since then it has been possible to use Frisian in all legal affairs including documents. Today, at the entrance of the court rooms in Leeuwarden, a bilingual sign informs everyone that it is permitted to use Frisian. In practice, Frisian is used in court cases only occasionally, due to hard-dying traditions, socio-psychological reasons and the lack of Frisian language proficiency on the part of defence lawyers.

The same act of 1997 prescribed that all certificates of birth, marriage and death in the province of Friesland should be drafted in both Dutch and Frisian. The consequence was that the use of Frisian during wedding ceremonies has increased a lot (De Vries 2003).

In the past, the use of geographical names, in particular place names, repeatedly was the topic of heated debates. As from 1997 the official name of the province is *Fryslân*, but both *Fryslân* and Friesland are commonly used. About half of the 31 municipalities have an official Frisian name. The official names are also placed on the signposts (in one language) while most road maps and car navigation systems show all names bilingually. As recently as 2005, the provincial government agreed with all municipalities (except one) to introduce Frisian-only names for canals, lakes and rivers.

3.3. Media

The media reflect that Frisian is mainly an oral language. There are no daily newspapers in Frisian. The two major daily newspapers contain a very small number of Frisian texts and one whole page in Frisian once a week. There is one general monthly magazine (*De Moanne*, 'the month' as well as 'the moon'). The traditional literary journals have in recent years got electronic competitors such as *Farsk* ('fresh') and *Doar* ('door') through the Internet. Young authors and poets also feel free to express themselves in both languages and they are perfectly biliterate.

The provision for radio and television is modest and Frisian is commonly used as a spoken language. The number of hours broadcast on the radio by the regional station *Omrop Fryslân* has increased considerably during the last decade, from 6.00 in the morning till 11.00 at night on all weekdays. In 1994, one hour of original daily TV-programming was introduced. Today, this is almost two hours (plus continuous re-runs). These programmes are well-received and have relatively high viewing rates. On its TV-channel, *Omrop Fryslân* has a continuous teletext service after broadcasting hours, which is the same news service as on its website. Because all items are written in Frisian it implies that *Omrop Fryslân* functions as the first all-Frisian newspaper on the Internet.

3.4. Cultural domain

An important aspect of status planning as well as corpus planning is the promotion of reading and writing in the minority language. First of all, literary texts as found in poetry, fiction, the theatre, and in children's literature can have a stimulating effect. The tradition of literary prizes dates back to 1947 with the awarding of a provincial prize for Frisian literature. Later on prizes were awarded for literary debuts, for translations, for lyrics and for children's literature. Annually around 100 new Frisian books are published, including 30 non-fiction books (Oppewal et al. 2006: 16). Since 1971 the annual *Sutelaksje* (an activity in which books are sold from wheelbarrows that are pushed from door to door) is the most successful reading promotion activity of the province. Every autumn during a six-week campaign books are sold by volunteers in over 100 villages. Another feature that marks the position of Frisian as an oral language is the strong cultural tradition of choir singing and brass bands as well as performances by amateur theatre companies in almost every town and village. These cultural traditions served as important factors of social cohesion in Frisian villages and as important transmitters of Frisian language norms for all generations in the 20th century when formal education in Frisian was mostly lacking. *Tryater* is the only professional theatre company whose performaces are in Frisian. *Tryater* successfully plays world repertoire as well as newly written dramatic work for full audiences (Oldenhof 2006).

For the promotion of Frisian song writing in 1990 the initiative was taken to organise an annual song contest *Liet* ('song'). The model of *Liet* has been exported and turned into an international song contest in lesser-used languages *Liet International,* which started in Leeuwarden in 2002 and was followed by an edition in Galicia in 2004 and in Sweden in 2006 and 2008 under the name *Liet-Lavlut*, a combination of Frisian and Sami.

Overall, these activities demonstrate that Frisian has a strong position in the cultural domain, in particular in forms where oral expression is important.

3.5. Economic and social affairs

The use of Frisian in commercial contacts can have an added value for business (Van Langevelde 1999). Frisian labels on products and on displays as well as in commercials on radio and television are increasing. However, the number of Frisian advertisements in the daily newspapers does not exceed 1%. On radio and television the situation is slightly better, but the total number of Frisian commercials is less than 10%. In contrast, the number of family announcements (for birth, marriage and death) in Frisian in the daily newspapers has increased from 10% in the 1970s to 40% in 2002 (De Vries 2003: 15).

In the health sector, the use of Frisian in contacts with older clients in particular is considered a positive factor. In most hospitals and homes for the elderly, the informal oral use of Frisian is common. In the latest language policy document of the province of Friesland, the chapter on the health sector has two spearheads: improving the situation for elderly people on the one hand and for young parents on the other. The aim is to reach at least 50% of all young parents, in particular those in mixed-language families. First of all, relevant information on raising children in Frisian and/or bilingually is delivered to expecting mothers and fathers. Secondly, parents of a newborn child get a "language bag" at the registrars' office. Thirdly, the *Afûk* in co-operation with the public library service is active with the *Tomke project*, a comprehensive reading-promotion project including booklets, CDs, an interactive website (*www.tomke.nl*) and a television show. These promotional activities are aimed at young parents and teachers and leaders of pre-school provisions (playgroups and day care centres).

4. Education

One hundred years of Frisian in education was celebrated in 2007. As mentioned before, the beginning of the teaching of Frisian was as an extra-curricular subject in a few schools. Today, the Frisian language still plays a small but a much more important role in education. Given this substantial period of time, the position of the Frisian language in education is modest, all the more so when compared to some other minority languages in Europe. The educational system in Friesland does not differ from the educational system in the rest of the Netherlands. As a matter of principle, schools have a lot of freedom and can choose their own educational methods and materials.

4.1. Pre-primary education

Pre-primary education is for children between the ages of 2.5 and 4. This type of education is not part of compulsory education in Friesland or the Netherlands. Playgroups are mostly privately run, sometimes by volunteers, under the supervision of the municipality. Children usually go to playgroups two mornings or afternoons per week. Day-care centres where children go several days a week or the whole week are usually larger in size than playgroups (Boneschansker and Le Rütte 2000). In 1989, the *Stifting Pjutteboartersplak* was established as an umbrella foundation of playgroups that create an all Frisian-speaking environment for young children. Their Frisian language playgroups accept both Frisian and Dutch-speaking children, and the children with Dutch as their home language will thus be immersed in Frisian. In 2005, the foundation was taken over by the *Stifting Frysktalige Berneopfang* (Foundation for Frisian-language child care). In the last few years, the number of day care centres and playgroups has grown steadily. In 2008, the foundation catered for almost 60 bilingual or Frisian-medium playgroups and day-care centres and looked after around 1,400 children. The most recent provincial policy plans show the ambition to increase the number of playgroups and day-care centres to 110 by the end of 2010.

4.2. Primary education

Children go to primary schools in the Netherlands from the ages of 4 to 12. The average size of primary schools in Friesland is about 130 pupils, which is substantially smaller than in the rest of the Netherlands (217 on average). There are 486 primary schools in Friesland with 62,815 children (2006/2007, Provinsje Fryslân 2008). The Primary Education Act lists a number of subjects and targets that all primary schools have to meet without prescribing the exact amount of hours and how the school needs to teach. The Frisian language has been a compulsory subject since 1980 and schools are allowed to use Frisian as a medium of instruction. Schools may ask the provincial government to be exempted from this rule, but only a very small number of schools have an exemption. In practice, however, about 6% of the primary schools do not offer any Frisian at all.

In an evaluation report of the Committee of Experts (European Charter 2004), the situation for primary education was described as "intolerable" because the average time investment for Frisian is only between 30 and 45 minutes per week. In a study by the Mercator Research Centre (De Jager and Van der Meer 2007), it was shown that an average time investment of 5–6 hours per week would be consistent with the undertakings of the *European Charter for Regional and Minority Languages*.

Thus, time spend on Frisian as a subject on average is very limited, and there has not been any change for years. About half of all primary schools use Frisian to some extent as a medium of instruction, mainly for the creative subjects or to teach physical exercise. The amount of time spent on Frisian is between 10 and 35% of the teaching time and usually more often in the lower grades than in the higher. The target attainment levels as defined in 1993 by the Ministry of Education were identical for Dutch and Frisian. The targets did not work for Frisian and were reviewed and modified in 2006. The new targets have been lowered and are supposed to better reflect actual educational practice, especially for Frisian as a first and as a second language.

Although the teacher qualification for Frisian is described officially in the Primary Education Act, teacher-training institutes are responsible for the content of the training and for the examinations for the qualification of teachers. The Inspectorate (Inspectie 2006) reported that only 67% of all primary school teachers have the qualification to teach Frisian.

In the year 1997, a small group of seven primary schools started a project to experiment with a model of trilingual education. The three languages used were Frisian, Dutch and English (Ytsma 2000; Gorter 2005). The experiment ended in 2006 and proved to be a relative success. The trilingual schools continue collaboration in a network which is already growing slowly (17 participating schools in 2007/2008). The goal is to establish full bilingualism for Frisian and Dutch, but for English the goal is to achieve better communicative skills on a basic and functional level. All three languages are used as medium of instruction; for grades 1 to 6, Dutch and Frisian are both used 50% of the teaching time. In grades 7 and 8, the division of time becomes 40% Dutch, 40% Frisian and 20% English. The whole experiment was evaluated through a longitudinal research project by the *Fryske Akademy*. Based on research in other multilingual areas, expectations were confirmed for this project in Friesland. The substantial extra investment of time in Frisian does not have an effect on the language proficiency of the dominant language Dutch, but the children have a much better command of Frisian compared to the control groups. The small additional amount of English instruction time does not lead to higher skill levels; it results in just a bit more confidence in the use of English by the pupils (Van Ruijven and Ytsma 2007).

4.3. Secondary education

Secondary education in the Netherlands is attended by 12 to 18-year-olds. In Friesland, there are 30 secondary school-institutes, some of which have different branches, so that there are 58 "establishments", with a total of 60,670 pupils (2006/2007, Provinsje Fryslân 2008). In 1993, Frisian became a compulsory subject in the lower grades of secondary education in the province of Friesland. The authority to give an exemption to individual schools was transferred in 2006 from the state to the provincial authorities. Of the 58 secondary schools, there are 10 that have such an exemption. Frisian is an optional exam subject in secondary education that is taken up by few students.

New target attainment levels for Frisian in 2006 for the lower grades differentiate between pupils with Frisian as their first and second language. A new teaching method *Freemwurk* was recently introduced. The method explicitly aims at achieving the key objectives through extra differentiation materials and it includes IT-methods of learning. Also, new materials have been developed for the highest grades. These methods can be used together with school television programmes and the magazine *Linkk* as well as with the electronic learning environment *Digischool*.

A survey conducted by the Inspectorate in 1999 and repeated 5 years later showed that the implementation of Frisian in the lower levels had not developed much. Over a third of the secondary schools do not offer Frisian lessons to their pupils. The schools that do offer Frisian lessons mostly do so in grade 1 for all students and in grade 2 as an optional subject. Only students who want to take their final exam in Frisian can follow lessons in the two higest grades (Inspectie 2006). The inspectorate concluded that the Frisian lessons do not contribute meaningfully to the linguistic and cultural development of the students. At school level, there is no clear idea of Frisian as a subject or about the use of Frisian as a medium of instruction (Inspectie 2006).

It must be concluded that the position of Frisian in secondary education is marginal, especially as a medium of instruction. The committee of experts of the *European Charter for Regional or Minority Languages* concluded in their evaluation report that the objectives concerning Frisian in secondary education had not been met. They recommended stronger measures (European Charter 2004).

4.4. Higher education

In Friesland, there are three institutes for higher tertiary training (*Hogeschool*, called "University of Professional Education" abroad). All three are in Leeuwarden: *Christelijke Hogeschool Noord Nederland* (CHN, the new name since 2008 is Stenden University), *Noordelijke Hogeschool Leeuwarden* (NHL) and *Van Hall Instituut*. In 2007, there were about 17,000 students for a broad range of study programmes. Stenden and NHL offer many courses, including teacher training, technical programmes, hotel management, administration and nursing. Van Hall Instituut offers studies mainly in the fields of agriculture and environmental management.

There is no university in the classical sense in Friesland. Frisian language and literature can be studied at the Universities of Amsterdam, Leiden and Groningen, and only in the latter as the main subject for a BA or MA degree. The number of students is small; during the year 2007/2008 only 15 students were registered for Frisian as their main subject in the four-year programme. Stenden and NHL provide primary teacher training, while secondary teacher training is provided only by the NHL. A common curriculum is being developed for Frisian as a subject as well as for Frisian as a medium of instruction. During the first two years of their training, students must follow a Frisian language course. In the third year, Frisian is optional. There are separate streams for Frisian and non-Frisian speaking students. Most students of Stenden and NHL obtain a certificate for Frisian. Since its foundation in 1938, the *Fryske Akademy* has held a central place in scientific research into the Frisian language, history and society. Important projects of the *Fryske Akademy* regard lexicography, a language database, a historical geographical information system, and multilingualism in schools and society in general. The latter mainly concerns sociolinguistic surveys and international comparative studies through the *Mercator European Research Centre on Multilingualism and Language Learning* (formerly Mercator-Education), which is a part of the *Fryske Akademy* and collaborates in European networks.

5. Conclusion

On a European scale, the Frisian language takes up an intermediate position. Out of 48 cases in the first *Euromosaic* study, the Frisian language group was ranked in 15th position (Nelde, Strubell and Williams 1996: 65). In overall strength, Frisian is similar to groups of regional minority language speakers of Gaelic in the United Kingdom or to speakers of Slovenian or Friulan in Italy. The Frisian language community is much weaker than German in Belgium or Catalan in Spain (Vila, this Volume). But at the same time the provisions and the infrastructure for Frisian are better than for Breton in France or for the Sámi languages (Svonni, this Volume).

In terms of number of speakers and goodwill among the population, Frisian still has the possibility of becoming an accepted language in education, the media and other domains of society. The developments at the European level of the Council of Europe and the European Union are of great importance. Perhaps these will incite Dutch state government to greater efforts for language policy or to devolve its powers and financial means to the regional and local authorities and thus give them the opportunity to strengthen and refine their support for Frisian.

According to the nine criteria developed by the UNESCO ad hoc group of experts on language endangerment (UNESCO 2003), Frisian could be conceived of as an endangered language, because some speakers of Frisian "cease to use it" or "use it in an increasingly reduced number of communicative domains" and "cease to pass it on from one generation to the next." However, if we were to apply the nine criteria to Frisian we would probably come to the conclusion that Frisian still is sufficiently vital to survive the 21st century.

References

Boneschansker, Engbert and Miranda le Rütte
    2000   *Pjuttepraat; Friestaligheid in Peuterspeelzalen en Kinderdagverblijven.* Leeuwarden: Economisch Bureau Coulon.

Bremmer, Rolf
    1997   Het ontstaan van het Fries en het Hollands. In *Negen eeuwen Friesland-Holland (Geschiedenis van een haat-liefde verhouding),* Philippus Breuker and Anteun Janse, (eds.), 67–76. Zutphen: Fryske Akademy/Walburg Pers.

Cenoz, Jasone and Durk Gorter
    2006   The linguistic landscape and minority languages. *International Journal of Multilingualism*, 3 (1): 67–80.

Cohen, Anthonie, Harold Ebeling, Klaas Fokkema and André van Holk
    1959   *Fonologie van het Nederlands en het Fries.* 's-Gravenhage: Martinus Nijhoff.

De Jager, Bernadet and Cor van der Meer
2007 *The Development of Minimum Standards on Language Education in Regional and Minority Languages.* Leeuwarden: Mercator European Research Centre on Multilingualism and Language Learning.

Dijkstra, Anne
2001 Lexicography of modern West-Frisian. In *Handbuch des Friesischen/Handbook of Frisian Studies,* Horst Haider Münske (ed.), 148–155. Tübingen: Max Niemeyer Verlag.

Eurobarometer
2005 *Europeans and languages, Special Eurobarometer 237 – Wave 63.4.* European Commission (*http://ec.europa.eu/public_opinion/archives/ebs/ebs_237.en.pdf*)

European Charter for Regional or Minority Languages
1998 *Explanatory Report.* (ETS no. 148) Strasbourg: Council Of Europe. (*http://conventions.coe.int/Treaty/EN/Reports/Html/148.htm*)
2004 *Application of the Charter in the Netherlands. 2nd Monitoring Cycle* A. Report of the Committee of Experts on the Charter. B. Recommendation of the Committee of Ministers of the Council of Europe on the Application of the Charter by the Netherlands. ECRML 8. Strasbourg: Council of Europe. (*http://conventions.coe.int/Treaty/EN/Reports/Html/148.htm*)

Foekema, Henk
2004 *Overdracht van de Friese Taal.* Amsterdam: TNS-NIPO.

Fokkema, Klaas
1948 *Beknopte Friese Spraakkunst.* Groningen: Wolters.

Gorter, Durk
2001 A Frisian update of reversing language shift. In *Can threatened Languages be saved? Reversing Language Shift: A 21st Century Perspective,* Joshua Fishman (ed.), 215–233. Clevedon: Multilingual Matters.

Gorter, Durk and Reitze Jonkman
1995 *Taal yn Fryslân: Op e Nij Besjoen.* Ljouwert: Fryske Akademy.

Gorter, Durk, Gjalt Jelsma, Pieter van der Plank en Klaas de Vos
1984 *Taal yn Fryslân (Undersyk nei Taalgedrach en Taalhâlding yn Fryslân).* Ljouwert: Fryske Akademy.

Inspectie
2006 *Inspectie van het Onderwijs – De Kwaliteit van het Vak Fries in het Basisonderwijs en het Voortgezet Onderwijs in de Provincie Fryslân.* Utrecht: Inspectie van het Onderwijs.

Jonkman, Reitze
1993 *It Leewarders (In Taalsosjologysk ûndersyk nei it Stedsk yn Ferhâlding ta it Nederlânsk en it Frysk yn Ljouwert).* Ljouwert: Fryske Akademy.

Nelde, Peter, Miquel Strubell and Glyn Williams
    1996   *Euromosaic – The Production and Reproduction of the Minority Language Groups in the European Union.* Luxemburg: Office for Official Publications of the European Communities.

Niebaum, Hermann
    2001   Der Niedergang des Friesischen zwischen Lauwers und Weser. In *Handbuch des Friesischen/Handbook of Frisian Studies*, Horst Haider Münske (ed.), 430–442. Tübingen: Niermeyer Verlag.

Oldenhof, Bouke
    2006   Van steen des aanstoots tot boegbeeld. Toneel, kleinkunst, film vanaf 1860. In *Zolang de Wind van de Wolken Waait. Geschiedenis van de Friese Literatuur*, Teake Oppewal et al. (eds.), 263–301. Amsterdam: Bert Bakker.

Oppewal, Teake et al. (eds.)
    2006   *Zolang de Wind van de Wolken Waait. Geschiedenis van de Friese Literatuur.* Amsterdam: Bert Bakker

Pietersen, Liewe
    1969   *De Friezen en hun Taal.* Drachten: Laverman.

Popkema, Jan
    2006   *Grammatica Fries.* Utrecht: Uitgeverij Het Spectrum.

Provinsje Fryslân
    2006   *Boppeslach. Underwiisnota Provinsje Fryslân. Plan fan oanpak Frysk yn it ûnderwiis.* Ljouwert: Provinsje Fryslân.
    2007   *De Fryske Taalatlas 2007. Friese Taal in Beeld.* Ljouwert: Provinsje Fryslân.
    2008   *http://www.fryslan.nl/fic* (Website with statistical information, accessed March 2008)

Sipma, Piter
    1913   *Phonology and Grammar of Modern West Frisian.* Oxford: Oxford University Press.

Tiersma, Pieter Meijes
    1985   *Frisian Reference Grammar.* Dordrecht: Foris.

UNESCO
    2003   Ad Hoc Expert Group on Endangered Languages 2003, Language Vitality and Endangerment. *http://portal.unesco.org/culture/en/files/ 8283/11195176347Language_Vitality_and_Endangerment.pdf/Lang uage%2BVitality%2Band%2BEndangerment.pdf* (accessed March 2008).

Van Bree, Cor
    1994   The development of the so-called Town Frisian. In *Mixed Languages*, Peter Bakker and Maarten Mous (eds.), 69–82. Amsterdam: Ifott.

Van der Avoird, Tim, D. Bontje, Peter Broeder, Guus Extra, R. Muis & N. Peijs
    2000   *Meertaligheid in Leeuwarden. De Status van Allochtone Talen Thuis en op School.* Tilburg/Utrecht: Babylon/Sardes.

Van der Bij, Jacob and Renze Valk
    2005   *Fries in het Voortgezet Onderwijs, een Echternachse Processie.* Leeuwarden: Fryske Akademy.

Van der Vaart, Jacob
    2001   De wenjende Fries. In *De aktuele steat fan Fryslân*, Piet Hemminga (ed.), 11–37. Ljouwert/Leeuwarden: Fryske Akademy.

Van Langevelde, Ab
    1999   *Bilingualism and Regional Economic Development. A Dooyeweerdian case study of Fryslân.* Ljouwert: Fryske Akademy.

Van Ruijven, Bernie
    2005   *Onderwijseffectiviteit in Fryslân.* Ljouwert: Fryske Akademy.

Van Ruijven, Bernie and Jehannes Ytsma
    2007   *'Trijetalige skoalle yn Fryslân': Onderzoek naar de Opbrengsten van het Drietalige Onderwijsmodel in Fryslân.* Leeuwarden: Fryske Akademy.

Vries, Oebele
    1997   From Old Frisian to Dutch: the elimination of Frisian as a written language in the sixteenth century. In *Language Minorities and Minority Languages*, Bruno Synak and Tomasz Wicherkiewicz (eds.), 239–244. Gdansk: Wydawnictwo Uniwersytetu Gdanskiego.

Ytsma, Jehannes
    2000   Trilingual primary education in Friesland. In *English in Europe: The Acquisition of a Third Language*, Jasone Cenoz and Ulrike Jessner (eds.), 222–235. Clevedon: Multilingual Matters,.

Zondag, Koen
    1993   The very beginning of the Frisian movement. *International Journal of the Sociology of Language,* 100/101: 193–201.

Hungarian as a minority language

Susan Gal

1. Introduction[1]

Hungarian speakers today live as migrant minorities and as regional minorities. As migrants, small numbers of Hungarian speakers are present in Western Europe, North and South America as well as Israel and Australia. Hungarian speakers also constitute one of Europe's largest regional minorities. Located in a relatively flat region bounded by the arc of the Carpathian mountains in the north and southeast and by the easternmost Alps in the west – Hungarian speaking minorities live in seven nation-states: Slovakia, Ukraine, Romania, Serbia, Croatia, Slovenia and Austria. Their settlement histories in these territories reach back as many as nine centuries. The present chapter provides a brief overview of their complex demographic, sociopolitical and sociolinguistic circumstances.

As part of the Austrian Empire and later the Austro-Hungarian Monarchy, Hungary was a multinational state in which, at the turn of the 20th century, non-Hungarians comprised nearly 50% of the total population. The Treaty of Trianon in 1920 ended the First World War and drastically revised Hungary's borders, redistributing two-thirds of its territory among the neighboring states. This border change resulted in a small, much more linguistically homogeneous Hungary, with only 7.9% non-Hungarian speakers, whereas about a third of the Hungarian speakers – roughly 3.3 million people – found themselves resident in the neighbouring states. These numbers have changed somewhat in the last ninety years, though the borders now are about the same as in 1920. Currently, the population of Hungary is 10.3 million, of whom 1.3% attests to speaking national languages other than Hungarian (Bartha, in press; Tóth and Vékás 2004). The combined population of the Hungarian-speaking regional minorities is currently estimated to be roughly 2.5 million.

While sharing a common history and often linked by kinship relations, the regional minorities created by the Trianon treaties differ from each other in many of their past and current circumstances. Their populations are of vastly different sizes, they have had historically different settlement patterns, different local interethnic relations and contrasting standards of living. Over the past ninety years, legal and educational contexts and minority politics have differed substantially among the five (recently expanded to seven) countries in which Hungarian speakers live. Although the ideology of ethnolinguistic nationalism is strong in the region, there have been variations in it over time. Each minority has been affected by the Hungarian state's diplomatic relations with the state in which they live. Contact and co-existence with at least five different languages has also had differentiating effects. From the late 1940s to 1989 most but not all Hungarian minorities lived in state socialist systems; since 2007, many but not all live in countries that have joined the European Union with its uniformly tolerant, sometimes supportive, yet only variably enforced minority policies.

Population figures that assess the size of minorities are always approximations; these are discussed in Section 2, including statistics about educational institutions and levels of attendance. Section 3 outlines the political circumstances of the Hungarian language and language politics in each country. Section 4 takes up sociolinguistic questions: the language ideologies of Hungarian speakers, patterns of bilingualism, language maintenance, standardisation and language planning efforts.

These descriptive sketches would be difficult to interpret without an orientation to the discursive fields – and political contests – out of which have emerged the several different genres of research on which this chapter draws. As a guide to further reading, I distinguish four approaches, noting the contrasting presuppositions with which researchers define their objects of study.

1.1. Research perspectives

A first approach is the perspective of this Volume. By omitting Hungary itself, and by setting the Hungarian minorities alongside "Catalan in Spain" and "Sámi languages in the Nordic countries and Russia," this Volume provides a decidedly European comparative frame, taking for granted that the topic is a legitimate question of regional, national, and supranational treaties and legal protections, not a dangerous irredentist project of political mobilisation or border revision. This stance assumes the existence of linguistic rights based on minority status itself, and assured by the presence of watchdog organisations such as the *European Bureau of Lesser-Used Languages* and the potential intervention of the Council of Europe or the European Union on behalf of regional languages. The accession of Austria,

Hungary, Slovakia, Slovenia and Romania to the EU makes this perspective appropriate, yet it has certain blindspots. Distinguishing sharply between regional and migrant languages, it neglects those large numbers of Hungarian regional minorities who have migrated to Hungary, Austria and further west since 1989.

This Euro-frame contrasts strikingly with earlier approaches. For almost fifty years of state socialism, discussion of these speakers was seen as a sensitive subject by official circles in Hungary and the bordering states. It was thought to raise the vexed topic of nationalist sentiment among governments and peoples who were supposed to have internationalist commitments. It threatened to recall long-standing grievances about Nazi-supported border changes in Hungary's favour during the Second World War, as well as Soviet-supported deportations and population transfers in the early postwar period that were rationalised on the basis of ethnolinguistic identities. After a brief, early phase of tolerance, the state socialist period saw waves of homogenising policies that bore down heavily on Hungarian speakers at various times in most of the circum-Hungary countries.

A second perspective is that of language scholars in Hungary today, what I call a metropolitan Hungarian view. This view gained leverage and state funding in the relatively open environment of the late 1980s. Until then, and during much of the socialist period the minorities had been present in linguistic descriptions largely as points on the Hungarian dialect atlas. The widespread and increasing bilingualism of the minorities was often ignored; its linguistic effects denied; patterns of bilingualism left unexamined. When mentioned at all, the minorities were judged lamentably "incorrect" in their speech, at least according to the powerful prescriptivist wing of Hungarian linguistics. The new wave of studies went against both prescriptivism and traditional dialectology with an insistence on empirical study of contemporary language use (Pléh 1995).

For the researchers in Hungary, a single terminology came to unify the objects of study: "Hungarians beyond the borders" (*határon túli magyarok*). The category unifies the different populations and highlights comparisons with Hungarian speakers inside Hungary. Since the 1990s, much valuable research has been produced from this perspective, stimulated in part by political circumstances. First, diverse voices of anti-communist opposition in the 1980s were united in the demand that the Hungarian government finally acknowledge support of Hungarian speakers in the neighbouring countries (Gal 1991). Second, scholarly study was further instigated when, after 1989, several neighbouring governments attempted to "nationalise" their populations by again instituting harsher linguistic constraints on Hungarian minorities. These policies brought issues of national identity and minority policy to crisis point within Hungary.

More broadly, the circumstances of the minorities since 1989, their large-scale westward and northward migration to Hungary, and debates about the proper role of the Hungarian state's policies towards them have divided right-wing from left-wing and liberal political stances in Hungarian domestic politics. Minority policy has become a platform for discussions of nationalism, multiculturalism, immigration, policy towards Roma, and social stratification. Studies of minority Hungarians from left or liberal positions usually appear in volumes that include studies of the much smaller number of national bilinguals within Hungary (German-, Slovak- and Romanian-speakers) and of Romani-speakers. They try to consider all multilingual cases together, to present an image of benign co-existence rather than nationalist bias (see, e.g., Pál et al. 2005). By contrast, right-wing or frankly nationalist books usually focus entirely on Hungarian minority speakers.

Metropolitan views are most apparent in the series of volumes that, starting in 1989, brought together for the first time since the First World War linguists from Hungary with linguists from the minority Hungarian populations (see, e.g., Győri-Nagy and Kelemen 1991; Kassai 1995; Borbély 2000; Lanstyák and Simon 2002; Kontra and Hattyár 2002). Such studies have been funded by independent foundations of various political stripes, by initiatives within the Linguistics Institute of the Hungarian Academy of Sciences and by new research institutes on minority affairs of the Academy. A major achievement of this perspective is the comprehensive comparative study, published in English, that is based on sizable samples of Hungarian speakers from all seven countries, organised and completed in the 1990s (Fenyvesi 2005; Göncz, in press). It grew out of the variationist study of language use in Hungary itself (Kontra 2005), and employed seasoned researchers from the minority populations as partners who administered questionnaires and tests on a wide range of language-related issues. It forms a rich source for my own report. Other, smaller projects have also brought together many of the same linguists in lively debates on language planning and standardisation (Kontra and Saly 1998). The fault lines in these scholarly disputes reflect areas of theoretical disagreement, and to a lesser extent fall along generational lines, not between metropolitans and minorities.

Nevertheless, research planned and published for and by minority populations takes a somewhat different approach; it is a third perspective – or, to some extent seven different ones. Minority linguists, like minority populations, prefer to be called Hungarians in Romania or Erdély (Transylvania), Hungarians in Slovakia, Hungarians of the Vajdaság (the north of Serbia) and so on, specifying an ethnonym and a geopolitical location. To some, the label of "Hungarians beyond the borders" implies a centralised viewpoint looking "out" and therefore sounds excessively bureaucratic. Studies formulated among minority intellectuals speak to others in minority situations (elites and non-elites) as well as to the Budapest political and intellecutal scene. They are broadly characterised by a concern for variations of everyday language use, an acceptance of bilingualism, an understanding of the subtleties and ambivalences of language loyalty and a close knowledge of the national educational and legal contexts. The Gramma Language Office in Dunajská Streda/Dunaszerdahely, Slovakia is exemplary (e.g., Lanstyák 2006; described in Lanstyák and Simon 2002); there are parallel workshops or at least cohorts of linguists in the other countries as well, usually based in departments of linguistics, and Hungarian or Finno-Ugric studies in universities.

Finally, a fourth set of approaches are those that originate outside the Carpathian region. These have distinctively different comparative frames. My own ethnographic research among Hungarian speakers in Austria aimed to compare their patterns of bilingualism to those of other bilinguals elsewhere in Europe (Gal 1979, 1987, 1993, 2005). Others have compared changes in the language policies of Slovakia and Romania – within the broader regional context – to show how democratic practices mediate international pressure (Kelley 2004; Csergő 2007). Still others have taken a micro-region and its interethnic relations as a comparative focus: A team of Finnish scholars conducted interviews in the multilingual Bànàt region of Romania (Hannonen et al. 2001; Laihonen 2004). Other spatial strategies target cities, as in the ethnographic work of Brubaker et al. (2006) on Hungarians and Romanians in Cluj/Kolozsvár, Romania, or Schwegler's (2007) ethnography of the Hungarian-speaking minority, their Slovak neighbours, and their cross-border contacts in the border city of Komárno/Komárom, Slovakia.

2. Demographic and educational perspectives

For an overall picture of the size, distribution, and socio-economic status of Hungarian speakers as regional minorities, we must turn to census materials. As many social scientists have remarked, the census is a valuable yet problematic source of evidence (see also Extra and Gorter, this Volume).

Language censuses present special concerns. The form of the census itself implies a cross-tabulation that puts each person into one exclusive category on each dimension measured. This is not a great problem when the dimension is "sex" or "age". But with language it creates a pressure towards linking each person with one language (monolingualism) and towards listing only standardised languages that have listable names, even if the respondent's everyday practices include divergent non-standard varieties, or several languages (Anderson 1991). Information about variation and bilingualism is simply unavailable from most national censuses; for this kind of evidence one must turn to smaller ethnographic studies.

The eight states of this report (including Hungary) have had catastrophic experiences over the last century with language censuses, as these have sometimes been coercive instruments of ethnonational politics. For example, language censuses in the Czech lands brought on violent riots in the final years of the 19th century (Hobsbawm 1991). Following the Second World War, ethnolinguistic identity was used as justification for denying citizenship to Hungarians in Slovakia, for deportation of Hungarian speakers in Subcarpathia (Ukraine), and of German speakers from Hungary – among many other examples. Local memories of these events survive, making any census question about language and ethnicity a fraught matter, most notably for the older generations. Respondents' attitudes towards the organisation that collects the data also have effects on how people respond. Census-takers themselves have often had divergent political agendas, choosing their questions accordingly. The form of the census question has predictable effects on the outcome. Inquiries about "nationality" give different results than those about "language," even in regions where the two are ideologically equated. The terms used to refer to language also have effects: "mother tongue", "usual language", "home language", "language of the community", "minority language", all potentially elicit different responses from a single person and historically have been the subject of heated debate in this region (Gal 1993).

Table 1 provides the number and percentage of Hungarians living as regional minorities in seven countries, indicating data source, year, and the census question. The percentage of ethnic Hungarians (by the relevant definition) in the total population of each country is also presented. Table 2 shows a further breakdown to highlight the percentage of Hungarians in regions/counties where Hungarians are concentrated in each country. The final column of Table 2 indicates what percentage of Hungarians in that country live in the regions indicated.

Table 1. Number and percentage of ethnic Hungarians in neighbouring countries according to the most recent census reports by national statistical bureaus*

Country	Total population (TP)	Ethnic Hungarians (EH)	% of EH in TP	Year of census
Romania	21,680,974	1,431,807 (ethnic affiliation *and* mother tongue as one category)	6.60	2002
Slovakia	5,379,455	520,528 (ethnic affiliation – mother tongue not available)	9.70	2001
Serbia	7,498,001	293,299 (ethnic affiliation – mother tongue not available)	3.90	2002
Ukraine**	48,457,000	156,600 (ethnic affiliation/nationality 149,396 (mother tongue)	0.30	2001
Austria	7,322,000	25,884 (language use – ethnicity not available)	0.35	2001
Croatia	4,437,460	16,595 (ethnic affiliation) 12,650 (mother tongue)	0.37 0.29	2001
Slovenia	1,964,036	6,243 (ethnic affiliation) 7,713 (mother tongue)	0.32 0.40	2002

* Romania: INSSE (Romanian National Institute of Statistics), Slovakia: Statistical office of the Slovak Republic, Serbia: Statistical Office of the Republic if Serbia, Ukraine: State Statistics Committee of Ukraine, Austria: Statistik Austria, Croatia: CROSTAT (Republic of Croatia Central Bureau of Statistics), Slovenia: Statistical Office of the Republic of Slovenia.
** Rounded figures (thousands) given only

Table 2. Number and percentage of ethnic Hungarians (on the basis of ethnic affiliation) in regions/countries where the Hungarian groups are concentrated

Country	Region	Ethnic Hungarian in the region (EHR)	% of EHR in total population in the region (TPR)	% of EHR in total number of Hungarian in the country (EH)
Romania	Transylvania*	1,415,718	19.6	98.9
	3 countries of the Szekler region (*Székelyföld*) only in Transylvania**	668,471	59.0	46.7
Slovakia	Trnava	130,740	23.7	25.1
	Nitra	196,609	27.6	37.8
	Banska Bystrica	77,795	11.7	14.9
	Kosice	85,415	11.2	16.4
Serbia	Vojvodina	290,207	14.0	98.9
Ukraine	Zakarpattia	151,500	12.1	96.7
Austria	Burgenland	4,704	1.7	18.1
(language use)	Vienna	10,686	0.9	41.3
Croatia	Osijek-Baranja County	9,784	2.9	58.9
	Vukovar-Sirmium County	2,047	1.0	12.3
Slovenia	Mura	not available		

* Consisting of the following countries (Hungarian name in parentheses): Alba (*Fehér*), Arad (*Arad*), Bihor (*Bihar*), Bistrita-Năsăud (*Beszterce-Naszód*), Braşov (*Brassó*), Caraş-Severin (*Krassó-Szörény*), Cluj (*Kolozs*), Covasna (*Kovászna*), Harghita (*Hargita*), Hunedoara (*Hunyad*), Maramureş (*Máramaros*), Mureş (*Maros*), Sălaj (*Szilágy*), Satu Mare (*Szatmár*), Sibiu (*Szeben*), Timiş (*Temes*).

** Consisting of Mureş (*Maros*), Covasna (*Kovászna*) and Harghita (*Hargita*) counties in the south-eastern part of Transylvania, it is the region with the highest concentration of Hungarians in Romania (traditionally it was called the *Háromszék* region).

To supplement these numbers, the following sections provide summaries of minority speakers' settlement patterns, social, religious and economic circumstances as well as educational issues[2] starting with the largest minorities and moving to the smallest.

2.1. Hungarian in Romania

This is the largest and most socially complex group, currently about 1,4 million people, located almost entirely in Transylvania, but divided into several territorially distinct populations within that province. The area around Cluj/Kolozsvár, a major city, is one such area. Another is on the northwestern border with Hungary, a third on the southern border with Hungary, near the city of Temesvár (the Bánát); a fourth is the compact, settlement zone known as the Szekler region (*Székelyföld*). A final area, is where the outlying Csángós are settled, outside Transylvania, in the province of Moldavia. This last is an isolated group, speaking a notably divergent linguistic form and with Hungarian ancestry, that has experienced particularly strong assimilationist pressure (Sándor 2005).

In Romania, as many as 56% of Hungarians live in settlements where they constitute the absolute majority; most of these are villages. Although cities are more linguistically mixed, 38% of Hungarians live in towns or cities in which they are a majority. Despite this relatively concentrated settlement pattern – which often signals institutional strength – there has been a steady decline in numbers since the 1950s when politically motivated resettlement of Romanians into Hungarian towns and villages accompanied urbanisation and industrialisation. Contributing to the loss of numbers is the low birthrate, compared to Romanians, and a steady stream of emigration to Hungary and beyond. Since 1992 as many as 200,000 people have emigrated, almost 12% of the population. The rate of intermarriage (circa 23%) also contributes to declining numbers since the children of such marriages are registered as Romanian, though this does not necessarily reflect linguistic practices (Benő and Szilágyi 2005).

Emigration is doubtless linked to the unfavorable socio-economic circumstances of Hungarians in Romania. They are underrepresented in white collar, administrative and professional work, being located instead in blue-collar work, handcrafts and construction. They are significantly less well educated than their Romanian counterparts by age. Finally, among Hungarians there are Reform Protestants (47%), Roman Catholics (41%) and a sprinkling of Unitarians. This distinguishes them from the majority population of Romanians who are overwhelmingly Eastern Orthodox.

The changing policies of the Romanian government in the state-socialist period had deleterious effects on Hungarian education, with decreases in the number of schools, and the frequent elimination of Hungarian classes and schools. By contrast, developments since 1989 have been supportive of Hungarian education, with Hungarian classes increasing at all levels, including higher education. The Law on Education of 1995 mandated toleration for the teaching of minorities in their mother tongue, if they constitute more than 20% of the population; the rights of minorities to learn their language and develop their cultural identities are protected. The system of Hungarian education in Romania is a large one, with 70% of Hungarian speaking children going to Hungarian kindergarten (circa 30 thousand, as of 2004–2005), more than 85% (circa 44 thousand) in Hungarian classes for grades 1–8, and 75% in Hungarian high schools. The figures are lower for post-secondary education or specialist training in trades. There is continuing tension about the lack of textbooks and a long-standing demand for a state-supported Hungarian-language university. Since the end of state socialism, private universities teaching in Hungarian or with Hungarian tracks have been established, as have religious seminaries, mostly with the help of funding by sister institutions in Hungary and/or the Hungarian government. The possibility of correspondence diplomas from Hungarian institutions of higher education is now a further alternative possibility.

A notable aspect of Hungarian education in Romania is the great range of student competence in Hungarian and Romanian. In areas of sparse Hungarian population, students know Romanian when they arrive in school and the Romanian taught as a second language is adequate to their needs. In densely Hungarian settlements, however, such classes are inadequate for fluency, potentially creating later problems for students in Romania. This discourages some parents from sending their children to Hungarian schools. Nevertheless, the numbers of Hungarian schools, especially secondary schools has increased markedly in the 1990s.

2.2. Hungarian in Slovakia

Slovakia's Hungarian minority – circa 520,000 in number – is concentrated on the border of Hungary, mostly in the southwest. The levels of concentration, however, are decreasing due to Slovak in-migration in recent decades. The Hungarian population is decreasing as a percentage of the country's population, and according to the latest census also decreasing in absolute numbers. It is estimated that about 90% of Hungarians in Slovakia speak Slovak. As in Romania, most of the population is rural, and lives in small settlements where they constitute a majority of the population. In contrast to the Romanian picture, however, only a few cities have Hungarian populations of any size; there has been little outmigration from Slovakia, and fewer marriages to Slovaks (17%). Most Hungarians are Roman Catholics; 11% are Reform Protestants, and some are Lutherans, within this largely Catholic country. As in Romania, in comparison to the majority population, the Hungarians are older, poorer, have lower levels of education, more unemployment and less desirable jobs. Indeed, as a result of the economic policies of the last few decades, the Hungarian areas have the worst socio-economic indicators in Slovakia and have been considered an underdeveloped zone (Lanstyák and Szabómihàly 2005).

The Slovak constitution and subsequent national laws – especially since accession to the Council of Europe and the EU – guarantee that in the Hungarian-speaking region, parents can choose Hungarian primary school for their children, although there are not enough schools to meet the demand. Roughly 80% of Hungarian speaking children go to Hungarian primary schools; this figure drops to 50% for secondary education and is even lower for technical education. There is no publicly funded higher education in Hungarian, so even those training to be Hungarian-language teachers are trained only partly in Hungarian. There are departments of universities where one can study in Hungarian in the social sciences and humanities. Several of the prominent Hungarian intellectuals in Slovakia obtained their degrees in Hungarian universities. While Slovak is taught in Hungarian schools, Hungarian is not taught in Slovak schools, so that parents who decide to send their children to Slovak schools give up all possibility of Hungarian educational input. Broadcast media from Hungary are accessible and preferred over Slovak sources; there are also Hungarian-language media in Slovakia.

2.3. Hungarian in the former Yugoslavia

Due to the extremely small numbers of Hungarian speakers in the relatively new states of Croatia and Slovenia, these countries will be discussed together with the much larger number of Hungarians in Serbia. Together they are a population of over 300,000. Hungarians are a majority in the easternmost geographical regions of the Serbian province of Vojvodina, especially along the Hungarian border. The population of this province has long been heterogeneous in language, ethnicity and religion. Besides Serbs (65%) and Hungarians (14%), Vojvodina also has sizable numbers of Romanians, Croatians, Slovaks, and Roma. In contrast to Romania and Slovakia, a majority of Hungarians live in towns (58%). The numbers of Hungarians have been decreasing, with a loss of 100,000 since 1961. Since the borders of Yugoslavia were more open than that of other eastern countries during the communist period, many migrated to Western Europe. During the wars of the 1990s, many moved to Hungary. Intermarriage has also had an effect: approximately 30% of recent marriages of Hungarians are with Serbians; the children are invariably registered as Serb. The majority of Hungarians in the former Yugoslavia are Roman Catholics. Through a stormy century of state-formation, dissolution and re-formation, the Hungarians experienced pressures to cease creating their own institutions and organisations. They work in blue-collar trades and have been underrepresented in higher education, in government work, the army and as economic leaders (Göncz and Vörös 2005).

There were relatively ample opportunites for education in Hungarian until the end of communism. Since 1991, the former system has been judged insufficiently national by its leaders and the minority rights taken for granted in earlier periods have been revoked. Serbian law now requires the public use of Serbian and the Cyrillic alphabet. Responsibility for the support of minority languages has been transferred to local councils. Bilingualism used to be required of officials in bilingual regions, but this too has ended. About 80% of Hungarian children attend Hungarian sections of Serbian schools for the primary grades. For secondary schools the rate is closer to 40%. Elementary classes in Hungarian are available if 15 students request it in any community. On the secondary level, Hungarian classes are started on a year-by-year basis so that there is no reliability of educational offerings. Because there is a shortage of textbooks (imports from Hungary are illegal) and a shortage of trained teachers (Hungarian students attend higher education at much lower rates than their Serbian counterparts), much of what is called Hungarian education has become bilingual education, where some subjects are taught in one language, other subjects in the other. Many bilingual programs turn out to be submersion or transition programs that take Hungarian-speaking youngsters into Serbian.

The Hungarians of newly independent Slovenia have a significantly different situation today than those in Serbia. In Slovenia they constitute a very small minority (circa 6,000), living near the border with Hungary. Constitutional guarantees of linguistic rights are backed by support of minority languages (Italian as well as Hungarian) at the national level. Minorities can initiate educational and cultural associations at their places of residence; the constitution also grants rights to vote on issues of education, mass information, and contact with other countries. In Slovenia, there are no Hungarian schools at all; those schools designated as "bilingual" provide some input in Hungarian, but tend to stress Slovenian. In the closed, small rural communities that make up the Hungarian region, bilingualism has become widespread in the last fifty years; language shift is far advanced among the younger generations. Many Hungarians were migrant workers in nearby Austria and Germany, where they earned money that was reinvested in their farms. But high school education is rare, higher education even rarer. Today, there are joint ventures with Hungarian firms and Hungarians in Slovenia enjoy access to Hungarian mass media (press, TV) in Hungary as well as their own publishing houses and folkloristic associations. An organisation for self-government represents them in Parliament.

2.4. Hungarian in Ukraine

The province of present-day Ukraine in which Hungarians are concentrated (Subcarpathia/Karpátalja/Zakarpattia) shares a border with Hungary. (This territory was formerly part of the Soviet Union and before that, after the Second World War, part of Czechoslovakia) Although their percentage in the province is dropping, the roughly 150,000 Hungarians continue to live in a relatively homogeneous block and are the largest minority of the province. Like those in Slovakia, they are overwhelmingly rural – 71% live in small villages, 70% in settlements where they constitute a majority. Traditionally, the Hungarians were the plains-dwellers, in contrast to the Ukrainians and others who were herders in the Carpathian mountains that ring the province. Today this division is not much in evidence, as Ukrainians have formed villages amidst Hungarian speaking lowland areas. Nevertheless, villages remain segregated by language.

In general, the levels of education and standard of living in the region are extremely low compared to neighbouring Hungary and also to other Ukrainian regions. Most Hungarians are either in agriculture or unemployed. Since this region was part of the Soviet Union until 1992, most Hungarian speakers claim to know either Russian or Ukrainian as a result of early education. There has been very little investment until a recent influx of Hungarian capital development through joint ventures. Because of the dire economic situation, a large percentage of the Hungarian speakers in Subcarpathia have plans to emigrate.

In principle, although Ukrainian is now the state language, minority speakers have a right to use their language in all spheres of social life in those geographical areas where they form a majority by nationality. These legal provisions are mostly for the large Russian minority in newly independent Ukraine, but they have effects on the much smaller number of Hungarians as well. Despite tolerant laws, minority languages are not used in local government, only in minority mass media (press, radio, TV) and in churches. In the one district (Berehove/Beregszász) where Hungarians constitute 67% of the population, there are primary schools where Hungarian is the language of instruction. Nevertheless, the situation of the linguistic minority is deteriorating culturally as well as economically (Csernicskó 2005).

2.5. Hungarian in Austria

Unlike the other groups we have discussed, the approximately 6000 Hungarians who constitute the regional minority of Burgenland, on Austria's border with Hungary, have not been the objects of obvious and sustained discriminative policies or practices, and they have been continuously part of the capitalist world. A very small group, they live in a few settlements, in the largest of which they are relatively concentrated in a few neighbourhoods. The Hungarian-speaking population is, on average, older than the German-speaking population of the province, suggesting both outmigration of younger Hungarians and failure to transmit the language across generations (Gal 1979). They are divided roughly equally between Catholics and Reformed Protestants, in an overwhelmingly Catholic country. Although primarily agricultural until the 1960s, the Hungarian population is now found mainly in service occupations and semi-skilled work; at the same time, their educational achievement is higher than that of German speakers: more high school diplomas, more college degrees (Bodó 2005).

This higher education, however, is largely in German, although the University of Vienna provides training for Hungarian teachers in its Finno-Ugric department. There is Hungarian education in the three elementary schools in the three small settlements of Hungarian speakers in Burgenland, and Hungarian is available as an optional subject elsewhere in the province. A major achievement of local politics by the minority was the establishment in 1987 of a separate Hungarian track in one of the most respected secondary schools (gymnasium) of the province. And since 1992, bilingual education in Hungarian-German and in Croatian-German has been available in Oberwart/Felőőr, the largest of the regional Hungarian settlements.[3]

3. Political processes

Ethnolinguistic nationalism, the language ideology (Woolard 1998) that presumes a natural, self-evident connection between national identity and knowledge of the language emblematic of the nation, is as firmly entrenched in the Carpathian area as elsewhere in Europe (see Extra and Gorter, this Volume). Control over the reproduction of the national language throughout a state's territory becomes a key sign of the state's sovereignty, as well as the justification and legitimation of the state's political power in the name of the nation. Yet, total homogeneity of linguistic usage within a state has never been achieved. Regional minority movements are themselves nationalisms, operating on the same principles, and competing with the majority to gain some measure of sovereignty over a single territory.

Within this broad framework, two ostensibly different definitions of nation have been embraced by elites in the post-Communist era: "cultural nation" and "political or civic nation". Hungarian minority leaders have emphasized the first, thereby attempting to assure audiences that in the demand for various degrees of minority autonomy over institutions of linguistic reproduction – schools, personal names, territorial signage – there are no risks for the political sovereignty of the states in which they live; no vision of border changes; no echoes of Hungarian political hegemony in the Carpathian region before the First World War. Linguistic scholars in Hungary who write about the minorities also invoke cultural nationalism, for the same reasons (e.g., Kontra 2005). By contrast, majority politicians in the circum-Hungary states have most often taken the "civic" stance. This was the Hungarian position before 1918, and is currently legitimated in the post-socialist region by pointing to its espousal by prestigious western states.

However, political theorists insist that "civic" and "cultural" nationalisms are merely two sides of the same coin. One position can easily morph into the other. After all, reproducing language and culture requires control over education, where loyalty towards a standardised national language is taught. This itself depends on political processes that secure jurisdiction over schools. Conversely, claims of cultural-linguistic unity are crucial for the justification of political autonomy. All the relevant post-Communist governments adopted nationalising stances to create legitimacy for new states (Slovakia, Serbia, Ukraine), or reinforce legitimacy for old ones (Hungary, Romania) by claiming strict control over the reproduction of national culture – and especially language. At the same time, newly instituted parliamentary procedures endowed minorities with more leverage to influence state policy, since numbers came to matter in the competition for votes.

In such electoral dynamics, the seven Hungarian minority populations are differently situated. In those states where there are large Hungarian minorities (Romania, Slovakia, Ukraine, Serbia), the language issue has remained the focus of political dispute for the twenty years since the end of communism, and has on occasion toppled governments. There was no such activity where the minorities are small (Austria, Croatia, Slovenia). Among the large ones, Ukraine and Serbia, not members of the European Union, both have minority problems – Russians in Ukraine, Albanians in Serbia – that far outweigh their (sizable) Hungarian speakers. In Serbia, the Hungarian minority's problems and protection have been dwarfed by war between the Yugoslav successor states, and religious or ethnolinguistic conflict among Serbs and Albanians.

Rather than civic *vs.* cultural nationalism, there is today a more complex political configuration in the region, one that is also influenced by the population size of the minorities. This configuration is well illustrated by an article in the Budapest daily *Népszabadság* (January 2008) in which a Slovak politician of the Slovak Nationalist Party was reported to have declared that: "There are no Hungarians living in Slovakia, just Slovaks who speak Hungarian (…) I submit that these people are not Hungarians, they are Slovaks who express themselves in Hungarian (…)" [my translation]. This, he averred, was both democratic and the exact parallel of France's categorisation system. Notice how the statement directly contradicts the preferred nomenclature of the Hungarian minority: "*szlovákiai magyarok*" ('Hungarians in Slovakia'). It asserts that loyalty to the state is more important than the (possibly distinct) language of some citizens. Furthermore, the newspaper, whose audience is primarily in Hungary, called this statement "ultranationalist" and "anti-Hungarian", thereby implying the appropriateness of a political response by Hungary.

The configuration to which the newspaper article draws attention consists of four intersecting interests, that of (1) "nationalising states" that aim to homogenize their populations, (2) "national minorities" often targeted for assimilation, (3) a linguistically related autonomous state (in this case Hungary) to which minorities turn, or which presumes to speak for them in an international arena (Brubaker 1995), and (4) the international arena itself with its institutions focused on linguistic minorities (Csergő 2007). Most important of such institutions are the Council of Europe (with its *European Charter for Regional or Minority Languages* and the Framework Convention), and the European Union; international NGOs and watchdog agencies are also significant. The aspiration of the post-Communist states to join the EU, and the conditionality to meet norms of linguistic policy as a prerequisite to membership, created the impetus for change in the restrictive, nationalising minority policies of the first post-Communist governments in Slovakia and Romania. As is well known, the various conventions, agreements and standards of the EU with respect to minority language issues are ambiguous, inconsistent and inconsistently enforced. There is not any single European norm. Indeed, as many have pointed out, states joining the EU give up sovereign authority over many important policy areas but generally retain control over institutions of national cultural reproduction such as education and other language-related issues. Nevertheless, the experiences of Slovakia and Romania, over the last decade, demonstrate the dynamics of language politics as these states responded to international pressure (see above, and Lanstyák and Szabómihály 2002; Kontra and Hattyár 2002; Brubaker et al. 2006).

However, it was not direct pressure from agents of the EU that created change. On the contrary, the trajectory of language policy, in the shadow of EU conditionality, was mediated by the debates of political parties in each state. Language issues – and therefore cultural reproduction – formed the focus for the creation of new minority political parties in Slovakia, and the renewal of the already existing political party for Hungarians in Romania after 1989. The majority parties too organised around the language issue, competing with each other for votes through different policy proposals about minorities. Splits among the majority elites – in the context of EU incentives – enabled some majority parties to form coalitions with minority parties and ultimately push through legislation that was relatively minority-friendly or at least satisfactory for EU membership. There were strategic alliances between majority parties that wanted more regional control or more popular sovereignty with less centralisation, and minority parties that wanted some sort of sub-state institutional autonomy in the areas of education and local government. Thus, plans for reduced centralisation by majority parties meshed with the goals of minority parties for sub-state institutional autonomy, thereby enabling compromises (Csergő 2007). Other minority situations throughout Europe provide useful guides for the Hungarian cases (Gál 2002).

One major result of EU pressure has been change in the legal arrangements governing the treatment of Hungarian minorities. Another has been change in Hungarian domestic politics. Popular support for treaties with the neighbouring countries was established, so that multiple bilateral agreements with Hungary, largely initiated by Hungarian diplomacy, have been the means towards economic cooperation. In turn, Hungarian investment in the minority regions has created incentives for assuring the linguistic rights of Hungarian speakers (Kelley 2004: 116–159). Furthermore, a network of institutions was designed and funded in Budapest to help Hungarians in other countries. An active program of lobbying by Hungary was initiated in European institutions on behalf of the minorities. On the domestic scene, successive governments in Hungary have been judged by voters in terms of their policies on behalf of the "Hungarians beyond the borders." One consequence was the occasional manipulation of this issue for electoral advantage. A more positive effect was that policies towards minorities inside Hungary were self-consciously designed to be exemplary, so as to gain the moral high-ground in Europe-wide discussions on treatment of minorities.

4. Sociolinguistic practices and problems

As information about the lives of ordinary speakers, national level statistics and political debates about language are deceptive, for they are far removed from the language ideologies and practices of the majority of Hungarian speakers. Ethnolinguistic nationalism as an ideology is firmly established in official circles and institutions, but it does not determine the experience of minority speakers. Despite the impression created by census tables, nationality and the corresponding language are not "things" that can be owned, nor essences of individuals and groups. Nationality and its linguistic counterpart are better thought of as events or practices of categorisation and language use that happen *between* people in interaction. In Romania and Slovakia, politicians and linguists have been in strong conflict about the Hungarian language. Yet, ethnographic research suggests that non-elite speakers in Cluj/Kolozsvár (Brubaker et al. 2006) and Komárno/ Komárom (Schwegler 2007) have customary practices of language choice that are not loaded with political meaning. Although frictions and misunderstandings occasionally arise, conflict is not continuously reproduced.

On the contrary, local speakers often resist the politicization of their speech practices by politicians: there is a marked difference beween elite and non-elite language ideologies (Laihonen 2001).

Nevertheless, state policies in each of the seven countries have had linguistic effects. Most obvious are the changes in education and administrative language use. Equally important have been Hungarian initiatives directed at the minorities, giving cultural and some socio-economic privileges in Hungary to Hungarians from the neighbouring states. Even without this controversial policy, travel across the borders for education, employment, tourism and business relations between monolingual Hungarians in Hungary and the minority populations have no doubt increased enormously. The end of communism has accelerated such movement, as have more lenient border regulations within the EU. This has expanded and changed the significance of competence in Hungarian. More local-level studies are needed to provide a full picture. Within the great variety of sociolinguistic matters, this chapter takes up two key areas: "status" issues (valuations, ideologies) and "corpus" issues (variation, terminology, registers).

4.1. Language ideologies and valuations

The available data show that Hungarian minority populations vary in their language attitudes by country, by the size of the minority, location near the border with Hungary and thus easy access to Hungarian mass media, and whether they live in contiguous minority settlements or in speech islands. Nevertheless, there are some general patterns. The minorities operate with a dual evaluative scheme: languages are judged by their efficacy in gaining economic mobility for speakers, and/or on aesthetic, cultural and literary grounds. With the economic lens, minority Hungarian speakers see the state languages as "better" than Hugarian, since their chances of upward social mobility are better with higher education in the state language. (Third languages such as English are omitted here.) The exception is Transylvania, where the existence of an almost full range of Hungarian institutions allows some mobility through the use of Hungarian (Brubaker et al. 2006). Migration to Hungary also lends Hungarian an added economic value for those minorities further east and therefore in economically less advantageous regions (Gal 1987). With the aesthetic and cultural lens, Hungarian is valued very highly by its speakers in all the countries under review. High proportions of Hungarian speakers report that they read Hungarian literary products, magazines and newspapers – many produced in minority regions by minority writers and journalists – and value Hungarian literary and cultural monuments (Fenyvesi 2005).

An exception to this generalisation is the border city of Komárno (Slovakia), across the Danube from Komárom (Hungary). There, the economic value of Hungarian – shopping in Hungary, retail trade to visiting Hungarians – has increased in the last decade (Schwegler 2007); the same burgeoning of border traffic has increased the value of Hungarian for the regional minority in Austria since 1989. In Austria the aesthetic and literary value of Hungarian have remained low, in competition with German which is seen as a world language (Gal 1987; Bodó 2005). The degree of aesthetic and "heritage" valuation of Hungarian is related to the presence (or not) of an intellectual elite who act as role models, and to the opportunity for schooling in the language. In Austria, Croatia and Slovenia such an elite has been lacking since the First World War and education has been revived only in the last few decades.

A further aspect of language valuation is the ranking by Hungarian speakers of the regionally distinct forms of Hungarian, including their own (Fenyvesi 2005). The Hungarian variety considered characteristic of Transylvania is valued most highly by all regions, probably in part because of the central place of Transylvania in the Hungarian national imaginary. Hungarians in Ukraine also rank their own forms as beautiful, perhaps because these are close to northern dialects on which the standard was based. By contrast, the Hungarians in Slovakia seem the most self-critical and devalue their own distinctive forms of Hungarian, as do those in Serbia, Austria and Croatia. An important explanation of this devaluation is that local forms ("dialect") are stigmatised in relation to standardised forms in Hungarian, as they are in all languages on the European continent (see final section).

Contact with monolinguals – in Hungary or in their home regions – creates typical dilemmas. In all the minority populations, Hungarian speakers are bilingual in very large proportions, while the majority populations are ordinarily monolingual. Because the pan-European norm is (still) monolingualism in the state language, minority Hungarian speakers are expected to accommodate to majority speakers in language choice. If they do not, the majority feel excluded and may charge Hungarian speakers with cliquishness or secrecy. Although minority speakers do indeed switch to the majority language in public settings or when a monolingual is present, they also feel policed because monolinguals retain the right to metacommentary questioning the use of Hungarian (Brubaker et al. 2006; Gal 1979; Schwegler 2007). The encounter with Hungarian monolinguals in Hungary can also be fraught and for some of the same reasons. Hungarian speakers in Hungary make no allowances for the linguistic effects of bilingualism. This, and the somewhat divergent local forms used by minority speakers are heard by metropolitan Hungarians as provincial and chronotopically "backward" or unsophisticated (Gal 2006), leading to the stigmatisation of those who use them.

But ideologies of language also vary somewhat by region (Baár and Ritivoi 2006) as do attitudes towards bilingualism. In the villages of the Bànàt (Romania), interviewees expressed a positive attitude about multilingualism, putting their three languages (Hungarian, Romanian, German) side by side and affirming that knowing all three is the ideal (Laihonen 2004: 88–89). For these speakers, general social tolerance is connected, ideologically, to the presence of multilingualism, and they identify both practices as characteristic of their region, an aspect of their identity. Local identities of this kind, with loyalty to a micro-region, form an important part of the sense of belonging of Hungarian minorities. In a striking pattern, questionnaire responses and small-scale ethnographic reports show that speakers are often more closely attached to the city, village or region in which they live than to the states of their residence or to the Hungarian "nation" as a whole (see Fenyvesi 2005; Bakó and Szoták 2005).

4.2. Language use patterns: registers and standards

The general pattern for the minority populations is that the public realm, municipal administration, police, legal system and often the workplace are the domains of the state language. Hungarian is used in domestic settings, in religious practice, often in school, in voluntary organisations and the local business world of shopping and subsistence. Those who live in largely minority settlements use the language much more broadly than those who do not. Children in such settlements enter school as Hungarian monolinguals. Hungarian is a language of reading, mass media – both local and from Hungary – and high culture such as theater, but it is often excluded from professional, occupational and workplace uses. In Ukraine, for instance, all medical interactions take place in Russian or Ukrainian, since there are no Hungarian-speaking doctors in the countryside. In Slovakia and Romania, engineers and other technical professionals live their work lives entirely in the state language, even if they use Hungarian at home, visit Hungary frequently and consume Hungarian mass media.

As a result of this restriction in the domains of use for Hungarian, linguists report that the Hungarian speech of bilinguals lacks technical and administrative registers (see Lanstyák and Szabómihály 2002; Péntek 1998 and reports in Fenyvesi 2005). Register stripping is but one reason that the speech of Hungarian minorities is often devalued by monolingual Hungarians and the bilingual speakers themselves. Codeswitching, borrowing and other contact phenomena are typical of bilingual populations, of course, yet in the pan-European regime of monolingualism and standard language, these features lead to stigma and to self-deprecation (Gal 2006). Judgmental encounters with purist linguists and teachers also create problems of self-confidence (see, e.g., Lanstyák 2006; Kontra and Saly 1998). A further source of stigma is the rural dialect forms that are often the home variety of the Hungarian minorities. In contrast to such regional forms, the idealised "standard" of Hungarian metropolitan elites is highly respected. Lacking in linguistic confidence, many Hungarian speakers in Slovakia overcorrect in the direction of the standard, often also insisting on extrapurist lexicon, which leads to pauses, hesitations and slower speech in formal situations.

Linguists speaking for the minority populations argue that language planning is essential in order to allow the minorities to acquire and maintain the metropolitan standard as a "High" variety of educated speech, public oratory, writing and humanistic scholarship, while not denigrating the "Low" and emotionally important contact-varieties that speakers bring from home to schooling (Lanstyák 2006). Intellectuals in the minority populations acknowledge the importance of the standard as a unifying force. This is also supported by Hungarian mass media. Yet, as in many other linguistic minorities, the linguists closest to the everyday problems of speakers argue that the goal of language planning should also include the expansion and enhancement of the local Hungarian varieties. They call for the creation of technical and administrative vocabulary that matches the lexical patterns of the various countries but is also aligned with that of Hungary. A strong element of status planning is also needed, they argue, so that the pan-European ideology of a standard that denigrates other varieties does not punish bilingual speakers.

Notes

1. I thank Adorján István for his research assitance and ethnographic insight; many thanks as well to Kassai Ilona, Bartha Csilla and especially Lanstyák István for his generous bibliographic and scholarly assistance. This research was supported by the Lichtstern Fund of the Department of Anthropology of the University of Chicago.
2. Information on education is based on reports at the website of the Hungarian Office to Develop Education Abroad [*Határon Túli Oktatás Fejlesztéséért Programiroda*] of the Education Ministry, which relies on the national statistics of each country. *www.martonaron.hu/htof/* accessed 1/2008.
3. This description pertains only to the regional Hungarian minority. It is a separate if related issue that there are large numbers of migrant Hungarian speakers in Austria, some of whom hail from minority regions, especially Romania, Slovakia and Vojvodina. In some of the larger cities, they have established educational institutions for the support of the Hungarian language.

References

Anderson, Benedict
    1991   Census, map, museum. In *Imagined Communities*, Benedict Anderson (ed.), 163–185. London: Verso.

Baár, Monika and Adreea Deciu Ritivoi
    2006   The Transylvanian Babel: Negotiating national identity through language in a disputed territory. *Language & Communication* 26: 203–217.

Bakó, Boglárka and Szilvia Szoták (eds.)
    2005   *Magyarlakta kistérségek és kisebbségi identitások a Kárpátmedencében.* [Identities in Small Regions with Hungarian Populations in the Carpathian Basin]. Budapest: Gondolat.

Benő Attila and Sándor Szilágyi
    2005   Hungarian in Romania. In *Hungarian Language Contact Outside Hungary*, Anna Fenyves (ed.), 133–165. Philadelphia: John Benjamins.

Bodó, Csanád
    2005   Hungarian in Austria. In *Hungarian Language Contact Outside Hungary*, Anna Fenyves (ed.), 241–264. Philadelphia: John Benjamins.

Bartha, Csilla
  in press   Myth and reality of linguistic others: The situation of linguistic minorities in Hungary. In *Les Langues Minoritaires: l'Expérience Hongroise et Centreüeuroéenne,* Ilona Kassai (ed.).
Borbély, Anna (ed.)
  2000   *Nyelvek és kulturák érintkezése a Kárpát-medencében* [Contact among Languages in the Carpathian Basin]. Budapest: Magyar Tudomànyos Akadémia.
Brubaker, Rogers
  1995   National minorities, nationalizing states, and the external national homelands in the New Europe. *Daedelus* 124 (2): 107–132.
Brubaker, Rogers, Margit Feischmidt, Jon Fox and Liana Grancea
  2006   *Nationalist Politics and Everyday Ethnicity in a Transylvanian Town.* Princeton, N.J.: Princeton University Press.
Csergő, Zsuzsa
  2007   *Talk of the Nation: Language and Conflict in Romania and Slovakia.* Ithaca: Cornell University Press.
Csernicskó, István
  2005   Hungarian in Ukraine. In *Hungarian Language Contact Outside Hungary,* Anna Fenyvesi (ed.), 89–132. Philadelphia: John Benjamins.
Fenyvesi, Anna (ed.)
  2005   *Hungarian Language Contact Outside Hungary.* Philadelphia: John Benjamins.
Gál, Kinga (ed.)
  2002   *Minority Governance in Europe.* Budapest: Open Society Institute, Local Government and Public Service Initiative.
Gal, Susan
  1979   *Language Shift: Social Determinants of Linguistic Change in Bilingual Austria.* New York: Academic.
  1987   Codeswitching and consciousness in the European periphery. *American Ethnologist* 14 (4): 637–653.
  1991   Bartók's Funeral: Representations of Europe in Hungarian political rhetoric. *American Ethnologist* 18 (3): 440–458.
  1993   Diversity and contestation in linguistic ideologies: German speakers in Hungary. *Language in Society* 22: 337–359.
  2006   Contradictions of standard language in Europe: Implications for the study of publics and practices. *Social Anthropology* 14 (4): 163–181.
Göncz, Lajos and Otto Vörös
  2005   Hungarians in the Former Yugoslavia (Vojvodina and Prekmurje). In *Hungarian Language Contact Outside Hungary,* Anna Fenyvesi (ed.), 187–240. Philadelphia: John Benjamins.

Göncz, Lajos
in press The language situation of the Hungarian minorities outside Hungary. In *Les langues minoritaires: l'Expérience hongroise et centre-euroéenne*, Ilona Kassai (ed.).
Győri-Nagy Sándor and Kelemen Janka (eds.)
1991 *Kétnyelvüség a Kárpát-medencében*. Budapest: Széchényi Társaság.
Hannonen, Pasi, Bo Lönnqvist and Gábor Barna (eds.)
2001 *Ethnic Minorities and Power*. Helsinki: Fonda Publishing.
Hobsbawm, Eric
1990 *Nations and Nationalism Since 1780*. New York: Cambridge Press.
Kassai, Ilona (ed.)
1995 *Kétnyelvűség és magyar nyelvhasználat*. [Bilingualism and Hungarian Language Use]. Budapest: Magyar Tudomànyos Akadémia.
Kelley, Judith
2004 *Ethnic Politics in Europe: The Power of Norms and Incentives*. Princeton: Princeton University Press.
Kontra, Miklós
2005 Contextualizing the sociolinguistics of Hungarian outside Hungary project. In *Hungarian Language Contact Outside Hungary*, Anna Fenyvesi (ed.), 29–46. Philadelphia: John Benjamins.
Kontra, Miklós and Helga Hattyár (eds.)
2002 *Magyarok és nyelvtörvények* [Hungarians and Language Laws]. Budapest: Teleki Foundation.
Kontra, Miklós and Noémi Saly (eds.)
1998 *Nyelvmentés vagy nyelvárulás?* [Language Rescue or Language Betrayal?]. Budapest: Osiris Kiadó.
Laihonen, Petteri
2001 Multilingualism in the Bánát: Elite and everyday language ideologies. In *Ethnic Minorities and Power*, Pasi Hanonnen et al (eds.), 11–45. Helsinki: Fonda.
2004 A romániai bánsági (bánáti) tolerancia és kétnyelvüség a nyelvi ideologiák tükrében [The tolerance of the Romanian Banat as seen through bilingual language ideology]. In *Tér és Terep* [Space and Field], N. Kovács, O. Osvát, and L. Szarka (eds.), 81–97. Budapest: Akadémiai Kiadó.
Lanstyák, István
2006 *Nyelvből nyelvbe* [From Language to Language]. Pozsony: Kalligram.
Lanstyák, István and Szabolcs Simon
2002 *Tanulmányok a kétnyelvűségről*. [Studies on Bilingualism]. Pozsony: Kalligram.

Lanstyák, István and Gizella Szabómihály
2002 *Magyar nyelvtervezés Szlovákiában.* [Hungarian Language Planning in Slovakia]. Pozsony: Kalligram.
2005 Hungarian in Slovakia. In *Hungarian Language Contact Outside Hungary*, Anna Fenyvesi (ed.), 47–88. Philadelphia: John Benjamins.
Pál, Tamás et al. (eds.)
2005 *Nemzetfelfogások: Kisebbség-többség.* [Concepts of Nation: Minority-Majority]. Budapest: MTA SZKI.
Péntek, János
1998 A kisebbségi iskolák kétnyelvüsége és kettösnyelvüsége. [Bilingualism and duo-lingualism of minority schools]. In *Nyelvmentés vagy nyelvárulás?* [Language Rescue or Language Betrayal?], Miklós Kontra and Noémi Saly (eds.), 299–304. Budapest: Osiris Kiado.
Pléh, Csaba
1995 Sociolinguistics in Hungary: A personal account. In *When East Met West: Sociolinguistics in the Former Socialist Bloc*, Jeffrey Harlig and Csaba Pléh (eds.), 125–142. Berlin/New York: Mouton de Gruyter.
Sándor, Klára
2005 The Csàngós of Romania. In *Hungarian Language Contact Outside Hungary*, Anna Fenyvesi (ed.), 163–185. Philadelphia: John Benjamins.
Schwegler, Brian
2007 *Confronting the Devil: Europe, Nationalism, and Municipal Governance in Slovakia.* PhD Disseration, Department of Anthropology, Univesity of Chicago.
Tóth, Ágnes and János Vékás
2004 A 2001.évi népi népszamlálási adatok rövid összefoglalása. [Short summary of the 2001 Census]. *Baràtsàg* 5: 4425–4432.
Woolard, Kathryn
1998 Introduction: Language ideology as a field of inquiry. In *Language Ideology: Practice and Theory*, Kathryn Woolard, Bambi Schieffelin and Paul Kroskrity (eds.), 3–47. New York: Oxford University Press.

Sámi languages in the Nordic countries and Russia

Mikael Svonni

1. Introduction

Sámi is spoken by the Sámi, an indigenous people living in Norway, Sweden, Finland, and Russia. Sámi has been spoken for thousands of years in Fenno-Scandia and Kola Peninsula and is apparently one of the oldest languages in the area. However, the 1900s have been a time of transition for the Sámi. Sámi society has changed in many respects, as regards people's livelihoods, economic conditions, patterns of habitation, cultural traditions and customs (Amft 2000). The changes in people's ways of life have also resulted in changing patterns of language use among the Sámi (Helander 1984).

The status of Sámi languages has attracted more attention during the last few decades, and reports on the on-going language shift among the Sámi have contributed to a rising interest in the language issue among the Sámi in general (Hyltenstam and Stroud 1990). However, the situation is not similar for all Sámi language groups. There is considerable variation across the regions within the traditional Sámi habitation area, which is called *Sápmi*. There are clear trends visible in Sámi language use: those Sámi who are pursuing traditional livelihoods, especially reindeer herding, tend to have a better knowledge of Sámi than the non-reindeer herding population; the younger generations have less knowledge than the older people; and finally, the language is weaker among the South Sámi and the East Sámi speakers than among the Central Sámi. Today, some of the smaller Sámi dialects are seriously endangered.

This chapter gives an overview of the Sámi population and the number of Sámi speakers, the Sámi languages and dialects, their history and their present legal status. After this, a description follows of the use of Sámi, in particular in education, in the media and in administration. Finally, processes of language shift and prerequisites for the Sámi maintaining their languages are discussed. The focus, however, is on the Sámi in Sweden.

2. Sápmi and Sámi population

Sápmi, or the Sámi core area traditionally called Lapland, consists of a large geographic area stretching from the east coast of the Kola Peninsula in Russia, across the northernmost districts of Finland, to the coastal and inland parts of northern and central Norway, including a region in Sweden from the far north down to the province of Jämtland (Figure 1).

Figure 1. Map of *Sápmi*, the traditional Sámi habitation area, divided according to the various Sámi languages

This settlement area actually comprises several geographic regions with correspondingly different traditional subsistence practices, including inland forests, where fishing, hunting and reindeer herding prevail; the Arctic Ocean coast where we find fishing, some hunting, and even farming in the fjords; and areas along rivers and lakes where fishing is the main occupation.

The Sámi have lived in this huge area for thousands of years. All this time, they were probably the only inhabitants, at least in the inland parts. The first contacts with Scandinavians were probably established before the Viking Age, probably in the South Sámi area. There are thousands of Scandinavian loanwords in the Sámi languages and only a few Sámi loanwords in the Scandinavian languages. It would be easy to conclude that the Scandinavians always have been superior to the Sámi, at least in some respect. However, recent research has challenged this view and has indicated close contacts between the Sámi and Scandinavians during the Viking Age and earlier (Zachrisson et al. 1997; Kusmenko and Riessler 2000; Kusmenko 2007). Kusmenko's point of view is that the Sámi did not have a suppressed position in the society during the Viking age; in fact, Sámi and Scandinavians were equal in a sense. During the Middle Ages, the Sámi lost their position in the society when agriculture had spread to areas where the Sámi were living and the Scandinavian population increased. The Sámi continued with fishing, hunting and reindeer herding and it was not until the period of industrialisation, which began at the end of the 19th century and continued well into the 20th century, that the Sámi culture began to change in a crucial manner, largely as a result of migration of Scandinavians into Sápmi. This immigration gradually began to have a profound impact on traditional Sámi economy and settlement patterns. Today, for example, there are only a few municipalities in Norway where the Sámi constitute a majority, i.e., *Guovdageaidnu* (Kautokeino) and *Kárášjohka* (Karasjok). There is one Sámi majority municipality in Finland as well, *Ohcejohka* (Utsjoki). In Sweden, the largest Sámi group lives in *Giron* (Kiruna), where they constitute 10–15% of the total population. The total Sámi population is currently estimated to be approximately 60,000, i.e., 30–35,000 in Norway, 17,000 in Sweden, 7,000 in Finland and 2,000 in Russia.

3. Sámi languages and dialects

Within Sápmi, a number of Sámi varieties are spoken that differ in phonology, morphology and syntax. There are also quite a large number of lexical variations. Sámi is typically divided into three main languages: East Sámi, Central Sámi, and South Sámi. These main Sámi languages are generally further subdivided into ten language varieties, as depicted in Figure 1. While the three main languages are mutually unintelligible, speakers of varieties that are close to each other geographically usually do not have difficulty in communicating.

South Sámi, which includes South Sámi and Ume Sámi, is spoken in Sweden and Norway by about 600–800 people. However, there are only a few Ume Sami speakers and the language is seriously endangered. Of the Central Sámi dialects, Pite Sámi and Lule Sámi are spoken in Norway and Sweden by about 800-1,000 people. Pite Sámi is seriously endangered as well, since there are only older people who have skills in that language. North Sámi, a Central Sámi dialect, is spoken by about 20,000 people in Sweden, Norway, and Finland. The East Sámi dialects – Inari Sámi, Skolt Sámi, Kildin Sámi, Akkala Sámi, and Ter Sámi – are spoken by about 800–1,000 people in Finland and on the Kola Peninsula in Russia, where the majority of speakers live. These numbers are estimates since no reliable statistics exist on the numbers of speakers.

The Sámi languages in Kola Peninsula are seriously endangered, mainly the Akkala and the Ter Sámi languages. There are only a few older speakers of these small Sámi languages. Kildin Sámi – which has the strongest position – is spoken by some 650 individuals, most of them older than 30 years of age (Sergejeva 1995). There are only some 20 speakers of Skolt Sámi in Russia; most of the Skolt Sámi speakers live in Finland. The Skolt Sámi group and the Inari Sámi group in Finland consist of approximately 500 people each. In the mid 1980s, the Inari Sámi group started language maintenance and revitalisation programmes for adult and also since 1997 successfully organised language-nest activities for children (Aikio-Puoskari 2001). Efforts to promote South Sámi skills among adults have been made in the South Sámi area as well (Huss 1999: 121–123).

4. Historic background

Sámi is a Finno-Ugric language and is most closely related to Balto-Finnic languages like Finnish and Estonian. According to a widely accepted theory, the Sámi and the Balto-Finnic languages have a common ancestor, Proto Sámi-Finnic. This proto language later branched off into two languages, Proto Sámi and Proto Finnic. This process started some 4,500 years ago, when Indo-European pre-agricultural groups of people arrived in the Baltic area (Sammallahti 1995; Korhonen O. 1997). The ultimate division of Proto Sámi and Proto Finnic was a consequence of the Proto German contacts with speakers of Proto Finnic, around 1,500 B.C., which had a profound influence on the sound system of Proto Finnic, and brought about crucial differences between the languages (Sammallahti 1995). Proto Sámi used to be considered as having been a uniform language until 800 A.D. and the Sámi were thought to have lived not further south than Bodö at the time (Korhonen M. 1988). However, recent studies in linguistics and archaeology (Sammallahti 1990; Bergsland 1996; Kusmenko and Riessler 2000; Zachrisson et al. 1997) suggest that over a thousand years ago Sámi lived much further south and that the division into the current dialects was in fact completed in 800 A.D. (Korhonen O. 1997: 83). Archaeological research in the South Sámi area in the 1990s shed new light on the history of the Sámi settlements in present Härjedalen and Jämtland. The findings indicate that Sámi have lived in this area and adjacent areas in present Norway more than one thousand years ago and grave findings suggest that the assumption that the Sámi always have had a suppressed position in the society was not altogether true (Zachrisson et al. 1997).

A decade ago German linguists in Berlin draw attention to linguistic phenomena in some of the northeastern Scandinavian dialects (eastern Norwegian and north-central Swedish dialects) in the area inhabited by both Sámi and Scandinavians one thousand years ago. They argued that these dialects have been influenced by the Sámi languages during the Viking Age and in the beginning of the Middle Ages with respect to vowel balance, level stress, metaphony and consonant lengthening. The process of Sámi influence on Scandinavian dialects was possible for the following reasons. First of all, the Sámi did not have a suppressed position in the society during the Viking age. In fact, the Sámi were superior to the Scandinavians with respect to skiing and hunting (among other things), and their hunting skills were extremely valuable because trading with skins was profitable both for the Sámi and the Scandinavians at that time. Secondly, at least the South Sámi were bilingual and many of the South Sámi were assimilated into the Scandinavian group; their Scandinavian language use was influenced by Sámi and their Scandinavian vernacular was later fossilised and became "standard" vernacular.

The Sámi were superior to the Scandinavians with regard to *noaidevuohta* (i.e., witchcraft) as well, and knowledge of *noaidevuohta* was accepted and quite common both among the Sámi and the Scandinavians during the Viking age and in the beginning of the Middle Ages, but was forbidden in connection wit Christianity. As a matter of fact, according to Norwegian laws in the beginning of the Middle Ages, Christian people were forbidden to make contact with people (i.e., Sámi) who utilised *noaidevuohta* (Mundal 2006), which in turn indicates that the Sámi were clearly present in the society.

5. The legal status of the Sámi languages

The Sámi languages enjoy legal status in Norway, Finland and Sweden, at least in some speech areas (Aikio-Puoskari 2001; Gaup Eira 2004). In 1987, the Norwegian Parliament (*Stortinget*) passed the Sámi Act, which included regulations with respect to language use. In 1992, special regulations were appended to the Sámi Act, one of which confirmed the status of Sámi as an official language in Norway. As a result, Sámi is now placed on the same level as Norwegian within the Sámi language administrative area, consisting of eight municipalities: *Kárášjohka* (Karasjok), *Guovdageaidnu* (Kautokeino), *Unjárga* (Nesseby), *Porsáŋgu* (Porsanger), *Deatnu* (Tana), *Gáivuotna* (Kåfjord), *Divtasvuodna* (Tysfjord) and *Snoasa* (Snåsa)(since 1 January 2008). Divtasvuodna is in the Lule Sámi area and Snoasa in the South Sámi area. The Sámi languages also achieved higher status with respect to their use in administrative proceedings, which for instance includes the legal right of individuals to use them in contacts with government authorities. The authorities in question are thus obliged to translate rules and regulations into Sámi. In addition, there are regulations regarding the right to use Sámi in legal proceedings. At the same time, amendments were made to the rules governing the comprehensive school system, specifically with respect to the use of Sámi in the classroom. According to this act, children living in Sámi districts now have the legal right to receive instruction in Sámi.

In Finland, a law came into force in 1992 regarding the government's use of Sámi. This legislation secures the right to use Sámi when communicating with authorities for those living within the so-called Sámi home district area, which includes the municipalities of *Ohcejohka* (Utsjoki), *Eanodat* (Enontekiö), *Anár* (Inari), and a part of *Soađegilli* (Sodankylä).

In Sweden, a proposal was put forward by a government commission (*samerättsutredningen*) in 1991, specifying regulations regarding the legal rights to use Sámi when communicating with authorities in domains of Sámi affairs, e.g., the administration of reindeer breeding. The commission's report, however, did not result in an actual language law at that time. As of 1 April 2000, legislation ensures the right to use Sámi when dealing with state authorities and in the law courts in Sweden. The law applies to municipal, state, regional, and local authorities in the Sámi administrative area, which includes *Giron* (Kiruna), *Jiellevárri* (Gällivare), *Jåhkåmåhkke* (Jokkmokk), and *Árjepluovve* (Arjeplog). According to the law, an individual has the right to use Sámi in all oral and written communication with authorities concerning official decisions related to that individual. Authorities are obliged to use Sámi in oral communications and to provide information so that a written answer can be translated orally to Sámi if so requested by an individual.

In the administrative area for Sámi, individuals have the right to use Sámi in the courts when a case is being heard that is related to the administrative area. Individuals also have the right to submit information in Sámi, to have the information dealing with the case translated orally, and to use Sámi in oral communication before the court. The administrative area for Sámi in Sweden includes the area where North and Lule Sámi are traditionally spoken. The South Sámi area is not covered by this legislation.

As a result of the seventh Nordic Sámi Conference in Gällivare in 1971, a Sámi Language Committee has been established. Nine members were elected on this committee, representing four dialects or language varieties: South Sámi, Lule Sámi, North Sámi, and Skolt Sámi. Since the Sámi Conference of 1974, the Inari Sámi also got represented in the committee, and since the Sámi Conference of 1992, the Sámi Language Committee has been further expanded to include Russian representatives. The committee initially concerned itself with orthographic issues, but also dealt with matters concerning standardisation, language preservation, and language laws. The Sámi Parliaments in Norway, Sweden and Finland have appointed Sámi Language Committees and the Nordic Sámi Parliaments in 1997 established a joint Sámi Language Council.

6. Language use

Sámi is spoken in a huge geographic area comprising parts of four different countries, where the majority languages are Norwegian, Swedish, Finnish, and Russian. This geographic distribution means that native Sámi speakers must also have skills in a majority language, because they have to be able to communicate with majority language speakers to varying degrees, depending on the speech environment in which they live. This is true, for example, in the work place, in mass media, in service organisations, and in government administration. The minority language is spoken primarily in informal domains, in particular within the immediate family and among close friends.

For natural reasons, the Sámi languages have an elaborate terminological system concerning phenomena within specific areas of traditional Sámi livelihood, for example, terms referring to the weather, to landscape features, to fishing, hunting, and reindeer herding. Among the reindeer herding Sámi in Sweden, whose proficiency in Sámi at the group level has the strongest position, the following seems to be apparent. Almost all of the North Sámi reindeer herders speak Sámi fluently. They use some Finnish and Swedish loanwords, but adjust them to the system of Sámi. In the Lule Sámi area many reindeer herders speak Sami as well, but far from all. A very typical way of speaking in this area is code-switching. They start a sentence in Sámi and complete it in Swedish or vice versa. Older Sámi in the Lule Sámi area speak in this manner as well. In the South Sámi area, the dominant language is Swedish, except for very few language islands. One might hear a few Sámi words, e.g., terms of greetings and also words for father, mother, dog, and reindeer. In the South Sámi case, Sámi does not function as medium of communication, instead it functions as marker of South Sámi identity (Svonni 1996). In recent years, however, the reindeer herding Sámi in the Lule Sámi area have begun to pay more attention to the status of Sámi among the reindeer herders and they have started to support young reindeer herders to promote their Sámi skills in connection with reindeer herding. However, because most Sámi work nowadays outside traditional livelihood, the use of Sámi within public domains such as education and administration has become more and more a crucial issue.

7. Language use in education

At the beginning of the 20th century, a school system was developed in Sweden that placed nomadic children on a lower educational level in comparison to non-nomadic Swedish children. After criticism of this system by the Sámi, however, conditions improved. In 1939, the Swedish Parliament (*Riksdag*) declared that the education of Sámi nomadic children should be equivalent to that of other children. During the 1940s, the duration of instruction in Sámi in so-called "nomadic schools" was increased to be commensurate with that of regular elementary schools of the time. Since the end of the 19th century, the language of instruction has been Swedish in Sámi schools, and it was only in the mid 1950s that Sámi was introduced as a subject.

In 1962, the Swedish Parliament agreed to a reorganisation of the Sámi educational system, which among other things implied that attending nomadic schools became optional. Until that change, nomadic schools had been compulsory for reindeer herding Sámi children (Svonni 1993: 49). As a further result of the reorganisation, Sámi became a mandatory subject in the schools, generally consisting of two periods of instruction per week. When home language instruction was introduced in Swedish elementary schools (*grundskolan*) in 1976 (see also Nygren-Junkin, this Volume), Sámi instruction increased in the Sámi schools as well, to comprise five to six periods per week at the most.

In Sweden, Sámi children can attend municipal nine-year compulsory schools or State-run Sámi schools. A special board, the *Sámi School Board*, is responsible for the operating of the Sámi schools. The Sámi School Board is appointed by the *Sámi Parliament*, a government body established in 1993 and elected by the people. Its mission is to examine issues dealing with the Sámi culture and society in Sweden. The Sámi schools are funded by the State and consist of grades 1 to 6. They provide Sámi children with an education that deals with Sámi matters and that is equivalent to an education in the Swedish nine-year compulsory school. Instruction is given in both Swedish and Sámi, and Sámi is taught in every grade of the child's schooling. Sámi schools are located in *Gárasavvon* (Karesuando), *Lattevárri* (Lannavaara), *Giron* (Kiruna), *Jiellevárri* (Gällivare), *Jåhkåmåhkke* (Jokkmokk), and *Dearna* (Tärnaby).

Some municipalities offer integrated Sámi education, which means that Sámi children attend municipal schools, with part of their education having a Sámi focus. This type of education is offered in grades 1–9. Pupils who have attended Sámi schools commonly choose an integrated Sámi education from grade 7. A municipality can make an agreement with the Sámi School Board to arrange integrated Sámi education for Sámi pupils in a compulsory school. The municipality will then receive State funding for providing this education. Sámi can also be studied as a mother-tongue language (previously referred to as "home language") in municipal nine-year compulsory schools and upper-secondary schools.

A new comprehensive elementary school curriculum came into effect in the academic year 1995/1996. In this curriculum, the objectives of Sámi instruction have been more clearly defined. It is now the responsibility of the Sámi schools to ensure that each student, upon completing the programme, will not only have gained knowledge of the Sámi culture, but also will have acquired the ability to speak, read, and write Sámi. However, the actual implementation of these goals has been questioned.

In Norway and Finland, nomadic schools have never existed, and both Sámi and other children attended the same schools. In fact, Sámi school children comprise a majority in some districts in the core area. The teaching of Sámi in Norway and Finland has been largely consistent with that of Sweden, since the medium of instruction was the majority language (Norwegian or Finnish), and Sámi was introduced as a subject in the school in the 1950s. Yet, while the medium of instruction was intended to be the majority language, Sámi could be used at the elementary school level, primarily as an aid to acquiring the majority language. During the 1970s and 1980s, the teaching of Sámi increased in all three countries to the extent that it has become the medium of instruction in many schools in Norway and Finland, and in some Swedish schools.

In Norway, there are more than 10 schools within the administrative area for the Sámi languages where Sámi is the medium of instruction. There are two upper-secondary schools in Norway where Sámi is the medium of instruction, i.e., in Guovdageaidnu and Kárašjohka. In Finland, Sámi education was developed in the 1980s (Aikio-Puoskari 2001). During that time, Sámi became the medium of instruction in several schools, both at the primary and secondary level of education, and the number of schools providing instruction in Sámi increased. In the beginning of the 1990s, it became possible to study Sámi as a first language in upper-secondary schools as well. All in all, North Sámi has a strong position in the most northern municipalities in Norway, both in compulsory and upper-secondary education, compared to Finland and especially to Sweden.

The teaching of Sámi languages in higher education in Sweden takes place primarily at Umeå University. It is also offered to a limited degree at Uppsala University. In Norway, Sámi languages are taught at the University of Tromsö, at the Sámi University College in Guovdageaidnu (North Sámi), at Bodö University College (Lule Sámi) and at Levanger University College (South Sámi). Higher education in Sámi languages in Finland takes place at the University of Oulu, and as a minor subject at the University of Helsinki and the University of Lapland (in Rovaniemi).

8. Language use in mass media, literature and administration

The domain of the mass media is another area where Sámi has a relatively strong position in Norway. Two Sámi weekly magazines are published in Norway. One of these, *Áššu*, has its editorial office in Guovdageaidnu, and the other one, *Min Aigi*, in Kárášjohka. They appear regularly, once and twice a week, respectively. Recently, the two Sámi papers have merged to one paper, *Ávvir*, which is planned to be a daily paper. By comparison, Sámi magazines are not published on a regular basis in either Finland or Sweden. The monthly magazine *Samefolket*, edited by a foundation supported by two Sámi organisations in Sweden, uses Swedish as the main language in articles, with the exception of a few pages in Sámi in each issue. In Finland, the North Sámi magazine *Sápmelaš* used to appear quite regularly, but these days appears less frequently.

There are a number of daily radio programmes in Sámi, primarily in Norway and Finland where they get more broadcasting time than in Sweden. In Sweden, Sámi programmes are broadcasted for 15 minutes every weekday morning and an hour every Saturday. In some areas in the northern parts of Sweden, there are Sámi programmes for an hour and a half every morning and one hour every afternoon from Monday to Friday. Generally, the programmes in Norway, Sweden, and Finland are produced in North Sámi. Since 2002, there are 10 minutes of daily TV news forecasts in North Sámi from Monday to Friday, which have now been increased to 15 minutes, in cooperation between TV companies in Sweden, Norway and Finland.

Another area where Sámi has increased in vitality over the past few decades is literature. Each year, new books of fiction and poetry by Sámi authors are published. The largest proportion of books is published in North Sámi, but some books are published in other Sámi languages and dialects as well.

Language legislation, especially in Norway and Finland, has given rise to an increased use of Sámi within government administration. In Norway, for example, the primarily Sámi municipalities utilise substantial resources in order to maintain bilingual administration. In accordance with the Sámi Parliament Act in Sweden, the Sámi Parliament works to promote a lively and dynamic Sámi culture and thereby initiates activities and proposes actions that promote the Sámi culture. The Sámi Parliament is also responsible for allotting government grants and funding for Sámi cultural events and activities as well as for working with Sámi language issues.

9. Process of language shift

The vitality of Sámi in Sweden has been analysed in a number of studies (Hansegård 2000; Hyltenstam and Stroud 1991; Hyltenstam, Stroud and Svonni 1999). Hyltenstam and Stroud (1991) examined how factors at the societal, group and individual levels influence processes of language shift versus maintenance among the Sámi in Sweden. At the societal level, factors that influence shift *vs.* maintenance within Swedish society as a whole include political and legal circumstances, the ideology of the majority population, language legislation, and economic conditions. At the group level, these factors include those conditions that regulate relations between the Sámi and Swedish society, but also factors that regulate internal relations among the Sámi, such as demographics, internal organisations, and the media. Factors at the individual level are those influencing personal choice of language use, e.g., in the process of primary socialisation.

The study suggests that a process of language shift is underway among the Sámi, and that it has advanced considerably in certain regions. This shift is occurring in spite of factors such as the growth of Sámi organisations and an increased ethnic consciousness, both of which promote language maintenance, particularly at the group level. Another factor that has a positive influence on Sámi language maintenance includes activities that facilitate language standardisation, modernisation and planning, such as educational programmes. At the individual level, where factors like language choice and socialisation come into play, the current situation has a negative influence on language maintenance, primarily because the opportunities to use Sámi in conversational contexts outside the family are extremely restricted. Many parents choose to use the majority language in raising their children, despite the fact that both of them speak Sámi. However, there are also activities going on among the Sámi to reverse the ongoing language shift (Huss 1999; Aikio-Puoskari and Skutnabb-Kangas 2007).

A recent study on the language situation of the Sámi in present-day Sweden (Svonni, forthcoming) included a questionnaire among the Sámi who are entitled to vote for the Swedish Sámi parliament, as well as the Sámi who are part of the reindeer-herding population or who have close relations with it, a total of 10,000 people. The study shows that approximately 45% of the Sámi have knowledge of Sámi, while 55% have none. Among those who know Sámi, almost 60% speak North Sámi, almost 20% Lule Sámi and slightly more than 20% South Sámi. Nevertheless, the results vary from region to region. In the most northern parts of the country, where North and Lule Sámi are spoken, the knowledge of Sámi is essentially better than in the area where South Sámi is spoken. There is also a marked difference between age groups. In the North and Lule Sámi regions, 60% of the oldest generation (60 plus) speak Sámi without any difficulties, while the corresponding figure for the middle generation (30–59 years old) is 45% and for the youngest generation (29 or younger) is 20%. In the South Sámi speaking area, less than 30% speak Sámi without difficulties in the oldest generation while the corresponding figure for the two younger generations is less than 10%. Interestingly, there are more people in the youngest generation in the province of Jämtland who speak Sámi without difficulties. This may be seen as an indication of a rising interest in South Sámi and revitalisation of the language. Further studies may confirm the existence of such a trend. The study also showed that the Sámi who have moved to areas outside the Sámi habitation area tend to shift language because the youngest generation in this group cannot speak Sámi without difficulties, while a better knowledge of the language is found in the middle generation (appr. 10%) and in the oldest generation (appr. 20%).

10. Prerequisites for Sámi language maintenance

As described above, there are various prerequisites for Sámi language maintenance in various areas. The conditions vary markedly from one Sámi language to another. In reindeer-herding and other traditional livelihoods, such as fishing and handicraft, both North and Lule Sámi are used on a fairly large scale, while South Sámi is only used within certain groups in the province of Jämtland. The traditional livelihoods still support the use of Sámi languages but with the decrease of the number of reindeer herders, the use of Sámi in other domains will rise in importance.

The language legislation of the year 2000 mentioned above does not cover municipalities within the South Sámi area in Sweden; only North and Lule Sámi areas are included. This has resulted in a situation where South Sámi will not be used by the authorities for information activities for instance, and there will therefore be no willingness to develop the South Sámi language. According to the language law, South Sámi, interestingly, is allowed in contacts with the authorities in the Lule and North Sámi areas. So far, the new language legislation has not contributed to any special improvement in the situation of North and Lule Sámi either, because only a very small number of people have taken the opportunity of using Sámi in contacts with the authorities. However, some general information has been translated into Sámi.

In Norway, language legislation covers all Sámi language areas, including the South Sámi area since 2008. In Finland, legislation covers all Sámi languages spoken in the country. Most of the Sámi schools in Sweden are situated within the North Sámi area (Gárasavvon, Lattevárri, Giron, Jiellevárri), one of them in the Lule Sámi area (Jåhkåmåhkke) and another one in the South Sámi area (Dearna). The possibilities to opt for a Sámi school are best for North Sámi speakers but they are also good for the Lule Sámi, because Jåhkåmåhkke is the centre of the Lule Sámi population. The Dearna Sámi School is situated in the province of Västerbotten, an area where South Sámi has a very weak position, rather than down in the South in the province of Jämtland, where the language is stronger. This implies that South Sámi does not receive much support from the Sámi School. The so-called integrated Sámi instruction apparently cannot give sufficient support to the development of the pupils' skills in Sámi because Sámi plays a restricted part in this instruction (Svonni 1993).

In the North Sámi area, the Sámi schools in the past few years have invested in teaching Sámi through a language immersion model, owing to the fact that most of the pupils do not speak Sámi when starting school. Sámi language activities are taking place in the North and Lule Sámi areas but not in the South Sámi area. Both in the North and in Lule Sámi areas, the Sámi schools play an important role in the development of Sámi.

South and also Lule Sámi are used in the media on a very small scale; North Sámi dominates the media. North Sámi thus receives the greatest support from the media, and also benefits from being the main Sámi language used in literature. The number of books published in North Sámi far exceeds the number of books published in Lule and South Sámi.

There has been a debate on creating a common Sámi language. However, Sámi speakers do not feel an affinity with a standardised Sámi language but with their own Sámi dialect. This means that a common Sámi language is a matter for the distant future, if it will be realised at all. There is no pronounced support among the Sámi for developing a common Sámi language or for establishing one of the Sámi languages as a common standard language. In practice, North Sámi moves towards a standard language, because 80–90% of the Sámi speakers speak North Sámi. In addition, there is substantial North Sámi language development work going on in connection with Sámi language legislation, while corresponding activities for the other Sámi languages are at present not taking place.

The North and Lule Sámi speakers usually live in areas where Sámi has a relatively strong position and they are concentrated in certain areas, for instance in Jåhkåmåhkke, Jiellevárri, Giron, and Gárasavvon in Sweden, in Guovdageaidnu and Kárásjohka in Norway, and in Ohcejohka in Finland. The relatively few South Sámi speakers, in turn, live dispersed over a large geographic area with few if any community centres for South Sámi. In Russia, the centre of the Sámi population is Lovozero, and most of the Sámi speakers in Russia live there.

In sum, the prerequisites for maintaining and developing North Sámi are available, while the speakers of the other Sámi languages and dialects have a much weaker position in that respect. The speakers of the smaller Sámi languages, however, are much more aware of the fact that their languages are endangered and they are trying in many ways to maintain them. Considerably more support and greater resources are required from the dominant society but also from the Sámi communities themselves, for instance through the Sámi parliaments, in order to prevent the extinction of more Sámi languages and dialects.

References

Aikio-Puoskari, Ulla
    2001   About the Sámi and the Domestic Legislation on their Language Rights. In *The Language Rights of the Indigenous Saami in Finland under Domestic and International Law*, Ulla Aikio-Puoskari and Merja Pentikäinen (eds.), 3–70. Juridica Lapponica 26. Publication of the Northern Institute for Environmental and Minority Law. Rovaniemi: Lapland's University Press.

Aikio-Puoskari, Ulla and Tove Skutnabb-Kangas
    2007   *When few under 50 speak the language as a first language: linguistic human rights and linguistic challenges for endangered Saami languages. Revitalizing the Periphery.* Proceedings of the conference in language revitalization, Inari, Finland, November 2002.

Amft, Andrea
    2000   *Sápmi i förändringens tid. En studie av svenska samers levnadsvillkor under 1900-talet ur ett genus- och etnicitetsperspektiv* [Sápmi in a Time of Change. A Study of Swedish Sámi living Conditions during the Twentieth Century from a Gender and Ethnic Perspective.]. (Kulturens Frontlinjer, Skrifter från forsknings-programmet Kulturgräns Norr 20). Umeå: Sámiska studier, Umeå Universitet. [Summary in English]

Bergsland, Knut
1996 *Bidrag till sydsamenes historie* [Contribution to the History of South Sámi]. Tromsø: Sámi dutkamiid guovddáš/Senter for samiske studier.

Hansegård, Nils-Erik
2000 *Dialekt eller språk? Om de västsamiska och norrbottensfinska skriftspråken* [Dialect or Language? On the Western Sámi and the Norrbotten Finnish Written Languages]. URSUS. Skriftserie utgiven av Finsk-ugriska institutionen i Uppsala 7.

Helander, Elina
1984 *Om trespråkighet. En undersökning av språkvalet hos samerna i Övre Soppero* [On Trilingualism. A Study of Language Choice among the Sámi in Övre Soppero]. Acta Universitatis Umensis. Umeå Studies in the Humanities 67. Stockholm: Almqvist & Wiksell. [Summary in English]

Gaup Eira, Inger Marie
2004 Sámegiella Davviriikkain. Stáhtus ja domenačielggadeapmi [Sami language in Nordic countries. Status and Domain Clarification]. *Dieđut nr. 4/2004.*

Huss, Leena
1999 *Reversing Language Shift in the Far North. Linguistic Revitalization in Northern Scandinavia and Finland.* Acta Universitatis Upsaliensis. Studia Uralia Upsaliensia 31. Uppsala.

Hyltenstam, Kenneth and Christopher Stroud
1991 *Språkbyte och språkbevarande. Om samiskan och andra minoritetsspråk* [Language Change and Language Maintenance. On Sámi and Other Minority Languages]. Lund: Studentlitteratur.

Hyltenstam, Kenneth, Christopher Stroud and Mikael Svonni
1999 Språkbyte, språkbevarande, revitalisering. Sámiskans ställning i svenska Sápmi [Language change, language maintenance, revitalization. The position of the Sámi in the Swedish Sápmi]. In *Sveriges sju inhemska språk – ett minoritetsspråksperspektiv* [Seven Domestic Languages of Sweden – A Minority Perspective], Kenneth Hyltenstam (ed.), 41–97. Lund: Studentlitteratur.

Korhonen, Mikko
1988 The history of the Lapp language. In *Handbook of Uralic Studies. Vol.1. The Uralic Languages. Description, History and Foreign Influences*, Denis Sinor (ed.), 264–287. Leiden: Brill.

Korhonen, Olavi
1997 Samiskan som språk och traditionskälla [Sámi as a language and a source of tradition]. In *Språkliga och kulturella gränser i Nordskandinavien. Två uppsatser* [Linguistic and Cultural Boundaries in Northern Scandinavia. Two Papers], Olavi Korhonen and Birger

Winsa (eds.), 53–106. Umeå: Kulturens Frontlinjer. Skrifter från forskningsprogrammet Kulturgräns Norr 7.

Kusmenko, Jurij
2006 Jätten Thjazi och det samiska elementet i nordisk mytologi [The giant Thjazi and the Sámi element in Nordic mythology]. In *Sápmi Y1K – Livet i samernas bosättningsområde för ett tusen år sedan* [Sápmi Y1K – The Conditions of Life in the Sámi Settlement Area one Thousand Years Ago], Andrea Amft and Mikael Svonni (eds), 11–28. Samiska studier 3. Skriftserie om samernas språk, kultur och samhälle utgiven av Sámi dutkan/Samiska studier vid Umeå universitet

Kusmenko, Jurij and Michael Riessler
2000 Traces of Sámi-Scandinavian contact in Scandinavian dialects. In *Languages in Contact*, Dicky Gilbers, John Nerbonne and Jos Schaeken (eds.), 209–224. Amsterdam/Atlanta: Rodopi.

Sammallahti, Pekka
1990 The Sámi language: Past and present. In *Arctic Languages. An Awakening*, Dirmid R. F. Collins, (ed.), 437–458. Paris: UNESCO.
1995 Language and Roots. *Congressus Octavus Internationalis Fenno-Ugristarum 1995. Pars I.* Jyväskylä: Moderatores.

Svonni, Mikael
1993 *Samiska skolbarns samiska. En undersökning av minoritetsspråksbehärskning i en språkbyteskontext* [The Sámi of Sámi Schoolchildren. A Study of Minority Language Proficiency in a Context of Language Change]. Acta Universitatis Umensis. Umeå Studies in the Humanities 113. Stockholm: Almqvist and Wiksell. [Summary in English]
1996 Saami language as a marker of ethnic identity among the Saami. In *Essays on Indigenous Identity and Rights*, Irja Seurujärvi-Kari and Ulla-Maija Kulonen (eds.), 105–125. Helsinki: Helsinki University Press.

Svonni, Mikael (ed.)
forthc. *Sápmi i siffror. En kvantitativ och kvalitativ studie om den Sámiska befolkningen i Sverige* [Sápmi in Numbers. A Qualitative and Quantitative Study of the Sámi Population in Sweden].

Zachrisson, Inger, Verner Alexandersen, Martin Gollwitzer, Elisabeth Iregren, Lars-König Königsson, Claes-Henric Siven, Norbert Strade and Jan Sundström
1997 *Möten i Gränsland. Samer och Germaner i Mellanskandinavien* [Meetings in Borderland. Sámi and Germans in Middle Scandinavia]. Monographs 4. Stockholm: Statens historiska museum.

Section III
Immigrant minority languages

New minority languages in the United Kingdom

Viv Edwards

1. Introduction

While linguistic diversity has been a defining feature of the British Isles for centuries, this diversity has assumed new proportions in the second half of the twentieth century and beyond. In the first of two large waves of migration, between the mid-1950s and the late 1960s, British citizens came from India, Pakistan, the Caribbean and from other former colonies in response to labour shortages created by the economic expansion following World War II. Increasingly stringent legislation meant that immigration had reduced to a trickle by the early 1970s, after which time most new arrivals were the dependents of those already in the country or refugees. The second wave of migration around the new millennium can be attributed to a number of factors, the most important of which are globalisation and the enlargement of the European Union.

This chapter will examine the linguistic ramifications of these migrations. It will explore the nature and extent of diversity as well as indicators of the ethnolinguistic vitality of the languages in question, including religion, the economy, the media and the arts, which determine the speed of language shift to English. Particular attention will be paid to the response of mainstream educators to the presence of large numbers of children speaking other languages, and to the responsibilities which minority communities have assumed for transmitting their languages to the next generation.

2. Terminology

As is often the case with new fields of study, discussions around linguistic diversity are plagued by terminological confusion. It is important therefore to explain at the outset, the choices I have made. Other chapters in this Volume speak of "immigrant languages". Possibly because of the longer history of large-scale migration, this term is unacceptable in the UK. Many of those who speak languages from the Indian sub-continent, for instance, are the second and even the third generation born in the UK. The use of "immigrant" is therefore both inaccurate and insulting.

Other terms are also problematic. "Community languages" – for many years the preferred term – has been criticised on the grounds that relationships between speakers of the same languages are not necessarily supportive, as is implied by the use of "community". "Minority languages" in a UK context must necessarily include both the "older mother tongues" – Gaelic, Irish and Welsh – and those of more recent provenance which are the focus for this Chapter. The use of "additional languages", adopted for instance by the *Valeur Project* (McPake et al. 2007), poses similar difficulties. While this term would be wholly appropriate for the discussion of *all* languages other than English, my focus is on the languages that have been part of the linguistic landscape only in more recent years. For that reason, my preference is for "new minority languages".

Terminological confusion also surrounds the teaching of these new minority languages. "Supplementary" and "complementary" tend to be used interchangeably in discussions of the non-mainstream school settings where these languages are taught.

3. The extent of diversity

Precise numbers of speakers of new minority languages are difficult to establish in any setting but pose particular challenges in the UK, where the only language data collected in population censuses to date relate to Welsh in Wales, Gaelic in Scotland, and Irish in Northern Ireland (Baker and Eversley 2000; Edwards 2004). Data on ethnicity offer some indications of the extent of diversity. The 2001 Census[1], for instance, points to important differences in the distribution of minority ethnic communities. Thus, while 2% of the population of England and Wales are Indian, this group constitutes 25.7% of the population of Leicester. Similarly, Bangladeshis form 0.5% of the population of England and Wales, but 33.4% of the population of the London borough of Tower Hamlets. It is not possible, however, to extrapolate from census data to the size of different language groups: some ethnicities (e.g., Indian) are associated with many different languages; and ethnicity is not, in any case, an automatic guarantee that a respondent is bilingual. Recent consultations on the form that questions on language might take give reason for optimism that the 2011 Census will address this unfortunate omission.

Various school surveys offer further indications. Baker and Eversley (2000), for instance, report that more than 300 different home languages are spoken by some 850,000 school children in the Greater London area. Each of the top ten languages – Bengali, Punjabi, Gujarati, Hindi/Urdu, Turkish, Arabic, English-based Creoles, Yoruba and Cantonese – is spoken by at least 40,000 school children. Extrapolating from the school survey data, they estimate that there are at least eighteen communities with more than 50,000 people; of these, French, Arabic, Spanish, Greek, Portuguese and Russian all have 200,000 or more speakers.

Information is also available on the languages spoken by children outside the capital. A survey of every local authority in England, Wales and Scotland (CILT 2005) reports that at least 300 languages are spoken by 702,000 children in England; the corresponding statistics for Wales are 98 languages spoken by 8,000 children, and 104 languages spoken by 11,000 children in Scotland. The researchers, however, suggest that these figures may be underestimates and the more comprehensive data generated by a language question in the 2006 Schools Census for Scotland confirm their suspicions. Scottish Executive (2007) reports that children in Scottish schools speak 137 different languages in addition to English, the most common of which were Panjabi, Urdu, Cantonese, Polish and Arabic. Hopefully, the inclusion for the first time in the 2007 School Census in England of a "Pupil First Language question" will lead to more accurate reporting of the languages spoken by children in this part of the UK, too.[2]

An important feature of the recent surveys is the changing nature of diversity, both in terms of the languages most commonly spoken – described by Vertovec (2006) as "superdiversity" – and the distribution of these languages. Whereas multilingualism was previously an urban phenomenon, there is now a greater presence of new minority language speakers in rural areas. CILT (2005) draws attention, for instance, to the changing populations in two rural settings – the Scottish Borders where Portuguese and Russian-speaking families have moved to work in the fishing industry; and to Wrexham, a small town in northeast Wales where at least 25 languages are now spoken in schools, including Portuguese, Polish, Tagalog and Shona. The most significant development, however, relates to the enlargement of the European Union from 15 to 25 member states in 2004. Of the previous EU countries, only the UK, Ireland and Sweden granted full work rights to nationals of the new accession countries. In the two years following enlargement some 427,000 East Europeans registered for work; with the addition of the self-employed, it is estimated that the total was in excess of 600,000 (Anseau 2006). Poles make up by far the largest proportion of these new arrivals (62%), followed by Lithuanians (12%) and Slovaks (10%).

3.1. Language standardisation

Standardisation is an important consideration in any discussion of linguistic diversity. It is often assumed that the language varieties spoken within ethnic minority communities are the same as the national or official language of the country of origin. Such an assumption is, at best, simplistic. Decisions about linguistic status are political and therefore contentious; in the words of a Yiddish saying: "A language is a dialect with an army and a navy". Thus while linguists consider that Danish, Swedish and Norwegian are part of a single dialect continuum, the perceived integrity of each language reflects political separation. In contrast, the differences between colloquial varieties of Arabic, such as Moroccan and Omani, are arguably greater than those found in the Scandinavian continuum. Yet, for cultural and political reasons, we normally refer to Arabic as a single entity. Similarly, we refer to both Cantonese and Putonghua as Chinese. It is important to remember, however, that the Putonghua used as a *lingua franca* by speakers from the People's Republic of China (PRC) in Britain and the Cantonese spoken by most families of Hong Kong descent are not mutually intelligible; conversations between Chinese from the PRC and Hong Kong in the UK often take place in English.

History, culture and religious affiliation sometimes influence the way in which speakers report their language. Muslim families from Pakistan, for instance, use a dialect of Panjabi in the home but identify themselves as speakers of Urdu, the language of religion and high culture. Most Bangladeshis come from the region of Sylhet and speak a highly distinctive variety that, according to some writers, is sufficiently distinct from Bengali to be considered a separate language (Husain 1991). Similarly, most Greeks speak a Cypriot variety that differs in significant ways from Standard Modern Greek; and most children of Italian heritage speak a southern variety.

The question therefore arises as to which variety – standard or non-standard – should be taught in an overseas setting. There is an inevitable tension between the pedagogical imperative to build on what children know already and the socio-cultural imperative to use the variety that has highest status in the home country. Thus, Cypriot heritage children in the

UK will have far less exposure to standard Modern Greek than their peers in Cyprus; the expectation of the community, however, is that they will be taught in standard Modern Greek.

4. Language maintenance and shift

New minority communities are by no means homogeneous. In many of the longer established communities, such as the Kwéyòl-speaking community in London (Nwenmely 1996), the shift to English is almost complete. In contrast, new arrivals will be proficient in their community languages. While the inevitable consequence of settlement in the UK is a shift from the language of the home to English, the speed and extent of this shift will depend on various factors, including individual acts of identity (cf. Le Page and Tabouret-Keller 1985) and the ethnolinguistic vitality of the community in question (Giles, Bourhis and Taylor 1977). There are many clues as to the ethnolinguistic vitality of new minority languages. The discussion which follows centres on four main areas: religion, the economy, the media and the arts.

4.1. Religion

Religious institutions such as the church, mosque, gurudwara or temple not only provide for spiritual needs, but fulfil an important cultural and welfare role in the life of many communities. Salverda (2006) reports that some 25 languages other than English are used regularly for religious purposes in London. The impact of the new Polish diaspora on the Catholic Church has attracted a great deal of attention. Leslie (2007), for instance, draws attention to the unprecedented demand in South-east England for mass and confession in Polish. In the Islamic community, Qu'ranic Arabic is used alongside many other languages. According to Reader (2002: 67, cited in Salverda 2006: 2), it is possible to buy versions of the Qu'ran at the International Islamic Dawah Centre near the London Central Mosque in a wide range of languages, including Albanian, Chinese, English, French, Korean, Polish and Spanish. New minority languages, of course, are a vehicle not only for worship but also for social interaction before and after worship and for the various social and cultural activities organised by religious groups.

4.2. The economy

Ethnic economies are an important feature of life in the UK. For instance, in Bangladeshi areas of East London, Mirpuri Panjabi areas of Bradford or Gujarati areas of Leicester, it is possible to find restaurants, travel agents and food and clothing shops run by and for the communities in question. Ethnic economies of this kind not only provide employment for large numbers of workers; they also create an environment where it is more natural to use the minority language to communicate with co-workers and customers from the same community. The Global London website with its strap line: *The world in one city: where to find almost everything ethnic and cultural in the multilingual capital* suggests that other languages can also be an attraction for outsiders. Tourists, for instance, are interested not only in the scenery but in new cultural experiences: other languages help create a sense of place and mark the destination out as different.

Mainstream businesses have only recently awoken to the fact that minority communities make up a significant market segment. Initiatives that target minorities rely heavily on the knowledge and experience of new minority language speakers. So, too, do the public and private agencies which provide services for minority communities.

New minority languages also play a role in global markets. Knowledge of other languages is now widely recognised as offering businesses a competitive edge. While English may be the language of wider communication for the educated elite, the great bulk of the world's population understand only the local language. Efforts to address the urgent need for language skills in business are currently spearheaded by the *Centre for Information on Language Teaching and Research* (CILT), the *National Centre for Languages*, and the *(Regional) Language Networks*[3] which aim to promote a greater national capability in languages for business and employment. Speakers of new minority languages are a key element in the national reservoir of language skills.

4.3. Ethnic media

The minority press is another indicator of ethnolinguistic vitality. Forty or so newspapers and periodicals serve many different language communities in the UK (Edwards 2004: 171–172). London is particularly well served with daily newspapers in Chinese (*Sing Tao*), Polish (*Dziennik Polski*) and

Italian (*London Sera* and *La voce sera*); it is also a major centre for Arabic publishing.

The minority press usually starts as a small-scale operation, with the same person often serving as journalist, editor, distributor, and printer. Many publications are family-owned and invest whatever they earn back into their enterprise. Although most titles remain in the hands of independent owners, there are exceptions. For instance, *Parikiaki*, the London Greek Cypriot newspaper, is affiliated with *Haravgi*, a newspaper in Cyprus.

In the newer communities, the minority press usually focuses on national and international news, and news and sports from the home country. In older more established communities, the assumption is that most readers will be able to access news in English and so the focus is on the home country. Newspapers try, of course, to address as wide an audience as possible and use language accordingly. Thus *Parikiaki* uses Greek for news that is likely to be of main interest to the migrant generation and English for information likely to appeal to younger people (Georgiou 2003).

Minority radio and TV, like the minority press, play a key role in the transmission of new minority languages and cultures. They are also an important medium of entertainment, with the potential to reach a much wider audience, including those who are illiterate in the minority language, in English or in both. Growing numbers of radio stations now carry programmes for minority communities; most cater for speakers of south Asian languages. Sometimes minority media are small, short-lived projects produced by families, groups and associations. Well over 100 aspiring community radio groups make use of a 28-day license once a year, often during religious celebrations, such as Ramadan and Vaisaiki (Georgiou 2003).

Digitalisation has, of course, created many new possibilities for minority media: according to one estimate, every third Cypriot household in one area of north London has a satellite dish in order to watch the evening news from Greece (Georgiou 2003). In other cases, local networks specifically target overseas communities. Networks such as Zee TV provide entertainment in English, Urdu and Hindi for viewers from the Indian subcontinent. Satellite TV would appear to serve different purposes for different viewers. Robins (2001) describes the case of a Turkish woman in her thirties who had come to London ten years previously, and who watches Turkish TV for the news, but British programmes for entertainment. Another woman who watched mainly Turkish television read British newspapers and so was well aware of what was going on around her. Far from retreating into ethnic ghettos, members of minority communities are well placed to move between and evaluate different cultural spaces.

Last but not least, the Internet has revolutionised communication in minority communities (Crystal 2001: 219–221). There has been a proliferation of websites dedicated to minority languages. The advantages of web publishing are clear to see: it offers a cheap alternative to traditional media, which is not constrained by legislation and allows for two-way interaction.

4.4. The Arts

New minorities have had an enormous impact on the cultural life in the UK. The presence of a wide range of art forms reinforces the distinctive identities of minority communities; it also gives English-speakers access to a much wider range of experiences and choices.

The rhythms, melodies and lyrics passed from one generation to the next in family events or social gatherings are strongly linked with the identity of the group. Indian weddings, for instance, are associated with an extensive repertoire of songs, serving a wide range of functions (Edwards and Katbamna 1989). Religious music such as Qawwali singing in the Pakistani community is another important focus for cultural and linguistic identity (Edwards 2004: 199). UK cities are a reservoir of talent. The *London Diaspora Capital* project, run by the arts charity Cultural Co-operation, is designed to exploit this rich potential, raising the profile of London-based artists from different national backgrounds.[4] The main tool is a web-based interactive database with audio-visual profiles of performers whose life journeys have converged in the capital. Global London[5] also provides extensive listings of minority cultural organisations.

The different traditions which meet in the UK often transcend linguistic and cultural barriers to create hybrid performances with a very broad appeal. The Yellow Earth Theatre[6] is a case in point. Its bilingual production of Shakespeare's *King Lear* addresses the miscommunication that arises from migration. Lear, in his Shanghai penthouse, hands over control of his global business empire to his daughters and asks them to justify their inheritance. The older sisters flatter their father in elegant Chinese but English-educated Cordelia, no longer fluent in her father's tongue, says nothing and the loss of face sends Lear into a fury.

Musical fusion is another manifestation of languages and cultures in contact. Take the case of Bhangra, the roots of which lie in the traditional

Panjabi music performed on festive occasions. Indians in the UK have used the same percussion instruments that provide the rhythms for traditional Bhangra as the foundation for strong melds with musical influences from the west. Since the early 1990s, it has gained popularity with mainstream as well as British Indian audiences, with bands like Apache Indian making an appearance in the UK charts.

5. New minority languages in education

The publication of the 1985 Swann Report, *Education for All*, was a defining moment in the teaching of new minority languages in the UK. It recommended that responsibility for new minority languages should lie with minority communities rather than mainstream schools, and that official support should be limited to the provision of accommodation, grants for books and teaching materials, in-service courses and advice.

In the absence of meaningful state support, various community groups assumed responsibility for teaching new minority languages. As well as providing for spiritual and welfare needs, religious institutions such as the church, mosque, gurudwara or temple have fulfilled an important educational role in the life of many communities. In some cases, governments have taken the lead. Thus community language teaching in Portuguese, Spanish, Italian and Greek is supported in varying degrees by the High Commission or Embassy in London. In other cases, classes have been organised by more informal groups of parents.

Provision burgeoned from the late 1970s onwards and there are currently an estimated 5,000 "supplementary", "complementary", "community" or "Saturday" schools in Britain.[7] Typically, these schools are staffed by volunteers and meet in community halls, temples and school classrooms. Some are scheduled on weekdays after school hours; others take place on Saturdays. CILT (2005) identifies some 61 different languages taught to children of school age in community settings.

5.1. Recent developments

There has been intermittent pressure on government to diversify language provision in response to the challenge of global markets. Official policy on this question has been rather contradictory. The Department of Education and Science (1988) accepted the validity of arguments for diversification of the modern foreign language curriculum and acknowledged the need for speakers of Japanese, Chinese and other Asian languages. However, it was not considered cost effective to provide teaching in these languages for pupils of compulsory school age. Several recent developments have signalled a significant policy departure from this position.

The Nuffield Languages Inquiry (1998–2000) was an important turning point. Acting on the recommendations contained in the final report (Nuffield Foundation 2000), the Department for Education and Skills (DfES) launched a strategy for language teaching in England in 2002 in which new minority languages are seen as an important element in cultural cohesion:

> In the knowledge society of the 21st century, language competence and intercultural understanding are ... an essential part of being a citizen. Language skills are also vital in improving understanding between people here and in the wider world, and in supporting global citizenship by breaking down barriers of ignorance and suspicion between nations. Learning other languages gives us insight into the people, culture and traditions of other countries, and helps us to understand our own language and culture. Drawing on the skills and expertise of those who speak community languages will promote citizenship and complement the Government's broader work on the promotion of social cohesion (p.13).

The UK position is thus in line with changing attitudes towards new minority languages in Europe. The Council of Europe *Guide to Language Education policies in Europe* (Beacco and Byram 2003) and the European Commission's (2003) *Action Plan for Languages 2004–2006* both promote diversification of language learning, including new minority languages.

The rapid increase in provision for Chinese teaching in mainstream schools is just one indicator of the change in attitudes. Between 10% and 13% of English secondary schools provide some Mandarin teaching, although much of this provision takes place outside normal curriculum time. Mandarin is also offered in a growing number of primary schools. From 2008 schools will be free to offer any major European or world language as their statutory modern foreign language for pupils aged 11–14. According to CILT (2006), at least 35 different community languages are taught during the school day or on school premises after school hours.

Most mainstream provision is targeted at the middle years of secondary school, as students prepare for public examinations at ages 16 (General Certificate of Education) and for university entrance (Advanced Subsidiary [AS] and Advanced or A-levels). Given current levels of diversity, however, relatively few languages are currently included: only 20 languages are examined at GCSE and A-level. Nonetheless, large numbers of students are being entered for examinations in community languages. In 2004, approximately 26,000 students were entered for GCSE examinations in new minority languages, and 12,250 students for AS and A-levels. Although both complementary and mainstream schools entered students for these examinations, the most common route was via mainstream schools.

An indicator of the low status associated with many minority languages has been the failure to make provision for study of these languages at tertiary level. Once more, however, there are signs of change. The *Routes into Languages Project*[8] is attempting to map provision for community languages in higher education in order to relate current provision to the needs of an increasingly multilingual population, and to consider how provision can be developed to meet emerging demand in business, public sector, aid and development fields.

5.2. Challenges and prospects

Contact between mainstream and supplementary education has until recently been minimal or non-existent. Different perceptions on the part of mainstream and community providers of the aims and usefulness of community language teaching are part of the ongoing problem. CILT (2005) suggests that complementary schools have a much broader vision, attaching importance to the culture, history and religion associated with the language, and enjoyment of language learning and opportunities to meet others from a similar background. Mainstream schools, in contrast, display a limited understanding that bilingualism is a valuable asset for both the individual and the wider society:

> Some feel that students are spending time and gaining credit for something that they are "naturally" good at and that this is a waste of resources (although it is never suggested that English-speaking students do not need to study the language formally at school because they are already "naturally" competent in the language). It is important to recognise that it takes many years of study for monolingual English-speaking students to acquire high levels of literacy in English, and the same is true for those who speak community languages. Students may gain varying levels of oral fluency at home or in their communities, but learning to read and write the language requires a different sort of attention, particularly when it involves a different script (CILT 2005: 3).

Even in those cases where mainstream providers offer enthusiastic support for community language teaching, they face a number of practical challenges, not least of which are the growing numbers of languages, many of which are spoken by very small numbers of students. Further, the linguistic profile of a school can shift considerably from one year to the next (CILT 2005).

Various policy developments may help to encourage more meaningful collaborations, including the requirement for Schools Inspectors to assess how well a school works in partnership with parents and local communities, including supplementary schools (OFSTED 2005), and the greater flexibility offered by the 2002 Education Act for school governing bodies to provide facilities that benefit families and the local community and to enter into agreements with other partners to provide services on school premises.

The availability of suitably trained teachers is a recurrent issue for both mainstream and community provision (Edwards 2004; CILT 2005), although some progress has been made on this front. Postgraduate qualifications in community languages are now available at eight teacher-training institutions in England. The limited opportunities for continuing professional development are another matter of concern. The National Resource Centre for Supplementary Education (the NRC) provides information, advice and resources to supplementary schools across England. The Supplementary Schools Network offers a forum for the sharing information on resources, training and funding. Some training is also provided by networks of community language teachers such as the UK Federation of Chinese Schools. Nonetheless, 40% of the community language teachers working in mainstream settings and 65% of those in community schools express concern about this issue (McPake, Tinsley and James 2007). In identifying possible ways forward, these authors point to the potential of partnerships between community languages and modern languages teachers in the same school or authority, between mainstream and complementary schools who have students in common, and between teachers of the same languages in different areas. Anderson (in press) provides further support for this position from the perspective of community language teachers.

Another useful initiative is the development of a series of Curriculum guides which offer a flexible framework for the design and delivery of courses in both mainstream and complementary sectors.[9]

5.3. Research on complementary education

Until relatively recently, the main focus for research on speakers of new minority languages has been on mainstream education settings and the acquisition of English. There is, however, a growing body of research which recognises the potential of the study of new minority language teaching and learning in its own right. Recent examples include Gregory's (1998, 2001) investigations of literacy practices in the Bengali community and the implications for mainstream schools; Parke et al.'s (2002) discussion of the importance of an appreciation of the full range of children's linguistic capacities in teaching and assessment in mainstream classrooms; contributions to Creese and Martin (2006) which examine the ways in which complementary schools teaching Gujarati, Chinese, Urdu and Arabic are involved in "transforming, negotiating and managing the linguistic, social and learning identities" of students, staff and parents (p.2); and Rosowsky's (2006) discussion of how two teachers fuse the literacy practices from both schooled and Qu'ranic literacies in a mosque school in northern England.

Attention has also been paid to the experience of teachers in community settings. Sneddon (2003) explores the role in the community group of some 18 teachers, what and how they teach, their relationships with children and families, their conditions of work, the challenges they face and the rewards of their chosen profession. Anderson (in press) examines insider perspectives on the professional development of teachers of community languages.

6. Conclusion

Precise numbers of speakers of new minority languages are difficult to establish because questions related to language in the population census are limited to Welsh in Wales, Gaelic in Scotland and Irish in Northern Ireland. Current estimates are based on recent school surveys; coverage is incomplete. It is nonetheless possible to detect two main trends over recent years. The first trend relates to the very large number of languages in use: at least 300 languages are spoken in England, and close to 100 languages in Wales and Scotland. The second trend concerns distribution. Whereas multilingualism was previously an urban phenomenon, there is now a greater presence of new minority language speakers in rural areas.

The language of communication in new minority communities is not necessarily the same as the national or official language of the country of origin. Many Chinese in the UK, for instance, speak Cantonese rather than Mandarin or Putonghua, the official language of China. Cultural and religious affiliations may also influence the way in which speakers report their language: thus Muslim families from Pakistan, who use a dialect of Panjabi in the home, identify themselves as speakers of Urdu, the language of religion and high culture. These sociolinguistic realities have implications for the provision of language teaching.

Language maintenance and shift are complex issues. While new arrivals are proficient in their community languages, in many of the longer established communities the shift to English is almost complete. The ethnolinguistic vitality of the community in question, however, exerts an important influence on the speed and extent of this shift. There are many indicators. Religious institutions such as the church, mosque, gurudwara or temple not only provide for spiritual needs, but play an important role in the cultural life of many communities, offering a range of opportunities for using new minority languages. Various aspects of economic activity offer similar possibilities. The ability to speak new minority languages plays a role in global markets; ethnic economies are an important feature of life in the UK; and minority communities make up a significant market segment in themselves. The minority press serves many different minority communities, as do minority radio and TV. New minority communities also have an enormous impact on the cultural life of the UK.

The refusal of the state in the mid-1980s to make provision for the teaching of new minority languages has meant that responsibility for the organisation of classes has fallen on minority communities. There are currently an estimated 5,000 "supplementary" or "complementary" "community" schools. In the last decade, however, there has been a significant softening of attitudes. Official policies now embrace new minority as well as European languages, such as French and German, with particular attention to world languages like Chinese and Arabic. Significant numbers of students are entered for public examinations in new minority languages.

In spite of the improved status of these languages, community providers remain the poor relation. Areas of concern in both mainstream and community settings include the shortage of suitably qualified teachers and the limited opportunities for continuing professional development, but these needs are particularly pressing for complementary schools. While one obvious way forward is to encourage more meaningful partnerships between mainstream and community providers, differences in perspective on the aims and usefulness between the two sectors make this difficult to achieve.

On balance, though, significant progress has been made in the last decade. There is a far greater awareness of the importance of accurate data on language in the formulation of education and social policy. Language questions in the 2011 Census are likely to relate to new minority languages as well as Welsh, Gaelic and Irish, and schools in England and Scotland are now collecting data on the languages spoken by pupils. The Languages Strategy for England embraces new minority languages as well as the small number of European languages traditionally taught in schools; accreditation is available in a growing number of languages; and the first serious attempt to map tertiary language provision to the needs of a multilingual population is under way. Schools Inspectors are now required to assess how well a school works in partnership with parents and local communities, including supplementary schools, while the 2002 Education Act makes it easier for governing bodies to provide facilities with partners such as complementary schools providing services on school premises. The growing interest of researchers is yet another indicator of the transformation of new minority languages from an issue of marginal interest to a matter of central concern.

There is, of course, no room for complacency. Many people do not subscribe wholeheartedly to the new discourse of inclusion which surrounds discussion of new minority languages, including some members of the government responsible for framing this policy. David Blunkett, for instance, illustrates his limited understanding of the role of language in a speech delivered in 2002 as Home Secretary where he makes reference to the "schizophrenia (associated with bilingualism) which bedevils generational relationships". Discussion of diversity is also taking place in an atmosphere of Islamophobia where ethnocentric assumptions run the risk of what Freud labels "the narcissim of small differences" (Bunting 2006).

Notes

1. *www.statistics.gov.uk/census2001/profiles/commentaries/ethnicity.asp#ethnic*
2. *www.standards.dfes.gov.uk/ethnicminorities/collecting/Pupil_First_Lang/*
3. *www.cilt.org.uk/employment*
4. *www.culturalco-operation.org*
5. *www.global-london.com*
6. *www.yellowearth.org*
7. *www.supplementaryschools.org.uk/site*
8. *www.lww-cetl.ac.uk/routes/index.htm*
9. *http://community.gold.ac.uk*

References

Anderson, Jim
    in press   Pre- and in-service professional development of teachers of community/heritage languages in the UK: insider perspectives. *Language and Education*.

Anseau, Julien (ed.)
    2006   *Social Indicators*. House of Commons Research Paper 06/49, pp. iii–vii. Retrieved from: *www.parliament.uk/commons/lib/research/rp2005/rp05-044.pdf*

Baker, Philip and John Eversley (eds.)
    2000   *Multilingual Capital: The Languages of London Schoolchildren and their Relevance to Economic, Social and Educational Policies*. London: Battlebridge.

Beacco, Jean-Claude and Michael Byram
    2003   *Guide for the Development of Language Education Policies in Europe*. Strasbourg: Council of Europe.

Blunkett, David
    2002   What does citizenship mean today? *Observer*, 15 September. Retrieved from: *http://observer.guardian.co.uk/race/story/0,11255, 792231,00.html*

Bunting, Madeleine
    2006   Jack Straw has unleashed a storm of prejudice and intensified division. *Guardian*, 26 October. Retrieved from: *http://www.guardian.co.uk/commentisfree/story/0,,1890821,00.html*

CILT, the National Centre for Languages
    2005   *Language Trends 2005: Community Language Learning in England, Wales and Scotland*. London: CILT. Retrieved from: *www.cilt.org.uk/research/languagetrends/2005/trends2005_community.pdf*

Creese, Angela and Peter Martin (eds.)
    2006   Interaction in complementary school contexts. Special issue of *Language and Education* 20 (1).

Crystal, David
    2001   *Language and the Internet*. Cambridge: Cambridge University Press.

Department for Education and Skills (DfES)
    2002   *Languages for All: Languages for Life. A Strategy for England*. London: DfES.

Department for Education and Science (DfES)
    1988   *Modern Languages and the School Curriculum: a Statement of Policy*. London: DfES.

Edwards, Viv
    2004   *Multilingualism in the English-speaking World: Pedigree of Nations*. Oxford: Blackwell.

Edwards, Viv and Savita Katbamna
    1989   The wedding songs of British Gujarati women. In *Women in their speech communities*, Deborah Cameron and Jennifer Coates (eds.), 158–74. London: Longman.

European Commission (EC)
    2003   *Promoting Language Learning and Linguistic Diversity: An Action Plan 2004–2006*. Retrieved from: http://ec.europa.eu/education/policies/lang/policy/index_en.html

Georgiou, Myria
    2003   Consuming ethnic media – constructing ethnic identities – shaping communities: The case study of Greek Cypriots in London. In *Race/Gender/Media: Considering Diversity Across Audiences, Content and Producers*, Rebecca Ann Lind (ed.), 311–329. Boston: Allyn & Bacon.

Giles, Howard, Richard Bourhis and Donald Taylor
    1977   Towards a theory of language in ethnic group relations. In *Language, Ethnicity and Intergroup Relations*, Howard Giles (ed.), 307–348. London: Academic Press.

Gregory, Eve
    2001   Sisters and brothers as language and literacy teachers: Synergy between siblings. *Journal of Early Childhood Literacy* 1 (3): 301–322.
    1998   Siblings as mediators of literacy in linguistic minority communities. *Language and Education* 12 (1): 33–54.

Husain, Jyoti
    1991   The Bengali speech community. In *Multilingualism in the British Isles*, Safder Alladina and Viv Edwards (eds.), Volume 11, 75–87. Harlow: Longman.

Le Page, Robert and Andrée Tabouret-Keller
    1985   *Acts of Identity*. Cambridge: Cambridge University Press.

Leslie, Robert
    2007   Poles keeping the faith. *BBC News* 26 October. Retrieved from: www.bbc.co.uk/kent/content/articles/2006/12/11/polish_religion_feature.shtml

McPake, Joanna, Teresa Tinsley and Ceri James
    2007   Making provision for community languages: issues for teacher education in the UK. *Language Learning Journal* 35 (1): 99–112.

McPake, Joanna, Teresa Tinsley, Peter Broeder, Laura Mijares, Sirkku Latomaa and Waldemar Martiyniouk
    2007   *Valuing All Languages in Europe*. Graz: European Centre for Modern Languages.

Nuffield Language Inquiry
    2000   *Languages: the Next Generation*. London: The Nuffield Foundation.

Nwenmely, Hubisi
  1996   *Language Reclamation: French Creole Teaching in the UK and the Caribbean.* Clevedon: Multilingual Matters.
Office for Standards in Education (OFSTED)
  2005   *Framework for the Inspection of Schools in England from September 2005.* Retrieved from: *www.ofsted.gov.uk/publications/ndex.cfm?fuseaction=pubs.summary&id=3861*
Parke, Tim, Rose Drury, Charmian Kenner and Leena Helavaara Robertson
  2002   Revealing invisible worlds: Connecting the mainstream with bilingual children's home and community learning. *Journal of Early Childhood Literacy* 2 (2): 195–220.
Reader, Lesley
  2002   *Book Lovers' London.* London: Metro Publications.
Robins, Kevin
  2001   *Beyond Imagined Community? Transnational Media and Turkish Migrants in Europe.* London: Goldsmiths College, University of London.
Rosowsky, Andrey
  2006   'I used to copy what the teachers at school would do'. Cross-cultural fusion: the role of older children in community literacy practices. *Language and Education* 20 (6): 529–42.
Salverda, Reinier
  2006   Multilingual London and its literatures. *Opticon* 1(1): 1–15. Retrieved from: *www.cilt.org.uk/commlangs/research.htm*
Scottish Executive
  2007   Pupils in Scotland. *Statistical Bulletin* 27 February. Retrieved from: *www.scotland.gov.uk/Publications/2007/02/27083941/123*
Sneddon, Raymonde
  2003   Every teacher has a story to tell: a pilot study of teachers in supplementary and mother tongue schools. *Bulletin of the Resource Unit for Supplementary and Mother Tongue Schools*, June. Retrieved from: *http://www.multiverse.ac.uk/viewArticle.aspx?subCategoryId=611&categoryId=608&qts=false&resource=false&contentId=274*
Swann, Lord
  1985   *Education for All. Report of the Committee of Inquiry into the Education of Children from Ethnic Minority Groups.* London: HMSO.
Vertovec, Steven
  2006   *The Emergence of Super-Diversity in Britain.* Working Paper No. 25. Centre for Migration, Policy and Society, University of Oxford. Retrieved from: *www.compas.ox.ac.uk/publications/papers/Steven%20Vertovec%20WP0625.pdf*

Immigrant minority languages in Sweden

Lilian Nygren-Junkin

1. Demographic perspectives

As a consequence of socio-economically or politically determined processes of migration over the past decades, Western European countries have a growing number of immigrant minority (henceforward IM) populations, which differ widely, both from a cultural and from a linguistic point of view, from the indigenous populations (Extra and Gorter 2001). Sweden is no exception in this regard and has gone from being a relatively homogenous society around the middle of the 20th century to becoming an increasingly multi-ethnic, multicultural and multilingual society.

Present-day Sweden has actually become one of the European countries that have the highest proportion of immigrants. Statistical data from 2004 show that around 12% of all residents in Sweden were born in another country, the same as for Germany and Austria. Higher levels were found only in Luxembourg (33%) and Switzerland (22%). If those born in Sweden whose parents were both born abroad are added, the proportion increases to 16%, and if those with one parent born elsewhere are included, over one fifth (22%) of the Swedish population were in 2004 part of the group that could be referred to as residents with some degree of immigrant background. (SCB 2004)

In spite of more stringent immigration policies in most European Union (henceforward EU) countries, the prognosis is that non-indigenous populations will continue to grow as a consequence of the increasing number of political refugees, the EU expansion and the opening of the internal European borders, as well as political and economic developments in other regions of the world (Extra and Gorter 2001). Sweden makes this prognosis look realistic. From the onset of the new millennium, Swedish immigration authorities have indeed become more restrictive about granting refugee status to asylum seekers. From an approval rate of over 50% in the mid-1990s, the proportion of successful asylum applicants in 2005 had dropped to approximately 10%. In the past year, though, Sweden has given exceptional treatment to refugees from Iraq, who according to recent reports were allowed to stay in Sweden in more than half of the cases. Asylum-seekers from other countries, however, are still more often sent back to where they came from than given refugee status in Sweden.

Reliable demographic and linguistic information on IM groups in EU countries can be difficult to obtain. In Sweden, data are collected by the Swedish Central Bureau of Statistics (SCB) and updated annually with information from the immigration authorities (*Migrationsverket*) about asylum-seekers, those granted temporary and permanent residency permits, and new Swedish citizens. In addition, the SCB gathers data on the demographic distribution in terms of gender, age, employment status, area of residence, and marital status (SCB 2003). In contrast, no information about (home) language use, mother tongue or language skills is collected by Swedish authorities, nor is there any language proficiency requirement to become a Swedish citizen that might have revealed the applicant's native language. It is thus hard to provide a reliable picture of how many speakers there are of the various immigrant languages in Sweden.

There are, however, ways of looking to other related sources of information in order to find out what languages are spoken by most people of foreign background living in Sweden. Country of origin and recorded nationality could be such criteria (at least in the case of monolingual birth countries), as can data from the national school system on requests for mother tongue instruction by pupils and parents of immigrant background. In Sweden as in most EU countries, population data based on nationality and/or birth country are available for the adult population. However, these widely used criteria have become less valid over time because of an increasing trend toward naturalisation and births within the countries of residence. To illustrate the discrepancy between the two criteria above, Table 1 gives an overview of the 12 largest IM groups in Sweden on December 31, 2001, based on the birth-country criterion versus the nationality criterion (SCB 2002).

The table shows strong criterion effects of birth country *versus* nationality. All IM groups are in fact strongly underrepresented in the nationality-based statistics. The reason for this is either that it has not been possible to "get rid of" the citizenship in the country of origin, or that some immigrants want to maintain the right to vote in the old country and perhaps still plan to move back there some time in the future. It is only since July 2001 that Sweden has allowed dual citizenship.

Table 1. The twelve largest immigrant groups to Sweden based on the birth country criterion versus the nationality criterion on December 31, 2001 (SCB 2002)

Groups	Birth country	Nationality	Difference
Finns	193,465	97,521	95,944
(former) Yugoslavs	73,274	20,741	52,533
Iraqis	55,696	36,221	19,475
Bosnians	52,198	19,728	32,470
Iranians	51,884	13,449	38,435
Norwegians	43,414	33,265	10,149
Poles	40,506	15,511	24,995
Danes	38,870	26,627	12,243
Germans	38,857	17,315	21,542
Turks	32,453	13,907	18,546
Chileans	27,153	9,896	17,257
Lebanese	20,228	2,961	17,327
Total	667,998	307,142	360,856

However, the birth-country criterion does not solve the identification problem either. The use of this criterion leads to non-identification in at least the following cases:

— different ethnocultural/language groups from the same country of origin (cf. Turkish *versus* Kurdish immigrants from Turkey);
— the same ethnocultural/language group from different countries of origin (cf. Chinese immigrants from China *versus* Vietnam);
— the increasing group of second, third and further generations (cf. the Greek and Italian communities in Sweden). (Nygren-Junkin and Extra 2003)

The degree to which IM families retain use of their original language into second, third or further generations varies greatly. Factors that influence the degree of language shift are both the perceived status/usefulness of the IM language and the social circumstances under which each family is living in terms of integration versus segregation, residentially as well as in the workforce, and access to other speakers of the same language outside the family. Mother tongue instruction in the family language can help maintain the use of a particular language, but mother tongue instruction is optional and voluntary, and it is known that not all pupils in Swedish school that have the right to such instruction request it or are provided with it, even though requested, due to lack of resources. Therefore, data on mother tongue instruction only offer a limited part of the over-all language picture (Frisell et al. 2004).

From the above, it becomes clear that collecting reliable information about the actual number and use of IM languages in Sweden is not easy to undertake. Given the decreasing significance of the nationality and birth-country criteria, collecting reliable information about the composition and language use among IM groups in Sweden is one of the most challenging tasks facing demographers. With the increasing proportion of elderly people in not only the general population but also among IM groups, a greater awareness of what languages are spoken by whom and where is becoming necessary, or at least desirable, due to the effects of language atrophy among many of the aged. It has been observed in Swedish elder-care facilities and hospitals that older immigrants, who perhaps ten years earlier spoke Swedish very well, later in life with the on-set of senility lose their ability to speak the second language they learned as adult immigrants to Sweden. Whether they still understand is difficult to ascertain, unless there is a staff member who knows the same IM language and can relate a given response to what has been said in Swedish. With relevant language data, this information could be used to attempt a care facility placement match between elderly persons who speak the same native language and bilingual staff that have proficiency in that language.

2. Demolinguistic perspectives

One way of obtaining data on IM languages used nationally can be to study the use of different languages locally in an area where the speakers represent all or at least most of the languages spoken by immigrants to Sweden. Such a survey was conducted among school children aged six to twelve in the city of Gothenburg in the winter of 2001–2002 as part of the *Multilingual Cities Project*, a six-nation/city European study (Nygren-Junkin and Extra 2003; see also Extra and Yağmur, this Volume). Gothenburg is Sweden's second largest city with a population of just over half a million. Due to the city's character of being both an industrial centre and a major port, many of its inhabitants are of immigrant background. They have arrived at different times in recent history and have come for different reasons and from different countries, thereby ensuring that most IM languages spoken anywhere in Sweden will be used somewhere by Gothenburg residents.

The children in Gothenburg schools that are born abroad or born to parents from other countries than Sweden make up a sizeable proportion of the school population as a whole – around 25% throughout the 1990s according to local school statistics – and the participation of Gothenburg schools therefore ensured a great variety in the different languages used by the pupils. As a result of this survey, it was however revealed that the officially collected school data on children of foreign background, i.e., the 25% that could be identified as first and second generation immigrants, did not accurately indicate how many pupils actually used another language than Swedish at home. The children surveyed came from 80% of all schools in Gothenburg and included all pupils aged six to twelve, not only those identified by the school system as entitled to home language instruction (henceforward HLI). The survey data showed that as many as 36% of the children reported using another language instead of, or in addition to, Swedish at home (Nygren-Junkin and Extra 2003). Therefore, it can be concluded that these data provide a picture of what IM languages are used in Gothenburg homes that is more reliable than the school statistics that are based on how many pupils are officially entitled to HLI. This entitlement is only assessed if mother tongue instruction is requested by a pupil's parents, or if the teacher has reason to believe that a pupil has another language than Swedish as his/her first language. In other words, if parents do not ask for HLI for the child and/or if the child speaks native-like Swedish, this pupil will not appear in the statistics as using or knowing any other language than Swedish.

With these data as the point of departure for this overview of IM languages in Sweden, the current chapter will report on these languages with a focus on the most frequently occurring ones rather than those with only small numbers of speakers. Language vitality, the degree to which a language seems to be well established among its users, will be commented on in order to reflect on the possibility for language maintenance or language shift, and these comments are based on the reported usage patterns among the participants in the survey. A description of HLI in the Swedish school system will also be provided in this chapter. First, however, follows a brief overview of the dominant patterns of immigration to Sweden since the end of the Second World War.

The post-war industrial boom that occurred in Sweden, a country untouched by the destruction and ravages of war, started in the late 1940s and reached its peak in the 1950s and 1960s, creating a need for imported manpower. This labour immigration resulted in hundreds of thousands of men and women moving to Sweden from other Nordic countries and from southern Europe. From Turkey, Greece, Yugoslavia and Italy, men came to work on the assembly lines in the Swedish car, steel and ship-building industries, and from Denmark, Norway and above all Finland, especially in the late 1960s, both men and women came to work in textile and mining as well as in the other manufacturing industries. Political events in Hungary in 1956, in Greece in 1967, and in Czechoslovakia in 1968 added refugees to the immigrants who had come to join the Swedish workforce (SCB 2004).

In 1967, the Swedish government took a decision to severely restrict the immigration of non-Nordic workers. The effect was that immigration levels decreased in the 1970s and changed character. Now a switch occurred from labour immigration to refugee and family reunification immigration, initially mostly from South America and Asia but, in the 1980s, countries in the Middle East and the crumbling Yugoslavia/Balkans were added to the list. Immigration from Africa only became significant in the 1990s, mainly from countries in northern Africa and the Horn of Africa, and today the Somali group especially stands out among refugee immigrants to Sweden. (SCB 2004) An even more recent phenomenon are the many Iraqis, who in 2006 and 2007 have been granted refugee status when they came to Sweden seeking asylum from the US-initiated war in their home country.

As a result of these demographic changes over the past half-century, a number of IM languages are now used in Sweden. Table 2 presents a ranking list of the languages referred to by the pupils that participated in the Multilingual Cities Project. All in all, 75 different home languages could be traced amongst primary school children in Gothenburg. It also becomes clear from this table that a small number of languages are frequently referred to and a large number of languages are mentioned rather or very infrequently. The twenty languages most frequently referred to are shown in Figure 1. Out of these twenty languages, seven languages have the status of national languages of EU countries, seven other languages originate from other European countries, and six languages originate from other continents. After the eight most frequently mentioned languages, the decline in the number of references is very gradual with no drastic differences (Nygren-Junkin and Extra 2003). It can even be argued that the cut-off point at twenty is arbitrary, since the two languages in twentieth and twenty-first position are listed with the same frequency reported, the ranking being determined solely on the basis of the alphabetic order of the languages Tigrigna and Vietnamese.

Table 2. Ranking list of references made to languages other than Swedish at home by Gothenburg primary school children

Nr.	Language	Frequency	Nr.	Language	Frequency
1	English	1,276	39	Amharic/Ethiopian	16
2	Arabic	871	40	Farsi	16
3	Kurdish	567	41	Japanese	15
4	Turkish	454	42	Wolof/Senegalese	14
5	Bosnian	437	43	Estonian	13
6	Spanish	402	44	Czech	13
7	Finnish/Suomi	378	45	Armenian	11
8	Somali	369	46	Sorani	11
9	Chinese	219	47	Azerbaijani/Azeri	9
10	Albanian/Tosk	212	48	Bahasa/Indonesian	9
11	Serbian	191	49	Mandinka/Manding(o)	9
12	Polish	184	50	Bulgarian	8
13	German	179	51	Korean	8
14	Croatian	167	52	Malay	8
15	French	141	53	Bengali	7
16	Macedonian	139	54	Sign language	7
17	Norwegian	122	55	Akan/Twi/Ghanese	5
18	Portuguese	111	56	Gujarati	5
19	Russian	90	57	Slovenian	5
20	Tigrignan	72	58	Slovak(ian)	5
21	Vietnamese/Eritrean	72	59	Swahili	5
22	Danish	70	60	Berber	4
23	Turoyo	70	61	Irish	4
24	Greek	64	62	Lithuanian	4
25	Romani/Sinte	62	63	Khmcr/Cambodian	3
26	Thai	61	64	Afrikaans	2
27	Italian	56	65	Lao	2
28	Hungarian	48	66	Nepali	2
29	Tagalog/Filipino	44	67	Bambili	1
30	Dari/Pashto/Afghani	36	68	Bisaya	1
31	Icelandic	34	69	Catalan	1
32	Romanian	33	70	Luo	1
33	Urdu/Pakistani	31	71	Moldavian	1
34	Hindi	26	72	Quechua	1
35	Turkmen(ian)	24	73	Telegu	1
36	Dutch	21	74	Uigur	1
37	Panjabi	19	75	Zaza	1
38	Hebrew/Ivrit	17			
	Total tokens				7,598

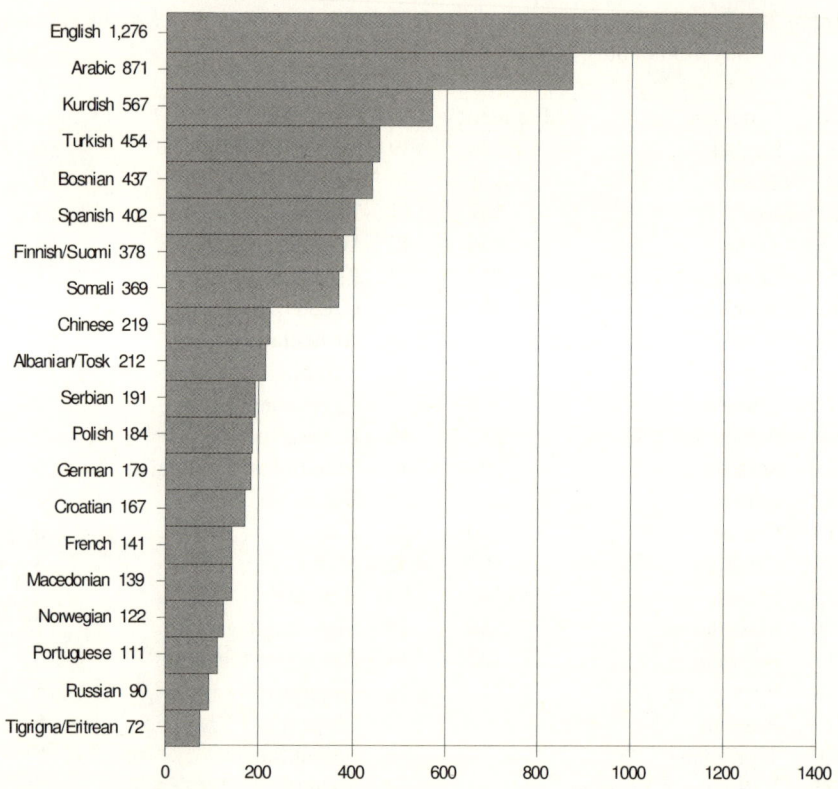

Figure 1. Bar graph of top-20 languages

The high status of English, with frequent use reported in Gothenburg homes, becomes apparent from its first place on the list. (Similar findings have been reported by Extra et al. [2001] regarding the city of The Hague in The Netherlands.) A look at the birth countries of parents whose children have indicated English as being used in the home reveals that over half of these parents were born in Sweden, thus pointing to a bilingual Swedish-English environment in these homes. Around a third of the parents were born in English-speaking countries, while the remaining parents appear to be using English in the home as a *lingua franca*.

Table 2 includes Chinese as one language, which can be argued to be an umbrella term for languages such as Mandarin, Cantonese, Hakka, and Wu. The same can be said for the term Kurdish, which includes at least the two major varieties Kurmanji and Sorani, the latter appearing separately on the list (in 46th place) while the former is not given its own place in the table.

Although the differences between these varieties may not be great, other closely related varieties such as Bosnian/Serbian/Croatian and Spanish/Catalan are treated as separate languages. In thirtieth place on the list is the combination Dari/Pashto which can also be argued represents two different languages, which are both official school and media languages in Afghanistan.

From the above emerges a picture of what the dominant IM languages in Sweden currently are. Due to refugee and family reunification immigration from the Middle East and northern Africa, the Arabic-speaking group is the largest, and there are also many Kurdish-and Turkish-speakers. The languages of the former Yugoslavia also have many speakers, including older immigrant workers and refugees from the Balkan wars. The Chinese group of languages has a large number of speakers as well. Spanish and Finnish have a comparatively long history in Sweden and are still languages represented by many speakers, including second- and third-generation users. The relatively recently arrived Somali-speaking group is also in the top ten, while the sizeable group of immigrants to Sweden from Iran (see Table 2) is either in the process of going through a language shift, as Farsi only appears in fortieth place, or may have had very few children aged six to twelve in 2001–2002 when the data was collected. Because of intra-EU immigration, German and French are among the larger IM languages in Sweden. Thanks to the longstanding open labour market within Scandinavia, many speakers of Danish and Norwegian can also be found living in Sweden (SOU 2002).

3. Sociolinguistic perspectives

Although immigrants to Sweden are expected to know or learn the Swedish language, Swedish is not officially the national language of Sweden. Nowhere in any law or any part of the constitution is it stated that Sweden is a "Swedish-speaking" country and that all official information shall be available in Swedish. In school, every pupil is required to study Swedish, which is one of three core subjects in the national curriculum, but the same is true for English. (The third core subject is Mathematics.) Indeed, Table 2 shows how widespread the use of English has become in homes that otherwise seem to be primarily Swedish speaking. Even every-day Swedish is increasingly interspersed with English words and expressions (Gunnarsson 2001).

Since the mid-1990s, there has been a law that defines five minority languages as official (historic) IM languages in Sweden – Finnish, Meänkieli, Saami, Romani and Yiddish (Hyltenstam 1999) – but Swedish is nowhere legally protected as the country's official majority language. In practice, however, it is the national language, and with English being a compulsory subject in the Swedish school system since the early 1960s, every Swede of working age has grown up to become more or less functionally bilingual (Boyd and Huss 2001). Immigrants to Sweden from English-speaking countries can actually be heard complaining about the difficulty they have in finding native speakers to practice their Swedish with, as most Swedes promptly switch to English as soon as they realise that they are talking to an English-speaker. To Swedes, English is a high status language.

Other languages that are benefitting from high status in Sweden are German – the largest EU language and the Swedish queen's first language – and French – in many ways still an international language although not a world language like English – as well as Spanish, which has experienced a surge in popularity over the past ten years. A few decades ago, Spanish was an IM language with its speakers coming to Sweden mostly from Latin America. Now, Spanish is the most popular foreign language among Swedish school children beside English, but unlike English, Spanish is not a compulsory subject. It has emerged as an international language in the western world, not least with the increasing presence of Spanish-speaking Americans in the media and the entertainment industry. Since the end of the Franco era, Spain has become more popular than ever for Swedes to visit and even buy a second residence. Also, with air travel becoming more affordable to more people, destinations in South and Central America are no longer out of reach for sun-starved Swedes on a winter holiday.

Turning to the status among other major IM languages, Chinese (languages) and Russian are held in high regard as indicated both in the data from the Multilingual Cities Project and in the courses offered by various continuing education facilities in Sweden. Both languages represent political powers that command international respect, and China's rise in the world economy is a likely positive factor. Other sought-after languages are Greek and Italian, both IM languages from the middle of the twentieth century and also languages with strong cultural associations. In addition, Greece and Italy are popular countries for Swedes to visit, and the two nations have a heritage that goes back to Antiquity.

Arabic, Kurdish and Turkish, the three highest-ranked IM languages after English on the Multilingual Cities Project list, do not appear to be given high status in the sense that they are reported as popular to study/ desirable to learn by the Gothenburg school children or frequently offered as continuing education options. It would seem safe to assume that these languages are not given very high status in Swedish society, nor are Somali, Bosnian or Albanian, which were also in the top ten on the Multilingual Cities Project list of IM languages frequently used in the homes of Gothenburg pupils.

Shifting the attention from language status to language vitality, a very different pattern emerges. In the Multilingual Cities Project report, language vitality is defined as the cumulative value of language proficiency, language choice (in interaction with the mother), language dominance, and language preference (see Extra and Yağmur, this Volume, for details). The results show that the top ten here are made up of:

1. Somali
2. Bosnian
3. Kurdish
4. Tigrigna
5. Turkish
6. Chinese
7. Arabic
8. Albanian
9. Macedonian
10. Russian

Of these, all except the Chinese and Turkish groups are made up of relatively recently arrived immigrants. It therefore appears that these language users have a particularly effective strategy in making the family language successfully transfer from one generation to the next, thereby preventing the loss of language skills through language shift.

4. Educational perspectives and home language instruction (HLI)

Data on home language use play a crucial role in the context of education. Such data not only raise the awareness about multilingualism in multicultural schools; they are indispensable tools for educational planning of both the teaching of the national majority language as a first or second language and the teaching of IM languages. In Sweden, with the introduction of the Home Language Reform in 1976/1977 (see below), it became mandatory for schools to submit information about their IM pupils to the National Department of Educational Statistics. This was necessary for the national school authorities to accurately plan the organisation and funding of IM education in the public school system and to reliably forecast the need for teachers of home languages and Swedish as a second language. Since 1995, the requests for HLI and for Swedish as a second language are reported to the municipal education authorities by each school director, if such a need is apparent. (It is thus no longer mandatory for a school to provide these data.)

Until 1997, the teaching of IM languages was referred to as HLI, but this term was then changed to mother tongue instruction in order to avoid the interpretation that these languages only had their place in the home and were not to be included in activities that took place elsewhere in society (Boyd 2007). However, the term HLI had been used for almost twenty years in the Swedish school system, and still is in many staff rooms and classrooms, so it will also be used in the rest of this chapter.

The following will focus on nine parameters for the teaching of IM languages at both primary and secondary schools in Sweden: target groups, arguments, objectives, evaluation, enrolment, curricular status, funding, teaching materials, and teacher qualifications (Nygren-Junkin and Extra 2003).

4.1. Target groups

Anywhere in Sweden, children of immigrant background are, at least officially, eligible to receive HLI. The children may be first, second or third generation immigrants to Sweden, as long as they have already developed some proficiency in the language, and use it in the home on a daily basis, the pupils are entitled to HLI. (No beginner level teaching is thus available in HLI.) The availability of this instruction is not limited to particularly large IM groups, nor is it restricted to certain socio-economic strata. Adopted children, who have developed a mother tongue other than Swedish, are also entitled to receive instruction in this other language.

Teacher availability can be a constraint on who receives HLI. Among recently arrived IM groups with few well-educated adults, it may prove impossible to find a speaker of their language that would be able to function as a teacher. Another problem arises when an x-speaking parent does not approve of the variety that the teacher of language x uses. If two or more languages other than Swedish are used in the home, the family may then decide to choose another home language for instruction through the public school system, or simply refrain from having the child participate at all. The participation in HLI has decreased with the changes made to the national curriculum guidelines of 1994 (Lpo-94). This document introduced not only a minimum group size requirement but also more stringent demands on the pupil's proficiency in the home language.

4.2. Arguments

The history of HLI in Sweden goes back longer than in most other countries in the western world. The Swedish inclusion of HLI in the public school curriculum was preceded by a vote in parliament in 1976 that approved this educational reform, the so-called Hemspråksreform ('Home Language Reform'). This reform was a logical consequence of another resolution by the Swedish parliament regarding the core objectives of Sweden's immigration policy. The bill, from 1975, states three main goals for this immigration policy: the equality goal, the freedom of choice goal, and the cooperation goal. The first objective concerns the right to equality in terms of quality of life and the right to a standard of living comparable to that of the indigenous Swedish population. Herein lies also the right to instruction in one's first language, or mother tongue, through the publicly funded school system, just as native Swedish children receive Swedish language instruction as a compulsory part of their curriculum (Hyltenstam and Tuomela 1996).

The rationale for requiring that schools offer HLI for IM children within the framework of the public school system thus had its roots in the notions of equal opportunity and social justice that underpinned much of Swedish policy and government practice in that era. Furthermore, there had already, since the 1960s, been early home language programs offered by school boards in certain municipalities in Sweden that opted to provide this kind of instruction, usually because of a high proportion of IM populations living in the area. The public school system thus became obliged, from 1977, to provide HLI to any pupil whose parents demanded it and who chose to participate. (These children were also to be taught Swedish as a second language.) The arguments for nowadays placing HLI outside the regular school hours and requiring a minimum number of participants are primarily based on limited resources and budgetary constraints.

4.3. Objectives

In the most recent curriculum guidelines (Lpo 94 1994), the acquisition of bilingual skills through HLI is supplemented with the added objective of developing a strong bicultural identity and dual cultural competence. This is different from the earlier national guidelines from 1980, where the focus was on setting objectives for language development in (potentially bilingual) IM school children. Here, the purpose of giving the pupil HLI was to further the child's emotional, linguistic, and intellectual development. However, the goal to attain is only defined as "active bilingualism" in both the earlier and the later curriculum documents, without any specification as to what this means in terms of performance and ability.

Among Swedish scholars in the field of bilingualism, a suggested objective is that the pupil shall reach spoken and written skill levels in both the mother tongue and Swedish that enable her/him to use both languages in any context where s/he desires to do so (Hyltenstam 1986; Tingbjörn 1986). Although this definition is still rather imprecise and does not identify any particular levels or performance, it does provide a broad functional objective with an individually determined target level, which narrows the field from the sweeping strokes of the national curriculum guidelines.

4.4. Evaluation

In general, formal evaluation of pupils' performance and progress is not a high priority in the Swedish public education system. Instead, informal evaluation meetings are held regularly, as a rule once per term, where the form teacher meets individually with the parent(s) of each pupil. During these talks the teacher informs the parents about the child's situation at school, both academically and socially. The emphasis is on the positive aspect of the child's accomplishments, and possible problems are dealt with from a constructive point of view, the purpose being to look for ways to improve the status quo rather than disciplining the pupil for what is now in the past.

Those who have participated in HLI get a mark in this subject when formal grades are issued, and unless there has been other informal contact between the parents and the home language teachers, this may be the first indication the parents get about how well their children are doing in this subject. At present, there is unfortunately little contact between home language instructors and other teaching staff, so it may be difficult for the form teacher to receive information about a pupil's progress as assessed by the home language instructor before meeting with the child's parent(s) for the informal evaluation talk.

When Swedish schools provide formally reported annual evaluations of the pupils in all subjects, they include the home language. Nationwide written examinations are held in grade 9 and in the last year of secondary school, the results of which are one factor in the evaluation of the children, together with class participation and other assessment instruments used by individual teachers. When applying to secondary and post-secondary education, the home language mark is counted as a regular subject mark, but not as one of the core subjects, i.e., Swedish (as a first or second language), English and Mathematics, in which a graduate must have at least a passing grade to be eligible for the next level in the education system.

4.5. Enrolment

During the first 15 years after the home language reform in Sweden (1977–1992), there was no minimum enrolment required for a child to be entitled to receive HLI. A group could literally be made up of just one pupil and the teacher. Prior to the reform, HLI could be provided by schools that chose to offer it, and the recommended group size was then at least five pupils. In 1991/1992, the Swedish school authorities returned to this model by suggesting a minimum group size of four participants and then, in 1994, by stating that a minimum of five children per municipality must be enrolled for the home language to be provided by the public school system (Lpo-94 1994). Still, this is not a large group, compared with similar criteria in other countries (see Extra and Yağmur, this Volume).

The pupils who belong to the same HLI group do not all have to attend the same grade or even the same school for their regular classes, and some may thus have to go to another location for their HLI in order for the group to reach the required size. The net result of this has been that HLI for smaller IM groups is frequently no longer available through the public education system in Sweden.

4.6. Curricular status

Two aspects of curricular status, time allotted per week and time of day when the classes are offered, have both been changed as a result of cost-reducing revisions to the home language reform that were implemented in 1992. The new curriculum guidelines of 1994 also affected the teaching of home languages in Swedish schools. With few exceptions, these changes have not resulted in improvements. The amount of time allotted to HLI was in the early days of optional provision of this instruction, i.e., before 1977, limited to 80 minutes per week. This limitation was officially removed with the home language reform of 1977, when schools became obliged to offer this kind of instruction, and the guiding principle was instead to be the needs of the individual pupils. However, most schools continued to limit the availability of HLI to the original 80 minutes, and nobody seems to have questioned this practice (Municio 1987). One reason for this could be that HLI at this time replaced other subjects during the school day, and too many substituted hours would have led to the pupils' missing too much learning in other subjects.

The average time given to HLI today still seems to be those 2x40 minutes a week, although there have since 1994 been other models available. These alternatives include just one as well as up to three 40-minute class periods of HLI per week at different stages in the compulsory school system, usually starting in grade 3 and continuing through grade 9. However, the pupil can only continue until a total of between 320 and 470 (depending on the instructional model) such class periods have been accumulated over a maximum of 7 school years, i.e., potentially each school year from grade 3 up to and including grade 9. According to a report written by the National Agency for Education entitled *Flera språk – fler möjligheter,* ('More languages – more opportunities') (Skolverket 2002) which covers many aspects of HLI in Sweden, it is in reality not uncommon that local schools decide not to implement the time restrictions stated in the curriculum guidelines.

With the curriculum guidelines of 1994 (Lpo-94), HLI is no longer to replace other scheduled class activities. The pupils now have more individual flexibility in designing their study programs, at least in theory, and home language can be one of these options that either the school can choose to include in its regular curriculum or the individual pupil can select as one of her/his courses. Otherwise, HLI is to be done outside the regular school day. This seems to be what has become the reality for most children receiving HLI. Just one year after these new rules, 65% of all municipalities reported that they had opted to schedule instruction in home languages after the end of the school day and that they had ensured that the minimum group size of five was implemented (Hyltenstam and Tuomela 1996). It appears that an even greater percentage of Sweden's municipalities follow those guidelines today, based on more recent reports from local schools to the National Agency for Education (Skolverket 2002).

This late afternoon instruction makes for a very long day, especially for younger pupils, and older pupils may find that HLI late in the afternoon leaves them with less time for homework or that it conflicts with other interests, such as sports. Participation in HLI can even be seen as counterproductive if it segregates IM children from Swedish pupils, with the former developing their first language skills while the latter engage in various athletic, creative or social activities after school. Thus, this change in scheduling can become an added burden when the minimum number of pupils necessary to start a HLI group has to be found.

In secondary schools, the changes in access to HLI have been less striking. If there is enough interest to get a group of at least five pupils, and there is a teacher available, a home language can usually be studied in lieu of a second or third foreign language. (English, the first foreign language, is compulsory also at the secondary level in the Swedish school system.) Over the three years of secondary school, a maximum of 190 class periods of HLI can be accumulated.

4.7. Funding

All funding for HLI in public education comes from the government and cannot be supplemented with funds from any other source. The national treasury distributes education funds to the municipal authorities with recommendations about how this school money should be spent. Since 1994, however, none of these funds are earmarked specifically for HLI. In practice, this means that a school board can decide to use money, whose recommended use is to pay for HLI, to replace broken windows or spend it on some other school need/activity, which is seen as a higher priority. School administrators and local authorities tend not to consider HLI a high priority. As a result, money for HLI only becomes available if the local school authorities decide that they can afford it (Skolverket 2002). What was once a very generous and truly democratic component in the Swedish school system has now become a bonus that the pupils may benefit from if circumstances permit.

The funding for the so-called independent schools in Sweden also comes from the public purse and is not to be supplemented with any infusions of funds from other sources. This school form is thus intended to be free of charge to the families who choose to have their children attend this type of school. There have been reports in the media about independent schools requesting extra contributions from the parents of their pupils, but these schools have without exception been reprimanded by the school authorities. The same is true for organisations wishing to sponsor a particular independent school, so an immigrant or cultural association cannot financially sponsor an independent school with a language or subject profile that the organisation in question would like to support. The amount of money an independent school receives from the government is determined by the number of pupils registered at the school.

Swedish school children have to choose one school type or the other. It is therefore not possible to, for example, attend a regular public school for most of the day and supplement one's education with some courses offered at an independent school, such as instruction in a certain home language that one's public school does not provide.

4.8. Teaching materials

Finding appropriate teaching materials for HLI has been a considerable problem ever since these programs were started. It soon proved inappropriate to import materials from where the languages were taught as majority languages. Not only was the content culturally unsuitable for teaching in the Swedish school system, but the language level, especially for the older pupils, was also too sophisticated for a child growing up in another social and linguistic context (Jacobsen 1981).

Generally speaking, though, considering the great heterogeneity of the children in a group of home language pupils, being taught together by the same teacher in the same room at the same time, the creation of teaching materials seems an almost impossible task except on an ad hoc basis. Informal sharing among instructors can take place, provided they get a chance to see each other, but home language teachers often operate quite isolated from one another. There are few venues for them meet, such as conferences or professional development days intended for home language teachers in particular. With recent government funding cut-backs in Sweden to schools in general and immigrant education in particular, the difficulty in finding proper home language teaching materials will most likely persist.

4.9. Teacher qualifications

When the home language reform was implemented in 1977, a new teacher-training program was also established at major colleges of education in Sweden, the home language teacher program. It was two years long and was initially available in seven immigrant languages: Arabic, Danish, Finnish, Greek, Serbo-Croatian (still considered one language at that time), Spanish, and Turkish. A few years later, Farsi was added. However, considering the need for trained teachers in these languages, the number of applicants to the program was limited. There was also criticism of the program as being too focused on language skill training and lacking in cultural content (Jacobsen 1981). The students enrolled in the program are reported to have complained about both a shortage of time and a lack of depth, the result of the wide spectrum of teaching situations and age groups these teachers were to face in the classroom. Consequently, the majority of home language instructors did not get and do not have this training.

Instead, there is a mixture of practices in place to secure teachers for various home languages. Most teachers working today are still employed after many of their colleagues lost their jobs in connection with the reduced funding of the programs in the early 1990's. Consequently, even though they may be lacking in terms of formal qualifications, they have several years of experience. Among them are academics with teacher training from their home countries or some other higher education or pedagogical training. Others were simply willing to do the job when somebody was needed and proved able to do it satisfactorily, in spite of not having formal qualifications (Skolverket 2002). The latter strategy can still become used if an instructor for one of the newer home languages is needed. The individual school (board) today has a great deal of liberty to recruit as they see fit, since the Swedish school system today is very decentralised.

The report from the National Agency for Education (Skolverket 2002) calls for improvements to the present working conditions for home language teachers in Sweden and emphasises the need for professional training and development. This document also suggests clearer home language guidelines in terms of not only instructional content and teaching methods but also objectives and funding. All these are factors that ultimately affect the teaching reality of home language instructors and contribute to raising the status of HLI among pupils, parents, other teachers and school directors. Those factors also determine the kinds of qualifications that are necessary to accomplish the goal of helping IM children in Sweden develop into active bilinguals and well-educated adults.)

5. Conclusions

The goal of developing active bilingualism in pupils from homes where other languages than Swedish are spoken, is essential for the maintenance of the linguistic capital Sweden has in its immigrant population. In an increasingly global economy with many Swedish companies becoming parts of multinational conglomerates, not just good English skills but also proficiency in other languages will become an asset in the international marketplace. Swedish know-how in the field of environmental issues is also vital to the survival of parts of our planet, many of them areas from where immigrants have come to Sweden. The bilingual children of these people can thus become key players in bridging the gap between the needs of the affected regions and the available Swedish research and technology. Working together in the same language can prevent misunderstandings and mistakes and can maximise the results of such cooperation.

Moreover, the children growing up in IM families can, with the proper language input and instruction in both Swedish and their home languages, become adults with the bicultural and bilingual skills necessary to build bridges between the indigenous and the IM communities. In a country like Sweden, where most urban areas today are characterised by segregation between these population groups, there is a risk that xenophobic political organisations become more powerful as a result of alienation and fear of the unknown among both ethnic Swedes and immigrants. With more successful integration of both second- and third-generation immigrants, born in Sweden and in many cases Swedish citizens, the future may turn a Sweden with many IM languages into a truly multilingual Sweden.

References

Boyd, Sally
   2007   Communication and community: Perspectives on language policy in Sweden and Australia since the Mid-1970s. In *Maintaining Minority Languages in Transnational Contexts*, Anne Pauwels, Joanne Winter and Joseph Lo Bianco (eds.), 141–179. London: Palgrave Macmillan.

Boyd, Sally and Leena Huss
   2001   Introduction. In *Managing Multilingualism in a European Nation-state. Challenges for Swedish*, Sally Boyd and Leena Huss (eds.), 1–12. Clevedon: Multilingual Matters

Extra, Guus, Rian Aarts, Tim van der Avoird, Peter Broeder and Kutlay Yağmur
   2001   *Meertaligheid in Den Haag: de Status van Allochtone Talen Thuis en op School*. Amsterdam: European Cultural Foundation.

Extra, Guus and Durk Gorter (eds.)
   2001   *The Other Languages of Europe. Demographic, Sociolinguistic and Educational Perspectives*. Clevedon: Multilingual Matters.

Frisell, Helena, Lilian Nygren-Junkin, Ingela Nyman, and Mikael Olofsson
   2004   *Kartläggning av svenska som andraspråk* [Survey of Swedish as a Second Language]. Stockholm: Myndigheten för skolutveckling.

Hyltenstam, Kenneth
   1986   *Politik, forskning och praktik. Invandrarspråken – ratad resurs?* [Politics, Research and Practice. Immigrant Languages – A Rejected Resource?] Stockholm: Forskningsrådsnämnden.
   1999   *Sveriges sju inhemska språk* [Sweden's Seven Indigenous Languages]. Lund: Studentlitteratur.

Hyltenstam, Kenneth and Veli Tuomela
   1996   Hemspråksundervisningen [Home language instruction]. In *Tvåspråkighet med förhinder? Invandrar- och minoritets-undervisning i Sverige* [Obstacles to Bilingualism? Immigrant and Minority Instruction in Sweden], Kenneth Hyltenstam (ed.), 9–109 Lund: Studentlitteratur.

Gunnarsson, Britt-Louise
   2001   Swedish tomorrow – A product of the linguistic dominance of English? In *Managing Multilingualism in a European Nation-state. Challenges for Swedish*, Sally Boyd and Leena Huss (eds.), 51–69. Clevedon: Multilingual Matters.

Jacobsen, Inger
   1981   Hemspråksundervisning och utbildning av lärare i hemspråk. [Home language instruction and the education of home language teachers]. In *Språkmöte. Svenska som främmande språk. Hemspråk. Tolkning*

[*Languages Meeting. Swedish as a Foreign Language. Home Languages. Interpreting*], Kenneth Hyltenstam (ed.), 156–177. Lund: LiberLäromedel.

Lpo-94
1994 *Läroplanen för det obligatoriska skolväsendet* [Curriculum Guidelines for the Compulsory School System.]. Stockholm: Utbildningsdepartementet.

Municio, Ingegerd
1987 *Från lag till bruk: hemspråksreformens genomförande* [From Law to use: The Implementation of the Home Language Reform]. Stockholm: Centrum för invandringsforskning.

Nygren-Junkin, Lilian and Extra, Guus
2003 *Multilingualism in Göteborg. The Status of Immigrant Minority Languages at Home and at School.* Amsterdam: European Cultural Foundation.

SCB
2002 *Personer med utländsk bakgrund. Riktlinjer för redovisning av statistiken. Meddelande i samordningsfrågor för Sveriges officiella statistik* 2002:3 [Persons of immigrant background. Guidelines for presentation of statistical data. Announcement on issues of coordination for Sweden's official statistics 2002:3]

2003 *Befolkningsstatistik 2003 Del 3. Folkmängden efter kön, ålder, födelseland och medborgarskap mm. Tidigare utgåvor samt dess föregångare* [Population statistics 2003 Part 3. Population according to gender, age, birth country and citizenship etc. Earlier issues and their predecessors.]

2004 *Efterkrigstidens invandring och utvandring. Demografiska rapporter 2004:5* [Post-war immigration and emigration. Demographic reports 2004:5].

Skolverket
2002 *Flera språk – fler möjligheter* [More Languages – More Opportunities]. Stockholm: Skolverket.

SOU (*Statens Offentliga Utredningar* [The government's official investigations])
2002 *EU:s utvidgning och arbetskraftens rörlighet* [The Expansion of the EU and the Mobility of the Workforce].

Tingbjörn, Gunnar
1986 *Skolan som resursförvaltare. Invandrarspråken - ratad resurs?* [The School as a Care-Taker of Resources. The Immigrant Languages – A Rejected Resource?]. Stockholm: Forskningsrådsnämnden.

Immigrant languages in Italy

Monica Barni and Carla Bagna

1. Objectives

Our objective is to describe the trends and changes in the linguistic space in Italy as a result of contact with the languages that have entered this space through migratory events during the last 30 years. This objective represents the main focus of studies carried out at the Centre of Excellence for Research – *Centre for the Study of the Italian Language among non-Italians and Immigrant Languages in Italy* of the Siena University for Foreigners. We take a semiotic approach, exploring all signs that cooperate in sense-construction processes. Given that language is viewed in terms of identity, we look at both languages and identities in contact (see De Mauro 1963, 2002, 2007).

In order to fully grasp the current linguistic situation in Italy, we need to understand the context and dynamics in which the "new" languages have come to interact in Italy. It is only after some analysis, albeit concise, of the Italian linguistic situation and its complex dynamics that we can appreciate whether, and if so which and how immigrant languages might be capable of playing a part in the reshaping of the Italian linguistic space, thus helping to strengthen the linguistic pluralism that has always been a key feature of this country.

The social phenomenon of migration has constituted a determining factor in the structuring of the linguistic situation in a distinctive manner in Italy compared to other European countries. This is true of both external and internal migration phenomena as well as immigration. One constant feature in analyses of migration, whether regarding the phenomenon itself, its linguistic consequences, or its political and educational contexts, is a certain inclination on the part of analysts to conceal and refuse to acknowledge its significance and the results of its influence. The aim of this chapter is to explain the reasons for this denial and to link phenomenological and quantitative data with linguistic data, overcoming the embarrassing yet all-too-common tendency to equate ethnic data with linguistic data (De Mauro 2005; Orioles 2006; Extra and Yağmur 2004), in order to shed light on the role of migration in the structuring of the Italian linguistic space.

Processes of both emigration and internal migration have played a decisive role in reducing the plurilingual space made up of dialects and historic minority languages which has always been a major feature in Italy, and in the diffusion of a unitary language spoken by all Italians. Today, however, with some 3,700,000 immigrants in Italy and around 500,000 minors within the education system, and with the increasingly structured progression towards rootedness, socio-demographic data indicates the presence of a critical mass that is bound to have implications on a linguistic level. This chapter aims to examine these implications. As we have mentioned elsewhere (Bagna, Barni and Vedovelli 2007), research with this aim in view must seek to identify the factors that may have a positive influence on the maintenance of immigrant languages, the types and networks of language use, the factors exerting pressure on the local linguistic space and those facilitating change in different directions: the maintenance *vs.* loss of new languages, the formation of new varieties through contact and the differing degrees of linguistic assimilation.

We will also analyse the language policy interventions put in place by the Italian State as regards the status of immigrant languages. Italy lacks specific legislation to safeguard immigrant languages on a national level, as is also the case on a European level (see Extra and Gorter, this Volume). Article 6 of the Italian Constitution ("The Republic safeguards linguistic minorities"), enacted in 1948, contains a general principle aimed at facilitating freedom of linguistic and cultural expression. It was another 50 years before the Italian State published law n°. 482/1999 (*Regulations for the protection of historic linguistic minorities*), recognising twelve minority language varieties. This law only recognises minorities that meet the criteria of being linked to a specific territory and being of long-standing, i.e., the so-called "historic minority languages" (Orioles 2007). Since there is no legislation regarding the recognition and safeguarding of immigrant languages, we will analyse the normative and operative choices adopted in the educational world. Schools, forced by everyday reality to confront the linguistic problem of immigration before other institutions, have found the need to respond to this social emergency. We will present both the directions put in place by the Ministry of Education and the operative practices and ways in which the educational world has responded to the arrival of foreign pupils, focusing particularly on the attention paid by the institutions to these languages and how they are received in schools.

2. Emigration and immigration in Italy: linguistic impact

Traditionally, Italy has always been a country of emigration. During the second half of the 19th century and the first half of the 20th, it is estimated that some 14 million Italians left the country. As De Mauro (1963) emphasises, the effect of emigration on the Italian linguistic situation was profound. In the social context of migration, language always acts as a catalyst, shaping forms of identity, and providing a focal point for the reformulation of identities. In the case of Italy, emigration played a fundamental role in the Italianisation of the country. Those emigrating from Italy above all were individuals from the regions and social classes with the highest rates of illiteracy and the most widespread use of dialects. In fact, Italian emigration, by thinning out the numbers of illiterate dialect speakers, made easier the work of the nationwide school system and the promotion of the development of literacy and thus the spread of the national language, Italian, to the detriment of dialect-based language use. Linguistic unification was also promoted by Italy's internal migration, which, from the 1950s, brought masses of dialect-speakers from southern Italy to the more industrialised regions of the North. All this, together with other factors (De Mauro 1963), led to the diffusion of a unitary Italian language (De Mauro et al. 1993), which, as De Mauro (1977) and, more recently, Orioles (2006) confirm, only followed the trend towards monolingualism that was already deeply-rooted in the Italian society, and especially in its ruling classes. In terms of language policy, the consequences of the rejection of plurilingualism were the imposition of a single language – in accordance with the 19th-century paradigm of *one nation/one language* and thus the failure, until a decade ago, to recognise even the historic minorities, and the diffusion in schools of a sort of pseudo-purist prescriptivism. Thus, driven by linguistic unification, dialects and other minority languages, whilst still an active part of Italy's linguistic repertoire, as can be seen from recent statistical enquiries (ISTAT 2007), have gradually seen their range of possible communicative uses dwindling (Vedovelli 2003). This policy has repercussions on the current situation.

In the past 30 years, the Italian society has experienced new conditions, marked by the increasingly large-scale arrival of a population of foreign origin. The latest socio-demographic data on foreign immigration in Italy are those produced by the annual *Dossier Caritas*, which, over the years, has established its position as the most reliable and careful observatory of immigration patterns in this country. The most recent Dossier (Caritas 2007a) shows that the number of immigrants is now some 3,690,000 people, which accounts for over 6.2% of the resident population. The Dossier shows us that there are more than 150 different nationalities represented by immigrants in Italy, the most numerous groups being Romanians, Moroccans, Albanians, Ukrainians, Chinese, Filipinos, Moldavians, Tunisians, Indians and Poles. The composition of the foreign population in Italy has changed repeatedly, due both to diachronic factors (differentiation of groups over time), and synchronic factors (presence of different identities with varying social connotations), often highly dependent on the conditions of the labour market and the geographic configuration of the country. This makes for a varied and complex demographic panorama, and therefore also a complex linguistic panorama. This aspect, however, and its effects on the Italian linguistic space, have been largely ignored in linguistic research, except for a handful of studies. Ever since the early 1980s, warnings were issued (Vedovelli 1981) of the problems arising from the emergence of the new social phenomenon of foreign immigration within the linguistic composition of an Italian society that was still seeking a balance between the unitary Italian language and traditional dialects and historic minority languages within national boundaries. Linguistic analyses focused primarily on Italian as an object of learning for immigrants (Giacalone Ramat 2003), in order to highlight and verify natural language acquisition sequences.

The Population Census (ISTAT 2001) also lacks questions on the languages spoken: foreigners resident in Italy are only asked about their country of birth and their citizenship. Paradoxically, the questionnaire for the 2001 census and the instructions for compilation were translated into 12 languages, including Chinese, Sinhala, Arabic and Polish, neither of which are historic minority languages in Italy, nor are they languages of neighbouring countries. This proves that, albeit vaguely, the presence of speakers of other languages in Italy was perceived, but the choice of languages for which translation was provided was in no way prompted by the self-evident criterion of the corresponding nationalities being represented most strongly in the Italian population at the time.

The various Caritas Dossiers also lack any systematic and constant research into the languages spoken by immigrants. In a report presented in 2001, the first on this topic, a figure was hypothesised, based on the nationalities declared, of the presence of at least 150 languages (Vedovelli and Villarini 2001). The 2007 Dossier simply provides a summary of various non-systematic studies performed on the matter in Italy. None of the other annual Dossier editions make any mention of languages.

Above and beyond the scientific significance of the lack of data on the ways and effects of entry of immigrant languages into the Italian linguistic space, and the blindness in the interpretation of available data, these failings lead to social and educational fall-out, so that legislation and interventions regarding immigrants and their communicative skills continue to remain non-structural emergency measures. By contrast, a systematic study to identify the distribution and vitality of immigrant languages constitutes a necessary cognitive tool for a policy of linguistic diffusion, and also for the planning of social interventions for immigrants by the institutions responsible for handling contacts. Several sectors come to mind: schools, for a better knowledge of the pupils' linguistic background and for planning activities aimed at maintaining their L1; or the health service, justice and production systems, for a more effective handling of social communication.

3. Research on immigrant languages in Italy

As we have pointed out, research in Italy has been almost entirely lacking in analysing the linguistic implications that emerge from statistical data regarding migratory phenomena, due to the difficulty faced by researchers in importing approaches from other areas such as semiotics into linguistic studies. This, however, makes it possible to handle the complexity of the phenomena involved in linguistic contact, which is also contact between identities, and to understand the implications of the "new-sense territories" that derive from contact. Thus, the question of *immigrant languages* has remained in the background when compared to the attention paid to the dynamics of immigrants' acquisition of Italian as a second language.

While De Mauro (1977) already spoke of "new minorities" and Vedovelli (1981, 1989) of "immigrant languages", in reference to the "non-territorial" and "non-historic" minority languages that had come to be a part of the Italian linguistic space, Italy does not seem ready yet to "acknowledge" or to "deal with" other languages. It therefore comes as no great surprise that research carried out in the period from the early 1980s to the end of the 20th century tended to be restricted to small areas of the country. Indeed, no Italian city has been the subject of any large-scale data collection similar to that carried out in the context of the *Multilingual Cities Project* (Extra and Yağmur, this Volume), and the micro-surveys on the linguistic repertoires of immigrant adults and minors in Italy have only served to illustrate the reality of specific locations, such as Pavia, Turin, Verona, Bergamo and Palermo (Chini 2004; Massariello Merzagora 2005; D'Agostino 2006; Valentini, in press).

A first step towards a more in-depth and systematic analysis of the complex situation in Italy, and of the dynamics that have developed here, was taken in 2001, when the above-mentioned Centre of Excellence for Research was established, with a view to monitoring the effects of the "new" languages entering Italy. At a 2002 conference on the theme of linguistic ecology (to which the outcomes of linguistic contact are also linked), an explanation was given (Bagna, Machetti and Vedovelli 2003) of the distinction made between the concepts of *migrant language* and *immigrant language*. This distinction is useful in describing the nature and effects of the interaction between the new plurilingualism and the local linguistic repertoire.

Migrant languages are defined as languages "passing through", used by migrant groups who drift around the social territory, non-cohesive and in relatively small numbers. For this reason, these languages are unable to put down roots and to leave traces of their presence in the linguistic contact make-up of the host community, or they succeed in doing so only sporadically. *Immigrant languages*, on the other hand, are those of numerically larger, stable groups, with intentions of putting down roots within a local community. These languages are used systematically by particular immigrant groups and are able to "leave their mark" in the linguistic contact make-up of the host community. Only the latter can hope to become part of the new plurilingualism of the Italian peninsula and, given that they are in a more stable and lasting situation of contact with the other language varieties present in the area, they are in a position to affect its communicative and linguistic make-up.

In light of the above, a language may be defined as *immigrant* because it is spoken by a community that is present in an area in quantitative terms, but that is also strong in qualitative terms. The latter aspect brings us back to the need for detailed studies on the types of use of languages within the area where groups have settled. We need to identify the parameters that enable us to establish whether the languages spoken by groups in a given area have the status of immigrant languages, with a certain degree of manifestation, visibility and recognisability (if not yet recognised), or whether these languages may potentially achieve this status. We also need to verify whether, for reasons which may be extra-linguistic, these languages alter, even superficially or temporarily, the Italian linguistic space. Hence, the logical choice is multi-level research, using a theoretical and methodological approach that takes into account the weight of many variables, in order to monitor the possible outcomes of linguistic contact. Only identifying the languages present within the country in quantitative terms does not provide information on the relations between the languages observed and their use, which is what the objective of research would be that seeks to obtain synchronic and diachronic results on the "behaviour" of immigrant languages.

4. Immigrant languages in Italy: focus on Chinese and Romanian

Questions like *How many immigrant languages are there in Italy, which languages are these, and where do they occur?* presuppose the identification of the immigrant languages present within a given area and the awareness that only with adequate tools is it possible to account for the complexity of a phenomenon such as linguistic contact. Only more "refined" multilevel tools can provide indications regarding the role, use and functions of what are "potentially" immigrant languages in a given area. These indications are often the fruit of a complex monitoring mechanism involving several disciplines, and providing a map that can be read from a range of perspectives. One of the first criteria that can be used to discuss immigrant communities is of a statistical-demographic nature. We know how many nationalities are present in Italy, which are the most numerous communities, and where in the country they have chosen to live. We also know that, by overlaying these areas, it is possible to obtain an initial map of linguistic presence and contact between different immigrant groups and Italian, with all its varieties and dialects. A second level of analysis involves the study of language use, with methods such as interviews and questionnaires. The *linguistic landscape* approach offers a more detailed exploration of the visibility of immigrant languages in a relatively circumscribed area (Bagna, Barni and Vedovelli 2007; Barni 2006, 2008; Barni and Bagna 2008).

Only by combining the results obtained from the various levels of observation is it possible to formulate hypotheses regarding the apparent dispersion or homogeneity of behaviours, attitudes and linguistic dynamics that may be established in a neighbourhood or a city. In any case, the simple presence of a group is not enough to justify talking of *immigrant languages* in a given area. The very condition of *immigrant languages* presupposes a presence which may show neutral features, if such a thing is possible, up to a certain level of pressure which may generate conflict in linguistic contact. The territory is constantly being reshaped by the linguistic pressures sustained or exerted, and by the language choices made by individuals and groups. This presence/pressure level needs to be detected, measured and analysed in terms of factors such as:

- the territory (urban area, rural area, presence and level of concentration of immigrants);
- the specific traits of each group (period of immigration, attitudes towards their own language and culture, etc.);
- the conditions of visibility and vitality of languages spoken by the groups (type of activities performed, percentage of minors in school etc.).

Thus, if we can initially derive the presence of immigrant languages from a statistical/quantitative analysis, their level of linguistic pressure and eligibility as an immigrant language derives from a range of factors. Furthermore, to qualify a language as *immigrant* in one Italian region or city may prove to be impossible in another area. For this reason we refer to the concept of linguistic pressure of immigrant languages in terms of the sum and weight of the dynamics generated by the presence and contact (in its various forms and manifestations) of immigrant languages with Italian and with other languages in a given area.

It is not possible to provide a list of the *immigrant languages* found in Italy: this varies according to the area and its characteristics. Indeed, the examples given below regarding Chinese and Romanian show that languages identified as fitting the definition of *immigrant* more so than others are closely tied to and dependent upon individual cities or provinces, and they may not fit the definition in other areas. The data presented are the fruits of territorial mapping activities performed by the Centre of Excellence. The mapping in turn is the fruit of the choice to combine several complementary approaches, and to use a powerful multi-mode method that could be used in different combinations and in conformity with the aims of research into different dimensions (investigating one or more languages) and levels (semiotic, macro- and micro-linguistic) (Bagna and Barni 2005; Barni and Bagna 2008). By analysing different mappings and the state of vitality and visibility of languages that may be considered immigrant, we can also verify the pressure conditions in the areas where they are spoken.

The decision to a focus on Chinese and Romanian is prompted by the fact that for these two languages the factors mentioned above combine in a range of different ways, giving rise to varied outcomes. Chinese has been present in Italy for quite a while and shows considerable visibility and vitality; Romanian, which has arrived more recently, has its own visibility and vitality mechanisms. Following the same format of analysis we could identify different modes of presence, use and visibility of immigrant languages in each area under investigation (regions, provinces, small- or medium-size towns *vs.* large cities).

4.1. The status of Chinese

Rome (Esquilino)

The *Municipio I* administrative area in Rome, which includes the Esquilino neighbourhood, is the area with the greatest number of foreigners in the city. In 2004, when the survey was carried out, 25,004 foreigners were living there (11.2% of Rome's total foreign population). This ratio has remained constant in subsequent years. It is the neighbourhood with the highest percentage of foreigners in relation to the number of residents: 20.4% (22.9% in 2006). In other publications we have dealt in detail with the survey of languages in the neighbourhood (Bagna and Barni 2006; Barni 2006; Bagna 2006), using statistical and demographic analysis and linguistic landscape. Twenty-four visible languages were identified, scattered unevenly across the area, and able to establish different relations with Italian and other languages. In the Esquilino neighbourhood, Chinese is the leading language in terms of dominance (quantitative prevalence of visible, written texts observed in the area) and autonomy, i.e., the capacity to be used in public communication without the use of Italian or other languages. It thus proves to be the language capable of exerting the most pressure on the area. Of the 851 texts observed, including 296 monolingual texts, 197 are entirely in Chinese. It is no mere accident that on the subject of the presence of Chinese, the document entitled *Esquilino dei mondi lontani* 'The distant worlds of Esquilino' (Caritas 2007b) emphasises that the neighbourhood feels "the alienating impact caused by the presence of ideograms [...], an indecipherable language that does not facilitate everyday communication". Such comments confirm the hypothesis that Chinese, a language capable of conserving its autonomy to a greater degree in a neighbourhood with high levels of plurilingualism, exerts pressure, manifested in its visibility and in strong vitality. It is no coincidence that this pressure led to the signing of a protocol between the City of Rome and the Chinese community on 11 May 2007. This document emphasises that the Chinese community must "improve shop signs and fittings, being sure to install signs written in Italian at the top, and in Chinese below". The City of Rome, on the other hand, must "facilitate the life and integration of the Chinese community by organising courses to enable them to learn Italian and to become familiar with the requirements of the law, particularly as regards integration, legality and trade; [...] make communication between institutions and foreign communities easier by translating laws and regulations into Chinese". Provisions of this kind clearly recognise the role of Chinese as the language of a minority community for which agreements are drawn up similar to those established for historic minorities. In the case of Chinese, however, the aims are different: not so much to maintain an ethno-linguistic identity, but rather to regulate and even limit the use of a specific language. This provision confirms the pressure of the Chinese language, which so strongly affects an area that laws are made regulating its use.

Prato

Prato is the municipality with the highest proportion of foreigners (23,621 people) amongst its resident population (185,631, data from 30 November 2007). Over 40% of these foreigners are Chinese (10,419). Based on this figure, we can hypothesise that Chinese may account for 44% of the languages spoken by immigrant groups, leading to pressure that can be seen particularly in certain areas of the city. Unlike the situation observed in Esquilino, however, the pressure and presence of the Chinese language in Prato is very wide-ranging: it concerns not only community choices or strategies of a commercial nature, but the handling of communication and public life in general. Compared with Esquilino, the domains of use of Chinese are broader, and the authors/sources of messages in Chinese (or Chinese and Italian) are not only members of the community itself, but also Italian institutions. In other words, the pressure of Chinese is exerted through both *bottom-up* and *top-down* mechanisms (Ben-Rafael et al. 2006), making it a unique case in Italy due to the intensity/range of this balance. Italian seems to seek out space within Chinese and vice versa, and in a situation such as that in Prato, it effectively becomes "one of the languages", subject to the dynamics of contact, comparison, choice or rejection by various groups of speakers.

Finally, as with Esquilino, the weight of the other immigrant languages comes into play; whilst they may not be able to exert the same level of pressure as Chinese, they still take part in the dynamics of visibility and contact.

4.2. The status of Romanian

The city and province of Rome

Romanians have been the largest immigrant community in the province of Rome since 2004, and on a national level too, their presence has increased considerably in recent years, to the point that they are now the largest immigrant group in Italy as a whole.

The data collected in Esquilino, both around the neighbourhood and at the market place, show few traces and texts in Romanian. Contained in only 13 of the 851 texts observed, and dominant in just 3, Romanian never appeared autonomously. It thus proves to be a language that relies on Italian or other languages. The group's preponderantly non-commercial presence and its subsequent lower visibility in terms of text production for public communication would appear to explain the result obtained. Nonetheless, these figures are counter-balanced by the linguistic vitality indexes (as against visibility), gathered in part through questionnaires and interviews with families and school children. Thus, we find a declared vitality, surveyed specifically in the municipalities of Mentana and Monterotondo near Rome for a total population of some 50,000 people, chosen as a new home by families of Romanian origin who have found the most favourable conditions for sedentarisation in this area. In these towns, the visibility of the Romanian language is of secondary importance, and is above all a result of vitality and established presence in the area. Indeed, it took at least 5–6 years of stable presence here before any writing in Romanian was observed within the public space. As from 2005, Monterotondo in particular has shown elements of visibility of the Romanian community, which was completely absent previously and which reinforces Romanian's role as an immigrant language. The very few traces previously observed had been produced exclusively by public bodies, so that the choice to use Romanian came from above, and not directly from the community itself.

Emerging from this analysis is a type of pressure that appears to be limited to the maintenance of the language of origin within the family. The very fact that Romanian is used in the private domain leads to a broadening of its use in the contexts of public communication, particularly where the authors of texts wish to emphasise links with their country of origin.

Florence

Florence is another city attracting Romanians in particular, who are the fourth largest immigrant group, numbering some 3,000 people (after Chinese, Albanians and Filipinos), and accounting for 8% of foreign residents. The city, however, seems impermeable to the presence of this community. The space of the central area, and particularly *Quartiere 1*, from San Lorenzo to Santa Croce, is crushed between Italian and English, and the weight of these languages of mass-communication and mass-tourism minimises the visibility of other languages, and thus of immigrant languages. Although *Quartiere 1* has the second largest number of Romanian residents, minimal traces of their language were found (5 in all), confirming the findings for Esquilino and the province of Rome.

Faced with the data from Rome and Florence, a question needs to be formulated: are the "partial" vitality and visibility illustrated sufficient to speak of a form of linguistic pressure (albeit limited and circumscribed) exerted by Romanian in these areas? We believe so, because this is one of the major groups present in the areas observed, and because the group shows the will to maintain their language of origin. This maintenance can be seen through a process of emergence that is slower and perhaps less well-organised than in the case of Chinese. The Romanian community is also caught between the drive towards permanent emigration and plans of return migration, on the one hand encouraging the maintenance of the language of origin, and on the other creating limited levels of pressure in the surrounding linguistic space. This pressure is clearly visible in strategic places, such as bus stations. In both Rome and Florence, the main language heard in these places other than Italian is Romanian.

4.3. Other immigrant languages

The examples of Chinese and Romanian in specific areas of Italy confirm the hypothesis whereby languages that can be defined as having *immigrant* status show traits that depend on the different contact conditions formed in the area where they have become established. Similar considerations as those observed for Chinese can be applied to Arabic in the Porta Palazzo area of Turin, where North African immigration was the first to arrive and settle. The considerations given for Romanian are also valid for Ukrainian, and in part also for Polish. These languages now all have their own recent or longer history of immigration to Italy. This history, which at times comes into the public eye following some dramatic news headline, affirms their status as immigrant languages. In part due to their previous linguistic history and paths of emigration, groups from the Balkans appear to encounter more complications in trying to define relations with their language of origin (sometimes immigrant language, other times migrant language) and with Italian. The motivations driving these groups to migration also include conflicts with linguistic implications.

This fact makes it even more imperative to analyse in detail another crucial context for immigrant languages: schools. As we shall see, legislative interventions and provisions made for the children of immigrants have failed to drive schools towards harnessing and valuing the linguistic and cultural repertoire of immigrant pupils. Schools do not know or recognise immigrant languages; they have not developed systematic actions to maintain immigrant languages, and in the same way they at times reject the linguistic heritage of indigenous pupils. More so than other agencies, schools have been involved right from the start in receiving pupils of foreign origin, but they have neglected (and to some extent continue to ignore) the linguistic heritage already available to pupils of foreign origin, both new-arrivals and those born in Italy.

5. Immigrant languages and the educational domain

With the development of increasing and permanent immigration, the Italian educational system, in addition to foreign adults attending literacy courses to learn Italian, saw the arrival of their children. In fact, Italian law n°. 40/98 on immigration guarantees the right and obligation for minors, including the children of illegal immigrants, to enrol in schools. During the year 2006/2007, there were more than 500,000 pupils with non-Italian citizenship attending school, accounting for almost 5.6% of the overall school population (MPI 2007). In the three-year period 2003–2005, the increase on average was 60,000–70,000 pupils per year: in some cases, the number of foreign pupils, especially in primary schools, accounts for more than 40% of total class numbers.

The categories of pupils present depict an educational landscape marked by multiplicity of citizenships: the number of countries of origin (the only data surveyed) of foreign pupils in our schools is calculated to be 191 (MPI 2007). The situation is not the same everywhere. Out of all the schools with at least 20% foreign pupils, 58 include pupils of just one or two nationalities, but another 216 include foreign pupils from over 20 different countries (MPI 2007). However, these data do not provide us with an accurate picture of the situation. The criterion used to identify foreigners within the school context, i.e., the nationality of pupils and their parents, is not adequate to describe a multicultural and multilingual environment (Extra and Gorter, this Volume). Pupils slipping through this net include those who already have the nationality of their adopted country, children of mixed couples, emigrants with Italian citizenship returning from abroad, adopted children, and nomadic children born in Italy who have acquired Italian citizenship. If, instead of the criterion of nationality, the languages spoken in their repertoires of origin were to be used, this would result in a far more accurate picture of the degree of multiculturalism, the numbers would certainly increase, and above all, the other linguistic varieties present in their repertoires of origin would be brought to light alongside the official languages.

And yet still today, although the presence of foreign/immigrant pupils is now a constant feature, it is difficult to get out of the attitude of astonishment at the news of emergency interventions, both in socio-political terms and in terms of educational operations. The speed of change in Italian schools is often cited as a justification: going from 50,000 foreign/ immigrant pupils in the year 1995/1996 to 430,000 in 2005/2006. However, both the relevant institutions and the educational world had already prepared procedures and responses in the late 1980s and early 1990s, but these were then either forgotten or remained limited to the location and period of their initial use.

One of the first institutional documents published in Italy on the education of foreign/immigrant pupils dates back to 1989: CM 30189, a memorandum of the Ministry of Education at the time, dealing with the "Inclusion of foreign pupils in compulsory schooling: promotion and coordination of initiatives for exercising the right to study". This is a highly innovative document, containing in germinal form the elements needed to set out an educational operation based on respect for individual rights in terms of multilingualism and multiculturalism. It both identifies the criteria around which to shape interventions, following the principles and values of the Italian Constitution and of relevant European legislation, and highlights the weak points in the educational system for the development of policies on diversity.

The first significant point to note is that the memorandum recognises the presence of foreign/immigrant pupils and their languages in the classroom as a constant feature, destined to increase in quantity. The text does not feature expressions such as "emergency", "teaching emergency", or "problem", typical of more recent legislative texts, but promotes structural intervention in the various stages of schooling. The central importance of the language issue is recognised, both from the point of view of learning Italian, a prerequisite for integration and social cohesion, and of maintaining the language of origin, as an instrument for the formation of identity (Vedovelli 2003). Respect for differences is elicited, in order to consolidate community living through reciprocal familiarity with languages and cultures on the part of both Italians and non-Italians. The necessity of training teachers in suitable skills is pointed out, recognising the need for specific training courses of L2 teachers, who should also be aware of the languages and cultures of their pupils.

In 1990, subsequent to the newly-enacted immigration law (L.39/1990), in a new ministerial memorandum (CM 205/90), the topic of "harnessing the language and culture of origin" is raised again. In this context, a concept that would enjoy great favour in the educational world in the years to come is introduced for the first time: intercultural education, considered as a structural condition of a multicultural society. A desire is expressed for the creation of intercultural education projects, valid for both Italian and foreign pupils at the same time, which give the educational task the "specific characteristic of mediation between the different cultures brought into the classroom by the pupils: not a mediation that limits the different cultural contributions, but one which constantly animates productive comparison between different models". As we can see, it is the cultural aspect that prevails. From then on, in ministerial legislation and documents on the presence of foreign/immigrant pupils in schools, the vague practice of intercultural education has been considered the most effective educational tool for promoting respect and peaceful community life, given that it implies reciprocal knowledge and understanding (Vedovelli 2003). In these same intercultural perspectives, languages are often pushed to the margins, thus contributing to the perceived contrast between "language" and "culture", as if language were simply a communicative tool, and not, as a semiotic system, a cultural form as well (De Saussure 1967, 2005; De Mauro 2002; Wright 2007). This lack of interest in languages has been prevalent both in theoretical studies and in practical applications. Furthermore, the focus is solely on the acquisition of Italian as a second language.

In contrast, the pronouncement of the National Council for Public Education, dated 15/6/1993, *The protection of language minorities*, contains a clear statement of the need to defend and preserve "national language minorities", i.e., historic ones, which are traditionally part of the country's linguistic repertoire, because "a language is much more that a set of sounds, letters, words and grammar: a language contains the collective memory of a community". Furthermore, the same text recognises the "new languages" brought by immigrants as minority languages, even if, since they are rather "remote from us", it is less important to study and understand them than the historic minority languages. Nonetheless, the document attributes the status of "minority" to immigrant languages. But nothing was done even to find out which languages these might be.

In legislation issued in the following years, the importance of intercultural education is again stressed, and there is continued reference to the presence of foreign/immigrant pupils in schools as a "problem", still referred to as an "educational emergency". A document issued by the Ministry of Education, Universities and Research, entitled *Guidelines for the reception and integration of foreign pupils* (March 2006) refers to the extreme rapidity with which schools have found themselves dealing with the arrival of foreign pupils, and to the lack of homogeneity in the presence of this phenomenon nationwide, which has driven schools to adopt differentiated responses. Particular emphasis is placed again on the fact that the acquisition of Italian as a second language must be central to the learning experience. Languages of origin are defined as an important resource for cognitive and emotional development, but in order to harness this resource a vague operative plan is proposed, assuming "a polycentric viewpoint involving both the families and public and private social agencies present in the area". Thus the maintenance of the languages of origin is delegated to people outside the school environment. The handling of changes brought about by this new presence and the elaboration and diffusion of reception protocols and best practices seem to boil down to programmes for learning Italian. Thus, we witness a more ethnocentric view, less designed to harness language diversity in schools.

As a consequence of this policy, many of the experiments performed at school show a degree of teacher responsibility, but unfortunately in most cases they have remained tied to a specific situation, restricted to single classes, and therefore destined to leave no lasting trace. The insistence in recent documents on intercultural education has contributed to simplifying and marginalising the complex linguistic question of languages in contact. As Vedovelli emphasises (2006), the linguistic perspective, always kept at the margins of demographic and sociological analyses, as well as anthropological and pedagogic ones which ought to be more sensitive to it, seems almost to constitute an intrusive guest whose role and relevance are not truly recognised. And yet nobody fails to declare or recognise the central nature of language in social integration, the urgency of solving the difficulties presented for immigrants in learning the new language, or the need for systematically planned and diffused language-teaching operations. The echoes of 19th-century thinking are still evident in the way in which the presence of immigrants is recorded: very little is known about their languages in Italy.

6. Conclusions

The plurilingualism of immigrant languages is by now a concrete fact, but it is still scarcely studied or considered, especially as a form of linguistic heritage to be taken into account for any interventions regarding citizens of foreign origin in the social, educational and employment spheres. We should begin by identifying immigrant languages as the languages of those groups that have modified and enriched the places where they live, due to their capacity to settle in an area and to carry out a migratory plan. The recognition of these people as *speakers* of languages other than Italian or Italian dialects, with their own language repertoires and with their own needs for maintenance of their language of origin and of contact with Italian (and not just to learn Italian) is an increasingly felt necessity. Hopefully, research on immigrant languages, based on increasingly large population samples of foreign origin, will make its results visible, in order to facilitate effective interventions for the "new" Italian plurilingualism. It still seems difficult to speak of *immigrant languages* as "new" minority languages, although that is what some of them have become, but this is partly due to the awkward handling of the question of minorities, both in Italy and elsewhere.

The current situation is burdened by a lack of systematic analysis of migratory phenomena from a linguistic viewpoint, and unfortunately this has consequences for linguistic and educational policies. This can be seen in the inability of public institutions to recognise and manage the richness and complexity derived from the presence of numerous languages. Initiatives in this direction are often delegated and handled autonomously by individual institutions or voluntary associations. In everyday practice, this manner of hiding the other languages and protecting Italian can even result in racist and segregationist attitudes that consider linguistic richness as something to be suppressed by schools and by civil society, for fear of immigrants getting better opportunities in the future than Italian pupils. Our conclusions stand in contrast to those of the study by Baker and Eversley (2000) on London, which highlighted the close link between the presence of many languages in the Britisch capital and their being a genuine form of social and economic capital. We also refer to the recent report on the effects for the European economy of the lack of language skills on the part of business operators (CILT 2007). The study reaches the conclusion that small European businesses would have a huge potential for increasing their exports if they would invest more in languages and would define coherent languages strategies. Indeed, it is those companies capable of improving their language skills that are best able to exploit the commercial opportunities offered by the EU market which, with a population of almost half a billion, is the most important in the world. As regards languages, the report confirms the importance of English as an international business language, but emphasises that, in order to successfully construct solid commercial relations, a range of other languages are necessary, not only European languages, but also languages such as Mandarin Chinese, Arabic and Russian, all of them being languages of immigrants in Italy.

There is an attitude of closure in Italy towards immigrant languages, just as there tends to be a lack of propensity towards plurilingualism. In 2007, the nationalistic approach of defending Italy's linguistic identity led to the initial approval in the Chamber of Deputies of the Italian Republic of an Article that is set to modify the text of the Constitution. The Article reads: "Italian is the official language of the Republic, in respect of the guarantees provided by the Constitution and by constitutional legislation". This acknowledgement was not even included in the earlier Constitution of the Republic, written in a historic context in which the recognition of the language of the newly-formed republic might perhaps have made more sense. We believe that the approval of this Article at this time is a sign of the desire to reaffirm the identity of the state with its language, exorcising the fear of diversity as the state feels threatened by the presence of others and their languages.

References

Bagna, Carla
    2006   Dalle 'lingue esotiche' all'italiano di contatto: scelte e strategie comunicative all'interno del mercato dell'Esquilino (Roma). In *Lo Spazio Linguistico Italiano e le "Lingue Esotiche"*, Emanuele Banfi and Gabriele Iannàccaro (eds.), 463–491. Roma: Bulzoni.

Bagna, Carla and Monica Barni
    2005   Dai dati statistici ai dati geolinguistici. Per una mappatura del nuovo plurilinguismo. *SILTA* XXXIV, 2: 329–355.
    2006   Per una mappatura dei repertori linguistici urbani: uovi strumenti e metodologie. In *La Città e le Sue Lingue. Repertori Linguistici Urbani*, Nicola de Blasi and Carla Marcato (eds.), 1–43. Napoli: Liguori.

Bagna, Carla, Monica Barni and Massimo Vedovelli
    2007   Italiano in contatto con lingue immigrate: nuovi modelli e metodi per il neoplurilinguismo in Italia. In *Minoranze Linguistiche. Prospettive, Strumenti, Territori*, Carlo Consani and Paola Desideri (eds.), 270–290. Roma: Carocci.

Bagna, Carla, Sabrina Machetti and Massimo Vedovelli
    2003   Italiano e lingue immigrate: verso un plurilinguismo consapevole o verso varietà di contatto? In *Ecologia Linguistica*, Ada Valentini, Piera Molinelli, Pierluigi Cuzzolin and Giuliano Bernini (eds.), 201–222. Roma: Bulzoni.

Baker, Philip and John Eversley (eds.)
    2000   *Multilingual Capital. The Languages of London's School children and their Relevance to Economic, Social and Educational Policies.* London: Battlebridge Publications.

Barni, Monica
    2006   From statistical to geolinguistic data: mapping and measuring linguistic diversity. *Note di Lavoro* 53. 2006:
            http://www.feem.it/Feem/ Pub/Publications/WPapers/default.htm.
    2008   Mapping linguistic diversity: immigrant languages in Italy. In *Mapping Linguistic Diversity in Multicultural Contexts*, Monica Barni and Guus Extra (eds.). Berlin: Mouton de Gruyter.

Barni, Monica and Carla Bagna
    2008   Mapping techniques and the linguistic landscape. In *Linguistic Landscape: Expanding the Scenery*, Elana Shohamy and Durk Gorter (eds.). London: Routledge.

Ben-Rafael, Eliezer, Elana Shohamy, Muhammad Hasan Amara and Nira Trumper-Hecht
- 2006 Linguistic Landscape as symbolic construction of the public space: The case of Israel. In *Linguistic Landscape. A new Approach to Multilingualism*, Durk Gorter (ed.), 7–30. Clevedon: Multilingual Matters.

Caritas
- 2007a *Immigrazione. Dossier statistico 2007.* Roma: Idos.
- 2007b *Esquilino dei Mondi Lontani – che tanto vicini non sono mai stati.* Roma: Caritas.

Chini, Marina (ed.)
- 2004 *Plurilinguismo e Immigrazione in Italia. Un'Indagine Sociolinguistica a Pavia e Torino.* Milano: Franco Angeli.

CILT, the National Centre for Languages
- 2007 *ELAN : Effects on the European of Shortages of Foreign Language Skills in Enterprise.* London: CILT.

D'Agostino, Mari
- 2006 Segni, parole, nomi. In *La Città e le Sue Lingue. Repertori Linguistici Urbani*, Nicola de Blasi and Carla Marcato (eds.), 207–222. Napoli: Liguori.

De Mauro, Tullio
- 1963 *Storia Linguistica dell'Italia Unita.* Roma/Bari: Laterza.
- 1977 *Le Parole e i Fatti.* Roma: Editori Riuniti.
- 2002 *Prima Lezione sul Linguaggio.* Roma/Bari: Laterza.
- 2006 Crisi del monolitismo linguistico e lingue meno diffuse. *Lingue e Idiomi d'Italia – LIDI* 1: 11–37.

De Saussure, Ferdinand
- 1967 *Corso di Linguistica Generale.* Introduzione, traduzione e commento di Tullio De Mauro. Bari/Roma: Laterza.
- 2005 *Scritti Inediti di Linguistica Generale.* Introduzione, traduzione e commento di Tullio De Mauro. Bari/Roma: Laterza.

Extra, Guus and Kutlay Yağmur (eds.)
- 2004 *Urban Multilingualism in Europe. Immigrant Minority Languages at Home and School.* Clevedon: Multilingual Matters.

Giacalone Ramat, Anna (ed.)
- 2003 *Verso l'Italiano.* Roma: Carocci.

ISTAT
- 2001 *14° Censimento Generale della Popolazione e delle Abitazioni.* Roma: Istat.
- 2007 *La Lingua Italiana, i Dialetti e le Lingue Straniere.* Roma: Istat.

Massariello Merzagora, Giovanna
   2005   Le "nuove minoranze" a Verona. Un osservatorio sugli studenti immigrati. In *Città plurilingui - Multilingual Cities*, Raffaella Bombi and Fabiana Fusco (eds.), 169–192. Udine: Forum.

Ministero della Pubblica Istruzione
   2006   *Linee Guida per l'Accoglienza e l'Integrazione degli Alunni Stranieri (http://www.istruzione.it)*.
   2007   *Alunni con Cittadinanza non Italiana Scuole Statali e non Statali, anno Scolastico 2006/2007 (http://www.istruzione.it)*.

Orioles, Vincenzo
   2006   *Percorsi di parole*. Roma: Il Calamo.
   2007   Modelli di tutela a confronto: promuovere la ricerca e la formazione o assecondare la deriva burocratica? In *Minoranze Linguistiche. Prospettive, Strumenti, Territori*, Carlo Consani and Paola Desideri (eds.), 327–335. Roma: Carocci.

Valentini, Ada
   in press   *La vitalità delle Lingue Immigrate: un'indagine a campione tra minori stranieri a Bergamo*. Studi Italiani di Linguistica Teorica e Appliicata – SILTA.

Vedovelli, Massimo
   1981   La lingua degli stranieri immigrati in Italia. *Lingua e Nuova Didattica*: 3–17.
   1989   Lingue immigrate. *Italiano & Oltre* IV (2): 83–87.
   2003   Condizioni semiotiche per un approccio interculturale alla didattica-linguistica: il ruolo del linguaggio verbale. *Studi Emigrazione XL*, 151: 505–521.
   2006   L'italiano L2 in Italia e nel mondo: la condizione delle giovani generazioni. In *Lingue in Contatto a Scuola. Tra Italiano, Dialetto e Italiano L2*, Immacolata Tempesta and Maria Maggio (eds.), 21–42. Milano: Franco Angeli.

Vedovelli Massimo and Andrea Villarini
   2001   Lingue straniere immigrate in Italia. In *Immigrazione, Dossier Statistico 2001*, Caritas, 222–229. Roma: Anterem.

Wright, Sue
   2007   The right to speak one's own language: reflections on theory and practice. *Language Policy* 6: 203–224.

Immigrant minority languages in Europe: cross-national and cross-linguistic perspectives

Guus Extra and Kutlay Yağmur

1. Introduction

Given the overwhelming focus on mainstream second-language acquisition by immigrant minority (henceforward IM) groups, there is much less evidence on the status and use of IM languages across European nation-states. Here, we present the rationale and kernel outcomes of the *Multilingual Cities Project* (henceforward MCP), a co-ordinated multiple survey study in six major multicultural cities in different EU nation-states. The project was carried out under the auspices of the *European Cultural Foundation*, established in Amsterdam, and it was coordinated by a research team at *Babylon, Centre for Studies of the Multicultural Society*, at Tilburg University in the Netherlands, in cooperation with universities and educational authorities in all participating cities. The aims of the MCP were to gather, analyse, and compare multiple data on the status of IM languages at home and at school, taken from cross-national and cross-linguistic perspectives. In the participating cities, ranging from Northern to Southern Europe, Germanic or Romance languages have a dominant status in public life. Figure 1 gives an outline of the project.

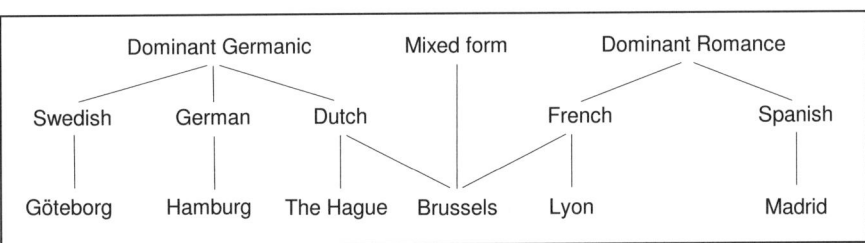

Figure 1. Outline of the Multilingual Cities Project (MCP)

The criteria for selecting a city to participate in this multinational study were that it should be prototypical for a multicultural environment with a great variety of IM groups, and that it should offer a university-based research facility that would be able to handle the local data gathering and local data analysis, and the final reporting of the local results. Given the increasing role of municipalities as educational authorities in all partner cities, the project was carried out in close cooperation between researchers at local universities and local educational authorities. In each partner city, this cooperation proved to be of essential value.

The rationale for collecting, analysing and comparing multiple home language data on multicultural school populations derives from four different perspectives:

— taken from a *demographic* perspective, home language data play a crucial role in the definition and identification of multicultural school populations;
— taken from a *sociolinguistic* perspective, home language data offer valuable insights into both the distribution and vitality of home languages across different population groups, and thus raise the public awareness of multilingualism;
— taken from an *educational* perspective, home language data are indispensable tools for educational planning and policies;
— taken from an *economic* perspective, home language data offer latent resources that can be built upon and developed in terms of economic chances.

Our method of carrying out home language surveys amongst primary school children in each of the six participating cities has profited from experiences in non-European English-dominant immigration countries with nationwide population surveys in which commonly single questions on home language use were asked. In contrast to such questionnaires, our survey was based on multiple rather than single questions on home language use and on cross-nationally equivalent questions. In doing this, we aimed at describing and comparing multiple language profiles of major IM communities in each of the cities under consideration. Local reports about the participating cities have been made available for *Göteborg* (Nygren-Junkin and Extra 2003), *Hamburg* (Fürstenau, Gogolin and Yağmur 2003), *The Hague* (Extra, Aarts, Van der Avoird, Broeder and Yağmur 2001), *Brussels* (Verlot, Delrue, Extra and Yağmur 2003), *Lyon* (Akinci, De Ruiter and Sanagustin 2004), and *Madrid* (Broeder and Mijares 2003). For the final cross-national report we refer to Extra and Yağmur (2004).

Table 1. Overview of the MCP database ([a] Dutch-medium schools only; [b] Reseau d'Education Prioritaire only)

City	Total of schools	Total of schools in the survey	Total of pupils in schools	Total of pupils in the survey	Age range of pupils
Brussels	117[a]	110[a]	11,500	10,300	6–12
Göteborg	170	122	36,100	21,300	6–12
Hamburg	231 public	218 public	54,900	46,000	6–11
	17 catholic	14 catholic			
Lyon	173[b]	42[b]	60,000	11,650	6–11
Madrid	708 public	133 public	202,000	30,000	5–12
	411 catholic	21 catholic	99,000		
The Hague	142 primary	109 primary	41,170	27,900	4–12
	30 secondary	26 secondary	19,000	13,700	12–17

Table 1 gives an overview of the resulting database, derived from the reports of primary school children in an age range of 4–12 years (only in The Hague were data also collected at secondary schools). The total cross-national sample consists of more than 160,000 pupils.

2. Distribution of languages across cities

The local language surveys amongst primary school children have delivered a wealth of yet unknown cross-national evidence on the distribution and vitality of IM languages at home. Apart from selecting one or more of the prespecified languages in each of the local surveys, pupils could also opt for self-references to other home languages by filling-out in handwriting the boxes provided for this objective.

The resulting database consists of a huge variety of self-references (types) and their frequencies of mentioning (tokens). In most cases, the pupils referred to entities that could be (re)traced as existing languages. In this context, the regularly updated database of *The Ethnologue* (*www.sil.org/ethnologue*; Grimes 1996) on languages of the world proved to be very helpful. In cases of doubt or lacking information, other resources were used, such as Comrie, Matthews and Polinsky (2003), Campbell (2000), Dalby (1999/2000), Giacalone Ramat and Ramat (1998), and Crystal (1997). Apart from self-references to known and hitherto unknown languages, the pupils also made references to countries that could not reasonably be traced back to languages or to other/unknown categories.

Table 2. References made by pupils in terms of types and tokens (x = not specified)

Municipality	Reference to languages		Reference to countries		Other/unknown references	
	Types	Tokens	Types	Tokens	Types	Tokens
Göteborg	75	7,598	8	40	10	20
Hamburg	90	16,639	12	229	10	92
The Hague	88	23,435	13	788	17	24
Brussels	54	12,737	9	186	7	11
Lyon	66	6,106	17	130	–	–
Madrid	56	2,619	x	x	x	x

In general, however, the resolution level of the home language question in the survey was very high, and relatively few references could not be traced back to languages. Table 2 gives a cross-national overview of the data under consideration.

Based on the overview of types and tokens of (re)traced home languages, the distribution of these home languages was specified in a ranked order of decreasing frequency. A common phenomenon in all participating cities, so familiar in type/token studies of word frequencies, was that few languages (types) were referred to often (tokens), and that many languages (types) were referred to rarely (tokens). Therefore, the most frequently mentioned home languages represent a very high proportion of the total number of occurrences/tokens in all cities.

Apart from Madrid, late-comer amongst our focal cities in respect of immigration, the proportion of primary school children in whose homes other languages were used next to or instead of the mainstream language ranged between one third and more than a half. The total number of languages other than Swedish/German/Dutch (The Hague/Brussels)/French/Spanish ranged per city between 50 and 90. The figures were 36% of the total student population in Göteborg, 35% in Hamburg, 49% in The Hague, 82% in Brussels, 54% in Lyon, and 10% in Madrid.

The outcomes of the local surveys were aggregated in one cross-national database. On the basis of the number of references made to home languages, the top 20 of the most frequently mentioned languages in each city were identified. Forty-nine languages were in the group of the top-20 list in the six cities. Out of these 49 languages, 19 languages were represented in 3–6 cities and 30 languages in only 1–2 cities. There were also unique references in the top-20 per city; most of these languages were either languages of neighbouring countries, languages of former colonies, or regional minority languages.

Table 3. Overview of the numbers of pupils (6–11 years) per reported language and city

Reported languages	Gö	Ha	tH	Br	Ly	Ma	Coverage
English	1,039	1,077	950	676	426	359	6
Arabic	768	464	1,391	1,608	2,789	662	6
Portuguese	88	360	88	77	259	202	6
Italian	51	192	92	361	255	43	6
Turkish	385	4,948	2,535	606	468	1	5
Spanish	328	431	288	389	353	–	5
German	148	–	156	119	91	45	5
French	118	17	185	7,327	–	157	5
Chinese	184	7	180	22	37	160	4
Kurdish	468	197	273	11	36	4	4
Albanian	186	410	5	107	62	3	4
Polish	163	1,729	16	33	3	100	4
Russian	70	1,652	14	32	11	37	4
Berber	4	–	1,334	214	145	37	4
Serb./Croat./Bosnian	795	460	46	29	26	6	3
Vietnamese	55	153	14	14	91	–	3
Somali	315	–	135	–	49	–	3
Urdu/Pakistani	27	238	294	32	1	3	3
Armenian	8	82	5	47	41	1	3
Romani/Sinte	51	219	6	8	3	1	2

For purposes of cross-national and cross-linguistic analyses, 20 of the most frequently mentioned languages in these cities were chosen.

Two criteria were used to select these 20 languages from the list of 49 languages. Each language should be represented by at least three cities, and each city should be represented in the cross-national database by at least 30 pupils in the age range of 6–11 years. Our focus on this age range was motivated by comparability considerations: This range was represented in the local databases of all participating cities (see Table 1). Romani/Sinte was included in the cross-national analyses because of its special status in our list of 20 languages as a language without territorial status. Two languages had an exceptional status: English "invaded" the local databases as a language of international prestige, and Romani/Sinte was solidly represented in Hamburg and Göteborg only. The concept of language group was based on the pupils' answers to the question whether and, if so, which other languages were used at home instead of or next to the mainstream language.

On the basis of their answer patterns, pupils may belong to more than one language group. Table 3 gives an overview of the resulting database.

As shown in Table 3, eight languages were represented in 5–6 cities, while eleven languages were represented in 3–4 cities. With respect to French, Brussels offers a special case, given the public and private status of both French and Dutch in this city (Verlot et al. 2003). There is a remarkable municipal distribution of two pairs of languages which are often in competition in their source countries, i.e., Turkish and Kurdish in Turkey, and Arabic and Berber in Northern African countries (in particular, Morocco). Only in Göteborg was Kurdish more strongly represented than Turkish, and only in The Hague were Berber and Arabic represented in balance. In our database, Kurdish hardly emerged in Brussels and Madrid. The same holds for Berber in Göteborg and Hamburg.

3. Specification of language profiles and language vitality

For all language groups mentioned in Table 3, pseudo-longitudinal and intergenerational profiles were specified and visually represented in graphs and tables. For each language group, three age groups and three generations were distinguished. The age groups consisted of pupils aged 6/7, 8/9, and 10/11 years old. The three generations were operationalised as follows:

— G1: pupil + father + mother born abroad;
— G2: pupil born in country of residence, father *and/or* mother born abroad;
— G3: pupil + father + mother born in country of residence.

The pseudo-longitudinal profiles consisted of age-specific information on:

— *proficiency* in the minority language in terms of language understanding, speaking, reading and writing;
— *choice* of the minority language in interaction with the mother, father, younger and older siblings, and best friends;
— *dominance* in the minority vs. mainstream language;
— *preference* for the minority vs. mainstream language.

In addition, age-specific and generation-specific information was provided on language vitality. The final aim was the construction of a language vitality index (henceforward LVI), based on the outcomes of the four dimensions presented above. Since Giles, Bourhis and Taylor (1977) introduced the concept of ethnolinguistic vitality, the focus has been on its the concept of ethnolinguistic vitality, the focus has been on its extra-linguistic determinants rather than on the empirical operationalisation of language use. Determinants have been proposed in terms of lists of factors, clustered in status factors, demographic factors, and institutional support factors, e.g., by Giles, Bourhis and Taylor (1977), or in additional factors such as cultural (dis)similarity, e.g., by Appel and Muysken (1987: 32–38). The proposed lists of factors suffer from various shortcomings that cannot be solved easily:

— the lists of factors are neither exhaustive nor mutually exclusive;
— different factors contribute in different ways to (lack of) vitality and may even neutralise each other;
— some of these factors are personal characteristics (e.g., age, gender, or educational level), whereas other factors are group characteristics (e.g., group size or group spread);
— moreover, a distinction has been proposed and found between the objective status of these factors and their subjective perception by minority and/or majority groups (Bourhis, Giles and Rosenthal 1981, Van der Avoird 2001);
— finally, no relative quantitative weight has been suggested for the proposed (clusters of) factors, which makes the establishment of a language vitality index and the verification of empirical outcomes unfeasible.

For a comprehensive overview of the origins of the concept "language vitality" and its theoretical and empirical development over time since Weinreich (1953), we refer to Achterberg (2005: 23–100), in the context of a case study on Slavonic languages in Germany.

In our research project, we took a different approach by focusing on the empirical operationalisation of language vitality rather than on its extra-linguistic determinants. The operationalisation of language vitality was derived from the following four reported dimensions:

— language proficiency: the extent to which the minority language under consideration is *understood;*
— language choice: the extent to which this language is commonly spoken at home *with the mother;*
— language dominance: the extent to which the minority language is spoken *best;*
— language preference: the extent to which the minority language is *preferably* spoken.

The focus of the chosen dimensions was on oral skills at home and not on literacy in order to give IM languages a fair chance of emerging in societal contexts in which the acquisition of literacy is rarely promoted, whether at home or at school (see also Section 7). Moreover, earlier analyses have shown that the four selected dimensions are highly correlated and lead to reliable scores (Extra et al. 2002: 129). The operationalisation of the first and second dimension (language proficiency and language choice) was aimed at a maximal scope for tracing language vitality. Language understanding is generally the least demanding of the four language skills involved, and the mother acts generally as the major gatekeeper for intergenerational language transmission (Clyne 2003).

In the analyses, the four above-mentioned language dimensions were compared as proportional scores, i.e., the mean proportion of pupils per language group that indicated a positive response to the relevant questions. The LVI is, in turn, the mean value of these four proportional scores. This LVI is by definition a value-driven index, in the sense that the *chosen* dimensions with the *chosen* operationalisations are weighted *equally*. The establishment of such an index makes it feasible to carry out cross-linguistic and cross-national comparisons of large databases in which equal criteria for such comparisons are used.

In this context, it should be mentioned that, from a conceptual point of view, the chosen dimensions are more closely related than in many other large-scale attempts to operationalise multiple human properties in terms of an index. An interesting case in point is the widely used *Human Development Index* (HDI), proposed by the United Nations in its annual UNDP reports. The HDI measures the overall achievements in a particular country in three basic dimensions of human development, i.e., life expectancy, educational achievement, and income per capita. For each of these dimensions, an index based on multiple values has been created. The ultimate HDI is based on the average of the three indices mentioned. In this case also, the chosen dimensions with the chosen operationalisations are weighted equally (for details see UNDP 2002). On the basis of the established LVI in our project, LVI scores have been calculated per age group and per generation, for each language group. On the basis of this categorisation, intergenerational shift can be estimated.

In all cases, the total population of age groups was always larger than the total population of generations. This discrepancy is the result of a predictably larger number of missing values (i.e., non-responses) for generation than for age. In the former case, references have to be made to the countries of birth of the pupil, the father, and the mother; in the latter case,

Table 4. Turkish language group: cross-national numbers of pupils and LVI per age group and per generation

	Age groups							
	Population				Vitality			
Cities	6/7	8/9	10/11	Total	6/7	8/9	10/11	Mean
Göteborg	124	115	146	385	69	67	66	67
Hamburg	1,384	2,381	1,183	4,948	66	62	65	64
The Hague	833	853	849	2,535	75	68	65	69
Brussels	225	213	168	606	73	75	71	73
Lyon	146	176	146	468	65	63	68	65
Total / Mean	2,712	3,738	2,492	8,942	70	67	67	68
	Generations							
	Population				Vitality			
Cities	G1	G2	G3	Total	G1	G2	G3	Mean
Göteborg	51	308	10	369	67	68	43	59
Hamburg	627	3,676	205	4,508	69	64	49	61
The Hague	539	1,842	46	2,427	73	68	62	68
Brussels	75	417	42	534	74	74	70	73
Lyon	78	308	24	410	70	64	65	66
Total / Mean	1,370	6,551	327	8,248	71	68	58	65

reference has to be made only to the age of the pupil. Language vitality indices for age and generation were calculated only if at least 5 pupils were represented in a particular group. Given the possible non-responses of pupils to any of the questions represented in figures and tables, all figures and tables were presented and interpreted in proportional values. In Table 4, we demonstrate the provided cross-national, pseudo-longitudinal and intergenerational information per language group for the Turkish language group (see Table 3 for the absence of data on Madrid).

4. Cross-linguistic perspectives on language vitality

Table 5 gives a cross-linguistic and pseudo-longitudinal overview of the LVI per language group and age group. LVI calculations have only been made if at least 5 pupils were represented in a particular age group and generation. Considering its non-territorial status, it is not surprising that Romani/Sinte emerged with the highest language vitality. English and German ended up in bottom positions given the fact that they often had a higher status at school than at home. When the average scores of the youngest and oldest age groups were compared, 11 language groups showed the highest scores for the former and 5 language groups for the latter. The largest interval between the scores emerged for Romani/Sinte. Strong maintenance of language vitality across the youngest and oldest age groups, with intervals of -1/0/+1 only, emerged for 8 out of the 20 language groups.

A different cross-linguistic and pseudo-longitudinal perspective is provided in Table 6, in terms of generations. Table 6 reveals significant differences between language groups in the distribution of pupils across different generations. In most language groups, second-generation pupils were most-represented and third-generation pupils least. Remarkable exceptions to this rule were Armenian and in particular Russian, with mainly first-generation pupils. Third-generation pupils were relatively well represented (>20%) for English, French, German, Italian, Romani/Sinte, and Spanish. In conformity with expectations, Table 6 shows a stronger decrease of language vitality across generations than Table 5 shows across age groups.

Table 5. Language vitality per language group and age group (in %, LVI in cumulative %)

Language group	Total pupils	6/7 years	8/9 years	10/11 years	Average
Romani/Sinte	270	76	71	64	70
Urdu/Pakistani	564	65	70	69	68
Turkish	8,942	70	67	67	68
Armenian	170	64	59	65	63
Russian	1,791	66	58	57	60
Serb./Croat./Bosnian	1,285	60	58	59	59
Albanian	765	63	56	58	59
Vietnamese	299	57	60	58	58
Chinese	561	56	58	60	58
Arabic	7,682	59	58	58	58
Polish	1,925	57	59	53	56
Somali	499	58	54	53	55
Portuguese	1,074	54	54	54	54
Berber	1,730	51	54	51	52
Kurdish	974	54	47	51	51
Spanish	1,789	47	49	47	48
French	7,787	47	40	44	44
Italian	994	39	40	39	39
English	4,527	37	33	39	36
German	559	35	31	32	33

All language groups show more or less decreasing language vitality across generations. The strongest intergenerational shift between G1 and G3 emerged for Polish (42%), Albanian (38%), Spanish (33%), and Portuguese (30%), whereas the strongest intergenerational maintenance of language vitality occurred for Romani/ Sinte and Turkish. The top position for language vitality of Romani/Sinte across age groups in Table 5, and its relatively strong maintenance across generations in Table 6, were also observed in earlier and similar research in the Netherlands (Broeder and Extra 1998: 70). The high vitality of Romani/Sinte was also confirmed by other studies on this language community (Acton and Mundy 1999; Kyuchukov 2002). One reason why language vitality is a core value for the Roma across Europe is the absence of source country references as alternative markers of identity – in contrast to almost all other language groups presented in Tables 5 and 6.

Table 6. Intergenerational distribution (in %) and intergenerational language vitality (LVI in cumulative %) per language group

Language group	Total pupils	Intergenerational distribution			Intergenerational language vitality		
		G1	G2	G3	G1	G2	G3
Albanian	675	39	56	5	72	51	34
Arabic	7,002	21	73	6	64	57	35
Armenian	153	49	42	9	69	55	–
Berber	1,656	20	78	2	59	50	45
Chinese	523	22	74	4	72	59	–
English	4,045	16	42	41	43	41	28
French	7,090	7	45	48	55	43	30
German	506	18	45	38	43	35	22
Italian	916	12	60	28	49	43	29
Kurdish	900	50	49	2	61	43	33
Polish	1,837	14	82	4	73	59	31
Portuguese	1,004	27	66	8	63	52	33
Romani/Sinte	231	35	41	23	76	66	65
Russian	1,616	81	16	3	64	–	–
Serb./Croat./Bosn.	1,191	38	58	4	71	50	–
Somali	464	38	58	5	70	50	–
Spanish	1,570	18	61	21	63	47	30
Turkish	8,248	17	79	4	71	68	58
Urdu/Pakistani	534	25	72	3	70	67	–
Vietnamese	270	12	85	3	60	57	–

5. Community language teaching in Europe

Across Europe, large contrasts occur in the status of IM languages at school, depending on particular nation-states, or even particular federal states within nation-states (as in Germany), and depending on particular IM languages, as national languages in other EU countries or not. Most commonly, IM languages are not part of mainstream education. In Great Britain, for example, IM languages are not part of the "national" curriculum, and they are dealt with in various types of "complementary" education at out-of-school hours (e.g., Martin et al. 2004).

Here, we present the major outcomes of our comparative study on the teaching of IM languages in the six EU cities and countries of the MCP under discussion. Being aware of cross-national differences in denotation, we will use the concept *community language teaching* (henceforward CLT) when referring to this type of education. Our rationale for the CLT concept rather than the concepts *mother tongue teaching* or *home language instruction* is the inclusion of a broad spectrum of potential target groups. First of all, the status of an IM language as "native" or home language is subject to change through intergenerational processes of language shift. Moreover, in secondary education, both minority and majority pupils are often *de iure* (although seldom *de facto*) admitted to CLT (in the Netherlands, e.g., Turkish is a secondary school subject referred to as "Turkish" rather than "home language instruction"; compare also the concepts of *Enseignement des Langues et Cultures d'Origine* and *Enseignement des Langues Vivantes* in French primary and secondary schools, respectively).

In all countries involved in the MCP, there has been an increase in the number of IM pupils who speak a language at home other than or in addition to the dominant language in primary and secondary education. Schools have largely responded to this home-school language mismatch by paying more attention to the learning and teaching of the dominant language as a second language. A great deal of energy and money is being spent on developing curricula, teaching materials, and teacher training for second-language education. CLT stands in stark contrast to this, as it is much more susceptible to an ideological debate about its legitimacy. While there is consensus about the necessity of investing in second-language education for IM pupils, there is a lack of support for CLT. IM languages are commonly considered sources of problems and deficiencies, and they are rarely seen as sources of knowledge and enrichment. Policy makers, local educational authorities, headmasters of schools, and teachers of "regular" subjects often have reservations or negative attitudes towards CLT. On the other hand, parents of IM pupils, CLT teachers, and IM organisations often make a case for including IM languages in the school curriculum. These differences in top-down and bottom-up attitudes were found in all the cities and countries investigated.

From a historical point of view, most of the countries involved in the MCP show a similar chronological development in their argumentation in favour of CLT. CLT was generally introduced into primary education with a view to family remigration. This objective was also clearly expressed in *Directive 77/486* of the European Community, on 25 July 1977. The Directive focused on the education of the children of "migrant workers" with the aim "principally to facilitate their possible reintegration into the Member State of origin". As is clear from this formulation, the Directive excluded all IM children originating from non-EU countries, although these children form(ed) the large part of IM children in European primary schools. At that time, Sweden was not an EU member state, and CLT policies for IM children in Sweden were not directed towards remigration but modelled according to bilingual education policies for the large minority of Finnish-speaking children in Sweden.

During the 1970s, the above argumentation for CLT was increasingly abandoned. Demographic developments showed no substantial signs of remigrating families. Instead, processes of family reunion and family formation occurred in the host countries. This development resulted in a conceptual shift, and CLT became primarily aimed at combatting disadvantages. CLT had to bridge the gap between the home and the school environment, and to support school achievement in "regular" subjects. Because such an approach tended to underestimate the intrinsic value of CLT, a number of countries began to emphasise the importance of CLT from a cultural, legal, or economic perspective:

— from a cultural perspective, CLT contributes to maintaining and advancing a pluriform society, in correspondence with the fact that many IM groups consider their own language as a core value of cultural identity;
— from a legal perspective, CLT meets the internationally recognised right to language transmission and language maintenance;
— from an economic perspective, CLT leads to an important pool of profitable knowledge in societies which are increasingly internationally oriented.

The historical development of arguments for CLT in terms of remigration, combatting deficiencies, and multicultural policy is evident in some German states, in particular North Rhine-Westphalia and Hamburg. In most countries in our study, however, cultural policy is tied in with the mainstream language to such an extent that CLT is tolerated only in the margins. Cultural motives have played a rather important role in Sweden. It should, however, be noted that multicultural arguments for CLT have not led to an educational policy in which the status of IM languages has been substantially advanced in any of the countries involved in our study.

6. Cross-national perspectives on community language teaching

Derived from Extra and Yağmur (2004), we give a cross-national overview of nine parameters of CLT in primary and secondary education that were taken into account in each of the six countries involved in the MCP, i.e., Sweden, Germany, the Netherlands, Belgium, France and Spain. CLT for primary school children came to an abrupt nationwide end in the Netherlands in 2004 as being "in contradiction with integration policies" according to Dutch government, and resulted in Dutch-only education in multicultural and multilingual schools (Extra and Yağmur 2006); the information presented is therefore in retrospect.

(1) *Target groups*
The target groups for CLT in primary schools are commonly IM children, defined as such in a narrow or broad sense. Narrow definitions commonly relate to the range of languages taught and/or to children's proficiency in these languages. The most restrictive set of languages is taught in Spain, i.e., Arabic and Portuguese only, for Moroccan and Portuguese (-speaking) children, respectively. A wide range of languages is taught in Sweden and Germany. The Netherlands, Belgium, and France take/took an intermediate position. Sweden and France demand from the target groups an active use of the languages at home and a basic proficiency in these languages. Special target groups in Sweden are adopted children; in Germany, ethnic German children from abroad; and in France, speakers of recognised regional minority languages. Sweden has the most explicit policy for access to CLT in terms of "home language" (nowadays, back to "mother tongue") instead of socio-economic status. The target groups for CLT in secondary schools are commonly those who participated in CLT in primary schools. *De iure*, all pupils were allowed to CLT in the Netherlands, independent of

ethnolinguistic background; *de facto*, most commonly, a subset of IM pupils took part. CLT for secondary school pupils is almost non-existent in Belgium, and limited to Arabic and Portuguese in a few secondary schools in Spain.

(2) Arguments
The arguments for CLT are formulated in terms of a struggle against deficits and/or in terms of multicultural policy. Whereas the former type of argument predominates in primary education, the latter type predominates in secondary education. The vague concept of "integration" utilised in all countries under discussion may relate to any of these arguments. Deficit arguments may be phrased in terms of bridging the home/school gap, promoting mainstream language learning, promoting school success in other ("regular") subjects, preventing educational failure, or overcoming marginalisation. Multicultural arguments may be phrased in terms of promoting cultural identity and self-esteem, promoting cultural pluralism, promoting multilingualism in a multicultural and globalising society, and avoiding ethnic prejudice. Whereas in the Netherlands and Belgium deficit arguments dominate(d), multicultural arguments tend to play a greater role in the other countries. Deficit arguments for CLT are almost absent in secondary schools, and multicultural arguments are commonly favoured in all countries.

(3) Objectives
The objectives of CLT in primary schools are rarely specified in terms of language skills to be acquired. The vague concept of "active bilingualism" has been a common objective in Sweden, whereas in Germany and Spain, reference is made to the development of oral and written language skills, language awareness, and (inter)cultural skills. In none of these cases have more particular specifications been introduced. In contrast, the objectives of CLT in secondary schools are commonly specified in terms of particular oral and written skills to be reached at intermediate stages and/or at the end of secondary schooling.

(4) Evaluation
The evaluation of achievement through CLT may take place informally and/or formally. Informal evaluation takes place by means of subjective oral and/or written teachers' impressions or comments, meant for parents at regular intervals, e.g., once per semester or year. Formal evaluation takes place using more or less objective language proficiency measurement and

language proficiency report figures, e.g., once per semester or year. Informal evaluation may occur in lower grades of primary schooling, formal evaluation in higher grades (e.g., in Sweden). In most countries, however, no report figures for CLT are provided throughout the primary school curriculum, and report figures for "language" commonly refer implicitly to proficiency in the mainstream language. If CLT report figures are given (e.g., in France), such figures commonly do not have the same status as report figures for other subjects. The evaluation of achievement through CLT in secondary schools takes place formally through assessment instruments and examinations. Here, report figures may have a regular or peripheral status. The former holds in particular for Sweden, Germany, and the Netherlands.

(5) *Minimal enrolment*
Minimal enrolment requirements for CLT may be specified at the level of the class, the school, or even the municipality at large. The latter is common practice only in Sweden, and the minimal enrolment requirement for children from different classes/schools in Sweden was five in 2004. Secondary schools in Sweden may also opt for CLT if at least five pupils enrol. All other countries are more reluctant, with minimal requirements for primary school pupils ranging between 10–20 (Germany, Belgium, France), or without any specification (the Netherlands, Spain). In the latter case, enrolment restrictions are commonly based on budget constraints.

(6) *Curricular status*
In all countries, CLT at primary schools takes place on a voluntary and optional basis, provided at the request of parents. Instruction may take place within or outside regular school hours. The latter is most common in Sweden, Belgium, and France. Germany, the Netherlands (until 2004), and Spain allow(ed) for two models of instruction, either within or outside regular school hours, depending on the type of language (in Germany), the type of goal (auxiliary or intrinsic in the Netherlands), and the type of organisation (in integrated or parallel classes in Spain). The number of CLT hours varies between 1–5 hours per week. If CLT takes place at secondary schools, it is considered a regular and optional subject within school hours in all countries under consideration.

(7) *Funding*
The funding of CLT may depend on national, regional, or local educational authorities in the country/municipality of residence and/or on the consu-

lates/embassies of the countries of origin. In the latter case, consulates or embassies commonly recruit and provide the teachers, and they are also responsible for teacher (in-service) training. Funding through the country and/or municipality of residence takes/took place in Sweden and the Netherlands. Funding through the consulates/embassies of the countries of origin takes place in Belgium and Spain. A mixed type of funding occurs in Germany and in France. In Germany, the source of funding is dependent on particular languages or organisational models for CLT. In France, source countries fund CLT in primary schools, whereas the French Ministry of Education funds CLT in secondary schools.

(8) *Teaching materials*
Teaching materials for CLT may originate from the countries of origin or of residence of the pupils. Funding from ministries, municipalities, and/or publishing houses occurs in Sweden, Germany, and the Netherlands, although limited resources are available. Source country funding for CLT occurs in Belgium and Spain. In France, source countries fund teaching materials in primary schools, whereas the French Ministry of Education funds teaching materials in secondary schools.

(9) *Teacher qualifications*
Teacher qualifications for CLT may depend on educational authorities in the countries of residence or of origin. National or statewide (in-service) teacher training programmes for CLT at primary and/or secondary schools exist in Sweden, Germany, and the Netherlands, although the appeal of these programmes is limited, given the many uncertainties about CLT job perspectives. In Belgium and Spain, teacher qualifications depend on educational authorities in the countries of origin. France has a mixed system of responsibilities: source countries are responsible for teacher qualifications in primary schools, whereas the French Ministry of Education is responsible for teacher qualifications in secondary schools.

7. Conclusions

The findings of the *Multilingual Cities Project* have delivered a wealth of hidden evidence on the distribution and vitality of IM languages at home and at school across European cities and nation-states. Apart from Madrid, late-comer amongst our focal cities in respect of immigration, the proportion of pupils in whose homes other languages were used next to or instead of the mainstream language ranged per city between one third and more than a half. The total number of traced "other" languages ranged per city between 50 and 90; the common pattern was that a limited set of languages were often referred to by the pupils and that many languages were referred to only a few times.

The findings show that making use of more than one language is a way of life for an increasing number of children across Europe. Mainstream and non-mainstream languages should not be conceived in terms of competition. Rather, the data show that these languages are used as alternatives, depending on such factors as type of context and interlocutor. The data also reveal that the use of other languages at home does not occur at the cost of competence in the mainstream language. Many children who addressed their parents in another language reported to be dominant in the mainstream language.

Among the major 20 non-national languages in the participating cities, 10 languages are of European origin and 10 languages stem from abroad. These findings clearly show that the traditional concept of language diversity in Europe should be reconsidered and extended. The outcomes of the local language surveys also demonstrate the high status of English among primary school pupils across Europe. Its intrusion in the children's homes is apparent from the position of English in the top 5 of languages referred to by the children in all of the cities (Table 3). This outcome cannot be explained as an effect of migration and minorisation only. The children's reference to English also derives from the status of English as the international language of power and prestige. English has invaded the repertoire of all of the national languages under consideration. Moreover, children have access to English through a variety of media, and English is commonly taught in particular grades at primary schools.

In addition, children in all participating cities expressed a desire to learn a variety of languages that are not taught at school. The results of the local language surveys also show that children who took part in instruction in particular non-mainstream languages at school reported higher levels of literacy in these languages than children who did not take part in such instruction. Both the reported reading proficiency and the reported writing proficiency profited strongly from language instruction. The differences between participants and non-participants in language instruction were significant for both forms of literacy skills and for all the 20 language groups under consideration. In this domain in particular, the added value of language instruction for language maintenance and development is clear. Owing to the monolingual *habitus* (Gogolin 1994) of primary schooling across Europe, there is an increasing mismatch between language practices at home and at school. The findings on multilingualism at home and those on language needs and language instruction reported by the children should be taken into account by both national and local educational authorities in any type of language policy.

The comparative overview of given parameters in Section 6 shows that there are remarkable cross-national differences in the status of CLT across European nation-states. There are also considerable differences between primary and secondary education in the status of CLT. A comparison of all nine parameters makes clear that CLT has gained a higher status in secondary schools than in primary schools. In primary education, CLT is generally not part of the "regular" or "national" curriculum, and, therefore, becomes a negotiable entity in a complex and often opaque interplay between a variety of actors. Another remarkable difference is that, in some countries (in particular France, Belgium, Spain, and some German federal states), CLT is funded by the consulates or embassies of the countries of origin. In these cases, the national government does not interfere in the organisation of CLT, or in the requirements for, and the selection and employment of teachers. A paradoxical consequence of this phenomenon is that the earmarking of CLT budgets is often safeguarded by the above-mentioned consulates or embassies. National, regional, or local governments often fail to earmark budgets, so that funds meant for CLT may be appropriated for other educational purposes.

The higher status of CLT in secondary education is largely due to the fact that across EU countries instruction in one or more languages other than the national standard language is a traditional and regular component of the (optional) school curriculum, whereas primary education is mainly determined by a monolingual *habitus* (Gogolin 1994). *Within* secondary education, however, CLT must compete with "foreign" languages that have a higher status or a longer tradition. It should further be noted that some countries provide instruction and/or exams in non-standard language varieties. In France, for instance, pupils can take part in examinations for several varieties of Arabic and Berber (Tilmatine 1997); Sweden offers Kurdish as an alternative to Turkish. From mid-2004 on, the EU member-states have been expanded with the inclusion of the national languages of ten new EU countries. This leads to the paradoxical situation that the national languages of, e.g., the three Baltic States are supported by more positive action ("celebrating linguistic diversity") in multilingual Europe than IM languages like Turkish, spoken by many more people across Europe.

CLT may be part of a largely centralised or decentralised educational policy. In the Netherlands, national responsibilities and educational funds are gradually being transferred to the municipal level, and even to individual schools. In France, government policy is strongly centrally controlled. Germany has devolved most governmental responsibilities to the federal states, with all their differences. Sweden grants far-reaching autonomy to municipal councils in dealing with educational tasks and funding.

In general, comparative cross-national references to experiences with CLT in the various EU member-states are rare, or they focus on particular language groups. With a view to the demographic development of European nation-states into multicultural societies, and the similarities in CLT issues, more comparative cross-national research would be highly desirable.

References

Achterberg, Jörn
   2005   *Zur Vitalität slavischer Idiome in Deutschland. Eine empirische Studie zum Sprachverhalten slovophoner Immigranten*. München: Verlag Otto Sagner.

Acton, Thomas and Gary Mundy (eds.)
   1999   *Romani Culture and Gypsy Identity*. Hatfield: University of Hertfordshire Press.

Akinci, Mehmet-Ali, Jan Jaap de Ruiter and Floréal Sanagustin
   2004   *Le Plurilinguisme à Lyon. Le Statut des Langues à la Maison et à l'École*. Paris: L'Harmattan.

Appel, René and Pieter Muysken
   1987   *Language Contact and Bilingualism*. London: Edward Arnold.

Bourhis, Richard, Howard Giles and Doreen Rosenthal
   1981   Notes on the construction of a "Subjective Vitality Questionnaire" for ethnolinguistic groups. *Journal of Multilingual and Multicultural Development* 2: 145–155.

Broeder, Peter and Guus Extra
   1998   *Language, Ethnicity and Education. Case Studies on Immigrant Minority Groups and Immigrant Minority Languages*. Clevedon: Multilingual Matters.

Broeder, Peter and Laura Mijares
   2003   *Plurilingüismo en Madrid. Las Lenguas de los Alumnos de Origin Inmigrante en Primaria*. Madrid: Centro de Investigación y Documentación Educativa.

Campbell, George
    2000   *Compendium of the World's Languages* (Volume 1 & 2). London: Routledge.
Clyne, Michael
    2003   *Dynamics of Language Contact.* Cambridge: Cambridge University Press.
Comrie, Bernard, Stephen Matthews and Maria Polinsky
    2003   *The Atlas of Languages.* Revised Edition. London: Eurospan Group.
Crystal, David
    1997   *The Cambridge Encyclopedia of Language.* Cambridge: Cambridge University Press.
Dalby, David
    1999/2000 *The Linguasphere Register of the World's Languages and Speech Communities* (Volume 1 & 2). Wales-Hebron: Linguasphere Press.
Directive 77/486
    1977   *Directive 77/486 of the Council of the European Communities on the Schooling of Children of Migrant Workers.* Brussels: CEC.
Extra, Guus and Kutlay Yağmur (eds.)
    2004   *Urban Multilingualism in Europe: Immigrant Minority Languages at Home and School.* Clevedon: Multilingual Matters.
Extra, Guus and Kutlay Yağmur
    2006   Immigrant minority languages at home and at school: A case study of the Netherlands. *European Education: a Journal of Issues and Studies,* 38 (2): 50–63.
Extra, Guus, Rian Aarts, Tim van der Avoird, Peter Broeder and Kutlay Yağmur
    2001   *Meertaligheid in Den Haag. De Status van Allochtone Talen Thuis en op School.* Amsterdam: European Cultural Foundation.
    2002   *De Andere Talen van Nederland.* Muiderberg: Coutinho.
Fürstenau, Sarah, Ingrid Gogolin and Kutlay Yağmur (Hrsg.)
    2003   *Mehrsprachigkeit in Hamburg. Ergebnisse einer Sprachenerhebung an den Grundschulen in Hamburg.* Münster/New York: Waxmann.
Giacalone Ramat, Anna and Paolo Ramat
    1998   *The Indo-European Languages.* London: Routledge.
Giles, Howard, Richard Bourhis, and Donald Taylor
    1977   Towards a theory of language in ethnic group relations. In *Language, Ethnicity and Intergroup Relations,* Howard Giles (ed.), 307–348. London: Academic Press.
Gogolin, Ingrid
    1994   *Der Monolinguale Habitus der Multilingualen Schule.* Münster/New York: Waxmann.
Grimes, Barbara (ed.)
    1996   *Ethnologue. Languages of the world* (13th Edition). Dallas: Summer Institute of Linguistics (*www.sil.org/ethnologue*).

Kyuchukov, Hristo (ed.)
2002   *New Aspects of Roma Children Education*. Sofia: Ictus.
Martin, Peter, Angela Creese, Arvind Bhatt and Nirmala Bhojani
2004   *Complementary schools and their communities in Leicester. Final report*. School of Education, University of Leicester.
Nygren-Junkin, Lilian and Guus Extra
2003   *Multilingualism in Göteborg. The Status of Immigrant Minority Languages at Home and at School*. Amsterdam: European Cultural Foundation.
Tilmatine, Mohand (ed.)
1997   *Enseignment des Langues d'Origine et Immigration Nord-Africaine en Europe: Langue Maternelle ou Langue d'Etat?* Paris: Inalco/Cedrea-Crb.
UNDP
2002   www.hdr.undp.org/reports/global/2002/en/pdf/backone.pdf and _backtwo.pdf.
Van der Avoird, Tim
2001   *Determining language vitality. The language use of Hindu communities in the Netherlands and the United Kingdom*. Dissertation, Tilburg University.
Verlot, Marc, Kaat Delrue, Guus Extra and Kutlay Yağmur
2003   *Meertaligheid in Brussel. De Status van Allochtone Talen Thuis en op School*. Amsterdam: European Cultural Foundation.
Weinreich, Uriel
1953   *Languages in Contact. Findings and Problems*. The Hague: Mouton.

Contributing authors

Dennis Ager
Professor Emeritus
Aston University
United Kingdom
e-mail: ad.ager@talktalk.net

Carla Bagna
Researcher of Educational Linguistics
Department of Science of Languages
and Cultures
Università per Stranieri di Siena
Italy
e-mail: bagna@unistrasi.it

Monica Barni
Associate Professor of Educational
Linguistics
Department of Science of Languages
and Cultures
Università per Stranieri di Siena
Italy
e-mail: barni@unistrasi.it

Viv Edwards
Professor of Language in Education
Institute of Education
University of Reading
United Kingdom
e-mail: v.k.edwards@reading.ac.uk

Guus Extra
Professor of Language and Minorities
Department of Language and Culture
Studies
Tilburg University
The Netherlands
e-mail: guus.extra@uvt.nl

Susan Gal
Metzl Distinguished Service
Professor of Anthropology and
Linguistics
University of Chicago
USA
e-mail: s-gal@uchicago.edu

Durk Gorter
Ikerbasque Research Professor
University of the Basque Country
Spain
e-mail: d.gorter@ikerbasque.org

Gabrielle Hogan-Brun
Senior Research Fellow
Graduate School of Education
University of Bristol
United Kingdom
e-mail: g.hogan-brun@bristol.ac.uk

Juliane House
Professor of Applied Linguistics
Rescarch Center on Multilingualism
Hamburg University
Germany
e-mail: jhouse@uni-hamburg.de

Justyna Leśniewska
Associate Professor
Institute of English Philology
Jagiellonian University
Poland
e-mail: justyna.lesniewska@uj.edu.pl

Zygmunt Mazur
Associate Professor
Institute of English Philology
Jagiellonian University
Poland
e-mail: zygmunt.mazur@uj.edu.pl

Cor van der Meer
Researcher and Management
Mercator Research Centre
Fryske Akademy
The Netherlands
e-mail: cvdmeer@fa.knaw.nl

Lilian Nygren-Junkin
Reseracher and Senior Lecturer
Department of Swedish
University of Göteborg
Sweden
e-mail:
lilian.nygren.junkin@svenska.gu.se

Alex Riemersma
Management and Researcher
Mercator Research Centre
Fryske Akademy
The Netherlands
e-mail: ariemersma@fa.knaw.nl

Mikael Svonni
Professor
Department of Language Studies
Umeå University
Sweden
e-mail:
mikael.svonni@samiska.umu.se
(mikael.svonni@hum.uit.no)

F. Xavier Vila i Moreno
Associate Professor of Catalan
Language and Sociolinguistics
Departament de Filologia Catalana &
Centre Universitari de
Sociolingüística i Comunicació
Universitat de Barcelona
Catalonia, Spain
e-mail: fxvila@ub.edu

Kutlay Yağmur
Associate Professor
Department of Language and Culture
Studies
Tilburg University
The Netherlands
e-mail: k.yagmur@uvt.nl

Author index

Aarts, Rian   316
Achterberg, Jörn   321
Acton, Thomas   325
Adams, Anthony   44
Adrey, Jean-Bernard   142
Ager, Dennis   87, 95, 101
Aikio-Puoskari, Ulla   236, 238, 242, 244
Akinci, Mehmet-Ali   316
Alladina, Safder   24, 34
Altarriba, Jeanette   77
Alterman, Hyman   15
Amft, Andrea   233
Ammon, Ulrich   8, 64
Anderson, Benedict   212
Anderson, Jim   264–265
Anseau, Julien   255
Ansell, Amy   22
Appel, René   321
Arel, Dominique   15–16, 21
Argelaguet i Argemí, Jordi   179
Armstrong, Nigel   90, 99
Arnau, Joaquim   180
Arzoz, Xabier   3

Baár, Monika   227
Baetens Beardsmore, Hugo   38, 42
Bagna, Carla   294, 298–301
Bajerowa, Irena   111, 113–115
Baker, Colin   42
Baker, Philip   254–255, 309
Bakó, Boglárka   227
Baldauf, Richard   144
Barbour, Stephen   6–7
Barni, Monica   4, 34, 50, 294, 299–301
Bartha, Csilla   207
Bartmiński, Jerzy   113, 116
Baumgarten, Nicole   70, 74, 75

Beacco, Jean-Claude   262
Beetsma, Danny   42
Benő, Attila   215
Ben-Rafael, Eliezer   302
Bergsland, Knut   237
Billig, Michael   181
Birnbaum, Pierre   91
Bloch, Joel   69
Blum, Alain   15
Blunkett, David   267
Bodó, Csanád   220, 226
Boneschansker, Engbert   199
Borbély, Anna   210
Böttger, Claudia   74
Bourdieu, Pierre   91
Bourhis, Richard   320–321, 257
Boutet, Josiane   101
Boyd, Sally   280, 282
Breatnach, Diarmaid   26
Bremmer, Rolf   185
Broeder, Peter   24, 36, 316, 325
Brubaker, Rogers   211, 223–226
Bührig, Kristin   74
Bulajeva, Tatjana   147
Bunting, Madeleine   267
Byram, Michael   262

Cameron, Deborah   80
Campbell, George   317
Carmichael, Cathie   7
Caubet, Dominique   34
Cenoz, Jasone   29, 42, 192
Chaker, Salem   34
Chaudenson, Robert   106
Chini, Marina   298
Churchill, Stacy   34
Climent-Ferrando, Vicent   166
Clyne, Michael   22, 322
Coelho, Elizabeth   42

Author index

Cohen, Anthonie 193
Comrie, Bernard 317
Cook, Vivian 67
Coulmas, Florian 38, 42
Craith, Máiréad Nic 3, 6, 31, 43
Creese, Angela 265
Crystal, David 68, 260, 317
Csergő, Zsuzsa 211, 223
Csernicskó, István 220
Culioli, Antoine 101
Curtain, Helena 44

D'Agostino, Mari 298
Dalby, David 317
De Jager, Bernadet 200
De Mauro, Tullio 293, 295, 297, 307
De Ruijter, Arie 8
De Ruiter, Jan Jaap 34, 36, 316
De Saussure, Ferdinand 307
De Swaan, Abram 69
Deciu Ritivoi, Adreea 227
Delrue, Kaat 316
Dewitte, Philippe 13, 34
Dijkstra, Anne 193
Dini, Pietro 137
Dubisz, Stanisław 113, 115, 120, 122, 125–126, 129
Dzięgiel, Ewa 122–124

Eberhard, Piotr 123–124
Edmondson, Willis James 72–73
Edwards, John 7, 16, 25
Edwards, Viv 34–35, 49, 50, 254, 258, 260, 264
Ehlich, Konrad 77
Eversley, John 34, 254–255, 309
Extra, Guus 3, 6, 10–11, 17, 21, 24, 34, 36–37, 45, 50, 66, 78, 186, 271, 273–276, 278, 281–282, 285, 293–294, 297, 306, 316, 322, 325, 328

Fase, Willem 36
Feischmidt, Margit 211, 223–226
Fenyvesi, Anna 210, 226–228
Ferrer i Gironès, Francesc 159
Firth, Alan 66, 70, 72
Fishman, Joshua 7, 9, 16, 34, 43, 80
Foekema, Henk 188–189, 192
Fokkema, Klaas 193
Fox, Jon 211, 223–226
Frisell, Helena 274
Fürstenau, Sarah 316
Fysh, Peter 94

Gadet, Françoise 95–97, 99
Gál, Kinga 224
Gal, Susan 209, 211–212, 220, 225–228
García, Ofelia 34, 42
Gaup Eira, Inger Marie 238
Genesee, Fred 42
Georgiou, Myria 259
Gerner, Kristian 137
Ghuman, Paul 8
Giacalone Ramat, Anna 296, 317
Giles, Howard 320–321, 257
Gogolin, Ingrid 34, 43, 316, 332
Göncz, Lajos 210, 218
Gordon, Raymond 26
Gorter, Durk 3, 6, 11, 17, 26, 28, 30, 34, 48, 185–186, 190–192, 200, 271
Graddol, David 13
Graesser, Arthur 77
Grancea, Liana 211, 223–226
Gregory, Eve 265
Grimes, Barbara 317
Grin, François 26, 31, 43
Grosjean, Francois 67, 77
Gubbins, Paul 7
Gudykunst, William 7
Guibernau, Montserrat 16
Guiguet, Benoît 15

Guinot, Enric 179
Gunnarsson, Britt-Louise 279
Győri-Nagy, Sándor 210

Haarmann, Harald 5, 7
Haberland, Hartmut 6
Habermas, Jürgen 64
Hannonen, Pasi 211
Hansegård, Nils-Erik 244
Hargreaves, Alec 92
Harvey, Charles 91
Hattyár, Helga 210, 223
Hedlund, Stefan 137
Helander, Elina 233
Hiden, John 137
Hobsbawm, Eric 212
Hoffmann, Charlotte 42
Hogan-Brun, Gabrielle 28, 38, 48, 135, 137–140, 142–143, 145–151
Holt, Mike 7
Houdebine-Gravaud, Anne-Marie 101
House, Juliane 64, 68, 70, 73–75
Husain, Jyoti 256
Husén, Torsten 34
Huss, Leena 236, 244, 280
Hyltenstam, Kenneth 233, 244, 280, 283–284, 287

Jacobsen, Inger 288–289
Jakobson, Roman 77
James, Ceri 264
Jamin, Mikaël 88, 97, 107
Jaspaert, Koen 34
Jenkins, Richard 16
Jessner, Ulrike 42
Jonkman, Reitze 186, 190–192
Jørgensen, Normann 34
Joseph, John 7

Kachru, Braj 67
Kaplan, Robert 144

Karaś, Halina 122–124
Kassai, Ilona 210
Katbamna, Savita 260
Kelemen, Janka 210
Kelley, Judith 211, 224
Kertzer, David 15–16, 21
Kontra, Miklós 210, 221, 223, 228
Korhonen, Mikko 237
Korhonen, Olavi 237
Kramsch, Claire 68
Kroon, Sjaak 34
Küppers, Anne 74
Kusmenko, Jurij 235, 237
Kyuchukov, Hristo 325

Laihonen, Petteri 211, 225, 227
Lam, Wan Shun Eva 69
Lanstyák, István 210–211, 217, 223, 228
Le Page, Robert 257
Le Rütte, Miranda 199
Leech, Geoffrey 68
Leslie, Robert 257
Lesznyák, Ágnes 70
Lieven, Anatol 137
Lipińska, Ewa 127
Lo Bianco, Joseph 34
Lodge, Anthony 28, 97
Luchtenberg, Sigrid 34

Machetti, Sabrina 298
Maclean, Mairi 91
Majewicz, Alfred 114
Marí, Isidor 174
Markowski, Andrzej 113
Mar-Molinero, Clare 7
Martin, Peter 35, 265, 326
Martyniuk, Waldemar 127
Massariello Merzagora, Giovanna 298
Matthews, Stephen 317
Mazur, Jan 128

McPake, Joanna 44, 254, 264
Metuzāle-Kangere, Baiba 136, 148
Mężykowski, Michał 117–118
Mijares, Laura 316
Mikołajczuk, Agnieszka 119
Milian i Massana, Antoni 164
Miodunka, Władysław 127
Monés i Pujol-Busquets, Jordi 160
Moring, Tom 26
Morris, Delyth 29
Motz, Markus 78
Mundy, Gary 325
Municio, Ingegerd 286
Muysken, Pieter 321
Myers-Scotton, Carol 77

Nelde, Peter 26, 28, 39, 202
Nicholas, Joe 24
Niebaum, Hermann 185
Nikolov, Marianne 44
Norgaard, Ole 137
Nwenmely, Hubisi 257
Nygren-Junkin, Lilian 273–276, 282, 316

Ó Gliasáin, Micheál 28
Ó Riagáin, Pádraig 26, 28
O'Reilly, Camille 28
Oakes, Leigh 7–8
Obdeijn, Herman 34, 36
Oldenhof, Bouke 197
Opper, Sylvia 34
Oppewal, Teake 197
Orioles, Vincenzo 293–295
Ortega y Gasset, José 77
Özçetin, Demet 75
Ozolins, Uldis 136, 138, 148

Pál, Tamás 210
Parke, Tim 265
Pauwels, Anne 34
Pawłowski, Adam 128–129

Péntek, János 228
Phillipson, Robert 43, 45, 64
Pietersen, Liewe 190
Pisarek, Walery 114, 119
Pla Boix, Anna 173, 175
Plasseraud, Yves 137
Pléh, Csaba 209
Polinsky Maria 317
Pons Parera, Eva 173, 175
Popkema, Jan 193
Poulain, Michel 15, 33
Pradilla Cardona, Miquel Àngel 166
Press, Jon 91
Price, Cathy 77
Priegnitz, Frauke 78
Probst, Julia 74
Pueyo i París, Miquel 174
Pugh, Stefan 28
Puzynina, Jadwiga 113, 119

Querol Puig, Ernest 176

Ramat, Paolo 317
Ramonienė, Meilutė 138, 147–148, 150
Reader, Lesley 257
Reich, Hans 34, 36
Reid, Euan 34, 36
Rex, John 16
Rieger, Janus 123
Riemersma, Alex 26, 30, 48
Riessler, Michael 235, 237
Riley, Philip 7
Robins, Kevin 259
Rodríguez, Jacinto 161
Rosenthal, Doreen 321
Rosowsky, Andrey 265

Salmon, Philip 137
Salverda, Reinier 257
Saly, Noémi 210, 228

Sammallahti, Pekka   237
Sanagustin, Floréal   316
Sándor, Klára   215
Sanford, Anthony   77
Satkiewicz, Halina   128
Schneider, Britta   7, 36
Schwegler, Brian   211, 224, 226–227
Seretny, Anna   127
Sibille, Jean   34
Simon, Szabolcs   210–211
Simsek, S. Cigdem Sagin   66
Singleton, David   126
Sipma, Piter   193
Skutnabb-Kangas, Tove   39, 42, 244
Sneddon, Raymonde   265
Solomos, John   22
Soltau, Anja   78
Spencer, Stephen   22
Spielmann, Daniel   68
Spolsky, Bernard   102, 104
Stevenson, Patrick   7
Stroud, Christopher   233, 244
Strubell, Miquel   28, 202
Svartvik, Jan   68
Svonni, Mikael   240–241, 244, 246
Swann, Lord   261
Szabómihály, Gizella   223, 228
Szilágyi, Sándor   215
Szoták, Szilvia   227

Tabouret-Keller, Andreé   257
Taylor, Donald   320–321, 257
Ten Thije, Jan   78
Tiersma, Pieter Meijes   193
Tilmatine, Mohand   34, 36, 333
Tingbjörn, Gunnar   284
Tinsley, Teresa   264
Tjeerdsma, Rommert   46
Torres-Guzmán, Maria   39, 42
Tosi, Arturo   34
Tóth, Ágnes   207

Tulasiewicz, Witold   44
Tuomela, Veli   283, 287

Ureland, Sture   28

Valentini, Ada   298
Valk, Renze   188
Van Bree, Cor   186
Van der Avoird, Tim   192, 316, 321
Van der Bij, Jacob   188
Van der Meer, Cor   26, 30, 48, 200
Van der Vaart, Jacob   192
Van Els, Theo   64
Van Langevelde, Ab   197
Van Londen, Selma   8
Van Ruijven, Bernie   188, 200
Vedovelli, Massimo   294–299, 307–308
Vékás, János   207
Verhoeven, Ludo   34
Verkuyten, Michael   16
Verlot, Marc   316, 320
Verschik, Anna   148–149
Vertovec, Steven   255
Vihalemm, Triin   149
Vila i Moreno, F. Xavier   160, 165, 175
Villarini, Andrea   296
Vörös, Otto   218
Vries, Oebele   185–186

Wagner, Johannes   70, 72
Walczak, Bogdan   120, 122, 125, 127
Weinreich, Uriel   321
Wenger, Etienne   68
Wicherkiewicz, Tomasz   114
Widdowson, Henry   67
Williams, Glyn   28–29, 202
Winter, Joanne   34
Woehrling, Jean-Marie   31
Wolff, Stefan   28

Woolard, Kathryn   179, 221
Wright, Sue   7, 307

Yağmur, Kutlay   10, 21, 34, 36–37, 45, 50, 293, 297, 316, 328

Ytsma, Jehannes   42, 200

Zachrisson, Inger   235, 237
Zeevaert, Ludger   78
Zondag, Koen   186

Subject index

active bilingualism, 284, 290, 329
additional language, 40, 44–45, 49, 79, 254
administrative (municipal) register, 15, 18, 228
affirmative action, 9, 15, 163–164
ageing, 47, 89–90, 97
Alliance Française, 13, 105
ancestral language, 9, 10
ancestry, 21–22, 127, 215
Arts, 102–103, 128, 253, 257, 260
awareness raising, 6, 24, 38–39, 42, 72, 90, 98, 104–105, 113, 119, 126, 165, 174, 267, 274, 281, 316, 329

bicultural identity, 50, 284
bilingual, 29, 32, 42, 66–67, 89, 104, 122, 125, 138, 143, 145, 149–150, 172, 178, 195–196, 198–199, 210–211, 218–219, 226, 228, 237, 243, 254, 260, 274, 278, 280, 284, 290
    education, 36, 42, 143, 218, 221, 327
    school, 143, 195
    skill, 50, 284, 290
bilingualism, 24, 42, 67, 136, 138–139, 144, 147–149, 170–171, 178, 200, 208–209, 211–212, 218–219, 227, 263, 267, 284, 290, 329
bilateral, 32
birth country/country of birth, 14–18, 21, 272–273
British Council, 13, 129

census, 15–16, 18, 21–22, 24, 26, 28–30, 111–112, 114, 122, 124, 126, 148–150, 158, 161, 186, 211–213, 217, 224, 254–255, 265, 267
    data, 15–16, 18, 21, 29, 122, 124, 148, 150, 254
    question, 21–23, 212
citizenship, 8, 15, 18, 33, 43, 136–137, 140–143, 212, 262, 272
city, 34, 157, 211, 215, 226–227, 258, 274, 278, 297, 299–304, 315–320, 332
co-construction of utterances, 72
collective identity, 16
Common European Framework of Reference for Languages CEFR), 38, 127, 141–142, 144
communicative style, 74–76
community, 6, 9–10, 44, 143, 254, 257, 261–266, 326
    language teaching (CLT), 10, 34–37, 261, 263–264, 326
complementary
    education, 265
    school, 263–267
convergence, 8, 14, 24, 43, 67
core value, 4, 7, 9, 16–17, 22, 36, 126, 325, 327
corpus planning, 48, 193–194, 197
Council of Europe, 31, 38, 43–44, 46, 170, 195, 203, 208, 217, 223, 262
covert translation (project), 74–76
cross-border language, 11
cross-linguistic perspective, 34, 315
cross-national
    data(base), 33, 318–319
    perspective, 4, 34

research, 37, 50, 334
cultural
    cohesion, 50, 262
    diversity, 8, 174
    identity, 4, 36, 66, 126, 327, 329
    pluralism, 32, 329
    policy/policies, 328
curricular status, 50, 282, 286, 330
curriculum, 31, 35, 45, 79, 119, 144–146, 195, 202, 242, 262, 264, 279, 282–284, 286, 326–327, 330, 333

decennial census, 16, 29
demographic
    change, 8, 138, 276
    shift, 32
diaspora, 10, 120, 126–127, 257, 260
Directive 77/486 of the European Community, 35–36, 43, 327
discourse marker, 73–74
divergence, 8, 43, 113, 122
diversity, 64, 66–67, 106, 163, 171, 174, 253–256, 262, 267, 306, 308, 310, 332–333
dominant language, 21, 23, 27, 31–32, 35, 122, 200, 240, 326
dual citizenship, 18, 272

economic migration, 32
educational
    policy/policies, 23, 42–43, 50, 143, 309, 328, 334
    provision, 9, 28, 31, 44
    system, 20, 31, 38, 40, 91, 104–105, 108, 159, 174, 198, 241, 305–306
English as lingua franca (ELF), 3, 45, 66, 79
equal treatment, 23
ethnic
    dilemma, 15

group, 7, 16, 112
identity, 7, 16
nationality, 18–19
origin, 16, 22, 128
ethnicity, 9, 14, 16–19, 21–24, 28–29, 87, 141–142, 150, 212–213, 218, 254
ethnocultural identity, 16
ethnographic research, 24, 211, 224
ethnolinguistic vitality, 49, 253, 257–258, 266, 321
EU policy/policies, 3, 13
Eurobarometer, 39–41, 64, 112, 129, 192
EUROCOM, 78
Euromosaic, 26, 30, 202
European Centre for Modern Languages (ECML), 38, 44
European Charter for Regional or Minority Languages, 26, 30–31, 39, 102, 104, 170, 194–195, 201, 223
European Commission, 18, 34, 40–44, 65–66, 107–108, 262
European Constitution, 8
European Framework Convention on National Minorities, 30
European Language Portfolio, 38, 127
European Language Survey Network, 30
European Union, 3, 18, 38, 63–66, 92–93, 106, 135, 140, 192, 203, 208, 222–223, 253, 255, 271
European Year of Languages, 3, 44
EuroStat, 14, 18, 33

family
    formation, 36, 327
    remigration, 35, 327
    reunion, 36, 92, 276, 279, 327

Subject index

foreign language, 11–12, 39, 44, 46, 48, 64–65, 67, 71, 73, 78, 99, 103, 105, 112, 115, 117–118, 120, 127–129, 144–146, 159, 192, 262, 280, 287
former colony, 15, 33–34, 253, 318
Francophone, 103–104, 106–107
Francophony, 104
French Academy, 95, 97, 100, 102–103

General Delegation for French and the Languages of France, 12–13, 97, 102–104, 107–109
globalization, 43, 76, 112, 135, 136, 174, 253
glocalisation, 42
Goethe Institute, 12–13
Group of Intellectuals for Intercultural Dialogue, 39

Hamburg ELF project, 70
hegemony of English, 43
heterogeneity, 7–8, 288
High Level Group on Multilingualism, 39
historic minority, 10, 294, 296, 308
home language, 16–17, 24, 37, 43, 199, 212, 241, 255, 275–276, 281–289, 316–318, 326, 328
    data, 21, 316
    instruction (HLI), 10, 34–35, 46, 50, 241, 275, 282–290, 326
    statistics, 23–24
    survey, 23, 50, 316
    use, 16, 23–24, 50, 281, 316
human development index (HDI), 322
human rights, 43, 69
Humboldt-Sapir-Whorf hypothesis, 77

hybrid language, 79

identification, 4, 14, 17–19, 23–24, 47, 68–69, 142, 176, 273, 299, 316
identity, 3–5, 7–9, 16–17, 22, 29, 36, 38, 42–43, 47, 50, 71–72, 94, 96, 114–116, 124–126, 136, 148–149, 166, 176, 210, 212, 221, 227, 240, 257, 260, 284, 293, 295, 302, 307, 310, 325, 327, 329
immigrant language, 4, 63, 66, 96–97, 99, 143, 192, 253, 272, 289, 293–294, 296–300, 302–305, 308–310
immigrant minority, 3, 6, 10, 32–34, 315
    children, 24, 34, 36, 43, 283, 284, 287, 290, 327–328
    group, 8–9, 14–15, 24, 32–33, 36, 40, 48, 50, 282, 285, 315, 327
    language, 3–4, 6, 10–11, 31–35, 42–44, 46–50, 63, 66, 96–97, 99, 275–276, 279–282, 290, 315, 317, 322, 326–328, 331, 333
    population, 32–33, 50, 271, 283
immigration, 15, 17, 21, 33, 47–48, 50, 89, 92, 97, 138, 160, 174, 178, 210, 253, 271, 275–276, 279, 293–296, 300, 304–305, 307, 316, 318, 331
    policy/policies, 32, 271, 283
inclusive approach, 3, 6, 42–45
indigenous minority language, 6, 47
Inspectorate, 200–201
integration, 8–9, 48, 50, 91, 112, 125, 136, 139, 141, 273, 290, 301–302, 307–308, 328–329

intergenerational
  erosion, 17
  minorisation, 8–9, 33, 43
  transmission, 9, 109
international
  communication, 8, 43, 45, 79
  institution, 93, 106, 108
  language, 13, 44, 93, 108, 280, 332
  migration, 8–9, 33
internationalisation, 43, 46

labour market, 47, 128, 279, 296
language
  activism, 28
  activity, 146
  assessment, 137, 140
  attitude, 28, 125, 150, 191, 225
  border, 6, 21
  contact, 113, 137, 186
  choice, 94, 144–145, 149, 165, 190–191, 224, 226, 244, 281, 299, 320–322
  community, 30, 87, 203, 325
  competence, 29, 126, 135–136, 141–142, 144, 146, 148, 169, 176, 180, 262
  distribution, 24, 316–318, 320, 325, 331
  diversity, 43–44, 50, 308, 332
  dominance, 281, 320–321
  dynamics, 48, 137, 148
  family, 26, 135
  for communication, 67–69, 79, 149, 175
  group, 9, 24–26, 28, 30–31, 97, 148, 185, 202, 233, 254, 273, 319–320, 322–325, 332, 334
  ideology, 28, 49, 151, 221
  in education, 31, 44, 48, 198, 203
  law, 139–141, 166, 194, 239, 245
  legislation, 21, 136–137, 151, 243–246
  maintenance, 9, 36, 43, 89, 126, 208, 244–245, 257, 266, 275, 294, 303–304, 308–309, 327, 332
  management, 28, 102–103, 135
  mismatch, 35, 326
  of identification, 47, 68–69, 176
  of instruction, 29, 145–146, 220, 241
  planning, 29, 108, 208, 210, 228
  policy/policies, 12–14, 28, 38, 42, 46–48, 63, 80, 87, 102, 107, 115, 118, 129, 135–136, 139–140, 149, 151, 162–166, 168–174, 176–178, 194, 198, 203, 211, 223, 294–295, 333
  practice, 137, 176, 180, 333
  preference, 74, 76, 150, 281
  proficiency, 38–39, 66, 79, 114, 117, 126–182, 137, 139–143, 186, 196, 200, 272, 281, 320–321
  profile, 316
  promotion, 4, 12, 14, 38, 144, 166, 174, 178
  quality, 160
  question, 16, 18, 20, 29, 255, 267, 318
  regulation, 140–141
  repertoire, 9, 38, 309
  rights, 43, 69
  schooling, 32
  shift, 9, 29–30, 35, 49, 104, 162, 219, 233, 244, 253, 273, 275, 279, 281, 325–327
  skill, 29, 37, 39, 116, 258, 262, 272, 281, 287, 289, 310, 322, 329
  status, 281

survey, 23–24, 50, 316–317, 332
teaching, 10, 31–32, 34, 37–40, 116, 119, 123, 127, 142, 146, 174, 258, 261–266, 289, 326
test(ing), 139, 142–143
transfer,
transmission, 4, 32, 36, 49, 108, 126, 188, 322, 327
variation, 32, 96, 101
vitality, 87, 108, 281, 320–325
vitality index (LVI), 320–325
Language(s) Other Than English (LOTE), 10, 23, 29, 45, 49, 254, 257
Language Policy Division (Strasbourg), 38
large-scale
data, 297
survey, 29–30
learning deficit, 32
legal status of language(s), 63, 238
lesser-used languages, 11, 65, 197, 208
lingua franca, 3, 8, 12, 43, 45, 47, 63, 66, 68, 79, 99, 128–129, 138, 144, 256, 278
linguistic
capital, 50, 290
diversity, 3, 5, 12, 14, 34, 38–39, 46, 63, 106, 163, 171, 253, 256, 333
heterogeneity, 7
landscape, 64, 79, 160, 192, 254, 299, 301
minority, 220
nationalism, 7, 64, 208, 221, 224
space, 293–294, 296–298, 304
literacy, 28, 145, 160, 162, 185, 189, 263, 265, 295, 305, 322, 332
literature, 13, 49, 67, 72–73, 105, 111, 114–115, 128, 137, 145, 162, 197, 202, 243, 246

majority language, 4, 9, 13, 42, 66, 165, 226, 239–240, 242, 244, 280–281, 288
majority language speaker, 9, 240
media, 14–15, 28–30, 49, 69, 99–100, 108–109, 113, 118–119, 160, 162, 164–165, 171–172, 175, 178, 186, 192, 196, 203, 217, 219, 220, 225, 227–228, 240, 243–244, 246, 257–260, 279–280, 288, 332
medium of instruction, 4, 31, 45, 78, 145, 195, 199–202, 242
Mercator Research Centre, 25, 200
migrant, 4, 33, 126, 192, 207, 219, 259, 298, 305
language, 4, 209, 298, 305
worker, 126, 219
migration, 6, 8–9, 11, 14, 16, 32–33, 43, 49, 210, 216, 220, 225, 235, 260, 271, 293–295, 304–305, 332
minorisation, 6, 8–9, 14, 16, 33, 43, 332
minority
language, 3–7, 9–11, 24, 26, 28, 30–34, 47–50, 126, 136, 147–148, 151, 164–165, 167, 170, 175, 177, 179, 197–198, 200–203, 212, 218–220, 223, 240, 253–255, 257–263, 265–267, 280, 294–297, 308, 309, 318, 320–321, 328
press, 49, 220, 258–259, 266
radio, 49, 220, 259, 266
TV, 49, 220, 259, 266
monolingual habitus, 43, 332–333
mother tongue, 10, 20, 22–23, 34, 36–38, 40, 44, 46, 63–66, 69, 79, 112, 122, 124–125, 128–129, 138, 147, 149,

350 *Subject index*

186–189, 192–193, 212–213, 216, 254, 272–275, 282–284, 326, 328
teaching, 10, 34, 326
multicompetence, 67
multicultural
context, 4, 16, 43
environment, 46, 306, 315
identity, 43
population, 16, 20, 23
society, 17, 45, 79, 271, 307, 315, 334
multiculturalism, 22, 24, 63, 66, 136, 210, 306
multilingual
city, 34
education, 44
society, 271
Multilingual Cities Project (MCP), 50, 274, 276, 280–281, 297, 315, 331
multilingualism, 3, 12, 22, 24, 38–39, 43, 46–47, 63–66, 74, 79, 106, 174, 192, 202, 227, 255, 265, 281, 306, 316, 329, 333
multiple identity, 148

national
identity, 7, 9, 29, 49, 94, 115–116, 124–125, 136, 210, 221
language, 3–5, 7, 11, 13–14, 38, 40, 44, 64, 78, 125, 129–130, 136, 138–139, 142–143, 147–149, 207, 221, 265, 276, 279–280, 295, 307, 326, 332–333
nationalising states, 222
nationalism, 7, 64, 71, 94, 173–174, 178, 208, 210, 221–222, 224
nationality, 7, 14–19, 21, 24, 92, 111–112, 116, 122–124,
129, 150, 151, 212–213, 220, 224, 272–274, 306
nation-state, 5–8, 10–13, 15–16, 24, 34–36, 43, 45–46, 48–49, 65, 79, 87, 96, 112, 207, 326, 331, 333–334
naturalisation, 15, 17, 137, 139–141, 272
neighbouring language, 44
new minority language, 10, 49–50, 254–255, 257–259, 261–263, 265–267, 297, 309
newcomer, 8–10, 174, 176
nomenclature, 10–11, 222
non-European language, 9, 10
non-national language, 44, 332
non-territorial language, 10, 28, 42, 297, 332
number of speakers, 24, 108, 120, 129, 186, 188, 203, 279

official language, 6, 9, 11, 13, 27, 29, 44, 46, 63–65, 88, 93–94, 100, 108, 111, 116, 140, 164–165, 169–170, 238, 256, 265–266, 306, 310
official state language, 3, 5–6, 8, 11, 14, 16, 27, 35, 43–44, 46–47, 111
Omrop Fryslân, 196
one language – one state, 9, 114, 178
operationalisation, 19–20, 22, 321–322
Organisation Internationale de la Francophonie, 13–14, 93, 109

pluralism, 32, 38, 50, 163, 171, 177, 293, 329
pluriform society, 36, 327
plurilingual
education, 42

European, 40
plurilingualism, 4, 8, 13, 38–42, 44–46, 104
policy maker, 9, 35, 46, 326
Polish Language Act, 116–118, 129, 130
Polish Language Council, 118, 130
population
    data, 15–16, 272
    group, 4, 14–18, 21, 24, 33, 290, 316
primary
    education, 144–146, 194, 199–200, 327, 329, 333
primary
    school, 10, 29, 36, 40–41, 43, 45–46, 49, 79, 145, 165, 192, 195, 199, 217, 220, 262, 276–277, 305, 316–318, 327–333
principle of subsidiarity, 38, 42
priority language, 45–46, 79

race, 21–22
refugee, 33, 253, 271–272, 276, 279
regional minority language, 3–4, 6, 8–11, 23–25, 26–28, 30–33, 42–43, 47–48, 89, 95–97, 102–104, 162, 193, 202, 318, 328
register, 15, 18, 67, 113–114, 123, 225, 227–228
religion, 20, 29, 49, 124, 218, 253, 256–257, 263, 266
religious
    denomination, 18–21
    institution, 49, 257, 261, 266
residence, 4, 15, 18, 33, 37, 40–41, 66, 125, 138, 219, 227, 272, 280, 320, 330–331
Russification, 151
Russophone, 138–139, 148

sample survey, 15, 18
school
    achievement, 36, 327
    curriculum, 31, 35, 45, 79, 119, 145, 242, 283, 327, 330, 333
    subject, 35, 45, 79, 142–146, 168, 172, 326
second language
    acquisition, 33, 315
    education, 35, 326
secondary
    education, 9, 11, 35–36, 143–146, 165, 195, 201, 216, 217, 242, 285, 326, 328–329, 333
    school, 10, 29, 35, 37, 40, 46, 91, 105, 115, 142, 144–145, 147, 168, 188, 192, 201, 216, 218, 221, 241–242, 262, 282, 285, 287, 326, 328–331, 333
self-categorisation, 16–17, 22, 24
social
    migration, 32
    structure, 89, 93
sociolinguistic survey, 28, 30, 190, 202
source country, 325, 331
standard, 28, 30, 38–39, 45, 79, 87, 90, 93, 95–100, 103, 113–115, 125–127, 145–147, 178, 186, 193, 219, 223, 226–228, 237, 246, 256–257, 283, 333
standardisation, 103, 119, 208, 210, 239, 244, 256
status planning, 192–194, 197, 228
subjectivity and addressee orientation, 75–76
superdiversity, 255
survey, 15, 17, 23–24, 26, 28–30, 48, 50, 115, 121, 126, 149–150, 180, 187–192, 201–202,

255, 265, 274–275, 279, 301, 317–318, 332

target country, 125–126
teacher
    qualification, 50, 200, 282, 289, 331
    training programme, 45–46, 79, 115, 331
teaching method, 45–46, 79, 144–145, 201, 289
titular language, 147, 150
Toubon Law, 102–103, 107
transactional communication, 47, 80
transitional education, 32
transnational
    citizenship, 8
    communication, 3, 45
trilingual
    education, 200
    school, 200
trilingualism, 42, 44, 139

UNESCO, 44, 46, 101, 108, 203
Unit for Multilingualism Policy (Brussels), 38
urbanisation, 47, 89–90, 93, 97–98, 215

Valeur project, 44
Victorian School of Languages, 45–46
visibility of language, 300
vitality, 9, 24, 28, 34, 49–50, 87, 108, 175, 243–244, 253, 257–258, 266, 275, 281, 297, 300–301, 303–304, 316–317, 320–325, 331

working language, 3, 27, 38, 63–64, 165